History of South Dakota

UNIVERSITY OF NEBRASKA PRESS, LINCOLN • 1975

History of South Dakota
Third Edition, Revised

By Herbert S. Schell

LINE DRAWINGS BY JACK BRODIE

Publishers on the Plains

UNP

Library of Congress Cataloging in Publication Data

Schell, Herbert Samuel, 1899–
    History of South Dakota.

    Bibliography: p.
    1. South Dakota—History. I. Title.
F651.S29 1975   917.83'03   74–18431
ISBN 0–8032–0851–0
ISBN 0–8032–5820–8 (pbk.)

First printing, 1961
First printing, Second Edition, 1968
Second printing, Second Edition, 1969
First printing, Third Edition, Revised, 1975

Manufactured in the United States of America

TO THE PIONEERS OF SOUTH DAKOTA

Contents

List of Maps and Charts

Following page 210 there is a 40-page pictorial review.

Introduction

THE EARLY HISTORY of South Dakota may be viewed as a series of protest movements against external forces. The first and immediate object of attack was the status of dependency under the territorial system to which the Dakota settlements were subjected beyond the normal period of federal tutelage. The second phase of the protest movement was the dissatisfaction expressed against alleged economic exploitation by railroads, grain warehouses, and other corporate interests in the form of excessive freight and elevator charges, high interest rates, and monopolistic prices. The reform movement led to regulatory legislation and to a program of state-owned enterprises that included a state-operated system of rural credits.

Despite the venture into state socialism, which should be construed as part of the contemporary campaign against "trusts" and "monopolistic prices," in recent decades South Dakota has been politically conservative. Differences between political parties over state issues have been more imagined than real: the distinction has been one of degree rather than a matter of basic principles. One writer has aptly referred to the state as having been "progressive in a conservative way" in recent years, applying practicality in its quest for political salvation. Since the early 1920's, South Dakota patently has been little inclined to erratic political behavior.

The interrelationship between the state and the federal government is of paramount significance: the impact of federal government has been continuously felt throughout South Dakota's history. Despite the relinquishment of political control under the Enabling Act of 1889, the public lands, the forests of the Black Hills, and the water resources of the Missouri Basin remained the property of the nation. The Indian lands and their occupants also remained outside the state jurisdiction. When new social forces tended to expand the activities of the federal government, problems formerly looked upon as local began to assume national importance. During the 1930's matters concerning public works and relief passed into the hands of the federal government. Since that time, questions concerning farm policy, public education, and transportation have become more and more of a national concern. The mobility of modern society has tended to obscure state boundary lines, and there has been a trend toward greater financial aid to state and local governments. In 1967 about one-third of the total governmental expenditures of the state of South Dakota came from the federal government; over one-third of the total federal revenues collected in the state were returned to it in the form of federal grants in aid. Whatever the propriety or wisdom of such financial assistance, federal aid undeniably is of tremendous importance in meeting the demands of modern society for public services.

Now, a full hundred years after the passage of the Organic Act on March 2, 1861, it is an appropriate time to present a full-scale history of South Dakota. The pioneering phases of the economic, political, and social developments have yielded to more urbane and mature approaches. South Dakota has, as it were, come of age. Moreover, the pick-and-shovel work in the vast body of available documents and other primary sources seems to have progressed sufficiently in most areas to warrant a synthesis on a wide basis.

The study of state history has values beyond its intrinsic interest. For one thing, knowledge drawn from the past is the key to an understanding of the present. Moreover, the colorful drama of bygone years can be a source of inspiration to us now: even though new conditions beget new problems, the vigor and resolution with which earlier generations dealt with the problems of their day can inspire a similar determination in present-day society. The history of South Dakota may also serve a useful purpose by giving us an insight into the history of the country as a whole, for historical forces clearly transcend state boundary lines. Only by comprehending its local facets can a general movement be evaluated properly; the history of a state, or even a community, may be regarded as a cross section of the nation at large. In the history of South Dakota, as in the history of her sister states, we find the grass roots for an understanding of general or national history no less than the history of the region.

In this volume, the author's aim has been to unfold the story of South Dakota's growth and development from prehistory to the present day, presenting the material chronologically within a topical framework. In connection with the latter, he has been particularly concerned to trace the growth of political institutions during the territorial period; he also has included a survey of the state's industrial activities, with the idea of providing a backdrop for the current campaign to attract industry to South Dakota.

For a proper understanding of the past, it is imperative to consider adjustments to environmental conditions. Since South Dakota occupies a transitional position between the Great Plains proper and the Prairie Plains, the variations in its economy as well as in farming practices are more than ordinarily significant, and the conditioning factors of climate and environment become an important theme for consideration. Any adequate survey of South Dakota history also must include an account of its large Indian population. The author has accordingly tried to cover the gamut of experiences under reservation life and to trace the progress made by the members of the Sioux nation.

Notwithstanding a century of progress, South Dakota still bears some aspects of a pioneer state. Its citizens remain precariously dependent upon an agricultural economy. There are, however, encouraging signs on the horizon: after a long, painful process of trial and error, agriculture has attained a greater degree of stability through a more rational land-use program; the Missouri River Development project and the prospects for further development of the state's varied physical resources, including oil and uranium, give great promise for the future; and there is evidence of other progress in the direction of diversification. On the strength of this outlook, South Dakota can begin its second century in a spirit of confidence and self-assurance.

History of South Dakota

CHAPTER 1

The Natural Setting

THE REGION of which the state of South Dakota is a part was born, geologically speaking, something like four billion years ago. About one billion, six hundred million years ago, the land in the area which is now South Dakota finally began to emerge—first the Black Hills and then the eastern part of the state, protruding like a finger pointing westward from Sioux Falls. After these crustal disturbances, South Dakota along with the rest of North America was subjected to many partial invasions of the sea. About sixty million years ago, the primeval ocean had receded entirely from this region, leaving the state as dry land in about its present form.

Later in geological time, during the Pleistocene epoch, ice sheets moved into the state from the north, blocking the streams flowing eastward from the Rocky Mountains and forcing the impounded waters to cut their way along the western edge of the massed ice, thus forming the present channel of the Missouri. Similarly, the ice shaped the surface features of the eastern region: it became a rolling prairie land studded with numerous lakes and overlaid in some places with a hundred to four hundred feet of glacial debris. The higher part of the coteau in the northeastern part of the state owes its height to these deposits. In all, four major ice sheets ground across the surface of the land in the eastern half of the state, building up moraine ridges, creating plains by leveling off high points and filling in low places, and leaving behind them their debris—boulders, gravel, and fine silt. The geological develop-

3

ments during these periods account for the character of South Dakota's soil as well as for its heritage of valuable minerals and other natural resources.

Described in the stripped-down terminology of the gazetteer, South Dakota today is a near rectangle of about 210 miles from north to south and 370 miles from east to west. It ranks sixteenth among the states in size, having an area of 76,995 square miles. Except for the Black Hills region, the land area is a tilted plateau, rising diagonally from a low elevation of 1,100 feet to 3,400 feet in the northwest corner. Because of the many different topographic features within its borders, the state has been hailed as the "Land of Infinite Variety"; and because of the diversity of topography, it has greater variations with respect to climate and natural resources than the states to the north and south.

TOPOGRAPHY

South Dakota lies within the two major physiographic provinces into which the western portion of the interior basin of the United States divides itself: the Prairie Plains or Central Lowlands and the Great Plains. The Missouri River, roughly speaking, forms the line of demarcation between these two provinces. Most of eastern South Dakota—in common parlance, the east-river area—is a continuation of the prairies of Iowa and Minnesota. The western half of the state, excepting the Black Hills, assumes all the environmental characteristics of the Great Plains Province which extends to the Rockies from Texas to Canada. The Black Hills which rise conspicuously above the surrounding plains may be regarded as an outpost of the Rocky Mountains and a separate physiographic province.

There are three main subdivisions of the Prairie Plains or Central Lowlands: the Minnesota Valley lowland; a lake-dotted highland in the northeast part of the state, designated as the Prairie Hills or Coteau des Prairie; and a lowland trough, from 50 to 75 miles in width, forming the James River Valley.

The Minnesota Valley lowland is an extension of the Minnesota River Basin. In South Dakota it comprises an area of some 720 square miles on the continental watershed formed by Big Stone Lake and Lake Traverse, the former draining into the Mississippi and the latter into Hudson Bay through the Red River of the North. The divide which separates Big Stone and Traverse lakes is so low that in periods of high water the waters of the two lakes commingle. The 50-mile trench in which the lakes lie is the lowest point in South Dakota, having an altitude of 960 feet above sea level.

The Prairie Hills, or Coteau des Prairie, is a rough highland with an elevation of over 2,000 feet above sea level, extending from the North Dakota border southward as far as Lincoln County. On its northeastern edge a 600-foot escarpment rises sharply above the Minnesota Valley and drops with equal abruptness into the

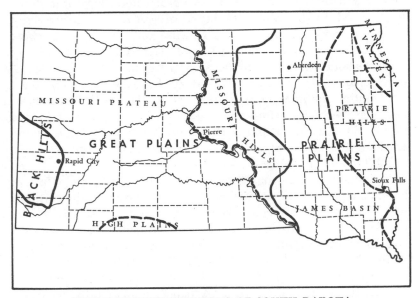

PHYSIOGRAPHIC DIVISIONS OF SOUTH DAKOTA

(Based on map, page 8, in E. P. Rothrock, *A Geology of South Dakota*, Bulletin No. 13, South Dakota Geological Survey, Vermillion, S. Dak., 1943.)

James Basin on the west from an elevation of 300 feet. The Dakota Basin or James Valley is a broad, nearly level stretch of land from 50 to 75 miles wide and 250 miles long. "So level is it that it takes water three weeks to travel the length of the state in the James River."[1] This valley was once the main spillway through which poured the waters from melted glacial ice. Despite its poor

[1] E. P. Rothrock, *A Geology of South Dakota*, Bulletin No. 13 (South Dakota Geological Survey, Vermillion, S. Dak., 1943), p. 24. The author has made extensive use of this reference in the preparation of this chapter.

drainage, the James Valley is one of the richest agricultural sections in the state.

The Great Plains Province has a rolling topography characterized by high buttes and rough canyons. Whereas the geological formation of the Prairie Plains must be explained in terms of glaciation and stream erosion, the Great Plains Province was developed by a process of aggradation. The land surface was raised in an eastward tilt by the same natural forces that formed the Black Hills and the Rocky Mountains, and was then built up further from rock debris carried eastward by streams and blown into dunes by the wind. In the course of time, rivers cut deep trenches across the plain, and the eroding forces of wind and running water wore away the softer parts of the rocks and clays. The western part of South Dakota thus generally became "a region of buttes and badlands separated by wide level uplands cut by deep narrow canyons."

Excluding the mountainous Black Hills, the Great Plains Province may be divided into three sections: the Missouri Hills, or Coteau du Missouri, flanking the James Valley; the High Plains, or Sandhills region, forming the northern edge of the Nebraska Sandhills; and the Missouri Plateau.

The Missouri Hills, or Coteau du Missouri, comprise a belt of hill country about thirty miles wide and extending to the Missouri River. Although, strictly speaking, this section is a subdivision of the Great Plains Province, it may be considered the transitional area in which the Prairie Plains Province merges into the Great Plains. The eastern border of the Missouri Hills is delineated by moraines, or belts of glacial hills, including the Bowdle and Lebanon Hills and the Bijou Hills. A fringe of high hills, separated by canyonlike valleys, forms the western edge of the Missouri Hills section.

The High Plains section is confined to a narrow strip of about 400 square miles along the Nebraska border in Bennett and Shannon counties. It is known locally as the Sandhills region because of the dunes formed from wind-blown sand loosened from the underlying sandy bedrock.

The Missouri Plateau, with an average elevation of about 2,800 feet, constitutes the largest topographic section in South Dakota. Although a butte and canyon topography predominates, there are wide expanses of nearly level tablelands within the area. The largest and most picturesque buttes occur in the northwestern corner of the state in Harding County.

"Bad land for crossing," or "mauvaises terres," said the Indians and the French, a descriptive term gladly adopted by both layman and scientist for the rugged badlands areas, which are fairly common in the Missouri Plateau section. Generally barren of vegetation, they have resulted from the erosion of softer clays and shales in the rock structure. A minor badlands is located in the northwestern part of the state near Slim Buttes and the East Short Pine Hills, but the most conspicuous and scenic, usually designated as the Big Badlands, lies along the White and Cheyenne rivers. Here, unwinding for a distance of more than a hundred miles, is a labyrinth of ravines and narrow ridges with buttes, domes, and spires of varied colors. These formations, sculptured by nature into myriad weird shapes, are composed of the harder types of strata that have resisted erosion. Laid bare by erosion and weathering, the rock materials not only have revealed the story of their formation, but also have yielded up the fossilized remains of many animals and reptiles. For years the Big Badlands has been a great attraction for scientists as well as tourists. The federal government sent a scientific expedition there as long ago as 1849; it was followed the next year by a paleontologist representing the Smithsonian Institution. Since that time, specimens and skeletons from this rich storehouse of ancient animal life have found their way into museums the world over.

The Black Hills, which have been aptly called a vest-pocket edition of the Rocky Mountains, are sufficiently different from the Great Plains to be regarded as a third distinct physiographic province of the state. This mountainous mass takes the form of an irregular dome-shaped uplift, rising 3,500 feet above the surrounding plain. Harney Peak, with its elevation of 7,242 feet above sea level, is the highest point in North America east of the Rockies. Two thirds of the Black Hills area lies in South Dakota; the other third forms a part of Wyoming.

The Missouri River drains the entire state with the exception of the Minnesota Valley lowland in the northeastern corner. In the eastern part, the principal tributaries of the Missouri are the Big Sioux, the James or Dakota, and the Vermillion, all flowing southward in the valleys formed by drainage from the glaciers.

The James River, with its source near the Canadian boundary in North Dakota, has been frequently referred to as the longest unnavigable river in the world. Because of the eastward slope of the Great Plains area, the rivers in that region flow in an easterly direction into the Missouri, with the exception of the Little Missouri, which drains the western portion of Harding County. The main rivers in the trans-Missouri region, from north to south, are the Grand, Moreau, Cheyenne, Bad, and White.

The rough, hilly area of the Prairie Hills section is dotted with many lakes. "Some of them are very deep and hold water during the longest dry spells, and others are very shallow and hold water only during wet seasons. They vary from large lakes, several miles across, like Lake Kampeska at Watertown . . . to small lakes, but a few yards in diameter, nestling deep in the kettles between knobby glacial hills."[2] The lakes, most of them spring-fed, offer excellent habitats for fish and wild fowl.

SOILS

The soils of South Dakota are among the most fertile to be found anywhere, yielding bountiful crops if the rainfall is adequate. Significant variations in soil types occur as a result of the diversity in the state's topography. Most of eastern South Dakota has a clay loam soil formed from the glacial drift. In the southeast along the Sioux River are rich wind-deposited soils, or loess, which make this section especially valuable for farming. These soils are identified with the Chernozem group in the classification generally used today. Chernozem soils are found in the temperate subhumid grassland plains in the central part of the United States where the precipitation ranges from eighteen to twenty-eight inches. They vary in color from an extremely dark brown to black, and are particularly well adapted to growing wheat and corn. Except for the Boyd-Holt soil area in the south-central part of the state along the Missouri River, the belt of Chernozem soils in South Dakota coincides with the Prairie Plains topography.

Within the Great Plains Province, excluding the small Boyd-Holt area, occur the Chestnut groups, comprising dark brown or dark grayish-brown surface soils and the Pierre soils distinguished by their heavy, sticky nature and moderately dark surface color, and by dense clayey or shaly subsoils. These are unglaciated soils

2 *Ibid.*, p. 18.

formed mostly from the weathering of various shales. When they receive adequate moisture, the smoother areas of both Chestnut and Pierre soils produce high yields of wheat and other small grains. They are, however, the typical soils of the cool and temperate semi-

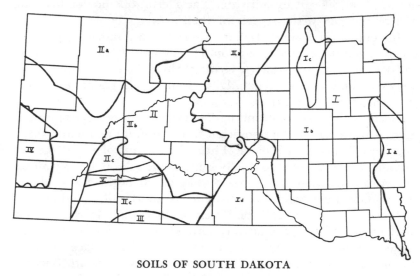

SOILS OF SOUTH DAKOTA

(Based on Fred C. Westin, Leo F. Puhr, and George J. Buntley, *Soils of South Dakota,* South Dakota Agricultural Experiment Station, Soil Survey Series No. 3, Brookings, S. Dak., March, 1959, p. 9.)

KEY

I—Chernozem Soils
  Ia, Moody
  Ib, Barnes-Parnell
  Ic, Fargo-Bearden (Beotia)
  Id, Boyd-Holt

II—Chestnut Soils
  IIa, Williams-Morton-Bainville
  IIb, Pierre or "gumbo" soils
  IIc, Rosebud

III—Valentine-Dune
  Sandhill Soil

IV—Gray Wooded Soils
  Thin lithosol soils on steep slopes, rock outcrop, and some Chestnut grassland soils

V—Rough
  broken land

arid grassland and are known for their value as grazing land. The Chestnut groups include various clay loams and sandy loams in the region along the Grand and Moreau rivers, in the south-central area below the White River, and in the northern and central parts of the Missouri Hills section of the Great Plains Province.

The Pierre shales, which have disintegrated slowly, form the ingredients for the heavy Pierre clay or gumbo soils. These do not absorb moisture readily; they form a slick mire when wet and tend to cake when dry. An intractable clay layer near the surface makes them difficult to cultivate. The Pierre soils predominate in the central and western parts of the state.

In south-central South Dakota along the Nebraska border is a small sandhills section several miles wide which supports native grasses excellent for livestock feeding. Since the sandy soils are so pervious, and rainfall generally so scanty, this region is poorly adapted to cultivated crops.

In addition to the conditioning influences of the geological formations, climate has been a significant factor in building up and shaping the soils of South Dakota. The difference in color and the accumulation of carbonates, chiefly lime, in the subsoil are explained in terms of rainfall. The brown soils, which begin at the Black Hills and extend eastward into the Missouri Hills section, are lighter in color than the Chernozem or black soils in the eastern part of the state. The relatively low supply of moisture has protected the heavy soil from the leaching that takes place in more humid sections of the state; consequently in western South Dakota, the lime horizon lies only about a foot below the surface of the ground. As one continues eastward where there is more rainfall, the layer of lime accumulation gradually thins out and drops to a lower depth. The heavy soils of the more arid areas also contain less humus from the grass cover and other matter than the soils in the more humid areas in the Prairie Plains section.

The native characteristic of the Prairie grassland is a turf of tall grass, chief of which is the big bluestem specie, growing rankly to a height of three feet and over. The tall grasses have a deep root system adapted to subhumid conditions. The line of demarcation between the tall grasses and the short grasses is almost identical with the western edge of the Chernozem or dark soils and follows closely the eighteen-inch rainfall line.

The short-grass species, which include grama, buffalo, and western wheat grass, are especially well adapted to the semiarid conditions of the Great Plains because they are drought-resistant. They have a shallow root system and the capacity to mature quickly. When rainfall is adequate, they grow more luxuriantly, western wheat grass at times attaining a height of two feet.

The transitional zone or belt between the Prairie and Great Plains sections is not constant, but shifts according to the moisture supply. In periods of low rainfall, conditions of semiaridity invade the normally humid areas in the eastern part of the state. Conversely, above-average rainfall will induce humid conditions in normally semiarid areas. Historically, it is this transitional zone between the James River Valley and the Missouri River which has presented the most serious problems of agricultural adjustment and adaptation. In this region, alternating cycles of copious and sparse rainfall profoundly affect farm production.

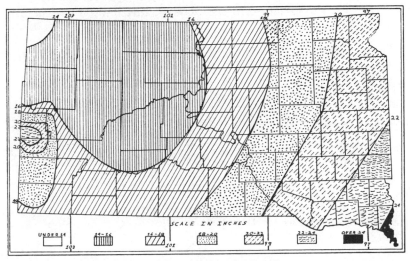

SOUTH DAKOTA AVERAGE ANNUAL PRECIPITATION, 1921–1950

(Based on map, page 3, in *South Dakota Agricultural Statistics, 1959*, South Dakota Crop and Livestock Reporting Service, United States Department of Agriculture, Sioux Falls, S. Dak., 1960.)

RAINFALL

The average annual rainfall in South Dakota is 19.12 inches, but the rainfall supply is quite variable, ranging from about 26 inches along the eastern border to 14 inches and under in Harding County in the northwestern corner. Thus the state possesses the characteristics of both semiarid and subhumid regions. The central part of South Dakota where the rainfall drops from the 20-inch to the 18-inch level is the transitional zone in which the Prairie Plains features merge into those of the Great Plains. This transitional area coincides roughly with the Missouri Hills section of the Great Plains Province. Here the features of the prairie grassland gradually blend into a Great Plains environment. No exact cartographic line can be drawn, however, to mark off the tall-grass from the short-grass country.

Variations in rainfall within the same locality are as significant for agriculture as the variations between different regions; any appreciable variability at a time when moisture is greatly needed has serious implications. Normally, three-fourths of the precipitation occurs between April and September, during the growing season. In fact, the variation in the seasonal distribution is generally

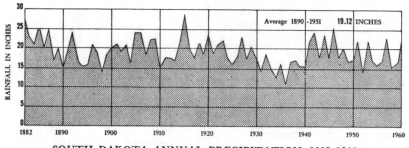

SOUTH DAKOTA ANNUAL PRECIPITATION, 1882–1960

(Based on *South Dakota Agricultural Statistics, 1959,* South Dakota Crop and Livestock Reporting Service, United States Department of Agriculture, Sioux Falls, S. Dak., 1960, p. 4.)

greater than the fluctuation in annual precipitation. As an example of extremes in rainfall, in the James River Valley a high of 40 inches in 1881 contrasts with a low of 14 inches in 1894.

Unfavorable moisture conditions may be intensified still further by a rapid rate of evaporation induced by a low relative humidity, high summer temperature, and persistent winds. In South Dakota evaporation can be as great a factor in crop failures as a deficiency of rainfall.

Because of their high elevation, the Black Hills receive more moisture, especially in winter, than the surrounding plains. Their several fertile limestone valleys are utilized by both farmers and stockmen. In the foothills, however, the environmental characteristics are those of the adjoining Great Plains Province.

The topographical and climatic peculiarities of the Upper Missouri Valley were for a long time misunderstood. Early explorers and military leaders, accustomed to humid regions, proclaimed the entire area unfit for cultivation, hence uninhabitable by white men. Their descriptive reports built up the myth of a "Great American Desert," the present state of South Dakota lying entirely within the region so designated. Settlement was discouraged as hazardous and experimental, and Indian policy and military strategy were shaped in accordance with the prevalent misconceptions.

To the military man whose thinking was limited to the elementary physical needs of timber and grain for the maintenance of a cavalry post, the rugged topography, the scarcity of trees, and the low rate of rainfall seemed confirmation of the popular view of semiaridity. One of those who reached the usual conclusions was Lieutenant G. K. Warren, who made important scientific and meteorological observations in the South Dakota country during the years 1855 to 1857—a period of severe drought. According to Lieutenant Warren, the Vermillion River marked the western limit of agricultural lands; he regarded the country bordering the James River as of no value for farming purposes and as having few resources.[3] As late as 1866 General W. T. Sherman declared that white settlement should be confined to the more humid areas where the accustomed patterns of farming might be carried out. It was his opinion that settlement should not be encouraged beyond the point where corn and grapes would grow.

The ability of some settlers to raise crops in the supposedly uninhabitable region and the advent of more propitious weather conditions combined to dispel the "Great American Desert" myth, but bred the equally misleading notion that the westward march of settlement had wrought progressive meteorological changes. According to this theory, cultivation of the soil had increased evaporation sufficiently to modify the temperature and to induce increased precipitation. The phenomenon of relatively high moisture coinciding with a heavy influx of settlers during the boom period of the late seventies and early eighties in eastern South Dakota appeared to confirm the idea that "rainfall follows the plow."

The recurrence of disastrous droughts was a rude shock to the

[3] See Gouverner K. Warren, "Explorations in the Dakota Country," in Lloyd McFarling, *Exploring the Northern Plains, 1804–1876* (Caldwell, Idaho: Caxton Printers, Ltd., 1955), pp. 220–231.

boosters of the boom period and compelled a re-examination of climatic conditions. Subsequently, a theory about weather cycles developed from an analysis of available meteorological records, which showed a picture of rainfall fluctuation from high to low in an almost rhythmical pattern. Although scientists have denied the existence of true cycles in rainfall, the long swings or trends revealed by tree-ring studies for the Upper Missouri Valley suggest some degree of periodicity in a progression of years of above- and below-average rainfall. In South Dakota the drought periods generally have lasted from five to nine years. The major significance of such variability in rainfall, whatever its scientific basis, is that it shows the need for land-utilization programs and the application of soil conservation principles.

So long as there was no adequate information about the land, the early settlers' efforts at adjustment were haphazard. The observations recorded by army officers and fur traders journeying through the region were not too reliable. Official weather reporting in the present state of South Dakota began in January, 1854, when the United States Army established a weather station at Fort Pierre; a second station was established at Fort Randall, November, 1856, and a third at the Yankton Indian Agency at Greenwood in 1859. Western South Dakota received its first weather station at Deadwood in January, 1878, and its second the following year at Fort Meade. The observations at the various posts were undertaken by medical officers. Voluntary observers, working through the Smithsonian Institution, began to submit reports from Yankton in 1860. The Signal Service Bureau began its services in the state at Fort Sully in 1872. From 1854 to 1892 as many as seventy-five different weather stations carried on meteorological observations, but the periods of observation were still too short and the records too incomplete to present a true picture.

The early settlers, moreover, lacked adequate information about the characteristics of the soil. There was no soil mapping by the United States Bureau of Soils until 1899. In the Great Plains region where the problem of adaptation and adjustment was most vital, no soil survey was made until 1912. In recent years better understanding of meteorological and soil conditions has made possible a more rational approach to the whole problem of effective land utilization and proper patterns of farm and ranch management.

CHAPTER 2

The First People on the Land

THE FIRST INHABITANTS of present-day South Dakota are unknown. Anthropologists and archaeologists have generally agreed that the ancestors of the North American Indians crossed from Asia to the Alaskan coast toward the end of the glacial age approximately fifteen to twenty thousand years ago. This migration, covering probably many thousands of years, gradually led to the occupation of the whole Western hemisphere.

PREHISTORIC OCCUPANTS

The first Dakotans had no knowledge of horticulture. They existed by hunting and fishing, using stone and bone weapons and tools—points, scrapers, hand axes, and other implements characteristic of Paleolithic or Old Stone culture. Fortunately, they were mighty hunters, for giant bison, sloths, elephants, and sabre-toothed tigers as well as camels, four-horned antelopes, and three-toed horses were roaming the land. In the course of time, for reasons unknown, these people disappeared from the region—probably about 5000 B.C.—and the animal life became extinct.

In 1946, archaeological evidence uncovered near the Angostura dam in Fall River County established the presence of an Indian camp site there about 5000 B.C. Altogether, archaeological explorations and surveys have brought to light nearly a thousand aborigi-

15

nal villages and camp sites within the state. Most of them are more
recent than the one uncovered in Fall River County.

Thanks to artifacts and other remains, it is possible to reconstruct
a partial picture of the Indian occupation in this area during the
late prehistoric period. After about 2000 B.C. one can begin to trace
events in the region with a fair degree of continuity.

From about A.D. 1000 on, a number of nomadic tribes occupied the
Black Hills region, some subsisting chiefly by hunting, others living
on the fruit of the abundant food plants that grow there. These
tribes, it is assumed, belonged to the various linguistic stocks then
dominant on the Northern Plains, and probably included Caddoan,
Athabascan, Shoshonean, and Kiowa groups.

East of the Missouri River, perhaps as early as A.D. 500, there appeared a group known as the Mound Builders, so named because
they erected low, broad, dome-shaped structures which mostly
were used as burial chambers. Primarily a hunting people who
lived in temporary villages, they were closely identified with similar
groups elsewhere in the Upper Mississippi Basin. Their mounds are
found for the most part along the Big Sioux River and in the vicinity
of Big Stone Lake, but other sites also have been located along
streams and lakes in eastern South Dakota. The Mound Builders
disappeared about A.D. 800, probably either annihilated in warfare or assimilated by other groups.

During the period from A.D. 1250 to 1400 an agricultural people
migrated out of southern Minnesota into present-day South Dakota.
These people are thought to be the ancestors of the Mandans who
were to occupy a strategic position along the Missouri River a few
centuries later.

THE ARIKARA

The Arikara, sometimes referred to as the Ree Indians, figured
prominently in the early history of the future state. This tribe was
the northern branch of the Caddoan linguistic family to which the
Pawnee also were kin. Apparently a long and severe drought was
the major factor causing the Arikara's migration northward along
the Missouri Valley from the Central Plains of Nebraska and Kansas.
It was during the sixteenth century, according to recent scholarship,
that they moved into the central part of South Dakota, and it was
there that they reached the peak of their cultural development.

The Arikara usually located their villages on high terraces along the Missouri to take advantage of the protection afforded by the deep ravines and the river bed. On the unprotected sides they put up a stockade of posts behind four- and five-foot ditches. Inside these fortifications were their earth-lodges, of which there might be from fifty to two hundred. The early earth-lodges were square; later on they were built in a circular form, no doubt because a round structure could be more easily heated from a central firepit. In the seventeenth century, which saw their period of greatest prosperity, the Arikara customarily maintained twelve villages, although at one time they are said to have had as many as thirty-two villages and four thousand warriors. After 1700, under pressure from the Sioux and other enemy groups they tended to concentrate the population in fewer villages, which were larger and more compact.

The industrious Arikara seem to have surpassed many of the contemporary tribes in their adaptation to the plains environment and in the skills called for by their way of life. For food, they depended mostly on crops of corn, beans, squash, and pumpkin, supplemented by game. In sign language among the neighboring tribes along the Missouri they were known as "corn-eaters," and the plant's prominence in Arikara ceremonials shows its importance in their economy. Their tribal government consisted of a loosely knit confederacy of subtribes. Each village had its own political organization which administered local affairs, and the leader of the largest band or subtribe usually was the head chieftain.

As a non-nomadic people living in a fixed habitation, the Arikara attained a high degree of self-sufficiency, supplying most of their wants from the raw materials at hand. From the bones of hunted prey came their tools and other implements, and their pottery cooking vessels were moulded of clay taken from the deposits along the riverbank. They excelled in basketry, and were skilled in dressing and decorating animal skins, and in adapting them to various uses. They also were active agents in exchange with neighboring nomadic tribes, bartering their surplus corn and vegetables and a kind of tobacco peculiar to them for meat products, skin, and buffalo robes.

By virtue of engaging in this trade the Arikara, along with the Mandans, were intermediaries in introducing horses to the Upper Missouri Valley and the region eastward. The trade in horses, which had become important merchandise in this area by 1760, probably was initiated by the Kiowa, Comanche, and Pawnee, who secured their supply from the Spaniards in the Southwest by direct purchase and by thievery. The horses were disseminated to the Northern Plains by a route which led from New Mexico and Texas across the High Plains to the vicinity of the Black Hills—the point of contact with the Arikara. Although they lived in fixed villages, the Arikara's buffalo hunts took them to the foot of the hills, and there they met with the Kiowa, Comanche, Arapaho, and Cheyenne in a trading fair. The horses which they acquired were, in turn, a significant item of barter in their trade with the Teton Sioux, who were migrating into the region from the east.

By the end of the eighteenth century the Arikara had fallen into a state of decline. Reduced by warfare and disease to two villages, they moved northward in 1795 from the mouth of the Cheyenne to the mouth of the Grand River. Because of their weakened condition they were forced to modify many aspects of their former organization, and some of the distinctive names of earlier villages were lost. Further deterioration followed the entrance of white fur traders into the region. In 1823 the Arikara villages were temporarily abandoned, and nine years later were evacuated permanently when the Arikara joined the Mandans, who lived along the Missouri in present-day North Dakota.

THE SIOUX

The Indian tribes which are most intimately associated with South Dakota's history are those of the Sioux or Dakota. Linguistically, they are of the Siouan stock to which also belong the Crows, Omahas, Iowas, Mandans, and related tribes which the first white men found occupying the western half of the upper Mississippi Basin. Originally, so it is believed, the Siouan peoples inhabited the Ohio Valley. In the period before the discovery of America they were forced from the region by the Iroquois and split into smaller groups, some dispersing eastward, others to the west. The largest group to migrate westward were the Dakota or Sioux.

The earliest definite information about the Sioux was recorded by French priests who came to Wisconsin during the 1640's. The Sioux at this time were occupying the timbered country west of Lake Superior on the headwaters of the Mississippi. In their own language they called themselves *Dakota* or *Lakota,* derived from *koda,* the Siouan term for friend, and signifying "an alliance of friends." But ironically enough, the name Sioux by which they are commonly known comes from a Chippewa word meaning "snake" or "enemy." Since the early French explorers were in closer contact with the Algonquins, of whom the Chippewa were a branch, it was an abbreviated form of the Chippewa designation that passed into the white man's language.

By the seventeenth century the Sioux parent group had expanded into seven major divisions, distinguished mainly by dialectic differences. Of these seven, four tribes—the Wahpetons, Sissetons, Mdewakanton (Med-ay-wah'kahn-ton), and Wakpekute (Wak-pay-koo'tay)—were known collectively as the Santee; the other divisions were the Yanktons, the Yanktonnais, and the Teton. The Teton tribe comprised seven subtribes: Oglala, Brûlé, Two Kettle, Sans Arc, Blackfoot, Hunkpapa, and Minneconjou. The Oglala is probably the oldest of the Teton subtribes, the others branching off from it when it became too large.[1]

On the early French maps the Santee divisions, which occupied the wooded and marshy area east of the Mississippi, are designated as the Sioux of the East. The other divisions, which ranged over the tall-grass prairies on the other side of the river, were appropriately identified as the Sioux of the West. Not long after the Sioux tribes had received their first visits from the whites, they began to move out of the headwaters of the Mississippi, following a course that led into the Minnesota Valley. From that region the Sioux of the West were to drift gradually westward until they reached the open plains in the Missouri Basin. Constant pressure from their Algonquin neighbors as well as the natural process of expansion which necessitated a more bountiful food supply were the factors which led the Sioux to migrate into the southern and western parts of Minnesota.

It seems likely that the Western Sioux were the first to feel the pressure from the Algonquin tribes. Until about 1670 the fierce Sioux warriors most often emerged the victors in their intermittent warfare with the Crees, a branch of the Algonquins dwelling north of them in the Rainy Lake country. But the tide turned when the Crees were supplied with guns both by the French, then penetrating the region west of Lake Superior, and by the British, who had arrived in the Hudson Bay area. The British, particularly, had enlarged the market for guns and ammunition. The Yanktonnais tribe, which lived nearest the Crees, was no doubt affected the most,

[1] Some anthropologists regard the subdivisions of the Teton Sioux as separate tribes. In this book they will be referred to as subtribes.

but nonetheless one of its subtribes, the Assiniboin, managed to remain on a friendly footing with their foes and actually severed all connection with the Sioux to join the Crees permanently.

When the Yanktonnais found themselves unable to withstand the attacks of the Crees, they began to retire southward, compelling a similar movement among the Yankton and Teton divisions. While the Yanktonnais were moving slowly up the Minnesota River, the Yanktons, an offshoot of the older branch and speaking the same dialect, had started into the region extending from the Blue Earth River to the Pipestone Quarry. The Tetons, either preceding or following the Yanktonnais, also occupied the prairies westward from the Blue Earth.[2]

Somewhat later, probably after 1735, the Santee, the Sioux of the East, in their turn were pushed out by a neighboring tribe—in this case, the Chippewas—who were well supplied with guns while the Santees still depended on the bow and arrow and stone weapons. Heading in a southwesterly direction, they left the northern and eastern, or wooded, parts of Minnesota, crossed the Mississippi, and ultimately occupied the lower valley of the Minnesota River.

According to Santee tradition, the growing scarcity of buffalo was the impelling factor in the migration of the Teton Sioux toward the Missouri River. On foot and in pursuit of the buffalo, the Oglala and the Brûlé drifted slowly westward in many small bands, moving into the James Valley during the first half of the eighteenth century and reaching the Missouri about 1760. The Oglala crossing of the Missouri some fifteen years later was probably made below the Great Bend, from which point they rapidly spread out over the country toward the Bad River. As recorded in a Sioux winter count (colored pictographs painted on a buffalo robe), in either 1775 or 1776 an Oglala war party moved far enough across the plains westward to discover the Black Hills, then occupied by the Cheyennes.

The Brûlé followed the Oglala across the Missouri to occupy the lands along the White River south of the Big Badlands. Finding the buffalo supply plentiful and having acquired horses, these southern Teton Sioux were soon well established in the trans-Missouri region, and before long their presence was felt by the several tribes in the Black Hills as well as by the Arikara along the Missouri and the Cheyenne River.

[2] George E. Hyde, *Red Cloud's Folk: A History of the Oglala Sioux Indians* (Norman: University of Oklahoma Press, 1937), p. 6.

The northern Tetons, sometimes called the Teton-Saones, and the Yanktonnais drifted across the coteau from the headwaters of the Minnesota River, probably reaching the Missouri a little later than the advance guard of the Oglala. From their location in the Cheyenne villages the Arikara blocked the Saone crossing of the Missouri until 1795; when they moved their villages north to the Grand River, the Cheyenne Valley was opened as a line of migration for the northern Teton bands. The Minneconjou appear to have been the first to cross the river. Unlike the Oglala and the Brûlé, many members of the north Teton maintained their camps on the east side of the Missouri until after 1800.

The Yanktonnais, who accompanied—or at any rate closely followed—the Tetons in their migration out of Minnesota, took over as their hunting grounds the country between the Missouri and the James, as far north as Devils Lake. The Yanktons moved into the Lower James Valley, and roamed the region while carrying on their hunting and trading activities. Their arrival compelled the rearrangement and relocation of the several tribes then in the Missouri Valley Basin. The Omahas and Iowas, who were settled on the north side of the Missouri above the mouth of the Big Sioux, withdrew southward into Nebraska; the Poncas, a part of the Omaha tribe, were also affected but managed to remain near the mouth of the Niobrara, where they built a strongly fortified village.

Although the several distinct divisions of Sioux were scattered over a vast expanse of territory, practical considerations continued to draw them toward the Minnesota country, which remained the major source of firearms and other European commodities until the early part of the nineteenth century. A distributing point for such goods had been maintained by the Santee on the Minnesota River since about 1700, and each spring it had been the scene of a Sioux trading fair. But after the Teton subtribes had become established in their new western hunting grounds, even though they now had horses, they were unwilling to travel so far for traders' goods. A new, more centrally located trading fair was established at Armadale Grove on the James River in what is now Spink County, and here each spring the Tetons met their Yankton, Yanktonnais, and Santee kinsmen to barter buffalo robes, antelope-skin shirts and leggings, and some of the horses acquired from the Arikara, in return both for native commodities such as walnut bows and red stone pipes and for guns and kettles and other goods of European manufacture which had been obtained from white traders on the Minnesota and Des Moines rivers. According to one white trader, sometimes as many as a thousand to twelve hundred lodges housing about three thousand men bearing arms were assembled at the Sioux market place.[3] The fair also served to maintain a community of interest among the different Sioux tribes.

A revolutionary change in their culture pattern was one consequence of the migration of the Western Sioux. In prehistoric times their mode of life had been shaped almost entirely by the natural conditions prevailing in a timbered country. Although there were small gardens in the southern part of their territory, theirs was essentially a hunting and gathering economy. They traveled mostly by boat; their diet consisted mainly of wild rice and berries gathered from the woods and swamps, fish caught in lake water, and game hunted down in the forest; their houses were of the type common to the region—shaped like loaves of bread, they were constructed on pole foundations, covered with earth and bark.

When they left the timbered region at the head of the Mississippi for the open prairies, the Western Sioux, traveling now mostly by land, exchanged boats for travois. They became accustomed to a new diet whose staples were furnished by the buffalo and by prairie plant life, and to light, transportable, skin-covered tipis instead of stationary dwellings. But this transition to a predominantly nomadic life did not take place overnight; rather, it was a gradual process whose final consummation was not attained until the Sioux moved into the Great Plains environment. Guns had become available to them as a result of contact with the whites; and the acquisition of horses, which served to strengthen and intensify nomadic traits, powerfully influenced the direction of their changing cultural pattern. New weapons, a new means of transportation, and a new environment worked together to transform the Teton Sioux and the kindred bands east of the Missouri into typical Plains Indians— mounted hunters who depended primarily on buffalo meat for subsistence.

The Western Sioux comprised an impressive proportion of the Great Plains Indian population: no less than one-sixth in 1780, by one estimate. Teton bands made up the larger part of this number. The Sioux domain extended from the Republican River in Kansas

[3] Annie Heloise Abel (ed.), *Tabeau's Narrative of Loisel's Expedition to the Upper Missouri* (Norman: University of Oklahoma Press, 1939), p. 122.

and Nebraska westward to the Rocky Mountains and northward to the Canadian border. Within this far-flung empire lay the major buffalo ranges, which they shared with other Plains Indians.

The Teton Sioux, in the opinion of anthropologists, represented the highest type, mentally and physically, of the Plains tribes. Along with the Cheyennes, they were regarded as the boldest and most capable warriors on the Northern Plains. When they made war, they were most often motivated by the desire to extend or protect their hunting grounds, to acquire horses, and to gain personal prestige—raiding a rival camp for horses was a good way for a young brave to earn admission to the warrior societies. Because of their intrepid nature and skilled horsemanship, the Teton Sioux were a formidable foe to whites and red men alike; and because they were unhampered by a settled village life, they were able to hold out for a long time against subjugation by force of arms.

For the Teton bands the early part of the nineteenth century was a period of great prosperity. A plentiful supply of game assured adequate subsistence for a population that increased fourfold, some authorities say, in the years from 1800 to 1825. Greater wealth in horses enhanced the social prestige of the tribal leaders; and, more important, the strategic position of the Teton Sioux along the Upper Missouri gave them a key role in the fur trade, whose western base was shifted from the Great Lakes to St. Louis in consequence of American occupation of the region. In their dual capacity of trappers and consumers the Teton Sioux were to profit from this traffic, receiving in exchange for their peltries a horde of metal tools, utensils, and luxury goods.

CHAPTER 3

French and Spanish Sovereignty on the Upper Missouri

UNTIL THE YEAR 1763 the Upper Missouri Valley was a part of the vast colonial empire set up by the French in North America. The French made their first permanent settlement at Quebec in 1608. Under the leadership of Samuel de Champlain they followed the St. Lawrence and its tributaries inland until they were upon the shores of Lake Huron and Lake Ontario. Favorable waterways leading beyond the St. Lawrence Valley and Lake Ontario made exploration into the interior easy: within a matter of half a century Frenchmen were penetrating the country beyond Lake Superior to make contact with the several Siouan tribes in the region, as well as with the Crees north of them. Pierre Radisson and his brother-in-law, the Sieur de Groseilliers, during their journeys in the western wilderness between 1654 and 1660, found the Sioux tribes on the headwaters of the Mississippi, where they visited them at the "lake where they live."

At first the French empire-builders paid scant attention to the western periphery of the Upper Mississippi Valley. Only a few fur traders occasionally appeared among the Cree and Sioux tribes for brief visits. One of these traders was Daniel Greysolon, the Sieur Dulhut, who decided to explore the country of the Sioux and Assiniboin tribes westward from Lake Superior in order to set up a trading domain. Dulhut—Duluth in the Anglicized form—started out in September, 1678, with seven white companions and some friendly Indians. After re-establishing contact with the Indians on Lake Superior, he retraced the route taken by Radisson and Groseilliers some twenty years earlier. From a base established in an Indian village on the shore of Lake Mille Lacs in the heart of the Sioux country, on July 2, 1679, he dispatched three of his men westward with a Sioux war party. It is quite probable that this group reached the coteau at Big Stone Lake, and here made their first contact with what is now South Dakota soil. Like others who had preceded him, Duluth eventually abandoned his project in order to give his full attention to the fur trade in the Wisconsin area.

At a little later period, Pierre Charles Le Sueur maintained occasional trading posts along the Minnesota River, one of them located in the vicinity of the present city of Mankato. There is evidence that small parties under Le Sueur's direction may have visited the Big Sioux Valley, including the site of Sioux Falls, between 1683 and 1700. At any rate, French maps by 1701 were showing clearer graphic details of Indian villages and the geography of the area.

Aside from such temporary and inconsequential excursions, the French continued to neglect the region beyond the Mississippi. Three major deterrents—one local, the others arising from external political and economic forces—explain their lack of interest in the Upper Missouri Valley. As in the case of the Iroquois who were blocking their way into western New York, the French had incurred the hostility of the Sioux tribes, then occupying a triangle lying roughly between the James River, Lake Superior, and the northern part of the present state of Iowa. The French were too closely identified with traditional Sioux enemies, whether Assiniboin, Cree, or Chippewa, to overcome suspicions of partiality. Unable to break through the barrier formed by the Sioux tribes, they withdrew the several trading posts and Jesuit missions they had established in the Sioux country at sporadic intervals prior to 1700.

In addition to their difficulties with the Sioux, the French were beset with colonial problems elsewhere. From 1689 to 1713 and the signing of the Treaty of Utrecht, almost continuous open warfare with their great rival, England, required them to concentrate on the defense of their settlements and colonial claims along the Atlantic seaboard to the neglect of their holdings in the Upper Mississippi and Missouri basins. And in any case, so long as the traffic in furs in eastern Canada and the Great Lakes region was heavy enough to satisfy their cupidity or to give them an advantage over their English rivals, the French had little incentive to stake out the virgin territory beyond the Great Lakes, with its attendant hazards and uncertainties.

At the end of the second intercolonial war (Queen Anne's War, 1701–1713), the French reconsidered their position in the interior of the continent. In the far north they had been forced to relinquish the Hudson Bay area to the British. At the same time excessive trapping, especially in Wisconsin, had led to diminishing returns. These considerations compelled the French to revise their policy with respect to the entire region west of Lake Superior. They began to reoccupy posts they had abandoned earlier, and sought to renew their close relationship with the Crees and Assiniboins in order to divert the flow of furs away from England's Hudson Bay outposts to their own posts on the Great Lakes. During the long interval of peace which lasted from 1713 to 1744, the French were able to extend their sphere westward from Lake Superior along a chain of lakes and rivers that collectively form "the crossroads of the continent."[1] Although the French failed to profit from the expansion because of their eventual defeat by the British, their explorations in the interior of Canada and in the Upper Missouri Basin beyond the continental watershed were among their greatest achievements in the New World.

THE LA VERENDRYE EXPLORATIONS

Key figure in these French activities along "the crossroads of the continent" was Pierre Gaultier de Varennes, the Sieur de La Verendrye. Born of a good family and a typical man of his time, La Verendrye spent his early years as a soldier. After a decade of active service, he settled down on a seigniory near Quebec where for a dozen years he carried on a licensed trade in furs with nearby Indians. In 1727 he was honored with the command of the fort at a trading post on the Nipigon River above Lake Superior, the westernmost permanent French establishment at the time.

[1] John B. Brebner, *Explorers of North America, 1492–1806* (New York: The Macmillan Co., 1933), p. 359.

Following his arrival in the autumn of 1727, he acquainted himself through a careful questioning of the many Indians gathered at the post with the nature of the fur trade and the part played by the tribes in the Hudson Bay competition. The geography of the region particularly commanded his attention, as little was known about the peculiar drainage system of lakes and rivers in the border country beyond Grand Portage. The concept of a Western Sea had especially engaged the attention of early explorers. The tales of the Indians (mainly based on hearsay, suppositions, and erroneous conclusions, but nevertheless convincingly told) fixed in La Verendrye a determination to turn explorer and discover the waterway that led supposedly into the interior of the continent.

With the information he secured from the Indians, documented by a crude map attributed to a Cree, and with the enthusiastic support of a Jesuit missionary who had established a temporary station among the Sioux, he convinced the Canadian governor of the feasibility of a search for the Western Sea. As the next step in his plan, in 1730 La Verendrye gained a trading monopoly for the Lake Winnipeg region. His principal fort he located on Lake of the Woods where he could deal with the Crees and Assiniboins and stabilize his trading operations. The anticipated profits from the fur trade were to provide the means for conducting his explorations.

In the next fourteen years La Verendrye, with the aid of four sons and a few other relatives, built a chain of posts along the lakes and rivers leading west and northwest of Lake Superior into a hitherto unexplored region. When he reached Lake Winnipeg, he made it his base of operations in his quest for a westward passageway that would lead to the Western Sea.

In 1738 La Verendrye struck southward for a visit to the Mandan Indians who had been represented to him as dwelling by a "Great River of the West." Leaving Lake Winnipeg on October 18, with a party of fifty-two persons that included his sons François and Louis-Joseph, by dint of a succession of wearying marches over the prairie, he reached his destination among the Mandans on December 3. La Verendrye and his men thus earned the distinction of being the first Europeans to attain the upper reaches of the Missouri River. Having been obliged to change his earlier plans for a prolonged stay, the elder La Verendrye was back at Fort La Reine on the Assiniboine River by February 10, 1739.

La Verendrye's determination to follow up his explorations in the Missouri Basin led to a second expedition, but vexing complications, arising mostly from intertribal wars waged by the Assiniboins and Crees against the Sioux of the West, prevented La Verendrye himself from returning to the Missouri. In his stead, he sent his sons, François and Louis-Joseph, who were accompanied by two experienced *voyageurs*. Louis-Joseph, who seems to have held the title of Chevalier, was the leader of the small party. On the first leg of what was expected to be a quick dash to the Western Sea, the brothers reached the Mandans on May 19, 1742, in an uneventful journey of only twenty days from Fort La Reine. After a period of waiting during which they familiarized themselves with the Mandan language and picked up further information about the region, the Frenchmen left on July 23 on an extended exploration of the Northern Plains. It was not until July 2 of the following year, after an absence of fifteen months, that they returned to Fort La Reine.

It is not easy to trace with any degree of exactness the route traveled by the second La Verendrye expedition. Identification of Indian encampments and the various geographic points mentioned in the La Verendrye journal is largely a matter of guesswork because of the vagueness of the terms. There is, however, incontrovertible evidence that during the early months of 1743 the La Verendrye brothers reached the west bank of the Missouri near the mouth of the Bad River in the central part of present-day South Dakota. A leaden plate attesting to this fact was discovered at Fort Pierre on February 17, 1913. According to the journal, the period from March 19 to April 2 was spent here with the "Gens de la Petite Cerise," the Little Cherries, undoubtedly a band of Arikaras who then occupied the area.

The journal kept by the Chevalier states:

I placed on an eminence near the fort a tablet of lead, with the arms and inscription of the King and a pyramid of stones for Monsieur le General; I said to the savages, who did not know of the tablet of lead that I had placed in the earth, that I was placing these stones as a memorial of those who had come to their country. I had very much wished to take the altitude of this place but our astrolabe had been out of service since the beginning of our journey, the ring being broken.[2]

The La Verendrye plate, which is eight and a half inches long, six

[2] See "Journal of the Trip Made by Chevalier de la Verendrye with One of His Brothers, to Reach the Western Sea" in *South Dakota Historical Collections,* VII (1914), 357.

and a half wide, and about an eighth of an inch thick, is now a prized possession of the South Dakota State Historical Society in its museum at Pierre. On one side is a carefully engraved Latin inscription: *Anno XXVI Regni Ludovici XV Prorege Illustrissimo Domino Domino Marchione de Beauharnois MDCCXXXXI Petrus Gaultier de Leverendrie Posuit.* The other side bears a French inscription, scratched on it with the point of a knife by a member of the party when the tablet was placed in the ground: *Pose par le chevalyet de Lav to jo Louy la Londette Amiotte le 30 de mars 1743.* The crude workmanship and the abbreviations have made it difficult to decipher and translate the inscription. Crouse, biographer of the elder La Verendrye, construes it as follows: "Placed by the Chevalier de la Verendrye, witnesses Louis, La Londette, Amiotte." In his opinion, the names are those of the three Frenchmen who actually witnessed the depositing of the plate: Louis-Joseph (the Chevalier) and the two *voyageurs* La Londette and Amiotte.[3]

The discovery of the La Verendrye plate on top of the hill overlooking the Missouri has strengthened the contention that the party was gazing at the Black Hills rather than the Big Horn range in Wyoming on New Year's Day, 1743, when it found itself "in the sight of the mountains." In view of the slow pace of travel, probably never over eighteen miles per day and usually much less, as well as the considerable time consumed in visitations at Indian encampments, it is improbable that the party got as far west as the Powder River Valley in Montana and Wyoming. The arguments expressed pro and con on this point are, however, inconsequential and have no relevancy to the importance that attaches to the expedition itself. Considering the area traversed, the difficulties involved, and the dangers braved, the expedition of 1742–1743 was a monumental achievement.

The La Verendryes fell into disfavor with the French government in 1744, bringing their activities to an end, but their work as explorers could not be discredited. The geographical knowledge acquired in the course of their explorations soon found a place

[3] Nellis M. Crouse, *La Verendrye: Fur Trader and Explorer* (Ithaca: Cornell University Press, 1956), p. 216. In a commentary on the various interpretations concerning the identity of the Chevalier, Crouse states, "We are inclined to believe that François was not present when the plate was buried—he may have been busy in the Indian village—hence his name does not appear on the plate." Several documents are extant referring to Louis-Joseph as the Chevalier; not a single one has been found assigning the title to François (*ibid.*, p. 217).

on French maps. Of particular importance was their discovery that
the Missouri had no western outlet, but flowed southward toward
the Gulf of Mexico.

THE PERIOD OF SPANISH SOVEREIGNTY

Under the Treaty of Paris of 1763 following the French and Indian
War, France ceded her possessions west of the Mississippi River to
Spain. This transfer of sovereignty, which was to usher in a forty-
year period of nominal Spanish rule for the Upper Missouri, brought
no immediate change to the area. The Spanish were still preoccupied
with their holdings in the Lower Mississippi Valley, where they
sought to strengthen their position. A major step toward this objective was taken in February, 1764, when they established a settlement
on the site of St. Louis, a short distance below the junction of the
Mississippi and Missouri rivers. From this vantage point the Spanish were able to gain exclusive control over the fur trade with the
adjacent Indian tribes. St. Louis underwent a rapid growth, eventually becoming the commercial center for the fur trade of the entire Mississippi Basin. The settlement at St. Louis, and the fortifications erected at the mouth of the Missouri, also served to prevent
the English from encroaching upon the fur trade in the Lower
Missouri Valley.

The upper country meanwhile was allowed to fend for itself.
Its Indian inhabitants, unaware of any change in political status,
continued to barter for merchandise that came from warehouses
based in Canada or in the Great Lakes region. Even with the information passed on to them by the French, the Spaniards had only
a limited knowledge of the region prior to 1790. French *coureurs
de bois,* who had moved into the Upper Missouri Valley after the
La Verendrye expedition, remained in the country, merely trans-
ferring their allegiance to British interests subsequent to the Treaty
of Paris.

British traders also were penetrating the region beyond the
Mississippi, and were especially active in the area along the Minne-
sota River. Other British fur traders, representing the Hudson's Bay
Company and the Northwest Company, came from the north coun-
try to the Mandan villages over the course followed by the La
Verendryes. This British infiltration not only impaired profits for
Spanish traders, but also constituted a constant threat to Spanish
sovereignty over the region. At first the Spaniards hoped to protect

their possessions in the upper country against English intruders
with a line of forts along the Mississippi, seeking in particular to
block trespassers from the mouths of the Des Moines and Minnesota rivers.

In the eyes of Spanish officials, the British intrusions into the
Mandan country posed an even greater threat to the Spanish empire
than their smuggling activities along the Mississippi. From their
limited knowledge of the Missouri River, the Spanish as late as
1785 were led to believe that its source lay beyond the Rocky
Mountains a little to the north of the source of the Rio Grande.
If the British were to establish themselves on the Upper Missouri,
it was feared they might readily follow these waterways to challenge Spanish control of New Mexico. It was also disturbing news
that at the time of the British advance into the Upper Missouri
Valley, out on the Pacific coast the Russians were moving southward toward California.

These fears of foreign aggression on the northern edge of its
colonial empire stirred Spain into action. To hold her outlying
possessions, she considered it necessary to move up the Missouri,
find the passageway to the Western Sea, gain the allegiance of her
Indian tribes, establish trading posts, eject intruders, and furnish
protection to the imperilled terrain. In contrast to the aggressive
spirit in which the French extended their control into the interior
by building forts and military posts, the Spanish policy was defen-
sive in character, necessitated by external danger. It was a policy of
protective expansion.

In 1790, while Spanish colonial officials were pondering over the
problem and seeking a more positive approach, the fur-trading interests at St. Louis were looking northward too. The trade among the
Indian tribes in the Lower Missouri Basin was so overcrowded that
it had become desirable to open up virgin territory.

The first Spanish trader to appear in the upper country was
Juan Munier, who in 1789 followed the west bank of the Missouri
River to the mouth of the Niobrara, where the Poncas had a fortified village. The next year Jacques D'Eglise, under a license which
permitted him to hunt on the Missouri, ascended the river all the
way to the Mandan villages, taking with him some merchandise for
trading purposes. D'Eglise obtained firsthand information about the
British traders from a Frenchman who had been living with the
Mandans for fourteen years, and who told him that the English

were carrying on a direct trade from their posts located about fifteen days' journey from the villages. By virtue of his discovery of the Mandans, D'Eglise requested exclusive rights of trade with them, but the Spanish authorities had other plans. When they denied his request, D'Eglise continued his independent activities.

A report transmitted by D'Eglise to the Lieutenant Governor of the Illinois province in October, 1792, seemed to confirm the fears held in official circles about British encroachments. To counteract British activities and to safeguard Spanish territory, plans were immediately drawn up for a frontal attack on the problem facing Spain in the Northwest.

THE MISSOURI COMPANY

A group of St. Louis merchants and traders met in May, 1793, to form a company "for the trade or commerce which may, now or in the future, be had with the tribes who live farther up than the Poncas, who are located on the upper part of the Missouri and in other places in which trade may be carried on . . . ."[4] They requested exclusive privileges of trade for a period of ten years so that the company might indemnify itself against the heavy expenses such an ambitious project would entail. Articles of incorporation were drawn up for the "Company of Explorers of the Upper Missouri" and received official approval a few months later. In this way, the Spanish hoped to realize the dual objective of establishing a trade monopoly with the Mandans and ousting the British from Spanish territory. Additional benefits were to accrue to the Spanish empire from the explorations, for everything possible was to be done "to discover the source of the Missouri River and to penetrate as far as the South Sea, upon whose shores are to be found the new Russian establishments formed above California . . . ."[5]

The Missouri Company, as it was commonly called, was headed by Jacques Clamorgan. Associated with him were prominent St. Louis fur merchants and traders, several of whom, like Clamorgan, had a close connection with official circles. In charge of its first expedition was Canadian-born Jean Baptiste Truteau, a former schoolmaster and a distant relative of Zenon Trudeau, the Lieuten-

[4] A. P. Nasatir (ed.), *Before Lewis and Clark—Documents Illustrating the History of the Missouri, 1785–1804* (St. Louis: St. Louis Historical Documents Foundation, 1952), I, 218.
[5] *Ibid.,* p. 236.

ant Governor of Illinois. D'Eglise, who had made two trips up the Missouri, had decided against joining the Missouri Company, preferring his independent status.

The directors of the new company specifically charged Truteau to proceed to the Mandan nation and establish an agency. He was requested further to obtain all available knowledge and information concerning other Indian nations, particularly the Shoshones, and to take note of the several rivers tributary to the Missouri and their relative distance from either St. Louis or the Mandans. He was to inform himself of the distance to the Rocky Mountains "which are located west of the source of the Missouri," and to establish friendly relations with the Indians beyond the mountains "and to find out from them, if they have any knowledge of the Sea of the West and if the waters of the rivers on the other side of Rocky Chain flow westward."[6] Finally, he was instructed to convoke a council with the Mandans so that they might place themselves under the protection and rule of the Spanish government and refrain from trading with the British.

Accompanied by eight men, Truteau set out from St. Louis in a pirogue, June 7, 1794. En route up river the Truteau party was passed by D'Eglise, anxious to arrive ahead of them so that he could secure for himself all the furs in the Upper Missouri region. He did agree to wait for Truteau, and kept his word, spending the winter at the Arikara villages. When he returned to St. Louis in the spring, his collection of furs included some that Truteau's men had obtained from a Cheyenne band.

After his encounter with D'Eglise, Truteau slowly made his way up the river, taking great pains to avoid detection by Indians who might wish to intercept him and prevent his establishing contact with the northern tribes. He entered what is now Union County on August 25, going into camp on the Big Sioux River near its mouth. He continued cautiously past the James River and finally, on September 14, approached the Ponca village above the mouth of the Niobrara. Although he succeeded in eluding this tribe, a few weeks later, after he had entered the region above the White River, Truteau had no alternative but to parley with a Sioux band. Among them were some Yankton Sioux from the Des Moines River who recognized him from his earlier trading days along the Upper Mississippi. Far from relishing his discovery that the greater part of

[6] *Ibid.*, p. 245.

the band were Teton Sioux, Truteau noted in his journal that "all *voyageurs* who undertake to gain access to the nations of the Upper Missouri ought to avoid meeting this tribe, as much for the safety of their goods as for their lives even."[7] The fact that he was en route to the nearby Arikara villages with a boatload of merchandise did not ingratiate him with the Tetons by whom he was virtually held captive. During the subsequent negotiations, the Indians helped themselves generously to Truteau's merchandise. Changing his plans, he decided to cache whatever goods remained, hide the pirogue, and proceed to the Arikaras on foot. After a week of dodging Sioux campfires, he and his men reached the mouth of the Cheyenne, only to find the villages unoccupied. The Arikaras had left two months earlier for a new village site on the Grand River farther north. Pursuing the journey northward to the Mandans now seemed out of the question. Although some members favored going on, the party retraced its steps to the cache, found the goods undisturbed, and proceeded down the river looking for a suitable place to pass the winter. On November 11, Truteau began building a cabin on the east bank of the Missouri above the site of Fort Randall in what is now Charles Mix County.

The following spring Truteau sent his pirogue back to St. Louis with furs he had obtained in trade with bands of Sioux, Omahas, and Poncas. Accompanied by a few men in two small canoes constructed at their winter camp, Truteau once more set his course northward in the direction of the Mandans. Again he failed to reach his destination. When he reached the new home of the Arikaras, he could find no transportation beyond their villages.

By July, 1796, a little more than two years after he had started up river, Truteau was back in St. Louis, and ended his direct connection with the Missouri Company. The length of Truteau's stay with the Arikaras is uncertain, but it is likely he spent the second winter with them. During his sojourn he was in a position to acquire considerable information, and he may have actually made a trip to the Cheyenne country in the vicinity of the Black Hills. He also dispatched letters to French traders among the Mandans, advising them to stop trading with the Indians in that area. In the course of his dealings with the Cheyennes, Truteau made inquiries about the Western Sea, asking whether, in their long journey be-

[7] *Ibid.*, p. 269. Truteau's "Journal" appears in full on pages 259–311, and in less complete form in *South Dakota Historical Collections*, VII (1914), 412–474.

yond the mountains, "they had not discovered some river the waters of which might possibly flow toward the setting sun." He received a positive reply. A Cheyenne war party had once reached a wide and deep river which seemed to flow in the direction of the winter sunset and which, moreover, was said to empty into a large body of water.

In the spring of 1795, Clamorgan had sent a second expedition up the Missouri, much larger apparently than that headed by Truteau. It was ordered to join Truteau at the Mandan villages and was, moreover, to go overland to the Rockies "in order to reach, if possible, by next spring, 1796, the shores of the Sea of the West." When this second expedition failed to progress beyond the Poncas, there was a third, headed by James Mackay, who was chosen as Truteau's successor in directing the business of the Missouri Company on the Upper Missouri. Mackay left St. Louis in the latter part of the summer of 1795 with a large cargo of merchandise. His project was expected to require six years for its full execution. The objectives of the expedition, according to Mackay himself, were to establish trade with the distant and unknown nations in the upper reaches of the Missouri and to discover all the unknown parts of the Spanish dominions as far as the Pacific Ocean. He was also to construct military posts wherever necessary to protect the trade against the British.

The lateness of the season prompted Mackay to pass the winter among the Omahas above the Platte. One of his lieutenants, John Evans, was sent up the river to make contact with the Arikaras and clear the way for a peaceful passage to the Mandans the following year, but the hostile disposition of a Sioux hunting party at the White River made Evans' hasty return advisable. During the early part of 1796 Evans ventured forth on a second attempt up the Missouri, spending some time with the Arikaras and finally reaching the Mandans in September. He took over the post maintained by British traders and hoisted the Spanish flag, thereby achieving one of the objectives toward which the Spanish energies were exerted. However, the dream of discovering a transcontinental passageway from the Missouri to the Pacific and effecting a consolidation of Spain's outlying provinces remained unfulfilled.

The return of Mackay and Evans to St. Louis in 1797 ended the exploring phase of Spanish policy on the Upper Missouri. By this date, Spanish traders from St. Louis were engaged in fairly regular activities up the river. Among them was the junior member of the firm of Clamorgan, Loisel and Company, organized in 1789 as a successor to the original Missouri Company. In 1800 Loisel received permission to form a trading establishment on the Upper Missouri. When his way up the river was blocked by the Sioux, he built a fortified post on Cedar Island about thirty-five miles below Fort Pierre. Fort aux Cedres remained a stopping place for traders and explorers until its destruction by fire about 1810. An agent of Loisel's, Pierre Antoine Tabeau, was expected to continue the work of exploration on the Upper Missouri for which Loisel was specifically commissioned in 1803. But Spain's time had run out. Three years before, in the secret Treaty of San Ildefonso, the Spanish had agreed to turn Louisiana back to France. In May of 1804, while on his way down the river from the Arikaras, Tabeau met Captains Meriwether Lewis and William Clark a few days' journey above St. Louis, and was informed by them of France's formal transfer of title to the region to the United States.[8]

The Louisiana Purchase of 1803 thus terminated the activities so zealously promoted by Spain in order to maintain her trans-Mississippi possessions. In her efforts to discover an overland route to the Pacific, Spain, like France, had presaged the accomplishments of Lewis and Clark and the expedition that did actually reach the "Western Sea."

[8] *Tabeau's Narrative of Loisel's Expedition to the Upper Missouri*, edited by Annie Heloise Abel and published by the University of Oklahoma Press in 1939, remains the best description available of the Upper Missouri region for that period. Although it was written anonymously, Tabeau's authorship has been acknowledged by historians.

"The Journal of Charles LeRaye," which first appeared in 1812 and was reprinted in *South Dakota Historical Collections*, IV (1908), 149–180, is generally regarded as a forgery. The journal purports to narrate the experiences of a French fur trader supposedly held prisoner by a band of Teton Sioux from 1801 to 1805.

CHAPTER 4

Opening the Way to the Western Sea

IN THE EARLY MONTHS OF 1803, while Napoleon Bonaparte was still making up his mind whether to sell the lands between the Mississippi and the Rockies, President Thomas Jefferson already was planning their exploration. Even before the treaty of cession was signed, Captain Meriwether Lewis and Lieutenant William Clark had been briefed on an expedition which would take them from St. Louis to the Oregon coast of the Pacific.

This project was no sudden whim on Jefferson's part; for at least twenty years he had been playing with the idea of exploring the region beyond the Mississippi. "Some of us here have been talking in a feeble way of making an attempt to search that country," he wrote in a letter of December, 1783, to George Rogers Clark, elder brother of William Clark. ". . . How would you like to lead such a party? tho I am afraid our prospect is not worth asking the question."[1] Three years later in Paris Jefferson had shown his interest again when he met John Ledyard, an erratic and intrepid adventurer who was nurturing a scheme to develop the Oregon fur trade for the Americans. Jefferson, then minister to France, lent moral

[1] James Alton James, *The Life of George Rogers Clark* (Chicago: University of Chicago Press, 1928) , p. 305.

37

support to the venture and even, so he later claimed, outlined Ledyard's east-west route. Having gone overland across Europe and Asia to Kamchatka, by boat to Nootka Sound, and then overland again to the latitude of the Missouri, he was to cross the continent to United States territory on the Mississippi. Since the Russians arrested Ledyard in Siberia in 1788, the feasibility of such a journey had to remain a matter of conjecture.

Time went by, but Jefferson did not permit his interest in exploration and in America's geography to slacken. From his study of the most recent maps, he concluded that the Columbia River interlocked with the tributaries of the Missouri for a considerable distance, making that river the best route to the Pacific. His name was again linked with a project for exploring the West when he was serving as Secretary of State. André Michaux, a gifted French botanist, had made several scientific trips in the southern states, and a journey through the wilds of eastern Canada to the Hudson Bay region. On his return from the latter in 1792, Michaux submitted to the American Philosophical Society a project for an overland trip to the Pacific by way of the Missouri "to make discoveries in the Western country."[2] Jefferson, as a Society committeeman, undertook to raise funds for such an expedition and enjoined Michaux to "find the shortest and most convenient route of communication" by following the largest tributaries of the Missouri that "would lead by the shortest way and the lowest latitudes to the Pacific Ocean." But these plans also came to nought when Michaux became involved in the intrigues of Edmond Genêt, the French minister, who was attempting to organize an expedition of American frontiersmen against New Orleans.

LEWIS AND CLARK

On January 18, 1803, two years after he became President, Jefferson sent a confidential message to Congress recommending a western exploring expedition. Funds of $2,500 were voted for the project, and Jefferson entrusted the command to his private secretary, Meriwether Lewis. At Lewis's request, his close friend William Clark was also named for the expedition, with the promise of a captaincy and a position of equality with the commanding officer. Although Clark was commissioned a second lieutenant and techni-

[2] Bernard De Voto, *The Course of Empire* (Boston: Houghton Mifflin Co., 1952), pp. 344–348.

cally outranked, Lewis regarded him with such respect and held him in such high esteem that the names of the two are irrevocably associated as partners and co-leaders.

Preparations for the expedition got under way rapidly. Captain Lewis spent several weeks in Philadelphia being schooled in astronomy and the biological sciences by members of the Philosophical Society and other savants. He also supervised the assembling of arms and equipment, and pored over maps and other materials about the western country. Elaborate instructions, which he received in April, 1803, acquainted Lewis with his duties. He was ordered "to explore the Missouri River, and such principal streams on it, as, by its course and communication with the waters of the Pacific Ocean . . . may offer the most direct and practicable water-communication across the continent, for the purposes of commerce." He was to take careful observations concerning the geography of the country, including such information as positions of latitude and longitude, climate, meteorological conditions, natural resources, and animal and plant life. A very explicit directive covered the matter of Indian relations. Captain Lewis was to treat them in as friendly a manner as their conduct permitted, assure them of the peaceful character of the exploring party, and acquaint them with the character, extent, and commercial interests of the United States. The over-all design of the expedition has been aptly summed up by Bernard De Voto:

As matters subsidiary to the great ones, it was to reconnoiter the trade, to assert American sovereignty over the West, to proclaim American authority over Indian tribes and British traders there, to settle whatever Indian problems it might encounter, and to lay a basis, the hope was, for a solution to the everlasting Indian Problem itself . . . . And it was to fill in a space in the map of the world that had been blank white paper up to now, and to add to the heritage of the Republic and of mankind as much knowledge as might prove possible.[3]

Captain Lewis completed his preparations at Pittsburgh, where, on August 30, he loaded his special equipment on large boats and proceeded to St. Louis, picking up Clark and several others at Louisville. Winter quarters were established opposite the mouth of the Missouri outside Spanish jurisdiction, and there they awaited the spring thaw that would open the river for navigation. They

[3] *Ibid.*, p. 430.

were a party of forty-five men, some of them drawn from the regular army, specially recruited for the expedition. Of these, seven soldiers and nine boatmen were engaged to go only as far as the Mandans for added protection and to assist in transporting the stores. The cargo included a large consignment of presents for the Indians.

On May 14, 1804, the expedition entered the Missouri on its journey upstream. Three boats were used: a keelboat, fifty-five feet in length and carrying twenty-two oars, and two pirogues, one of six and the other of seven oars. Two horses were led along the river bank to be used in hunting. Since formal transfer of Upper Louisiana under the treaty of purchase had been made on March 9, the expedition was fully under American jurisdiction.

Facing all the hazards surrounding navigation on the Missouri, the party slowly made its way upstream, now and then meeting fur traders on their way to St. Louis with cargoes of furs from the upper country. Pierre Dorion, a member of one of these parties, was engaged as an interpreter, a position for which his more than twenty year residence among the Sioux seemed sufficient recommendation. By the middle of August the expedition was passing the Omaha villages of eastern Nebraska and approaching the Big Sioux River. A tragedy befell it on August 20 in the death of Charles Floyd, one of the three sergeants. On the top of the bluff near Sioux City about a mile below the commemoratively named Floyd River, his body was interred "with the honors due to a brave soldier." A monument erected a century later marks the burial site.

On August 22 the expedition passed the mouth of the Big Sioux and made camp on the South Dakota side of the Missouri near Elk Point. The next fifty-four days through October 13 were spent along the Missouri channel either fronting or lying entirely within the present state of South Dakota. The party maintained forty-two different camp sites during the period, all but seven presumably on South Dakota soil. Up until this time it had passed through Indian country held in close fealty by the St. Louis trading interests. No such subservience existed above the Big Sioux. Here the British traders, capitalizing on the intertribal trade between the Upper Missouri and Minnesota Indians, maintained a sphere of influence. In the Sioux country, the Lewis and Clark Expedition entered on a new phase of its activities. The tenuous political hold of the United States government in this region required adroitness and finesse from the captains in their treatment of the Indian tribes, and the accounts in their journals indicate they were keenly aware of their responsibilities.

The first several days were not especially eventful.[4] When the party reached the mouth of the Vermillion River, the two captains, accompanied by ten men, walked a distance of about nine miles to "a large mound in the midst of the plain" known today as the Spirit Mound, then referred to as "the Mountain of little people or spirits." They enjoyed the delightful prospect of the plain and witnessed "numerous herds of buffalow," but had not yet seen any signs of Indians.

After twice setting the prairie on fire to signal the Sioux of their approach, they made camp on the Missouri near the present town of Yankton, probably on the Nebraska side, and there awaited the arrival of a large delegation of Yanktons. On August 30 a two-day conference began under a large oak tree with the flag of the United States hoisted close by. The Yanktons gave assurances of their peaceful interest, following up with an earnest plea for traders. Captains Lewis and Clark took the opportunity to learn more about the various Sioux tribes of which relatively little was known. All they found out they carefully recorded in their journals.

Pausing along the way to examine what they thought to be ancient fortifications opposite Bon Homme Island, the party proceeded past the Niobrara to the Ponca River; they found the Ponca village deserted because of the hunting season, and finally arrived at the building constructed by Truteau in 1794. The captains misnamed it the "Pawnee house" through a confusion of the word "Ponca" with "Pawnee" on the map they consulted. After they had passed the Big Bend of the Missouri, they came across the remains of a great number of Indian camps, a clear indication of their proximity to the Teton Sioux. On September 24 they reached the mouth of a stream which they named the Teton River. Camping nearby, they made preparations for a council with the Teton band in the area.

During the next four days the Teton Sioux, who had earned the sobriquet "the pirates of the Missouri," put on a performance that taxed the patience of the Americans. Only firm action by Captain Clark, taken at a risk of actual hostilities and bloodshed, caused the

[4] The main incidents of the Lewis and Clark Expedition can be followed in Bernard De Voto (ed.), *The Journals of Lewis and Clark* (Boston: Houghton Mifflin Co., 1953).

Indians to desist from their bullying tactics; they apparently had intended to prevent the expedition from advancing farther up the river. After quite a delay, the expedition finally set sail, fully convinced of the perverse nature of the Teton Sioux.

As Lewis and Clark continued northward past the mouth of the Cheyenne River, they saw a number of old Arikara villages, some of them only recently abandoned. To avoid any chance of molestation, they kept their distance from several groups of Sioux on shore who called for the party to land. On October 8 they reached the Grand River and came within sight of the Arikara villages. For five days they remained in the vicinity, holding council with the Arikara chieftains and visiting their three villages.

The stay with the Arikaras was in sharp contrast to their experience with the Sioux along the Teton, or Bad, River. The explorers found the Arikaras civil and receptive to the speeches impressing upon them the magnitude and power of the country whose subjects they had become. The Arikara tribe was then in the midst of a senseless war with the Mandans, and at their request Lewis and Clark agreed to serve as peacemakers, agreeing also to allow an Arikara chief to accompany the expedition to the Mandan nation. The cumulative data gleaned at the Arikara villages from white and Indian informants were extremely important to the expedition. Of special value to them were the conversations with some Cheyennes who were visiting the Arikaras at the time.

The expedition resumed its voyage on October 13 and was soon in Mandan country. During the long winter season of 1804–1805, spent in camp at Fort Mandan, the captains directed their energies toward three objectives: promoting intertribal peace in order to guarantee the peaceful passage of the Missouri for the fur trade; providing themselves with lighter equipment for the shallower passage upstream; and, what was more important, gathering from various sources all possible information about the unexplored region beyond. In what proved to be a master stroke, they succeeded in attaching a young Shoshone woman, Sacajawea or Bird-Woman, to the expedition through the expedient of employing her husband, Charbonneau, a French *voyageur* who had secured her from Minnetaree captors. Sacajawea later became the intermediary in dealings with the Shoshone, or Snake, tribe beyond the Divide, from whom the explorers secured horses and other necessary supplies. Without Sacajawea's intimate knowledge of that region, the expedition might well have failed.

By April 7, 1805, everything was in readiness for the final and most formidable stage of the overland trip. The keelboat was returned to St. Louis, carrying surplus supplies, specimens, and official dispatches. It made a short stop at the Arikara villages to take on board an Arikara chief whom Dorion was escorting to Washington in accordance with plans made the previous year. The main body of the expedition, comprising thirty-two persons and Sacajawea's two-month-old baby Baptiste, left Fort Mandan for the uncharted Rockies. During the next seven months, in one of the most remarkable exploits in the history of exploration, the two captains and their party made the crossing to the Western Sea, glimpsing the Pacific for the first time on November 15.

After a disagreeable rainy winter on the Oregon coast, the party began its return trip on March 23, 1806, reaching the villages of the Minnetarees and Mandans on August 12. Here they held several councils and renewed a pledge of friendship with the Indians. After considerable coaxing, Captain Clark induced a Mandan chief, Big White, to return with the expedition to St. Louis and to visit the Great Father in Washington. Accompanied by Big White and his family, the party left the Mandans on August 17. The passage downstream through present-day South Dakota took only fifteen days as compared to fifty-four days required for the upriver voyage two years earlier. Several councils were held with the Arikaras during a two-day stopover, which was not without its explosive moments. The pledge of peace given the year before had been violated by the Arikaras, and charges and countercharges were hurled by Big White and the Arikara chiefs before the captains managed to effect a reconciliation. After making their way cautiously through the Teton Sioux country, the homeward-bound explorers came to the Big Sioux River, and nineteen days later reached St. Louis.

Widely acclaimed for their feat, Lewis and Clark were entrusted with important positions in the administration and military establishment of the West. But Meriwether Lewis was not to serve his country much longer. In 1809, after two years as Governor of Louisiana, he died at the age of thirty-five. It is generally believed he took his own life. Captain William Clark was commissioned a general of the militia and became Indian agent for Louisiana Territory. He was later appointed Governor of Missouri Territory and held other positions of public trust up to the time of his death in 1838.

The Lewis and Clark Expedition asserted American sovereignty over the Upper Missouri Basin; and it directed official attention to the formulation of an Indian policy that would promote peace between the tribes, open the Missouri to unhampered passage for American traders, and lessen the danger of British infiltration. Above all, the expedition supplied a voluminous body of information of a scientific nature, utilizing especially Clark's skills in map-making and sketching plants and bird life.

The meteorological observations made by Lewis and Clark concerning the comparative aridity of the region were subsequently to become an important factor in fastening the "Great American Desert" concept upon the Northern Plains. The expedition chanced to occur during an extended period of severe drought.

SAFEGUARDING AMERICAN SOVEREIGNTY

News about the success of the exploring party had an immediate impact on the fur trade. While the expedition was still in the field, individual traders began to hasten up the Missouri to stake out promising fields for enterprise. On their return trip Lewis and Clark noted such signs of recent activity as the remains of a trading post built by a Robert McClellan on the James River during the winter of 1804–1805. Below the Vermillion they saw two boats and several men on shore, and upon landing met James Aird, a British trader from Prairie du Chien. Captain Lewis reported that trade with the Yankton Sioux on the James River had more than trebled in volume during 1806.

Since he considered the promotion of the American fur trade the major means of holding Upper Louisiana under control, Lewis was deeply concerned by the operations of British fur traders in the Northwest. The Spanish had failed to meet British competition on even terms and consequently had not won the allegiance of the tribes on the Upper Missouri. According to Lewis, "The Indians were friendly to the British merchants, and unfriendly to the Spanish, for the plain reason that the former sold them goods at a lower rate."[5] Unless the American traders were able to supply the Indians, the government would lose its influence over the tribes, and the Northwest frontier would be placed in jeopardy.

[5] Elliott Coues (ed.), *History of the Expedition under the Command of Lewis and Clark* (New York: Francis P. Harper, 1893), III, Appendix I, "Essay on an Indian Policy," p. 1222.

The whole problem of frontier defense was thus intimately bound up with the fur trade and Indian policy. Lewis and Clark had made a good beginning in establishing cordial relations with the upper tribes; the main exceptions were the Teton Sioux, who had appeared somewhat chastened by the curt manner in which Captain Clark handled them. As a means of further strengthening the new ties of allegiance, representative chiefs of the western tribes were sent to the States so that they might be properly impressed with the greatness and might of the United States.

The Indian trade was conducted under a system of licensing. Congress had passed a law in 1802 designed "to regulate trade and intercourse with the Indian tribes and to preserve peace in the frontiers." This legislation was extended to the region beyond the Mississippi as soon as title to the Louisiana Purchase passed to the United States.

In consonance with the views of Captain Lewis and fur merchants of St. Louis, James Wilkinson, as Governor of Louisiana and Superintendent of the Indian Department, issued a proclamation in August, 1805, denying any subjects of a foreign power permission "to enter the Missouri River for the purpose of Indian trade."[6] Moreover, no merchandise could be carried into the Indian country unless manufactured in the United States or imported by "Citizens of the United States or persons resident within the Territories thereof." All agents and interpreters were to take an oath of fidelity to the United States and abjure allegiance to all other powers. Wilkinson clearly directed his proclamation at the British.

From the return of the Lewis and Clark Expedition in 1806 until the Treaty of Ghent in 1815, American concern over competition with British fur traders shaped the government's basic policy toward the western tribes. Events in the Upper Missouri Basin during this period are all closely related to this concern and must be reviewed in this light.

American policy in the Upper Missouri Basin received a major setback in September, 1807, when the Arikaras attacked a small military escort which was returning the Mandan chief, Big White, to his people. The Mandan chief and his entourage had been attached to a larger party of Teton Sioux who were being returned from St.

[6] Clarence E. Carter (ed.), *The Territorial Papers of the United States*, XIII, "The Territory of Louisiana-Missouri, 1803–1806" (Washington: Government Printing Office, 1948), p. 203.

Louis. Each group of Indians had its own military escort, the one accompanying the Mandans being commanded by Ensign Nathaniel Pryor, a veteran of the Lewis and Clark Expedition. Two groups of fur traders and trappers also accompanied the party, one pointing for the Sioux country, the other, headed by Pierre Chouteau, Sr., making for the Mandan villages. When Ensign Pryor's party reached the Grand River, the Arikaras, who were currently at war with the Mandan nation, blocked its passage. Spurning Chouteau's conciliatory gestures, they began a general attack which lasted an hour. The casualties among the fur traders included three dead and seven wounded; there were three wounded in Pryor's party. Big White, refusing to risk an overland journey with his family, was returned to St. Louis.

The Arikara attack upon the military escort had alarming implications: failure to keep the Missouri open to uninterrupted passage for Americans would redound to the advantage of the British and strengthen their hold over the tribes within the region. Meriwether Lewis, who had succeeded General Wilkinson as Governor of Louisiana Territory, was most anxious that the Arikaras be severely punished "as well for the reputation of our Government, as for the security which it would give to the future navigators of the river Missouri."[7] The American government, accordingly, made extensive preparations to repair the serious damage to American prestige and to promote more favorable conditions for American trading interests. Big White was safely escorted to the Mandan country in 1809 at an expenditure of more than four thousand dollars. The Arikaras, however, in no wise altered their uncertain behavior, merely resigning themselves temporarily to the display of force. For years they continued to plague the whites, posing as friends one day and committing depredations the next.

THE ASTORIANS

As part of their plan to gain control over the western fur trade, the Americans also hoped to enter the Oregon country. Prime promoter in this movement was John Jacob Astor, who had organized the Pacific Fur Company in June, 1810. In order to launch the project and establish Astoria as a central post at the mouth of the Columbia River, he organized two expeditions, one by sea and the other by land. The overland party, known as the Astorians, was to

[7] *Ibid.*, XIV, "The Territory of Louisiana-Missouri, 1806–1814," p. 348.

follow the route of the Lewis and Clark Expedition. Headed by Wilson Price Hunt, a partner of Astor, the party left St. Louis on March 12, 1811, and arrived at the Arikara villages on June 12. Two Englishmen, Thomas Nuttall and the naturalist John Bradbury, whose published journals comprise an invaluable contemporary source, accompanied the Astorians on this first stage of the expedition. The numerous reports about the unfriendly proclivities of the Blackfoot tribe in Montana led Hunt to abandon his original plan of following the Missouri and Yellowstone rivers. Obtaining horses for the land journey from the Arikara and Cheyenne Indians, he struck out overland from the Missouri on July 17. The course took him along the Grand River toward the northern foothills of the Black Hills and across the Big Horn Mountains. This first overland passage westward across the present state of South Dakota was made by a party of 62 persons, with 118 horses, 76 of them loaded down with merchandise and equipment.

Although the Hunt party reached Astoria the following May, Astor failed in his attempt to establish the fur trade in the Oregon country under American auspices. The Northwest Company arrived upon the scene shortly after the founding of Astoria and eventually succeeded in gaining control of the American post.

The war with Great Britain produced a crisis for the American fur traders in the Upper Missouri Basin. It not only threatened the complete suspension of the trade, but also gave British traders an opportunity to draw the Sioux and other tribes to their side, eliminating American competition. In this contest for the control of Upper Louisiana, the loyalty of the Indian tribes was of paramount importance to the Americans. The British relied heavily upon the Indians in their efforts to wrest the Great Lakes region and the Upper Mississippi Basin from the United States. The Santee, or Minnesota Sioux, were virtually allied with them and in a position to draw the western Sioux tribes into the British sphere.

The agent chosen by the British officials to execute their plans was Robert Dickson, a Scot who had been carrying on trading operations with the Sioux for more than twenty years. He was married to the daughter of a chief of the Cut Head Yanktonnais band and lived with his family at his principal post, on Lake Traverse. James Aird, whom Lewis and Clark met near the Vermillion River in 1806, was one of his associates. Armed with blankets and other goods, Dickson began to align the Indians on the British side, trusting his persuasive powers to convince them that they were fighting for the privilege of trading with the British as well as for their lands. His success is indicated by the presence of Sioux, Winnebagoes, and other Indians from the Upper Mississippi Basin in the British army. Among them were a number of Yanktonnais, led from their haunts along the James River and Big Stone Lake by Red Thunder, Dickson's brother-in-law. These Sioux allies actually participated in the British capture of Michilimackinac in 1812.

The American government was fully aware of the British activities among the Indians of the Northwest. To neutralize Dickson's activities, in the summer of 1814 it named Manuel Lisa subagent of the Missouri tribes above the mouth of the Kansas. Soon after Lisa's appointment, rumors reached the Santee Sioux along the Mississippi that Teton bands from the Missouri were organizing a war party against them. Although such rumors were part of the propaganda disseminated by a friendly Sioux, Lisa reported later that at the war's end forty chiefs were cooperating with him in planning an expedition of several thousand warriors against the tribes of the Upper Mississippi.

Following ratification of the Treaty of Ghent which ended the war, the United States, in July, 1815, conducted negotiations with the various Indian tribes at Portage des Sioux above St. Louis. Manuel Lisa was on hand with a delegation of forty-three chiefs and headmen from the loyal tribes along the Missouri. Upon the restoration of peace, Lisa turned again to the fur trade on the Upper Missouri, and Robert Dickson also resumed his business, although for a time he found it discreet to remove to British soil. Upon Dickson's death his family returned to Lake Traverse.[8]

Despite the indecisive nature of the war with Great Britain, the American position on the frontier was definitely strengthened as a result. To forestall any possible recurrence of the "British menace," steps were taken to assure American dominance in the fur trade. In 1816 Congress enacted a measure which prohibited granting trading licenses to any aliens except by presidential permission. The law was not strictly enforced, and licenses continued to be issued in the name of American citizens while British traders were nominally hired as boatmen or interpreters. But British interests were feared no longer; by this time, they had generally withdrawn from the field.

[8] Numerous descendants of Robert Dickson have lived in South Dakota throughout the years.

CHAPTER 5

The Saga of the Fur Trade

CONDITIONS WERE virtually ideal for the fur trade in the Upper Missouri Valley. The various water courses teemed with beaver and other small animals, while the woody fringes along their banks supplied the wood for fuel, boats, trading posts and other structures, and served as shelter in bad weather. The major streams provided the most practical means of transport for both incoming merchandise and outgoing peltries. The region was also an important source for articles of commerce derived from the buffalo. In contrast with eastern North America where smaller pelts constituted the chief items, in the region west of the Mississippi River buffalo hides were a major ingredient in the trade. Before 1815 relatively few buffalo skins had been marketed. Subsequent years saw a tremendous increase in the popular demand for both robes and tongue, and these came mostly from the buffalo ranges of the Upper Missouri Basin.

The native tribes that occupied the Missouri Valley played a key role in the fur trade. Their main villages, whether the fixed abodes of Arikaras and Mandans or the temporary camps of Sioux, were in the most favorable locations along the main stream or at the mouths of its tributaries. At these strategic sites the successful passage of the Missouri depended entirely upon the variable mood of the Indian inhabitants.

After the War of 1812 the Sioux tribes were placed in an enviable position by the rapid expansion of the fur trade. So long as it dealt mostly with the smaller pelts, the western fur trade had little attraction for the natives. The early traders found it necessary to import white trappers who carried on their activities along the various streams during the winter season. Pelts gathered by the Indians did not add up to sufficient volume for profitable operations. But when the products of the buffalo became important items in the traffic, the Indian attitude toward the trade changed. The Teton Sioux, who occupied the northern buffalo range, were the major beneficiaries of this expansion, and the period from 1815 to 1850, the most active years of the fur trade, coincided with their greatest prosperity. The huge quantities of buffalo robes shipped out of their country brought great personal satisfaction as well as wealth to the Tetons. As their economic status improved, they lost their earlier indifference to and contempt for the white traders, and became more peaceful and friendly.

The large number of trading posts maintained at one time or another within the present confines of South Dakota is a good index of the primary position held by the several Sioux tribes. It has been estimated that there were more than a hundred of these establishments. They were scattered over the entire area from the Big Sioux to the Black Hills with the heaviest concentration in the central region along the Missouri where the main Teton camps were located.

The most important fur post was situated near the mouth of the Teton or Bad River at Fort Pierre. In its day this establishment vied in importance with Fort Union at the confluence of the Yellowstone and Missouri rivers. Some of the smaller posts were primarily gathering stations where pelts and robes were collected from neighboring Indians; they also served at times as winter quarters for trappers. The small posts were generally adjuncts to a larger post maintained by the same trading firm. Such subsidiary posts were located at one time or another on Elm River in Brown County, at the fork of the Cheyenne, and on the upper reaches of the White River.

The peak of the fur trade on the Upper Missouri was probably reached during the fourth decade of the century. During the year 1830, according to a contemporary estimate, the shipments to St. Louis from the country above the Big Sioux included 26,000 buffalo robes, 25,000 pounds of beaver fur, 37,500 muskrat skins, 4,000 otter skins, and 150,000 deer skins. A large proportion of the buffalo robes and beaver pelts, it can be assumed, came from the Sioux country.

The fur trade was a highly organized business requiring a heavy outlay of capital and considerable business acumen and entrepreneurial ability. It was international in character: the greater part of the merchandise carried into the interior for trade with the Indians was of European origin; most of the fine pelts obtained from the beaver, otter, mink, and other animals and some of the coarser items, such as buffalo robes and deer skins, found a European market. Although the fur companies regularly employed trappers and hunters who, working for fixed wages, followed the beaver streams or hunted down the buffalo, most of the furs and hides in the Sioux country were obtained in trade with the native tribes. The Indian wants were satisfied with a variety of goods ranging from firearms, ammunition, and utensils of various sorts to the gaudiest trinkets. Articles of American manufacture used in the trade included rifles, guns, shot, ball, tin and brass kettles, silver work, and tobacco. Goods imported from England were blankets, Indian calico, colored cloth, leather belts, beads, thread, needles, and thimbles. The Indians also acquired from the whites a liking for flour, sugar, salt, pepper, and even coffee. Whiskey, which was contraband, entered the trade surreptitiously.

The western fur trade centered in St. Louis. All the goods for the Indian country were shipped to this point and transported to their destination by river craft. The bulky cargoes of furs and peltries, gathered up at the wilderness posts, came down the river for final shipment by St. Louis merchants to New York and London.

THE FUR COMPANIES

One of the leading St. Louis traders was Manuel Lisa, a dominant figure in the business until his death in 1820. He has been characterized as a man of great boldness and restless energy, endowed with an exceptionally acute business sense. Born of Spanish parents and fortified with considerable experience acquired in the Missouri trade during the Spanish regime, he was the first to sense the well-nigh unlimited potentialities revealed by the Lewis and Clark explorations on the Upper Missouri.

Immediately following the return of Lewis and Clark to St. Louis, Lisa laid plans for an extensive trade with the Crow and Blackfoot nations. In 1807, accompanied by some twenty-five boatmen and trappers, he made his way by keelboat to the mouth of the Big Horn River where he established a post frequently referred to as Fort Lisa. He returned to St. Louis the following spring with a rich cargo of furs, and in 1809 organized the St. Louis Fur Company. He also established trading stations among the Blackfoot, Mandans, and Arikaras, but the hostile attitude of the Crow and the Blackfoot soon caused the abandonment of all the posts above the Mandans.

After the outbreak of war with Great Britain and the consequent collapse of the Upper Missouri trade, Lisa retired to Council Bluffs, where a new Fort Lisa was built in 1812. During the war he performed valuable services for his country as Indian agent for the Upper Missouri tribes, and upon the re-establishment of peace resumed his trading activities. His company, which he reorganized several times, finally became the Missouri Fur Company with himself as president. As a trade organizer, Lisa spent much of his crowded life on the Missouri. In his numerous trips up and down the river, two of them to the Yellowstone country, he must have traveled more than twenty-five thousand miles.

Lisa's death occurred just as the western fur trade was entering its most prosperous era. The Missouri Company continued in existence several years longer under the management of Joshua Pilcher who tried to carry out Lisa's original plan to enter the Blackfoot country. This effort ended in failure too, as did an attempt to enter the Rocky Mountain area. Pilcher's operations continued to decline, ending finally in the dissolution of the company by 1830. The demise of the Missouri Fur Company, the oldest to operate out of St. Louis, was in no small measure due to the growing ascendance of two larger companies, the Rocky Mountain Fur Company and the Western Department of the American Fur Company.

A group of St. Louis traders, led by General William H. Ashley, formed the Rocky Mountain Fur Company in 1822. Closely associated with Ashley was Andrew Henry, an earlier partner of Manuel Lisa in the ill-fated attempt to enter the Yellowstone trade. The company had only a twelve-year existence, but it attained an importance second to none in its western expeditions and discoveries of new hunting grounds. It made little effort to cultivate trade with the Teton Sioux, although at one time it did maintain a small post at Fort Brasseau at the mouth of the White River.

Under the direction of Andrew Henry, a post was established at the mouth of the Yellowstone. From this vantage point, during the spring of 1823 Henry tried unsuccessfully to push the trade into the country of the Blackfoot Indians. To assist Henry, General Ashley brought a large expedition up the Missouri, but the Arikaras treacherously blocked his passage when he appeared before their villages above the mouth of the Grand River. It was not until the middle of August, upon the conclusion of an indecisive military campaign against the Indians, that Ashley was able to proceed. Henry, who had brought military aid to the Ashley party, returned to the Yellowstone Valley with about eighty men, taking the same general course as that of the Astorians in 1811, across the northwestern part of what is now South Dakota.

In that same autumn some of Henry's men, following the North Platte, crossed South Pass to enter the rich beaver country of the Green River Valley. The operations of the Rocky Mountain Fur Company were at once transferred from the Arikara villages.

In 1826 General Ashley assigned the management of the company to Jedediah Smith and two associates, retaining, however, the right to supply the merchandise and receive the furs in payment. On the western side of the Continental Divide the familiar trading post of the Upper Missouri Valley gave way to the annual rendezvous, a predetermined point to which a corps of professional trappers called the "mountain men" brought the season's catch. Until the dissolution of the company in 1836, the hardy spirits identified with the Rocky Mountain Fur Company continued their search for fresh hunting grounds, exploring mountain valleys, discovering new passes, crossing the deserts of Utah and Nevada, and leaving their mark in diverse ways upon the geography of the Far West.

The American Fur Company dominated the fur trade along the Missouri. Incorporated in New York by John Jacob Astor in 1808 to broaden his operations as a fur merchant, the firm was able within a decade to control the Great Lakes and the Upper Mississippi region from its base at Mackinaw. In 1822 it established a branch at St. Louis. The area tributary to Mackinaw was called the Northern Department, while the new field of operations embracing the posts on the Missouri and also the lower posts on the Mississippi and the Illinois River became the Western Department.

Astor's patient efforts to form alliances with St. Louis traders met with success when Bernard, Pratte and Company assumed the management of the Western Department in 1827. The connection made with this powerful firm, which included members of the famous Chouteau family, was followed almost immediately by the equally important absorption of the Columbia Fur Company.

The Columbia Fur Company had been formed in 1822 by Joseph Renville, a former British trader on the Red River of the North.

Renville had been thrown out of employment as a result of a merger in 1821 between the Northwest and Hudson's Bay Company. Associated with him were Kenneth McKenzie and William Laidlow, who had been similarly affected by the consolidation of the British firms. For their field of operations Renville and his partners concentrated on the wide area between the Mississippi and the Missouri, placing their main post at Lake Traverse. The facile mode of traffic afforded by the Upper Missouri for bulky buffalo robes and skins gave the Columbia Fur Company a natural advantage over the Hudson's Bay Company, whose cargoes were carried overland.

When the American Fur Company found the competition with the Columbia Fur Company too formidable, it took the young firm into partnership. Under the terms of the consolidation, effected in July, 1827, the Columbia Fur Company withdrew from the region of the Great Lakes and the Upper Mississippi to manage a subdepartment in the Upper Missouri Valley above the Big Sioux. Without any change in organization, the retiring company became the Upper Missouri Outfit for the Western Department of the American Fur Company.

At the time of consolidation, the main post for the Columbia Fur Company on the Missouri River was Fort Tecumseh, situated a short distance above the mouth of the Teton or Bad River. Other posts were maintained along the Missouri below Fort Tecumseh and also on the James and the Big Sioux. In September, 1828, the Upper Missouri Outfit moved into the Yellowstone country for the Assiniboin trade, establishing Fort Union at the mouth of the Yellowstone River. During the next few years further expansion carried the trade into the Crow and Blackfoot country. In 1834 John Jacob Astor sold out his interests in the American Fur Company, disposing of the Western Department to Pratte, Chouteau, and Company, successor to Bernard, Pratte and Company. In 1838 the St. Louis firm became Pierre Chouteau, Jr. and Company, under which name the business was continued for more than twenty years.

Pierre Chouteau, Jr., the guiding spirit in the Western Department, was one of several illustrious members of a well-known fur trading family. His grandfather was one of the founders of St. Louis. In 1809, at the age of twenty, he accompanied his father up the Missouri in the interests of the Missouri Fur Company. A man of exceptional business ability, he acquainted himself thoroughly with every detail of the trade. The introduction of the first steamboat, the *Yellowstone,* to the Upper Missouri in 1831 may be regarded as Chouteau's greatest achievement.

STEAMBOATS ON THE UPPER MISSOURI

The departure of the *Yellowstone* from St. Louis marked the beginning of a new phase in the history of the Upper Missouri Valley. Carrying trading goods, the *Yellowstone* reached Fort Tecumseh on June 19, 1831, and made the return trip to St. Louis after a brief stopover, arriving on July 15 with a rich cargo of buffalo robes and peltries, and ten thousand pounds of buffalo tongues. The *Yellowstone*'s maiden voyage proved the feasibility of steamboat transportation on the Upper Missouri. The following year the boat made a second trip, this time reaching Fort Union. Pierre Chouteau, Jr., went along as a passenger in order to take part in a christening ceremony for a new post named in his honor and built as a replacement for Fort Tecumseh. The name of the new post was soon shortened to Fort Pierre.

By virtue of the saving in time and manpower as well as its larger cargo capacity, the steamboat soon replaced the keelboat as the main craft for the upriver voyage. Each spring a boat left St. Louis with the necessary goods for a year's trade, carrying along employees of the American Fur Company and, on occasion, missionaries, scientists, and others not directly identified with the fur trade. After all business matters in the fur country had been attended to, the boat returned with the cargoes of furs and peltries contributed by the trading posts along the way.

Because of the various obstacles encountered on the Missouri River, piloting a boat on its waters was a special branch of the art of navigation. The rate of speed varied with the physical conditions. The *Yellowstone* took about eighty days, including the time spent at Fort Pierre and other posts, to cover 1,760 miles from St. Louis to Fort Union; on the return trip, it averaged about one hundred miles per day. One of the fastest trips recorded for the fur trading period occurred in 1847 when a steamboat made the passage to Fort Union in forty days and the return trip in fourteen. The outmoded keelboat at best could make only eighteen miles a day upstream, and usually it averaged only twelve. Other types of river craft such as rafts and mackinaw boats continued in use for downriver transportation during the off season, especially for the lighter weight furs.

The period from 1827 to about 1840 was the heyday of the fur trade on the Upper Missouri. By the time the Western Department of the American Fur Company had become securely entrenched in the business, the supply of beaver and other fine furs in the country below the Big Sioux had become negligible. It was the region along the course of the Upper Missouri and its numerous tributaries that provided the unprecedented volume of furs and peltries. But here, likewise, the beaver meadows soon began to show signs of depletion.

The decline in the supply of pelts coincided with a depressed market for dressed fur in Europe, occasioned largely by a growing preference for silk in the manufacture of men's hats. Buffalo products, including robes and tongue, and the skins of deer and other animals remained in fairly large supply and continued to dominate the market for another decade or two. These articles of trade, however, came mostly from the posts in the upper reaches of the Missouri. In the Sioux country, the fur trade was in decline by 1850. The beaver had all but disappeared from the scene, and buffalo robes were more difficult to procure. For the Sioux tribes, the fur-trading era had practically come to an end by mid-century.

THE FUR TRADE AND INDIAN POLICY

Any attempt to evaluate the contributions made to American history by the fur trade must begin with a consideration of its impact upon the Indians. The entire industry centered in the Indians whether as the actual procurers of the pelts and skins or merely as the occupants of the domain from which this source of wealth was drawn. Basic to the welfare of the trade was an Indian policy that not only provided amicable relations between fur trader and native, but also curbed intertribal warfare, which was always very disturbing to the trade. As has been noted, the government established a licensing system, buttressing it with regulations designed to control the traders within the Indian country. Whenever peaceful relations were broken, the government tendered military protection. It also provided inspection machinery for enforcing the ban on spirituous liquors in the Indian trade.

The official relations between the government and the Indians were entrusted to Indian agents expressly provided as the occasion required. Since the fur trade was the main contact with the western tribes, Indian policy was all too frequently subordinated to the fur interests. Most of the subagents appointed to the Sioux tribes along the Missouri were fur traders primarily interested in the welfare of the American Fur Company.

Memories of earlier British intrigues among the Indians of the Northwest continued to influence the thinking of American officials during the peace that followed the War of 1812. The colony established in 1814 by Lord Selkirk near the international border in the Red River Valley was an especial matter of concern since it seemed to menace American sovereignty as well as the fur trade. The obsessive preoccupation with foreign activities led Secretary of War John C. Calhoun to draw up a comprehensive plan designed both to extend and protect the Indian trade and to counteract British influence.

Calhoun's plan, which originally envisaged a military post at the mouth of the Yellowstone River, was later amended in favor of an intermediate post at the Mandan village and a second post either at Council Bluffs or at the Great Bend in the heart of the Teton Sioux country. Calhoun also proposed a post at the mouth of the St. Peter's or Minnesota River on the Mississippi. He contemplated two expeditions for the execution of the project, one to proceed up the Missouri River, the other up the Mississippi to the mouth of the Minnesota.

The War Department, acting under orders from Calhoun, made extensive preparations for the Missouri phase of the project, engaging steamboats for the transportation of a military force of about a thousand men, including a scientific corps under Major Stephen H. Long. Colonel Henry Atkinson was placed in command. Major Benjamin O'Fallon, Indian agent for the Missouri district and brother-in-law of Governor William Clark, was to accompany the troops. The ascent of the Missouri began in July, 1819. After a series of delays and mishaps arising mostly from an unwise decision to utilize steamboats, the troops reached Council Bluffs during September and October. Only one steamboat, *The Western Engineer,* carrying Major Long's engineers, succeeded in making the voyage to this point. The rest of the troops were compelled to resort to keelboats for the greater part of the trip.

The Missouri Expedition, sometimes called the Yellowstone Expedition of 1819, made no effort to advance beyond Council Bluffs. Colonel Atkinson selected a site for a military post on the Nebraska side above the bluffs, and here was established Fort Atkinson. Although Congress refused to appropriate additional funds and Secretary Calhoun's plans could not be carried farther, nevertheless he had succeeded in pushing the military frontier into the heart of the fur country. While Fort Atkinson was under construction on the Missouri, the Mississippi Expedition had proceeded to the mouth of the Minnesota River where it established Fort Snelling. These new posts strengthened American prestige among the Indians and constituted a symbol of security for the fur trade.

The treacherous attack of the Arikaras upon General Ashley's party of fur traders on June 2, 1823, resulting in the loss of fourteen killed and eleven wounded, provided the garrison at Fort Atkinson with an opportunity to demonstrate its punitive powers. Colonel Henry Leavenworth, in command of the post, responded immediately to Ashley's frantic call for military assistance. The troops, numbering 220 men, set out partly by boat and partly on foot, with Leavenworth in command. Joshua Pilcher, head of the Missouri Fur Company and special agent to the Sioux tribes for the occasion, attached a party of 40 civilians to the expedition. On reaching the Sioux country, Pilcher secured from 400 to 500 recruits from the Teton Sioux. Ashley supplied some 80 additional men from his own group. Before reaching their destination the forces were joined by an additional 350 Sioux warriors who were eager to engage in common warfare against the traditional Arikara enemy.

Faced by Colonel Leavenworth's formidable Missouri Legion composed of regulars, mountain men, boatmen, and Indians, the Arikaras soon seemed ready to sue for peace. After some parleying of which the fur traders did not approve, Leavenworth, without the assent of Agent Pilcher, put his signature to a treaty whereby the Arikaras agreed to restore the property taken from the Ashley party and no longer to molest the fur traders. The negotiations over the return of property broke down, and the Arikaras escaped under cover of darkness. Forced to acknowledge complete failure in his mission, Leavenworth gave orders to embark. Before the Arikara villages were lost to view, they were seen to be enveloped in smoke, greatly to the regret of Leavenworth, who placed the blame for their destruction upon Pilcher and his fur traders.

While the Leavenworth Expedition had the practical effect of further aggravating the hostile attitude of the Arikaras toward the whites, the Arikaras were no longer a barrier to the river traffic at Grand River. After wandering about over the plains, they returned temporarily to the old village site in 1825. Ten years later a detachment of dragoons from Fort Leavenworth found them near the forks of the Platte River in western Nebraska. Not long after, they made their way up the Missouri beyond the Grand River, locating above the Mandans in the present state of North Dakota.

THE ATKINSON-O'FALLON COMMISSION

The general restlessness among the Indians, accentuated by occasional acts of hostility against the fur traders as well as intertribal warfare, moved the government to formulate a general peace policy. After Congress had authorized treaties with the several tribes along both the Mississippi and the Missouri, the treaty-making campaign up the Missouri was placed in the charge of Henry Atkinson, now a general, and Benjamin O'Fallon, who was chosen in his capacity as Indian agent for the Missouri tribes.

The Atkinson-O'Fallon Commission, quite properly called the Yellowstone Expedition of 1825, embarked from St. Louis in nine keelboats with an escort of 476 men. One of the boats was loaded with goods of various sorts, including guns, blankets, and tobacco for distribution to the Indians as presents. The main purpose served by the large force was to impress the Indians with the might and importance of the United States government.

During the course of the Atkinson-O'Fallon expedition a total of twelve treaties were signed. A military parade with a special display of the artillery pieces preceded each treaty council, and the distribution of the presents concluded the negotiations. The treaties, all alike in content, acknowledged the supremacy of the United States, admitted the Indians to the friendship and protection of the government, and provided for the conduct of the fur trade under the sole auspices of American citizens. These were the first formal treaties negotiated by the United States with Upper Missouri tribes.[1]

The Atkinson-O'Fallon Commission had been expected to establish a line of military posts, but such a course of action was no longer considered necessary. General Atkinson found no evidence of British influence behind the Indian disturbances. Moreover, Major Long had taken a small party from Fort Snelling into the Red River country at Pembina in 1823, and in his opinion no forts were

[1] See Russell Reid and Clell G. Gannon (eds.), "Journal of the Atkinson-O'Fallon Expedition," *North Dakota Historical Quarterly*, IV (October, 1929), 5–56.

necessary to hold the country. The whole area west of Lake Superior was to him nothing but "a sterile dreary waste" three or four hundred miles in width and fourteen hundred miles long, and consequently secure against foreign attack. Any disturbances requiring military attention, he maintained, could easily be handled by troops from the posts already established at Fort Snelling and Fort Atkinson.

The Fort Atkinson post was vacated in 1827, and at a new site at a lower point on the Missouri Fort Leavenworth came into being. There were no posts in the Indian country. Occasional patrols of dragoons from Fort Leavenworth and the military posts along the Mississippi searched the plains for trespassers and provided whatever policing was needed.

The Sioux tribes along the Missouri gave the military branch little cause for concern. Here, in the words of Doane Robinson, "the Yanktons and Tetons were pursuing the even tenor of their way, trading peaceably on the river, at the James, Fort Lookout and Fort Pierre, hunting the buffalo, trapping the beaver, drinking the abominable whiskey spirited into the country by the traders, and diverting themselves by an occasional foray against the Pawnees, Poncas, Crows, Rees, Mandans, and even the far off Arapahoes. . . ."[2]

All the tribes in the region were under the supervision of a superintendency at St. Louis. A general agent for the tribes of the Upper Missouri was stationed at Council Bluffs. Subagents were appointed from time to time to assist him in maintaining relations with specific bands. An annual distribution of presents helped to keep the Indians friendly and loyal in their attachment to the United States government. In spite of the inspection service at Fort Leavenworth, traders continued to smuggle whiskey up the river.

The Indians felt the impact of the fur trade in many ways. It enriched the native economy through the material comforts derived from metallic cooking utensils and other tools that were obtained by barter. The introduction of firearms increased their hunting operations and added to pleasures derived from the chase as well as to material wealth measured in terms of buffalo robes. The requirements of the trade for peaceful conditions also tended to make the tribes more orderly and less given to family feuds.

There is also a debit side to the ledger. In addition to the political

[2] Doane Robinson, "A History of the Dakota or Sioux Indians," *South Dakota Historical Collections,* II (1904) , 166.

vassalage to which they became subject, there were deteriorating influences which accompanied the fur trade. The liquor which flowed freely into Indian country in spite of prohibitory legislation was demoralizing in its effects. The white traders frequently victimized the Indians, taking advantage of them in every possible way. The fur trade eventually broke down the Indians' economic independence, making some of the articles of barter an economic necessity. In the process of exchange, the advantage in the bargaining usually rested with the white trader. Finally, there was the corrupting influence of the trading post where the Indians only too often were exposed to the white man's vices without the compensatory benefits of his virtues.

EARLY VISITORS TO THE UPPER MISSOURI

Not all the activities in the Indian country of the Upper Missouri were related to the fur trade. The return of the Lewis and Clark Expedition in 1806 excited the interest of various scientists in the region. Among the first attracted was Henry M. Brackenridge, Pittsburgh-born lawyer and son of a famous Pennsylvania jurist and author. During a sojourn in St. Louis in 1811, he was moved by the spirit of adventure to join a trading expedition led by Manuel Lisa. At this same time Wilson Price Hunt's Astorian party was accommodating the British botanists, John Bradbury and Thomas Nuttall, with transportation to the Arikara villages. Bradbury was employed by the Liverpool Botanical Society to visit the United States to investigate and collect native plants. Brackenridge was especially interested in natural history, geography, and Indian antiquities. The writings of both men are among the most extensive and reliable accounts of the period.

The Upper Missouri also attracted some members of the ruling class in Germany. Prince Paul of Wurtemberg made three trips to the United States devoted to exploration and a study of the natural sciences. On the first, in 1823, he ascended the Missouri River with fur traders in a keelboat as far as Fort Atkinson; from there he traveled overland northwest to the White River and then northeast to a fur post operated by Joshua Pilcher on the Missouri above the present city of Chamberlain. His carefully written account of this trip was published several years later in Germany, but very little is known about a second trip which he took to the upper tributaries of the Missouri in 1830.

A better known German visitor was Maximilian, Prince of Wied, whose studies of the native races and the flora of Brazil in 1815 and the Missouri Valley in 1833–1834 established him as an exploring naturalist of the highest rank. He took passage for Fort Union on a steamboat in 1833, spending the winter at Fort Clark. With him was Charles Bodmer, a Swiss artist, who made the illustrations for Prince Maximilian's *Travels in the Interior of North America,* first published in German and translated into English in 1843. The book is generally regarded as one of the most comprehensive and most accurate accounts of the Upper Missouri Basin at that time. It includes an excellent description of the trading post of Fort Pierre.

The famous artist George Catlin began his great career of sketching and portrait painting among the western Indians in 1832. He was the special guest of Pierre Chouteau, Jr., on the *Yellowstone*'s first ascent to Fort Union. Catlin spent fifteen days of the upward trip at Fort Pierre. Spread out in the vicinity of the post were about six hundred Indian lodges, and here he made careful observations of Teton life and drew the likenesses of some outstanding Indian chiefs. He also made a painting of the fort and sketches depicting the buffalo hunt and Indian dances. Although his personal accounts are not so trustworthy as those of Maximilian, Catlin made a lasting contribution through his pictorial representation of Indian life.

John James Audubon, who had been studying and painting birds and mammals for many years, went up the Missouri to Fort Union in 1843 to complete his investigations for a work on the *Quadrupeds of North America.* He was accompanied by a party of four, including a taxidermist and a fellow artist-naturalist. Like the other visitors, Audubon kept a daily journal which has become an invaluable source of information about the region he traversed.

Between 1836 and 1840 the upper basins of the Mississippi and Missouri were the scene of a topographical survey directed by Joseph Nicolas Nicollet, a distinguished French scientist. Nicollet, who had located in St. Louis, was encouraged by the Chouteau family in his plans to explore the Upper Mississippi Valley. After his preliminary reconnaissance during 1836 and 1837 to determine the sources of the Mississippi River, the United States government commissioned him to make a geographical and topographical map of the whole region. John C. Frémont, newly commissioned as second lieutenant in the topographical corps, was assigned to the Nicollet party as chief assistant. An expedition, outfitted and equipped by the

Chouteau firm, was transported up the Mississippi during the summer of 1838 to survey the region westward along the Minnesota River. Traveling in one-horse carts which were driven by the company's employees, the Nicollet party explored the prairie plateau of western Minnesota and eastern South Dakota, visiting the Red Pipestone Quarry and the region northward to Lake Kampeska, thence eastward to the Minnesota.

It fell to Frémont to explore and name the chain of lakes within the region. Thus were named Lake Poinsett in honor of Frémont's benefactor, Joel Poinsett, statesman and diplomat who introduced the poinsettia into the United States from Mexico; Lake Preston for a United States Senator; Lake Benton for his prospective father-in-law, Senator Thomas Hart Benton; and Lake Albert for an army engineer.

The following season the Nicollet survey was extended to the Upper Missouri Valley. Leaving St. Louis in early April of 1839 on the steamboat that was taking the annual supplies to the Chouteau Company's northern posts, the scientific group reached Fort Pierre in June. During July the party crossed the Missouri plateau in a northeasterly direction toward the James Valley and then went up the river to the vicinity of Devils Lake. Heading for the Minnesota River and the Mississippi for their return to St. Louis, the explorers followed the Red River of the North to Big Stone Lake, traversing some of the same ground covered the previous summer in eastern South Dakota. The drafting of the first accurate maps for the region and the names assigned to the numerous lakes were tangible results of these explorations. For Lieutenant Frémont, the famous Pathfinder of the 1840's, these visits to the Missouri watershed were an invaluable apprenticeship and a training school for later explorations beyond the Rockies.

Priests and missionaries were among the early visitors to the Upper Missouri Valley. In the 1830's resident priests along the Lower Missouri took passage on upbound steamboats to minister to the spiritual needs of the whites congregated at Fort Pierre and other fur posts, at the same time not neglecting opportunities for missionary work among the natives.

Father Pierre DeSmet, a Belgian who came to St. Louis in 1820, visited some Indians near the mouth of the Vermillion in 1839, but his mission took him the following year to the Flathead Indians in the Oregon country. His occasional journeys up the Missouri en route to the Pacific mission field acquainted him with the Teton Sioux to whom he generally confined his labors from 1849 until the time of his death in 1873.

The fur-trading community at Fort Pierre also received occasional visitations from the Minnesota country. Stephen Return Riggs, Protestant missionary, undertook the journey in 1840 from his mission among the Santee Sioux on the Minnesota River. Father Alexander Ravoux in 1842 visited an Indian camp on the James River within the present confines of Brown County and two years later made a trip to Fort Pierre.

By the midpoint of the nineteenth century the fur trade had become decadent. The virtual disappearance of the traffic in furs could not, however, restore to the Indian tribes their earlier economic independence. Their mode of life was in a state of transition, in large measure a result of the fur trade. As for the white participants in the trade, many formed permanent connections with the natives and elected to remain in the region. During the subsequent period of settlement they exerted a stabilizing influence on Indian relations, and rendered various services to the government as scouts and interpreters. Impermanent as the fur trade was, it had left its unmistakable imprint upon the region.

CHAPTER 6

The White Man Comes to Stay

DURING THE 1850's momentous developments were under way in the Upper Missouri Valley, altering the status of the native tribes and paving the way for white settlements. The events that ushered in a new era for the region were closely identified with the westward migration across the central plains toward Oregon, Utah, and California. The forces of expansion had extended the national boundaries and inspired a mass movement to the regions beyond the Rockies. The emigrant trails leading to the Far West which disquieted the Indians on their hunting grounds also inspired plans for transcontinental railroads and awakened interest in permanent white occupation of the fertile valleys along the Missouri and its tributaries.

Although the region between the Missouri River and the crest of Rockies from the Canadian border to Texas originally had been set aside as Indian country, the concept of a "permanent Indian frontier" was fast breaking down by 1850. Several treaties soon opened tribal lands to prospective settlers west of Iowa and Missouri. The controversial Kansas-Nebraska Act, passed by Congress in 1854, created the territories of Kansas and Nebraska out of the unorganized area. Nebraska Territory comprised the region from the fortieth to the forty-ninth parallel; it shared the Upper Missouri Valley with Minnesota Territory (created in 1849), the Missouri River serving as boundary between them.

By the time Nebraska Territory was created, an advance guard of settlers was trickling northward from the mouth of the Platte. Settle-

65

ments also began to appear on the Iowa side of the Missouri along
the Boyer, the Little Sioux, and the Floyd rivers. At the mouth of the
latter, Sioux City was founded in 1855. The following year a townsite location was sought at the falls of the Big Sioux in what was soon
to become Dakota Territory. A treaty with the Yankton Sioux followed in 1858 to make room for white settlers between the Big
Sioux and the Missouri.

MILITARY OCCUPATION OF THE SIOUX COUNTRY

As more white men entered the territory, tensions increased between the whites and the Teton Sioux, particularly the Brûlés and
Oglalas who frequented the plains from the headwaters of the
White River to the North Platte. Indian resentment of the emigrant
trains bound for the Far West soon turned to open hostility, and the
government took specific steps to provide protection for the trail
along the North Platte. A military post appeared at Fort Kearny in
1848; the following year the fur post of Fort Laramie was purchased
from the American Fur Company and provided with a garrison. Another military post was established at Fort Riley in 1853.

Despite the efforts to keep the Indians in good humor and peaceably disposed toward the emigrants, an incident affecting a Brûlé
band at Fort Laramie pushed peaceful relations to the breaking
point. Efforts to arrest a Minneconjou brave accused of killing a
stray cow belonging to a Mormon emigrant led to the annihilation
of a small punitive expedition under Lieutenant J. L. Grattan on
August 19, 1854. The Brûlé band involved in the affair became
openly hostile and began to make raids along the emigrant trail.
The military authorities placed the entire blame for the Grattan affair upon the Teton Sioux and determined to move into the country
north of the Platte in force to punish the offenders.

A formidable expedition of about a thousand men was sent out
the following year under the command of General William S. Harney. Forts Kearny and Laramie were designated as depots for the
collection of troops and supplies, and a third depot was to be located at some suitable point on the Missouri in the vicinity of Fort
Pierre. Despite some adverse opinions about the suitability of Fort
Pierre as a supply depot, army representatives concluded negotiations for its purchase in April, 1855, agreeing to pay Chouteau and
Company $45,000 for the dilapidated, outmoded fur post, which was
to accommodate four companies of cavalry and six of infantry. Six

companies of infantry arrived by steamboat during July and August to put the new military post in readiness for the main body of troops.

In the meantime, General Harney was en route from St. Louis to the Sioux country. Through the energetic efforts of Thomas Twiss, the new Indian agent at Fort Laramie, all friendly Sioux were warned to move south of the North Platte River at once or else face attack from the military. On September 3 Harney came upon a party of Brûlés led by Chief Little Thunder who were encamped with a few Oglalas on the Blue Water opposite Ash Hollow, several miles above the North Platte. Immediately upon the discovery of the Brûlé camp, Harney made plans for an attack. To gain time for his cavalry to reach their position, he carried on a half-hour parley which was abruptly broken off when his men charged the Indians from two directions. Eighty-six Indians were killed, including some women and children; Harney's losses were four dead and several wounded. Whether Little Thunder had hostile intentions is debatable. Why he failed to heed the admonitions of Agent Twiss to keep south of the Platte is not certain. In his camp, however, were found papers and other articles that definitely linked members of his band with the Grattan incident.

From Ash Hollow, Harney proceeded to Fort Laramie, which he reached on September 16. After holding council with several Sioux bands, Harney led his forces into the heart of the Teton country. He followed a course along the White River from its headwaters into the Big Badlands, then crossed over to the Cheyenne, and advanced to the Teton, or Bad, River. Advised by his scouts that the hostile Indians had retired northward beyond the Cheyenne, he decided to go into winter quarters at Fort Pierre.

Upon his arrival on October 19, Harney expressed his dissatisfaction with the conditions that existed at the new post. "I have never visited a post where so little had been done for the comfort, convenience and necessities of the troops," he reported to his superiors two months later.[1] The landing at the river was poor, there was no building timber, fuel, or forage within close range, and most of the buildings were in such a state of decay and dilapidation that they were beyond repair. The owners of the old trading post had made a good bargain. Now that the fur trade was on the decline, $45,000

[1] "Official Correspondence Relating to Fort Pierre," *South Dakota Historical Collections,* I (1902), 413.

was no mean sum for a post whose only virtue was its strategic location. Making the best of it, General Harney placed his force of nearly twelve hundred men in winter quarters along the Missouri within an eighteen-mile radius from Fort Pierre, excepting one detachment which he wintered between the White and the Niobrara. Fort Pierre was practically uninhabitable, and Harney determined to spend neither time nor money on its repair.

After a careful survey of the region between the Big Sioux and the Moreau rivers, General Harney decided to locate a new post on the west bank of the Missouri in Nebraska Territory thirty miles above the mouth of the Niobrara. Here, on June 26, 1856, he laid out Fort Randall. A garrison remained at Fort Pierre during the following winter; in the spring of 1857, it was also transported to the new post, together with all movable stores and property. The old post at Fort Pierre reverted to the traders in 1859 when the government defaulted in its payments.

The military occupation of the Sioux country was the first step in the white man's advance into the Upper Missouri Valley. Fort Pierre and its successor, Fort Randall, were the first military posts to be established in the region. A treaty which Harney negotiated with the Teton Sioux at Fort Pierre in March, 1856, recognized the right of travel over the Oregon Trail and between Fort Laramie and Fort Pierre, but the treaty was never ratified by the United States Senate.

The involvement with the Teton Sioux made it imperative for the army to assemble more information about the geography and topography of the Northern Plains. Lieutenant G. K. Warren, who had made observations in 1855 along the route of travel pursued by Harney's command, now made a more thorough reconnaissance of the Upper Missouri and also explored the area north of the Platte within the present states of Nebraska, South Dakota, and Wyoming. He concluded that military occupation of the Sioux country was essential for the safety of the whites as well as for the protection of the Indians. The maps he drew up were intended to facilitate military operations within the region. He anticipated a need for additional posts along the Missouri, particularly among the Yanktonnais and the northern subtribes of Teton Sioux who, in his opinion, should have been made to feel the full might of the government before the Harney expeditionary forces were disbanded.

The exhaustive reports submitted by Warren, together with the accompanying maps, represented an outstanding geographical achievement. They supplied the first reasonably accurate information about the Black Hills and the surrounding country. The observations on the geological and physical features, including notes on the soil, vegetation, and animal life, remain an invaluable storehouse of information to the present day.[2]

The explorations begun by Lieutenant Warren were continued in 1859–1860 by Captain William F. Raynolds. Working with him was Dr. F. V. Hayden who had been in charge of the earlier geological investigations under Warren. The Raynolds expedition left Fort Pierre in July, 1859, to explore the northern section of the Black Hills where, two years earlier, a hunting party of Minneconjous had prevented Lieutenant Warren from making a full reconnaissance. Raynolds led his party into the Powder River Valley and along the upper reaches of the Missouri and Yellowstone rivers. The Warren-Raynolds explorations of the terrain occupied by the Crows and the Teton Sioux provided information that was useful later in laying out military roads and planning strategy.

The newly established Fort Randall in the heart of the Sioux country symbolized the military control of the Northern Plains. Auxiliary posts in the Teton country, suggested by Lieutenant Warren, were believed unnecessary. The Teton Sioux had consented to white travel through their country along the Platte and over the trail along the White River from Fort Pierre to Fort Laramie. As for actual settlement, Warren shared with other military men and explorers the common opinion about the Great American Desert. Warren felt strongly "that continuous settlements cannot be made . . . west of the 97th meridian, both on account of the unfavorable climate and want of fertility in the soil."[3]

THE YANKTON TREATY OF 1858

While these activities were occupying the military authorities on the Great Plains, the Yankton Sioux east of the Missouri River began to feel the impact of an advancing line of white settlement. As measured by Indian standards, the Yanktons had fallen upon bad times.

[2] See E. G. Taylor, *Gouverneur Kemble Warren* (Boston: Houghton Mifflin Co., 1932), pp. 18–44.

[3] Lieut. G. K. Warren, "Exploration in the Dakota Country, in the Year 1855," *Sen. Exec. Doc.* 76 (Serial 822), 34 Cong., 1 Sess., 1856, p. 6. The official reports of Warren's explorations during 1855, 1856, and 1857 are reprinted in *South Dakota Historical Collections*, XI (1922), 58–219.

From their main camp overlooking the Missouri a few miles west of the James River, they could clearly read the signs of impending changes. In their impoverished condition, they were hardly strong enough to resist the establishment of communications across their lands between Sioux City and the new military post at Fort Randall.

The Yanktons, moreover, were under heavy pressure to relinquish a portion of their domain to make room for the whites who were experiencing one of the periodic land booms that characterized frontier history. By the terms of the Minnesota statehood bill passed by Congress in 1857, the western boundary of the new state was placed a short distance east of the Big Sioux River. The agricultural lands westward to the Missouri were left as unorganized terrain, and the prospect for a new political division carved out of the western part of Minnesota Territory made the whites especially anxious to enter the Indian country.

The firm of D. M. Frost and Company, then operating several licensed trading posts among the Indians above Sioux City, took the initiative in promoting a treaty with the Yanktons. Frost was a former army officer who had resigned his commission in 1853 to engage in the Indian trade. Associated with him was John B. S. Todd who had left Harney's command at Fort Pierre in September, 1855, to become Frost's partner. Their headquarters was at Sioux City where they operated a general store. They also planted trading posts at strategic points along the Missouri and the Big Sioux, their main post being on the James River near the present city of Yankton. Todd, from his position as sutler at Fort Randall, took personal charge of the firm's operations in the Sioux country.

Todd was in charge of the Indian negotiations. The leading Yankton chief, Struck by the Ree or "Old Strike," as he was called by the whites, philosophically reconciled himself to the changing order and looked with favor upon the proposed reduction of the tribal lands. Charles F. Picotte, a half-breed living with the Yanktons, played a prominent part in the conversations as interpreter. The customary junket to Washington was undertaken, even though the details had been virtually agreed upon. The treaty delegation included Todd, Picotte, Struck by the Ree, and fourteen other chieftains. Among the latter was Smutty Bear, who led a small faction opposing the treaty.

Under the terms of the treaty signed on April 19, 1858, the Yankton tribe was to withdraw to a reservation tract of 400,000 acres along the east bank of the Missouri in the present confines of Charles Mix County. The ceded lands lay within a triangle formed by the Big Sioux and Missouri rivers and a line roughly drawn from Fort Pierre to Lake Kampeska. In consideration for the cession, the government agreed to pay $1,600,000 in annuities over a fifty-year period, besides executing certain other provisions for the benefit of the tribe. Picotte received a special grant of a full section for his services as interpreter.

There was the further specification that "all other persons (other than Indians, or mixed bloods) who are now residing within said ceded country, by authority of law, shall have the privilege of entering one hundred and sixty acres thereof, to include each of their residences and improvements, at the rate of one dollar and twenty-five cents per acre."[4] This provision was undoubtedly the handiwork of Frost and Todd, as it permitted them to occupy prospective town-sites under cover of their trading license issued prior to the treaty. During the latter part of 1858 their agents actually occupied several choice claims on what became the townsite of Yankton.

Following the announcement of the Indian treaty, a few "sooners" appeared here and there during the summer of 1858, but a military detachment from Fort Randall moved down the valley to the mouth of the Big Sioux and destroyed the buildings and landmarks erected by the trespassers. The troops, however, did not disturb the squatters identified with the Frost and Todd enterprise at Yankton, nor did they bother whites who had intermarried with the natives and were therefore considered legal residents. Several such individuals lived along the Missouri between the Vermillion and the Big Sioux rivers at the time.

By 1859 nearly a thousand prospective settlers had gathered along the Iowa and Nebraska border, awaiting the ratification of the treaty by the United States Senate. The greater number lined the Nebraska side opposite the present town of Vermillion where there was feverish activity in townsite speculation. The treaty was ratified on February 17, 1859, but a disagreement over the interpretation of its provisions further delayed settlement. The whites assumed they could legally enter the cession within a year from the signing of the

---

[4] See Charles J. Kappler, *Indian Affairs—Laws and Treaties* (Washington: Government Printing Office, 1903), II, 586–590, for text of treaty.

treaty, once it was ratified. The Indians were of a different mind. They insisted that the provisions for their removal were inoperative until a full year had elapsed from the date of ratification.

An ugly situation developed when the whites tried to enter the cession after April 19, the anniversary of the signing of the treaty. Major A. H. Redfield, the agent assigned to the Yanktons, was hopeful that the Indians would gradually withdraw from the ceded lands. When he received instructions in April to establish an agency at Greenwood, he made immediate preparations to carry out the treaty stipulations. By the time he came up the river, over two thousand Indians were encamped in the vicinity of Yankton. Opposition to the treaty had again developed under the leadership of Smutty Bear, and there was sharp criticism of both Picotte and Struck by the Ree. By the time the agent arrived, Struck by the Ree had again carried the day for ceding the land.

On July 10, 1859, Major Redfield reached the Yankton camp on the steamboat *Carrier,* bringing with him annuity goods as well as construction materials. After putting the excited Indians in good humor by a judicious distribution of trinkets, the agent announced that they would receive the rest of the annuities and presents at their new agency. When the steamboat slowly proceeded on its way up the river, the Indians began to strike camp. Soon many of them were on their sixty-five-mile land journey to Greenwood. On July 13, when the *Carrier* reached the agency site, Redfield stored the treaty goods under tents until the work on temporary structures was completed. In the absence of any proclamation, July 10 may be regarded as the official opening of Dakota Territory.

TOWNSITE COMPANIES ON THE BIG SIOUX

The speculative activities that led to the Yankton Treaty of 1858 and the subsequent establishment of settlements along the Missouri at Bon Homme, Vermillion, and Yankton coincided with similar efforts to plant townsites along the Big Sioux. Here the Indian title was not in immediate question. Under the Treaty of Traverse des Sioux, negotiated in July, 1851, the Santee Sioux had ceded all the lands east of the Big Sioux River except for a reservation area consisting of a ten-mile stretch along the Minnesota River eastward from Big Stone Lake and Lake Traverse.

During the summer of 1856 a townsite company was formed at Dubuque, Iowa, for the express purpose of establishing the prospective capital of a new territory at the falls of the Big Sioux. A few months later, two agents arrived in the region to take possession of a townsite claim of 320 acres, but unfriendly Indians drove them away. In May, 1857, other representatives of the Dubuque company successfully occupied the townsite to which they gave the name of Sioux Falls. A month later representatives of the Dakota Land Company appeared; finding the choicest site already occupied, they selected a second tract of 320 acres adjoining the first townsite, and named it Sioux Falls City.

The Dakota Land Company was a St. Paul concern, also formed in 1856 to boom townsites within the region outside the boundary of the new state of Minnesota. The company comprised an ambitious group of Democratic politicians, including Governor Samuel A. Medary and his son as well as members of the Minnesota legislature. The latter had conveniently created seven new counties in the unsettled portion of Minnesota Territory, two of them in the Big Sioux Valley. With the aid of a Democratic administration in Washington, the townsite operators hoped to create a new territory and locate its seat of government.

Members of the Dakota Land Company were instrumental in securing an appropriation from Congress in 1856 for an emigrant road from Fort Ridgely on the Minnesota River to a connection with the Oregon Trail at South Pass. The Fort Ridgely–South Pass road was actually surveyed and marked out in 1856 and 1857, passing through the present towns of Woonsocket and Wessington Springs. Both the superintendent and the chief engineer of the road were identified with the Dakota Land Company, which anticipated the selection of promising townsites along the route within the Sioux Valley. But plans for the road came to nothing and the promoters did not realize their ambitions.

The Dakota Land Company began its operations on the Big Sioux in June, 1857, by locating townsites at Medary and Flandreau in addition to Sioux Falls. Medary was favored to become the capital of the new territory until the Yanktonnais tribe of Sioux refused to honor the Traverse des Sioux Treaty and compelled the abandonment of the Medary and Flandreau settlements. The settlers at Sioux Falls, however, refused to heed the Indian demands for their withdrawal from the locality, and erected crude fortifications of logs and sod to which they gave the name Fort Sod.

Although the Sioux Falls townsite was spared for the time being, the uneasiness created by the Indian alarm caused the departure of nearly half its occupants, and there were few subsequent newcomers. The remaining settlers were more closely identified with the Dubuque townsite company, but the townsite speculators from St. Paul continued to direct the political activities in behalf of a new territorial organization.

Governor Medary had appointed county officials for the two counties in the Sioux Valley, Midway and Big Sioux, in which "Sioux Falls City" was located. Anticipating a new territory immediately following the admission of Minnesota to statehood, the townsite promoters proclaimed an election for October, 1857, to select a delegate to Congress to represent the area left outside the new state. Alpheus G. Fuller was given a certificate of election to Congress at Medary by the county officials of "Midway County." At the same time, the settlers went through the formality of electing a territorial legislature. This body met at Sioux Falls shortly thereafter and extended the laws of Minnesota Territory over the proposed new territory which by common consent was called Dakota. The unauthorized legislature also memorialized Congress for a territorial organization. The president of the legislative council was designated as governor of the squatter settlement.

Upon his arrival at Washington in the spring of 1858, "Delegate" Fuller found his claim successfully contested by the incumbent delegate from Minnesota Territory, who argued that his seat in Congress was not vacated by the admission of a portion of the territory to statehood. Although Congress accepted the argument, it shortly passed a resolution to the effect that the settlers remaining outside the jurisdiction of the new state were not entitled to a delegate until specifically authorized by appropriate legislation.

In the meantime, the squatter government at Sioux Falls continued its uncertain existence. The settlement on the Big Sioux had a population of about twenty-five at the time, including two women. At a second election in September, 1859, another territorial delegate was chosen. Fuller was once again a candidate, but Jefferson P. Kidder, a recent arrival from St. Paul, was declared elected by an alleged vote of 1,938 against 147. The townsite promoters "canvassed" over a thousand votes for Midway County, notwithstanding its complete evacuation during the preceding year.

Kidder went to Washington, properly armed with certificates of election including one signed by the "acting governor of the portion

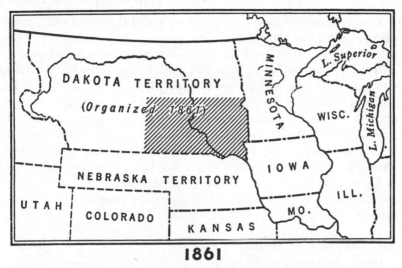

1861

1868

of Minnesota without the state limits now called Dakota." Like Fuller before him, he argued that the enabling act which provided for Minnesota's admission did not repeal the original territorial jurisdiction over the portion left outside the new state. He claimed to represent a constituency of from eight to ten thousand people. Congress, however, chose to ignore Kidder's claim to a seat as well as the pleas of his "constituents" for a territorial organization.

The pretense followed by the Dakota Land Company in its political endeavors was carried over into its business activities. In the issues of the *Dakota Democrat,* a townsite sheet which appeared on July 2, 1859, as well as in printed circulars, the company described its operations in glowing terms. Such place names along the Big Sioux as Commerce City, Eminija, and Renshaw, as well as Medary and Flandreau, continued to appear on official maps as late as 1864 as evidence of the far-reaching influence exerted by the townsite speculators. When the Missouri Valley was opened to settlement during the summer of 1859, the Dakota Land Company pretended to have planted townsites all along the Missouri from the mouth of the Big Sioux to old Fort Lookout above the present site of Chamberlain.

THE CREATION OF DAKOTA TERRITORY

While the promoters of the Sioux Falls townsite project were pressing their claims for recognition at Washington, spokesmen for the Missouri Valley settlements were actively engaged in counterlobbying. Frost and Todd, eager to have the seat of government placed on the Missouri, likewise initiated a movement for a territorial organization in the fall of 1859. Todd, who had influential connections at the national capital, quietly discussed the matter with the settlers and called a meeting at Yankton on November 8. Frost made a forceful speech in support of the movement for a territorial government and, with Todd's help, drafted a petition to Congress. Following the Yankton meeting the two promoters took the petition to Vermillion where they arranged a similar mass meeting and picked up more signatures.

Every settler on the Missouri slope was said to have signed the memorial to Congress. Armed with a petition bearing 428 signatures, Captain Todd set out for Washington to exploit his political connections. While he did not meet with success on this trip, he found it easy to deflate the exaggerated claims of his rivals in the Sioux Valley, thus insuring the failure of Kidder's mission. While the election statistics certified by Kidder included a heavy vote for the Missouri Valley settlements, actually not a single vote had been polled in that region. In presenting his claims, Todd was able to match Kidder's faked returns with the signatures of genuine settlers, even though the list of signers may have been similarly padded.

During the winter of 1860–1861 Todd resumed his lobbying activities. To bolster his efforts, another mass meeting was held in Yankton in January and another memorial drawn up. According to Kingsbury, "this document was neatly enrolled and signed by 478 pioneers, which probably included the entire population of the territory and possibly some of Picotte's kindred. . . ."[5] Congress, by this time in a responsive mood, passed a bill creating Dakota Territory to which President Buchanan appended his signature on March 2. In setting up the new territory, Congress detached from Nebraska Territory that portion lying north of the 43rd parallel, thus placing the entire Upper Missouri Valley under a single jurisdiction. The news of Todd's success at Washington reached Yankton on March 13 and, according to a contemporary, "on that night hats, hurrahs, and town lots 'went up' to greet the dawning future of the great northwest."[6]

[5] George W. Kingsbury, *History of Dakota Territory* (Chicago: S. J. Clarke Co., 1915), I, 169.
[6] Moses K. Armstrong, *History and Resources of Dakota, Montana, and Idaho* (Yankton, 1866), reprinted in *South Dakota Historical Collections*, XIV (1928), 38.

CHAPTER 7

The Sixties—Decade of Uncertainty

THERE WAS NO GREAT RUSH of settlers to Dakota Territory. The boom of the fifties had run its course, and the newly opened area was not sufficiently alluring to start another. Moreover, the nation's preoccupation with the Civil War and the problems arising from Indian disorders during the decade of the sixties combined with other factors to make the Territory's future a matter of uncertainty.

The first settlers generally located in the counties along the Missouri slope. Excluding the government employees at the Yankton agency and the fur traders scattered throughout the region, in 1860 the population in the southeastern section of the Territory was approximately five hundred. Yankton, Vermillion, Bon Homme, and Elk Point were the leading settlements. The fertile lands on the Missouri bottom between the Vermillion and the James rivers attracted a number of settlers, many of them Norwegians. In Union County two extensive settlements came into being, one extending from the Big Sioux crossing at Sioux City to Elk Point, the other located along Brule Creek farther up the Sioux Valley.

Yankton was the mother town of the Dakotas. Todd and his associates especially favored the location and established a townsite on the 160-acre tract available to them under the terms of the Indian treaty. But in spite of ambitious preparations for its establishment, Yankton drew few inhabitants at the outset. After its selection as the territorial capital in 1862, it grew faster and soon outdistanced the other towns, but the adjacent countryside failed to keep pace with

78

the farming communities in Clay and Union counties. Although most of the lands in Yankton County in the James Valley and along the Missouri were taken by 1864, most of the claims remained unimproved, being held by townsmen for a rise in value.

The migration to Dakota followed the customary pattern of movement to the frontier. The majority of settlers came from nearby states: the census of 1860 showed nearly 25 per cent of the population were natives of Minnesota and Wisconsin. The settlers usually traveled by covered wagon across northern Iowa or through southern Minnesota. A route from the south led by steamboat up the Missouri. The river passage especially recommended itself during the early sixties so long as St. Joseph, Missouri, was the nearest railway point. When Marshalltown, Iowa, was reached by railroad in 1864, it became a prominent outfitting point for the Dakota frontier.

The townsite speculators at Sioux Falls failed to profit from the flow of people into the Missouri Valley. After the failure of their petition to Congress during the winter of 1859–1860, most of them returned to their former homes. The remaining settlers moved to Yankton in August, 1862, when Indian hostilities forced them out of the Big Sioux Valley.

The largest organized group to settle in Dakota during the early period was the so-called New York Colony. This immigration had begun with a plan to settle in a compact community on the western prairies under the terms of the Homestead Law of 1862. After an inspection tour of the several Missouri Valley states and territories by its officers, the "Free Homestead Association of Central New York" which promoted the colony chose a tentative location along the James River near Yankton. Nearly a hundred families enrolled in the association. In the spring of 1864 they traveled by train to Marshalltown, Iowa, where they hunted up conveyances to carry them the last three hundred miles. Upon reaching the Territory after a four-week journey by covered wagon, the association gave up the original plan for a single settlement. In the end probably only thirty families became permanent settlers, but this number represented a substantial increase at a time when the Territory's growth was at a standstill or even in danger of shrinking.

The Indian uprising which began in Minnesota in August, 1862, caused a temporary abandonment of all the settlements in Dakota Territory except Yankton. Many settlers fled before marauding bands of Santee, never to return. Dakota, it has been estimated, lost at least half its farm population as a result of the Santee outbreak. Despite the military measures taken by the government, the Indian menace did not disappear until 1866. The settlers, moreover, were faced with other adversities in the form of droughts and grasshopper infestations, particularly during 1864 and 1865. Many left the new land in dismay, carrying with them tales of woe that made Dakota an uncomplimentary byword for several years.

Those who stayed had a hard lot. Crops often failed, and professional men and businessmen lost clients and customers. The settlers looked for auxiliary employment whenever they could find it. The Indian wars were a boon in this respect, supplying work for teamsters as well as an opportunity for military service. The disbursements of the federal government in connection with the military activities were a godsend to the settlements. A sharp increase in steamboating that resulted from both the military campaigns and the Montana gold rush also furnished increased opportunities for employment.

WAGON ROADS, RIVER TRAFFIC, AND RAILWAYS

The Dakota settlers hoped particularly to benefit from the gold discoveries along the tributaries of the Upper Missouri in Montana during the early 1860's. The tiny settlements lay athwart what many regarded as the shortest and most practical land route to the mines. The sight of Montana-bound emigrants crowding into Yankton hotels and spreading their tents over the townsite during the early months of 1864 brightened the prospects for the Dakota villages as outfitting points.

In response to demands from business interests in Minnesota and northwestern Iowa for overland routes to the mines, Congress on March 3, 1865, authorized the construction of three wagon roads through Dakota. One, intended to give St. Paul a direct route through central Dakota, was to run from the Minnesota border to Fort Thompson, thence north to the Cheyenne River and up the Belle Fourche along the northern edge of the Black Hills. A second road, designed to accommodate the settled areas of Dakota Territory and northwestern Iowa, was to begin at the mouth of the Niobrara and run along the southern base of the Black Hills. These two roads were to make a juncture with a military road projected through Wyoming to Virginia City along the Bozeman Trail. A third route was to run from Sioux City through the Dakota settlements along the military road to Fort Randall and up the Missouri to a connection with the Minnesota-Cheyenne project. The greater portion of the Congressional appropriations for the improvement of the Fort Randall road was to be used for bridging the Big Sioux near its mouth.

Work on the wagon-road projects started at once. W. W. Brookings of Yankton was placed in charge of the Minnesota and Cheyenne River road. Assembling a small crew of Yankton residents, he set out in June for the two-year-old post of Fort Sully, below Fort Pierre, where General Sully was expected to attach a large cavalry force to the expedition. Although a change in plans left him without military escort, Brookings decided to survey the route as far as the forks of the Cheyenne, but the all-too-numerous signs of hostile Indians forced his crew to backtrack to the Missouri and stake and mark the eastern section of the road instead. The route led to the Minnesota border near Pipestone in a direct line from Fort Thompson past the present-day towns of Wessington Springs and Forestburg.

Brookings and his associates unquestionably wished to exploit the projected route along the Cheyenne River as a means of entering the Black Hills. Indian hostilities, however, compelled the abandonment of the survey, and the subsequent treaty was to seal off entry to the Black Hills.

Sioux City interests were the main champions of the Niobrara–Virginia City wagon road. The task of surveying and opening up this route was assigned to Colonel James A. Sawyers, a resident of Sioux City and a man with considerable military experience. His surveying party, accompanied by a military escort which included twenty-five members of the Dakota cavalry, succeeded in reaching Virginia City during the summer of 1865 in spite of much annoying interference by the Indians. The following season Sawyers led a second expedition to survey, shorten, and otherwise improve the wagon road, but this time he had no military protection. A short while later all plans for the Niobrara route were abandoned.

The Sioux City–Fort Randall road, unlike the other two wagon-road projects, benefited Dakota materially. Federal appropriations not only resulted in permanent improvements, but also provided the needy settlers with new opportunities for employment. The most important phase of the project was the construction in July, 1867, of a bridge over the Big Sioux near its mouth. The bridging of the Vermillion followed a few months later. During the early part of 1869 a bridge was also constructed on the James River near Yankton. The improvement of the road was mainly a matter of straightening and shortening its course. There was no effort to extend the Fort Randall road to the Cheyenne River.

The failure of the government to maintain facilities for overland travel to the Montana gold fields left the Missouri River as the only means of ingress from the East during the Indian disorders. Fort Benton, successfully reached by steamboat in 1859, was the terminal point for the river traffic. Earlier, only a few boats had plied the Upper Missouri; now Fort Benton became the destination of an ever-increasing number of boats that covered the entire 2,300 miles from St. Louis.

Although the military activities were important, the mining camps provided the major stimulus for the increased volume in river traffic. Eighteen steamboats passed up the river in 1863, carrying huge cargoes of freight as well as thousands of passengers to the gold mines. Thirty-one different boats reached Fort Benton in 1866. In that year, thirty-six steamboats passed Yankton during the months of April and May, nearly all of them headed for Montana. The high point in the river traffic came in 1867 with thirty-nine arrivals at Fort Benton.

In their passage up the river, the steamboats made short calls at Vermillion and Yankton, not infrequently bringing in bulky cargoes for the merchants' shelves or discharging a few passengers. During the autumn many of the returning miners, whether crowding the decks of the steamboats or traveling in mackinaw boats, stopped long enough in the river towns to display their buckskin sacks of gold nuggets. The increased tempo in steamboating brought into being an army of woodchoppers who braved the risk of hostile Indians to set up woodyards above the settlements and supply fuel for the boats.

The Montana gold rush brought into being new territorial organizations. The territorial officials at Yankton made no effort to assert their authority over the mining settlements in the Rocky Mountain region. When the Territory of Idaho was created in 1863, it embraced the present states of Montana and Wyoming. The following year Montana Territory was established in order to provide a separate jurisdiction for the Montana mining towns, and Wyoming was attached again to Dakota, remaining under its jurisdiction until 1869.

At the same time that Dakota settlers were trying to reap benefits from the Montana gold rush, they became interested in securing an extension of the proposed transcontinental railroad. While Congress had the Pacific Railroad bill under consideration during May, 1862, the Dakota legislature at Yankton incorporated the Missouri and Niobrara Valley Railroad Company. In addition to listing two Congressmen and two stockholders of the Union Pacific Company, the lawmaking body designated almost its entire membership as charter members of the corporation. Under the provisions of the territorial enactment, the railroad was to start at some point on the Big Sioux River and follow the Missouri through Elk Point, Vermillion, and Yankton to the Niobrara Valley and up it "in order to reach, by the shortest and most practicable route, the South pass of the Rocky mountains."[1]

After a short period of dormancy, the Dakota corporation came to life in 1864 when Congress amended the original Pacific Railroad Act empowering the President of the United States to designate a company other than the Union Pacific to build a branch railroad or feeder from Sioux City. Since the branch was to follow the most direct and practicable route westward to a point on the main line, the Dakota company had hopes of receiving the official designation. An important stake in the matter was a land grant of ten alternate sections for each mile of construction.

A rival Iowa group, however, hurriedly formed the Sioux City and Pacific Railroad Company and began to construct a line from Sioux City to a connection with the Chicago and North Western near the town of Missouri Valley; from here it planned to build a short line westward across the river to Fremont, Nebraska, on the Union Pacific. The projected road was to run for a total distance of nearly a hundred miles in the form of an oxbow with its terminus at Fremont, just five miles west of a north and south line drawn through Sioux City. The Iowa group succeeded in having its line accepted as the Sioux City branch. Champions of the Dakota project failed in their efforts to have the action rescinded, and the official designation of the Sioux City and Pacific line remained unchanged. Thanks to this maneuver by Iowa railroad interests, Sioux

[1] *Private Laws . . . of the Territory of Dakota,* 1862, pp. 21–28.

City was assured of an early railway connection while the Dakota settlements continued without rail facilities.

THE SANTEE UPRISING

Even more disconcerting and discouraging to Dakota Territory than the fruitless efforts to secure emigrant roads and railroad connections were the Indian wars that ran their ugly course from 1862 to 1868. The Indian hostilities were touched off on August 18, 1862, by an uprising of the Minnesota, or Santee, Sioux on the reserve set aside for them along the Minnesota River. As Minnesota troops were rushed to the scene of trouble, large numbers of Santees fled across the prairie toward the Missouri, carrying the war into Dakota Territory. Many of the fugitives left Minnesota by way of Big Stone Lake and drew the Yanktonnais in the Upper James Valley into the conflict. The uprising initiated a series of events that ultimately affected the entire Northern Plains region.

The Santee uprising posed a serious defense problem for the Dakota settlers. Some military authorities actually favored the evacuation of the settlements: anticipating a major conflict in the Upper Missouri Valley, they wished to give undivided attention to the hostile Indians in preference to standing guard over a few widely scattered settlements.

Fortunately, the settlements were not entirely defenseless. A company of cavalry had been organized the preceding spring for patrol and garrison duty in response to President Lincoln's call for volunteers. The timely show of force by these troops against marauding bands along the Missouri halted the stampede out of the Territory in early September, and was undoubtedly an important factor in keeping the Yankton Sioux friendly. The residents of Yankton sought protection within hastily constructed fortifications. Returning settlers also erected stockades at Vermillion, Brule Creek, and Elk Point.

Although the area between the Big Sioux and the western limits of Bon Homme County was constantly patrolled by the Dakota cavalry, in October the governor took steps to raise eight companies of volunteer militia. The arrival of troops from neighboring states several weeks later obviated the necessity for such local military organizations. A portion of the recruits were, however, formed into a second company of cavalry and mustered into service in March, 1863. Dakota Territory thus furnished two companies of troops of nearly a hundred each. Since this number exceeded the estimated draft quota, it was not necessary to apply the national conscription law to Dakota Territory during the Civil War.

During the summer of 1863 a few disturbances near Yankton brought further alarm to the settlements. These incidents made the territorial authorities more vigilant, and they assigned the two local companies to constant scouting and patrolling duties. Military camps were maintained for a few years at various points between Brule Creek near the Big Sioux and the Yankton Agency at Greenwood. During the summer of 1865 the War Department also placed troops at Fort James near the mouth of Firesteel Creek on the James and at Fort Dakota on the site of Sioux Falls in order to screen the settlements against possible raids from the north.

In October, 1865, a small band of Santees entered the Brule Creek settlement in Union County and killed a settler who was out haying. This was the last incident arising from the Indian war in the southeastern section of the Territory. The army evacuated Fort James the next fall. The post at the falls of the Big Sioux was continued until 1870.

Following operations against the fugitive Santees in the Upper Missouri Valley during 1863 and 1864, the military confined its activities to garrisoning the military posts and keeping friendly and hostile Indians apart. A line of forts ran from the Minnesota border at Fort Abercrombie into the heart of the northern Indian country. The military cordon included Fort Sully, established by General Alfred Sully in the fall of 1863 at a site six miles below Fort Pierre. Three years later the War Department moved the post to a new site on the east bank of the Missouri some thirty miles north of the old site, where it remained in existence for thirty-one years.

Other forts serving as outposts during the sixties were Fort Union at the mouth of the Yellowstone, Fort Berthold in the Mandan country, and Fort Rice above the mouth of the Cannonball River. Fort Wadsworth (renamed Fort Sisseton in 1876) was erected in the fall of 1864 on the coteau forty miles east of the James River at Kettle Lakes, in what is now Marshall County. This post furnished protection against the hostile Santees from Minnesota for friendly Sisseton and Wahpeton bands who had returned to their haunts in the lake region west of Big Stone Lake.

The Indian war meanwhile had spread to the northern subtribes of Teton Sioux. The wild Hunkpapas, who roved from the Missouri to the Powder River Valley under Sitting Bull's leadership, were bound to become involved when hostile Santees fled to the rugged badland region of the Little Missouri. This region was the scene of intensive military operations under General Sully during the summer of 1864. At the same time, other hostiles, including bands of Oglalas and Brûlés as well as Cheyennes and Arapahoes, were moving into the Powder River country from the region of the Platte, rendering travel across the Northern Plains to the Montana gold fields extremely hazardous.

For the purpose of stabilizing the northern frontier and keeping the traffic lanes open, the military authorities undertook a campaign to bring the Teton Sioux and other hostile tribes into subjection. They also sought to maintain a line of forts along the Bozeman Road projected to the gold mines from Fort Laramie. The government's decision to open a wagon road through the Powder River country led to the conflict commonly known as Red Cloud's War, for the chieftain of the Oglalas. The Indians were determined to keep their hunting domain inviolate.

THE EDMUNDS COMMISSION

At the very time the army was focussing its attention upon hostilities in the Powder River country, Newton Edmunds, Governor and ex officio Superintendent of Indian Affairs in Dakota Territory, initiated a movement for peace among the Sioux along the Missouri River. Assured in his own mind that peaceful relations could be restored without such extensive military operations as the army contemplated, he appealed to the President for support. Lincoln was quick to give it, and used his personal influence in securing a $20,000 appropriation from Congress for a peace mission.

The determined opposition of military leaders to the peace-by-negotiation proposal of Governor Edmunds reflected sharp divergencies in opinion respecting Indian policy. The question resolved itself basically into a debate over army versus civilian control. In the acrimonious discussion that followed, the case for civilian control was strongly championed by eastern humanitarians who joined the Indian Bureau in opposing "fire and sword" methods. The military authorities, who strongly resented any meddling with their plans for subjugation, branded the peace advocates impractical sentimentalists and scoffed at their proposals as so much "milk and water." Conversant with the lax code of ethics all too prevalent among civilian personnel in the Indian service, army officers were impatient with any view not in agreement with their own, and were generally inclined to impugn the motives of their antagonists, especially if the latter included civilians even remotely interested in Indian contracts. In particular, General Pope, commander of the newly created military division of the Missouri, regarded treaty-making with gifts and annuities as tantamount to bribery, and insisted on punitive measures instead.

While the proponents of the peace policy found many supporters in the frontier communities along the Missouri, admittedly there was no unanimity of opinion on the subject among the civilians. Those who stood to profit from the Indian wars were not overly eager for a cessation of hostilities. This group included not only businessmen and farmers, but also many teamsters who found their services in heavy demand, especially during the winter months when steamboat transportation was halted. Both Sioux City, which served as a military depot until the summer of 1866, and Yankton were benefiting from the military activities.

After a delay caused by the opposition of the military who wished to strike a crushing blow which would make the disaffected tribes sue for peace, the peace machinery was finally set up in August, 1865. President Johnson, Lincoln's successor in the White House, appointed a mixed commission of civilians and military men to treat with the Sioux as well as with other tribes in the Upper Missouri region. The Northwestern Indian Commission met at Yankton on September 20 and chose Governor Edmunds as its chairman.

At a council called in October at the original site of Fort Sully below Fort Pierre, the Edmunds Commission made nine separate treaties with members of the seven subtribes of Teton Sioux as well as two bands of Yanktonnais. Congress later ratified all these agreements. The tribes pledged themselves to peace, and, in consideration of small annuity payments, agreed to withdraw from overland routes already established or contemplated through their country. The Lower Brûlé agreed to a permanent reservation along the Missouri north of the White River. Agencies for the other subtribes were fully implied in some of the other treaties.

Because of the lateness of the season further negotiations were suspended until the following summer, when the Edmunds Commission again journeyed up the river, arranging treaties with Teton Sioux at Fort Rice and with other northwestern tribes, including the

Cheyennes, at Fort Berthold and Fort Union. The agreements negotiated in 1866 were later superseded by the Laramie Treaty of 1868
and therefore never ratified.

The treaties negotiated in 1865 and 1866 failed to bring peace to
the Northern Plains. The warfare which broke out in the Powder
River area involved Indian groups not immediately under the jurisdiction of Governor Edmunds' superintendency and had, moreover,
altered materially the conditions under which the Commission had
to work. The chieftains who signed the Fort Sully treaties in October,
1865, represented only a part of the Teton groups. They were mostly
friendlies who kept close to the river, "stay-around-the-fort people,"
as the wild bands of Teton Sioux derisively called them. Some of
them had intermarried with whites. While these agreements were
being drawn up, close to four hundred lodges of Teton Sioux in the
Little Missouri and Powder River regions were engaged in open warfare to keep the whites out of their hunting grounds.

However meager its results in view of Red Cloud's War, the Edmunds Commission nevertheless served a useful purpose in stabilizing conditions along the Missouri. Steamboat traffic became less
hazardous, and the settlements in the southeastern corner of the
Territory once more felt secure. The treaties negotiated in 1865 and
1866, moreover, foreshadowed the agency system soon to be established among the Tetons and Yanktonnais.

THE LARAMIE TREATY OF 1868

A separate peace commission undertook negotiations with the
hostiles in the Powder River country during the summer of 1866, using the Fort Sully treaties negotiated by the Edmunds Commission as
a basis for discussion. The provision concerning overland routes,
however, proved a stumbling block, and the Indians would not sign
until the whites agreed to a complete abandonment of the Powder
River region. The treaty terminating the hostilities was finally concluded at Fort Laramie on April 29, 1868, and was ratified by Congress on the following February 16.

The Laramie Treaty superseded the treaties of 1865 and 1866 in
many respects. Under its terms the area in Dakota Territory from the
Nebraska line to the 46th parallel between the Missouri River and
the 104th degree of longitude was set aside as the Great Sioux Reservation. The area north of the North Platte in Nebraska and between the 104th meridian and the Big Horn Mountains remained

unceded. The military posts within the unceded region were removed, and the Bozeman Road leading to the mines was closed. The treaty thus abandoned the entire Powder River country to the tribes. The Indians in return withdrew all opposition to the construction of the Union Pacific and pledged themselves not to attack or molest emigrant trains upon ceded lands. At the same time, they reserved hunting rights in the region above the North Platte as well as along the Republican and Smoky Hill rivers "so long as the buffalo may range thereon, in such numbers as to justify the chase."

The Dakota settlements received the news of the Laramie Treaty with loud protestations. They were inclined to view the provisions as a measure of appeasement designed to guarantee peace and order on the Central Plains at the expense of the Upper Missouri region. Despite the disappointment of the Dakota inhabitants, the decision of the peace commissioners to close the Bozeman Road and to seal off the Black Hills was a logical one. The nearly completed Union Pacific, already well on its way through Wyoming by the time of the negotiations, had established the supremacy of the Platte overland route, besides giving promise of an early connection with the Montana gold fields from the Utah Valley, thus eliminating any need for a military road through the Powder River country. Moreover, the concept of the Great American Desert was still held to be valid, especially by military men. The parching droughts which coincided with the Indian wars of the 1860's seemed to confirm the earlier views of explorers and soldiers about the region. An army officer on a tour of inspection of Dakota posts in 1866 convinced himself that the country north of the Vermillion River would never be settled by whites; he suggested that Congress dissolve Dakota Territory and divide up the whole area into Indian reservations. In view of such opinions, the region west of the Missouri River above the Nebraska line seemed ideally suited for the Great Sioux Reservation.

The decision to withdraw from the Powder River country also led to the abandonment of the wagon-road project along the Cheyenne River in Dakota Territory and of plans for a military post at the northern base of the Black Hills. The treaty provisions served to seal off the Black Hills entirely, thus forcing a postponement of their entry. Fortunately, by the time the Indian wars had come to an end, conditions had improved in the agricultural communities along the Missouri, thus ending the uncertainties of the sixties and paving the way for the Territory's initial boom.

INDIAN AGENCIES AND RESERVATIONS

Several new Indian agencies had come into being since the Ponca Agency had been established along the Niobrara River under a treaty negotiated in 1858 and the creation of the Yankton Agency in 1859. The first of the new agencies was established at Fort Thompson on the Crow Creek Reservation in 1863 as a direct result of the Santee uprising in Minnesota.

In that year, the federal government, under pressure from Minnesota settlers, undertook to remove the Winnebagoes and the remaining Santees from their Minnesota reservations to the unsettled Missouri Valley above Fort Randall in Dakota Territory. The Indians were transported by steamboat from Minnesota. The Santees, 1,306 in number and mostly women and children, began to arrive in May as soon as the site had been selected. The Winnebagoes, numbering 1,945, came a month later, and were placed adjacent to the Santees. A single stockade surrounded the three agency buildings erected for them. When crop-raising efforts failed, supplies had to be brought in that fall from Minnesota by wagon train to keep the transplanted Indians from starving.

The Winnebagoes, although peaceful, had been forcibly removed from their homes, and they did not like the arrangements made for them. They were unhappy in their new surroundings and disposed to quarrel with their Santee neighbors. Within a month they were hard at work making canoes, threatening to leave for Nebraska to join the Omaha tribe which was kin to them. By early December, one-third of the Winnebagoes were gone, and the rest soon followed. The Omahas welcomed the Winnebagoes, and, under a treaty negotiated in March, 1865, gave up the northern third of their reservation to the newcomers.

The Santees, though more docile, were dissatisfied too. By early 1866 complications began to arise at Fort Thompson when several hundred Lower Yanktonnais and Tetons, comprising mostly starving bands of Brûlé and Two Kettles, crowded into the reservation from the Dirt Lodges directly east on the James River and from the vicinity of old Fort Sully. The Brûlés, who were a party to the treaties negotiated at Fort Sully the preceding October, claimed a share of the provisions and supplies, although the agent had barely enough for the Santees. Moreover, the number of Santees was augmented by the arrival of kinsmen recently released from prison in Minnesota. As a means of reducing the congestion, the Santees were removed to a separate reservation in northern Nebraska in April, 1866. Two years later they were permanently placed at an agency eighteen miles below the mouth of the Niobrara. The removal of the Santees thus made Fort Thompson available to the western Sioux bands who had gathered there.

Under the treaty negotiated by the Edmunds Commission, the Lower Brûlés committed themselves to a permanent location on the west bank of the Missouri above the White River. By 1867 they were settling down in the locality, and the following spring the government selected an agency site for them fifteen miles above the mouth of the White and adjacent to the Crow Creek Reservation. Buildings were put up and farming operations begun. The agent at Fort Thompson administered the affairs of the Lower Brûlé agency, including the drawing of rations.

During 1868 the government also established agencies for bands of Minneconjous, Sans Arcs, Two Kettles, and Blackfoot below the mouth of the Cheyenne River, and for Hunkpapas, Yanktonnais, and other Blackfoot bands at the mouth of the Grand River. These agencies served the northern bands of Teton. Most of the Minneconjous and Hunkpapas, however, refused to accept the "generosity" of the government and continued their nomadic existence for several years longer.

The Laramie Treaty of 1868 called for a central agency for the Brûlés, the Oglalas, and other bands who had participated in Red Cloud's War. The government accordingly chose a site at the mouth of Whetstone Creek, eighteen miles above Fort Randall, and General Harney began to construct buildings in accordance with the treaty provisions. The only Indians to locate at that point, however, were the so-called "Loafers," about a thousand in number, who had seceded from Sioux and Cheyenne bands. Many of these were mixed bloods. Although there were 4,500 Indians drawing subsistence at Whetstone by 1870, the agency was not serving its purpose. Following a trip to Washington by Red Cloud, Spotted Tail, and other chieftains, the federal government decided to move the Whetstone Agency to Nebraska for Spotted Tail and his band of Brûlés. In the fall of 1870 a new site was selected on the White River 225 miles west of the Missouri. The following year the Oglalas chose a new location on the North Platte just west of the Nebraska-Wyoming boundary, thirty miles below Fort Laramie. This became the Red Cloud Agency.

The policy of establishing agencies for the Indians and encouraging them to become self-supporting also led to an agency for the Sisseton and Wahpeton tribes of Santee who occupied the lands in the vicinity of Big Stone Lake. These Indians had not been involved in the Minnesota uprising of 1862. Under a treaty negotiated with them in 1867, the Lake Traverse or Sisseton Reservation was set apart for them as well as the Fort Totten Reservation south of Devils Lake for groups who had fled into the northern part of the Territory.

CHAPTER 8

Organizing the Territorial Government

THE ORGANIC ACT of March 2, 1861, gave Dakota a form of government that was to remain in effect until statehood. The Territory was under the direction of a governor who also served as superintendent of Indian affairs, a secretary, three judges, and other minor federal officials. The administration of the public lands was in the charge of a register and a receiver at the land office and a surveyor general. The legislative authority was vested in a council and house of representatives. A delegate to Congress had the customary privilege of discussion and debate in that body, but was denied a vote. The federal government paid the salaries of all these officials as well as the expenses of the Legislature.

President Lincoln made the first territorial appointments. During the month following his inauguration, he chose his close friend and personal physician, Dr. William Jayne of Springfield, Illinois, for the governorship. Jayne arrived at Sioux City in the latter part of May, and set out by horse and buggy for Yankton, which was to be the seat of government until the Legislature could make an official selection. Vermillion, then a village of about a dozen residences and also an aspirant for capital honors, hopefully extolled its virtues to the Governor as he stopped off for an hour's visit, but the choice of Yankton apparently had been prearranged. The hand of J. B. S.

Todd is evident in the selection of Yankton as the temporary capital. Todd, a former resident of Springfield, was a personal acquaintance of Governor Jayne and a cousin of Mrs. Abraham Lincoln, thus not without influence in the President's household.

In Yankton an unpretentious log cabin served the Governor as executive mansion. After a census had been taken, he divided the settled areas into legislative districts, ordered an election for September 16, and scheduled the first legislative session for the following March. At the same time he created three judicial districts, assigning a judge to each. Having set the wheels of government in motion, Jayne left for his Illinois home, returning to Yankton in time for the meeting of the lawmaking body.

Political activities got under way immediately. On June 1, even before any governmental machinery had been installed, Vermillion endorsed a resident as candidate for Congress, staging a mass meeting which may be regarded as the first political convention held in the Territory. It was followed by a convention at Yankton to endorse J. B. S. Todd, and a gathering at Bon Homme which placed a third candidate in nomination. Two newspapers played a prominent part in the campaign: *The Weekly Dakotian,* established at Yankton in June, beat the drum for Todd, while the Vermillion *Dakota Republican,* which began to appear irregularly in July, supported the local candidate. Todd, the most influential man in the Territory, was the winner by a safe margin. No party lines were followed, but in this first election the majority of the legislators and Todd as well formerly had been identified with the Democratic party.

THE FIRST TERRITORIAL LEGISLATURE

The first Territorial Legislature, dubbed the "Pony Congress" by one of its own members, convened on March 17, 1862. Bon Homme County was favored with both the speakership of the lower house, comprising thirteen members, and the presidency of the nine-man council. The best source of information concerning the session is a series of letters in the *Sioux City Register* contributed by a member of the lower house, Moses K. Armstrong, using the pseudonym "Logroller." This weekly recital, often facetiously written and satirical in tone, contains excellent characterizations of the lawmakers as well as being a faithful chronicle of events.[1]

[1] Portions of these letters appear in Moses K. Armstrong, *The Early Empire Builders of the Great West* (St. Paul: E. W. Porter, 1901).

The first legislators were mostly men of high caliber. The majority were young, and few had been prominent in public life before coming to Dakota. Given to the rough-and-tumble ways of the frontier, they were representative of their locale, and their conduct at times would not have befitted the decorum of older capitals. Succeeding legislatures during the sixties varied little from the first. There was the same disposition to mix horseplay with serious business.

Important matters of policy had to await the settlement of the all-absorbing capital question. Yankton and Vermillion were the leading aspirants. Because of the smallness of the legislative body, it readily lent itself to manipulation, and Yankton was not slow in arranging a deal to assure itself of the prize. But before the session had advanced very far, Yankton's well-laid plans threatened to miscarry. For some reason, probably because of his insistence upon giving an apportionment measure priority over the capital bill contrary to a previous agreement, Speaker George M. Pinney of Bon Homme became involved in a personal row with the Yankton schemers and deserted the combination. Pinney failed in his effort to amend the council bill by substituting Bon Homme for Yankton, and although he succeeded in having "Vermillion" written in by a seven to six vote of the lower house, the council refused to concur.

There was intense excitement over the bill, and in the heat of the controversy Yankton partisans threatened Pinney, who appealed to Governor Jayne to prevent violence. The Governor sent a small detachment of troops to the lower chamber, and the house, resentful of this action, voted an immediate adjournment. When Pinney resigned the speakership the following day, he ironically nominated a twenty-two-year-old colleague wholly unversed in parliamentary procedure as his successor.

After some bargaining, the house finally accepted Yankton. On the same day that Yankton became the capital a bill was introduced locating a territorial university at Vermillion and was given final approval later in the session. Clay County interests considered an educational institution a fair trade. The location of a penitentiary at Bon Homme also figured in the compromise. Yankton assuredly had the best of the bargain; Bon Homme remained a straggling community without any public institution, while Vermillion's reward was not to materialize until twenty years later.

The first Legislature applied itself seriously to setting up governmental machinery in conformity with the Organic Act. It gave legal status to local units and attended to the various problems of law and order. As Kingsbury states, "Nearly every legitimate subject was covered by various enactments and the general sentiment was that the legislative body had acquitted itself very creditably in covering the field of necessary legislation so thoroughly."[2] The drafting of comprehensive civil and criminal codes was considered the major contribution.

In the work of code-writing, the lawmakers borrowed freely from older states. The code of civil procedures was adopted from Ohio. In the 1863 session a justice code was enacted, and two years later a probate code. Thus at an early date Dakota Territory had attempted to cover the entire field of law codification. As imperfections were quite apparent, the Legislature in 1865 adopted new civil and criminal codes which had been prepared by a special commission in the state of New York. These codes were designed for a mature society, and the Dakota legislators made little effort to adapt them to local needs. Subsequent sessions had to supply deficiencies. An attempt in 1875 to prepare a complete revision finally yielded the so-called Revision of 1877.

The first Legislature convened in two adjacent private buildings, and a saloon conveniently nearby was the main rendezvous for legislators and lobbyists with important matters of state to settle. A capitol building had been built in time for the opening of the second session of the Legislature, and this privately owned structure served as the capitol until 1869.

The members of the first Legislature were apportioned among the several settlements in accordance with the Governor's proclamation. The Red River region was accorded a representative in the lower house, but was attached to the Sioux Falls settlement in forming a council district. To allay the dissatisfaction over this apportionment, the Legislature formed the Red River settlements into separate council and representative districts. At its second session, the Legislature reapportioned its membership, granting a larger representation to the communities along the Missouri at the expense of more sparsely settled areas, but leaving the Red River representation unchanged.

Although the census and election returns showed many inhabitants living in the Red River settlements near the Canadian border, this population was made up mostly of half-breeds and individuals

[2] Kingsbury, *History of Dakota Territory*, I, 210.

whose American citizenship was in question. Since, in addition, the region was still unceded Indian domain, the Legislature in December, 1863, abolished the counties in the Red River Valley. A treaty with the Chippewa Indians during the summer of 1864 finally gave the northern section a legal status, and it was permitted to elect a member to the lower house in 1866. A separate council district was not created until 1871.

The whites who were scattered over the Indian country along the Missouri, particularly those at Fort Randall and in the vicinity of the Ponca and Yankton agencies, also presented a serious apportionment problem. Charles Mix County had been created adjoining the Yankton Reservation, while west of it, beyond the Missouri, lay Gregory and Todd counties. Even though Clay, Union, and Yankton counties were accorded greater representation, the less populous counties were definitely overrepresented. On a few occasions legislators were elected by less than twenty votes. Moreover, the worst election irregularities occurred in the border counties. A few years later the Legislature remedied the situation by abolishing the counties on the edge of the Indian country, thus disenfranchising the residents.

Yankton's accommodations were at first so limited that federal officials did not care to expose their families to the primitive living conditions there. A few, including Governor Jayne, installed their wives in Sioux City; others, who anticipated a brief tenure, never brought their families west. Only one territorial official made his home in Yankton in 1862. Many of the officials were absent during the winter months; in fact, absenteeism was so prevalent that at times there was not a single official available for taking into custody prisoners held for capital crimes.

Aside from its favorable location on the Missouri, Yankton's selection as the capital soon enabled it to outstrip the other towns. The leading governmental offices were there, and it became the seat of residence for the leading officials. The meetings of the Legislature drew lobbyists and other visitors, and brought economic gain to the community. The bulk of the federal appropriations for territorial purposes was expended in Yankton. To the envy of other localities, the capital city seemed to be living off the fat of the land. Yankton businessmen and politicians dominated the Territory for two decades, and the "Yankton ring" became a popular target for attack in political circles.

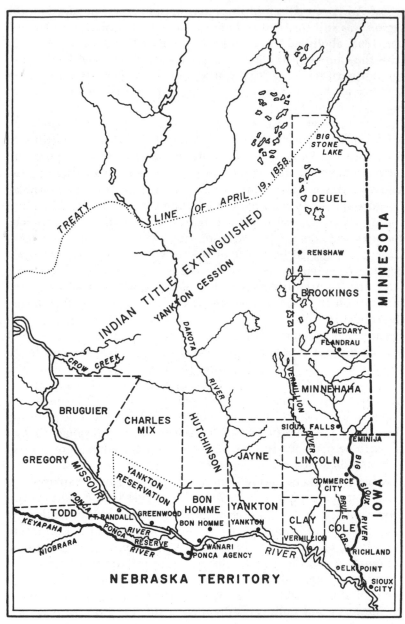

DAKOTA COUNTIES, 1862

PUBLIC SURVEYS AND THE LAND OFFICE

The urgent need for machinery to administer the public lands was an important factor in the agitation for a territorial organization. The Organic Act provided for a surveyor general and for the establishment of the Yankton land district; the land office was to be located at whatever point the executive branch at Washington might direct. The surveyor general's office was opened at Yankton on July 1, 1861. In addition to its administration of the public surveys, until July, 1862, this office also discharged the duties incidental to the filing of claims. Township lines had been run under the jurisdiction of the Iowa surveyor general in the vicinity of Sioux Falls during the summer of 1859 and in the settlements along the Missouri River during the following year. All the records and papers pertaining to these activities were immediately transferred to Yankton when the new office was established. While it was possible to have public surveys made prior to 1861, there were no legal means for the settlers to secure claims. In the meantime, the law of squatters' rights prevailed. The settlers at Yankton organized a claims club in the fall of 1859, as was customary on the unorganized frontier. A constitution and bylaws were drawn up and claims faithfully recorded. A squatters' court adjudicated rival claims.

When Vermillion became the seat of the land office in April, 1861, dissatisfaction arose over Lincoln's choice of officials. The Vermillion settlers, who were contesting the claims of J. B. S. Todd to the townsite, did not regard the location of the office and the appointment of Todd's personal friends as mere coincidence. Fearing a decision by the land officials in Todd's favor, they succeeded in having the appointments withdrawn, and the surveyor general assumed the duties of both the register and receiver until the following year, when new appointees took charge.

The duties at the land office were exceedingly light for several years. Few claims were filed. Much of the land was at first acquired by tendering land scrip. The first pre-emption filing within the present limits of South Dakota was made on August 1, 1861. Todd made the first cash entry for a pre-emption claim. The Vermillion land office had the distinction of recording one of the first homestead entries in the United States when Mahlon S. Gore, then editor of the *Dakota Republican* at Vermillion, filed a claim in the Brule Creek settlement a few minutes after midnight on January 1, 1863. He failed to prove up on his claim.

EARLY TERRITORIAL COURTS

Vermillion was the scene of the first term of court in August, 1861. Although three judicial districts were set up and a judge appointed to each district, court sessions convened at irregular intervals. Most of the cases originated in the Indian country, usually involving contraband traffic in whiskey. Other litigation grew out of trespassing on timber lands. The contemporary records show that for several years the courts frequently had no business to transact. As a consequence there was considerable absenteeism on the part of the judges: not a single one was on hand for the first session of the Supreme Court scheduled for May, 1862, and not until 1865 was a "full bench" possible at a Supreme Court session. During the early years of the Bon Homme–Fort Randall district, court was seldom held, and no justice assigned to the district established residence in it until 1867.

The judges who served during the early territorial days rarely represented the best in legal talent. In most cases they were appointed to their four-year term more out of consideration for their political qualifications than for their knowledge of the law. One chief justice was so ignorant of courtroom procedure that rather than expose himself to embarrassments on the bench at the territorial capital he had himself transferred in 1871 to a newly created district in northern Dakota. But apparently he did not altogether escape from his troubles, for in 1872 the United States attorney found it expedient to have the chief justice granted a leave of absence so that prospects would be better for conviction in criminal cases.

The administration of justice was greatly impeded by the vastness of the territorial jurisdiction and a generally lax attitude toward maintaining law and order. Crimes committed beyond the settlements often went unpunished, and legal processes were not easily served in the remote regions, even when offenders were apprehended.

The *cause célèbre* of the 1860's was the William Barry case, which involved the alleged murder of a British army officer on a June night in 1867. The setting of the alleged crime was a Missouri River steamboat, on the river below Fort Buford in the northern reaches of the Territory. Private Barry, an acknowledged member of the anti-

British Fenian society, was on sentry duty at the time. His superiors released him from custody on the plea that the incident occurred during the performance of duty. A few months later, at the insistence of the British government which was sufficiently interested to give the affair an international overtone, Barry was arrested by the civil authorities and remanded to Yankton for trial. Here he was released because of the inability to locate any material witnesses. Under further prodding from the British Foreign Office, Barry was rearrested in Montana in July, 1869, and again taken to Yankton. Difficulties in subpoenaing witnesses caused postponement after postponement of the trial until finally on November 11, 1870, after a few hours of deliberation a Vermillion jury, amidst the plaudits of a large crowd, returned a verdict of not guilty.

Frontier juries were generally disposed toward tolerance and inclined to temper justice with mercy. Trespassers caught in the act of cutting timber on government land were not easily convicted if they were merely seeking house logs and firewood. The small number of convictions obtained from local juries was a constant source of embarrassment for enforcement agents. The dismal record of not a single conviction out of a total of thirteen criminal cases during the year of 1870 prompted the following apology from the United States attorney for Dakota Territory:

> I regret at present such a record of acquittals and no convictions. The results of the year are most discouraging. I have labored zealously for better results, but I fear they will not come, until there is a revolution in public sentiment, and motives of action here upon the frontier, and some changes in the constitution of the Courts also.[3]

The appointment of Peter C. Shannon as Chief Justice in 1873 marks the end of the frontier phase in the history of the territorial courts. He introduced many needed reforms and adopted new rules of court procedure. One of his first official acts was to correct the lax procedure previously followed in granting divorce decrees. The improved state of the judiciary was soon reflected in a higher percentage of convictions in criminal cases.

LOCAL GOVERNMENT AND SCHOOLS

The administrative branch of government evolved slowly. For several years, aside from the activities connected with legislative

[3] Warren Cowles to Attorney General A. T. Akerman, December 31, 1870, Justice Department, Chronicle Files, Dakota, National Archives.

sessions, there were few administrative duties for either the governor or the territorial secretary. The Legislature in 1862 provided for an auditor and a treasurer at an annual salary of fifty dollars each, and these offices were duly filled. Warrants aggregating nearly five hundred dollars were issued by the auditor in 1863, but remained unpaid, as did the salaries of the auditor and treasurer. The federal government shouldered the military expenses incurred by the Territory during 1862. Before 1865, no revenue of any kind was raised for the support of the general government. Although property assessments were made in Yankton County in 1864 and in other counties the following year, little property was on the tax list.

At its first session, the Legislature created a number of counties and provided for county organizations in the settled areas, but there was very little attention to matters of local government until 1865. Except for an occasional license fee, there was little or no revenue. County boards generally limited their work to calling elections and enabling other county officers to qualify. Village governments were authorized in 1862, but these generally remained inactive for a few years. Yankton was the first city to become incorporated, receiving a charter from the Legislature in 1869.

Despite the early enactment of school legislation, there were no organized school districts before 1865. No school tax had been levied and no school moneys of any kind collected. During these years, private neighborhood schools provided some educational facilities. Vermillion had a private school during the winter of 1859–1860. A three-month term was conducted at Bon Homme in the spring of 1860 in what appears to have been the first schoolhouse in the Territory. The first permanent schoolhouse was built at Vermillion during the winter of 1864–1865. By that time private schools were serving half of the potential school population.

The public school system had its real beginnings with the appointment of James S. Foster as territorial superintendent of public instruction in August, 1864. Foster, a member of the New York Colony, brought to the office a wealth of experience gained in school work before his arrival on the Dakota frontier, as well as a zealous devotion to the ideals of education, as part of a New England heritage. He made a careful study of the school situation and within a year was able to report substantial progress. The number of school districts increased with the influx of new settlers, and by 1868 educational work had begun to function on a high plane.

POLITICS IN TERRITORIAL DAKOTA

The early Dakota settlers were, above all things, proficient in the art of politics. During the first decade party lines were either not well defined or were obfuscated by factional feuds. Gross irregularities characterized the early elections. Bribery, vote buying, and illegal voting were openly charged and often proved. The same tactics were pursued at nominating conventions. Political factions in an attitude of "rule or ruin" resorted to every known device to win. Party splits and contested elections were the order of the day. The decorum of the Legislature often suffered seriously under the strain of politics. Factional fights within the Republican party and a chronic disregard for law brought threats from Congress in 1864 to annex Dakota to Nebraska.

Petty rivalries and animosities between federal officeholders were the cause of much of the hectic character of early Dakota politics. Designing and eager to promote their personal ambitions, these officials not infrequently sought control of the local political organization or tried to build up a following that might lead to such control.

The leading elective position was that of delegate to Congress, and all other issues were subordinated to the contest for this office. The Congressional delegate was virtually the head of his party. His ability to reward followers with the spoils of office became the measure of his success. However, national politics, dictating territorial appointments from Washington, frequently interfered with his efforts to dominate the political situation.

The game of politics began with the first territorial officials. Since the Republican party was a mixture of old-line Whigs, Free Soilers, and antislavery Democrats, President Lincoln found it expedient to divide the federal patronage among these diverse elements. The Free-Soil wing was especially well represented in the bevy of federal officeholders that descended upon the raw Dakota frontier during the summer of 1861. Governor Jayne, personal friend of the President and brother-in-law of Senator Lyman Trumbull of Illinois, Chief Justice Philemon Bliss, former abolitionist Congressman from Ohio and protégé of Salmon P. Chase, and Surveyor General George P. Hill, protégé of Senator Zachariah Chandler of Michigan, all were Free-Soilers. Other officeholders, appointed from the more conservative wing, included former Democrats. Closely associated with the latter was J. B. S. Todd. Todd, although not a Republican, had considerable political influence in the nation's capital, as has been told.

The election in September, 1861, which had named Todd as delegate to Congress, was simply a prelude to that of 1862 in which the settlers also chose county officials as well as members of the lower house. Union County also had a county seat contest. This was the first general election.

Governor Jayne wished to become delegate to Congress, and ran as the Republican and Union candidate with the official backing of the Republican party. The incumbent, Todd, was the nominee of the so-called People's Union party, and had the support of many of the settlers who resented the Governor's intrusion in politics. A number of federal officials also aligned themselves with the Todd element. Each candidate claimed support on the strength of his personal influence at Washington, Jayne identifying himself with the dominant political elements in the Republican administration and Todd capitalizing on his kinship with the President and his many other connections in the national capital.

Many irregularities confused the results of the election of 1862 which was held on Monday, September 1, during the excitement over the Santee outbreak. At Brule Creek settlers were preparing to flee to Sioux City, but were unwilling to forego their franchise and were anxious that the county seat be located in their area. They opened the polls on Sunday evening, allowed minors and nonresidents to vote, and even stuffed the ballot box; the polls were also regularly opened the following morning. Half-breeds and nonresidents cast votes both in Charles Mix County and in the Red River Valley, where a hundred extra ballots were thrown in for good measure to swell the returns for Todd. Although a number of ballots were rejected because of irregularities, the canvassing board accepted the returns from Brule Creek and declared Jayne elected by a small margin. The Pembina returns, which happened to be mostly for Todd, did not reach Yankton in time to be canvassed. Todd at once instituted contest proceedings.

The disputed election also involved the make-up of the Legislature. When it convened, there were contesting delegations for the three southern counties in which the worst irregularities occurred. It was such a tangle that the lower house could not be organized until the seventeenth day of the session. Since the decision on the disputed seats would have a bearing on Todd's contest in Congress, neither side would yield: each organized the lower house to suit itself. Governor Jayne extended official recognition to his partisans, but the council denied the legality of his intervention and the deadlock continued with two rival bodies in the lower house. When a compromise finally was reached, it was mostly a victory for the Jayne supporters, although a Todd supporter became the speaker.

Jayne was admitted to his seat in Congress in January, 1864, pending the final outcome of the contest proceedings. In May, Congress conceded the election to Todd, rejecting the Brule Creek returns which were mostly for Jayne but accepting the equally questionable Red River votes which were overwhelmingly for Todd.

When Jayne resigned the governorship in March, 1863, the selection of his successor was a matter of great moment to the Territory. In its bid for the appointment, the Jayne faction represented itself as the loyal element supporting the Republican administration at Washington against "Copperheads and secession sympathizers." Its choice for the high honor was Newton Edmunds, a native of Michigan and chief clerk in the surveyor general's office. Edmunds had endeared himself to the settlers by his early devotion to the Territory's interests. He also had important political connections in Washington where an older brother held the important position of Commissioner of Public Lands. Philemon Bliss, the Chief Justice and an outspoken critic of Jayne, received the full support of the opposing political faction.

The forces marshalled behind Edmunds were particularly bitter in their opposition to Bliss because of his part in the 1862 campaign. In campaigning against the Chief Justice, they depicted the Territory as largely settled by a turbulent and disloyal population which would consider the appointment of Bliss a Copperhead triumph. Lincoln preferred not to take sides and offered the governorship to a Wisconsin lame-duck congressman who declined it. The matter finally was resolved six months later when the appointment went to Edmunds.

The civil jurisdiction of Dakota was in its infancy when the new governor assumed his duties. Less engrossed in politics than his predecessor, Governor Edmunds directed his full energies toward putting the machinery of government in running order. His relations with the Legislature were friendly and harmonious, and it supported his views on fiscal matters and public education. Governor Edmunds also applied himself more assiduously to his duties as Superintendent of Indian Affairs than had Jayne. Most of his time was taken up with matters concerning Indian policy and related problems. As Governor, he was at the head of the Indian Service in Dakota, being directly responsible to the Indian commissioner at Washington. The Ponca, Santee, and Yankton agencies were under his jurisdiction. Many of the employees, including some of the agents, owed their appointments to him. Although the agents were not directly subordinate to him, the Governor was in a position to exert pressure on them. Contracts for beef and other supplies for the Indian agencies were generally filled by Yankton and Sioux City residents, and the Governor disbursed the federal funds appropriated for these purposes. It was this aspect of his duties in connection with Indian affairs that made Newton Edmunds, as well as other early governors, so vulnerable to charges of collusion in fraudulent bidding and misappropriation of funds.

The election of 1864 brought to the forefront of Dakota politics Dr. Walter A. Burleigh, agent to the Yankton tribe. A man of boundless energy and unquestioned ability, but unscrupulous and ruthless in his political methods, Burleigh was a controversial figure for nearly a decade. He was intimately identified with the ambitions of both Bon Homme and Yankton, and was tireless in his efforts to develop the Territory's resources. In the political field he was allied with the Jayne faction.

Burleigh began to work for a seat in Congress during the summer of 1863 when he took over editorial control of the *Weekly Dakotian*. From this vantage point he announced his candidacy. Bliss had similar aspirations, and a rival newspaper, *The Dakota Union,* was started by George W. Kingsbury to advance the Bliss candidacy.

Just as the Bliss campaign got under way an unexpected announcement came from Todd, who had recently won his contest for Jayne's seat, that he intended to stand for re-election. Faced with the loss of his Democratic supporters to Todd, Bliss withdrew, giving Burleigh a clear field for the nomination. In the interest of party harmony, *The Dakota Union* immediately suspended publication until after the election, at which time it merged with the *Dakotian* to become the *Union and Dakotaian* under Kingsbury's management. Burleigh won an easy victory over Todd. He became a warm supporter of President Johnson and succeeded in having nearly all local appointments bestowed upon residents of the Territory.

The gradual break over Southern Reconstruction between President Johnson and the Radical Republicans at Washington had repercussions on Dakota politics. The cleavage in the Territory followed the national pattern: Burleigh, with the support of Democrats, headed the pro-Johnson faction, and the regular Republicans, which included Edmunds, aligned themselves with the Radical Republicans. At first Governor Edmunds was able to work in harmony with Burleigh; he won Burleigh's approval for his Indian peace policy and, during the summer of 1865, even secured his unqualified endorsement for his reappointment. But by the end of the year Burleigh was showing a hostility toward Edmunds which negated the Governor's efforts to hold himself aloof from the quarrel between the President and Congress.

The main source of Burleigh's animosity derived from the current investigation of his official conduct during his four years as Indian agent on the Yankton Reservation. Allegations against Indian agents and "Indian rings" were a conversational staple on the Dakota frontier, but so peculiar was the state of affairs at the Greenwood Agency that a Congressional committee was moved to visit there in August, 1865. The Governor, as Indian Superintendent, placed his office at the Committee members' disposal; they heard the testimony of Yankton chiefs and were sufficiently impressed to recommend a special investigation by the Indian office.

Burleigh, who had made a hurried trip from Washington to be on hand for the occasion, blamed Edmunds for permitting the committee on the reservation and for allowing the Indian chiefs to testify. Having characterized the investigation as political persecution and a conspiracy to defeat his re-election as delegate to Congress, he set out to eliminate Edmunds from the political scene and to replace him as governor with Andrew J. Faulk of Pennsylvania, who was Burleigh's own father-in-law. To undermine Edmunds' influence, Burleigh opposed his Indian peace policy and accused him of official misconduct in connection with Indian contracts.

Charges against Edmunds were submitted to President Johnson in April with the recommendation that he be removed and that Andrew J. Faulk of Pennsylvania be appointed in his place. The decision was an easy one for Johnson. The Edmunds family, through its close association with Senator Chandler of Michigan and other Radical Republicans, had not endeared itself to the President. In July he removed the Governor's brother, James M. Edmunds, from office as Commissioner of Public Lands; two weeks later, in August, he retired Newton Edmunds from public life in Dakota Territory.

Burleigh, experiencing no difficulty in winning re-election in the fall, had now reached the zenith of his political power. He engaged in an open feud with the Indian Bureau, missing no opportunity to attack its policies in Dakota. As for the personal charges facing him, a special agent had returned to Washington from the Yankton Agency in July, 1866, with a fantastic amount of evidence of payroll padding and ingenious ways of misappropriating Indian funds, and had recommended further investigation. A few months later a second special agent, appearing at a political gathering in the company of Burleigh, publicly exonerated him from all charges. The election of 1866, which apparently condoned his misconduct, had placed Burleigh in an even stronger strategic position, and the investigation was not followed up.

The campaign of 1868 is memorable for the uncommon number of candidates for the office of delegate, and for the appearance of the first distinct organization bearing the Democratic label. At this time there was a large population living along the line of the Union Pacific in the western part of what was then Dakota Territory, but was about to be organized under the independent jurisdiction of Wyoming Territory. Eligible to vote in the Dakota election, they greatly outnumbered the voters in the Missouri Valley, and this added a measure of uncertainty to the outcome.

The Republicans nominated S. L. Spink, the Territorial Secretary, and a group with which Burleigh was identified put up Jefferson P. Kidder of Vermillion. Burleigh, ever a political opportunist and apparently hopeful of winning with the help of the Wyoming voters, threw his hat in the ring three weeks before the election. During the last week of the campaign a Democrat living in the Wyoming settlements also announced his candidacy. On election day Spink was the victor, winning by a large plurality.

CHAPTER 9

The Early Seventies—Progress and Problems

BETTER TIMES SEEMED AT HAND for Dakota Territory by 1868. Favorable weather conditions and a temporary respite from the grasshopper plague as well as the pacification of the Indians contributed to the improved conditions. The major factor, however, was the railroad. The completion of the Sioux City and Pacific Railroad to Sioux City in 1868 gave the settlers in Union and Clay counties access to eastern markets for their wheat, and also was an indication that rail service soon would be extended to the Dakota settlements.

By the spring of 1867 the domain west of Elk Point was thickly dotted with new homes, and settlers were moving up the Big Sioux. Settlements began to spill over onto the bench lands north and west of Vermillion. The census figures for 1870 show a population of approximately ten thousand for the area now comprising South Dakota. While the actual yearly increase must remain a matter of conjecture, records of the Vermillion land office as well as various contemporary accounts indicate that the majority of the new settlers arrived during the three-year period from 1867 to 1870.

As migration into the Yankton cession gathered momentum, the line of settlement advanced rapidly up the James, Vermillion, and Big Sioux rivers and across the intervening prairies once considered suitable only for stock-raising. Homeseekers also advanced into Brookings, Hanson, Hutchinson, Lake, Moody, and Turner counties.

New county organizations followed to accommodate the new settlers. A new land office appeared in 1870 at Springfield on the Missouri, and in 1873 a third was opened at Yankton for the benefit of the homesteaders advancing up the James Valley. Because of the many land filings in the Big Sioux Valley, the land office at Vermillion was moved to Sioux Falls in 1873.

To serve the tide of migration in the northern part of the Territory, a new land office was opened at Bismarck, and one which had been located at Pembina in 1870 was moved to Fargo in 1874. Before 1878, however, over ninety per cent of the total entries were filed with the land offices in the southern part of the Territory.

The marked improvement in the fortunes of the Dakota settlements reflected a general upturn in economic conditions throughout the nation. The feeling of optimism ran particularly high in the Upper Mississippi Valley where the Panic of 1857 and the Civil War had interrupted earlier plans for railroad construction westward into the Missouri Valley. Under the stimulus of the new boom, several projects began to take form. In Dakota Territory during the period from 1867 to 1872 four different companies were organized to promote railway construction to Yankton, and five others to build lines from some specified river town into the interior of the Territory. Connections were sought not only with lines expected to reach the Big Sioux, but also with the Union Pacific in the south and the Northern Pacific in the north.

BRINGING IN THE RAILROAD

Anticipating an early railroad extension from Sioux City, Dakota and Iowa residents organized the Dakota and Northwestern Railroad Company, receiving a charter from the Territorial Legislature in January, 1867. On the list of incorporators was John I. Blair, the builder of the Sioux City and Pacific. Several months later, the company made a preliminary survey from the Big Sioux River to Yankton, preparatory to a petition for a federal land grant. It was not the purpose of the company to build and equip the road; its avowed functions were to build up vested corporate rights, secure Congressional aid in the form of a land grant, and then dispose of the franchise to reputable railroad capitalists.

In the meantime, the territorial delegate from Dakota was pressing Congress with a request for a land grant. Anticipating a favorable outcome, the railroad promoters actually laid a mile of grading at

Elk Point. They were influential enough at Washington to get a bill through the Senate granting the Dakota and Northwestern Company ten alternate sections of land on either side of the road from the Big Sioux River to Yankton and up the James Valley to the northern boundary line of Dakota Territory. The bill passed the Senate in June, 1870, but could muster only thirty votes in the House the following March.

The failure to get a land grant caused much dissatisfaction in Dakota Territory, especially at Yankton. Hitherto, Congress had been very liberal in extending government aid, bestowing lavish land bounties through indirect grants in Iowa and Minnesota and direct grants to the Union Pacific and Northern Pacific corporations. But by the time the settlements in southeastern Dakota were seeking help, Congress was opposed to further land grants and the Dakota settlers had to rely upon their own resources to attract railway capital.

When Congress denied a land grant to the Dakota and Northwestern project, Yankton businessmen organized the Dakota Southern Railway Company for the express purpose of constructing a line from the territorial capital to some undetermined point on the Iowa border. Anxious to divert from Sioux City the upriver traffic in government supplies to military posts and Indian agencies, Yankton was looking for a direct connection with the newly constructed Illinois Central line at Le Mars, Iowa. The Dakota Southern Company was free, however, to connect with Sioux City if necessary.

The desires of Yankton businessmen to bypass Sioux City ran counter to the economic interests of Elk Point and Vermillion, located, as they were, on the direct line between Yankton and Sioux City. It is, therefore, not surprising that little financial support for the Yankton company came from Clay and Union counties. In the meantime, the Dakota and Northwestern organization was kept alive, the headquarters being moved from Yankton to Vermillion.

The promoters of the Dakota Southern did not waste any time in pushing their project. After some inquiry in Chicago financial circles, they decided to secure a local subsidy in the form of either territorial or county bonds. Such action, however, required authorization from the Territorial Legislature, and that body was not to convene for another two years. There was some question whether the chief executive under the Organic Act could convene a special session of the Legislature, but the territorial secretary, in the absence of Governor Burbank, agreed to call a special session for April 18. Upon his return to Yankton, Governor Burbank asked Washington for an opinion on the legality of the special session, and on the first day of the session received the telegraphic message: "The attorney general is of opinion that the extra session is authorized." Two days later the lawmakers granted authority to organized counties and townships to vote aid to railroad corporations.

As they were adjourning the following day, the legislators learned that the telegram should have read "unauthorized." A telegrapher had committed an error in transmitting the message from Omaha. Undismayed by the news, the lawmakers concluded their meeting with a memorial to Congress, asking that the unauthorized session and its proceedings be legalized. Kingsbury reveals the prevailing mood when he states: "The Yankton legislators and citizens joined with the visiting members in deploring the outrage committed by the unknown telegraph operator, but there was so little body to their expressions of regret, that they were accused of shedding 'crocodile tears.' "[1]

The promoters of the Dakota Southern set confidently to work. They secured stock subscriptions, payable in real estate, labor, and supplies, and interviewed construction companies in Chicago, New York, and other eastern cities. Next, they held an election in Yankton County for the purpose of voting $200,000 in twenty-year bonds bearing eight per cent interest. The question carried by a vote of 542 to 126 with about two-thirds of the voters participating. In the town of Yankton 463 favored the bond issue and 59 opposed it. The Yankton interests, still hopeful of a direct connection with the Illinois Central, had a reconnaissance made to the Big Sioux in the direction of Le Mars.

Two months after the Yankton election the promoters of the Dakota and Northwestern Company asked Clay County to vote $60,000 in bonds to aid their project, but the Clay County voters rejected the question by an overwhelming margin. Shortly thereafter, the Dakota Southern secured a perpetual lease of the Dakota and Northwestern franchise.

The uncertainty over the status of the bond subsidy was removed on May 27, 1872, when Congress enacted a measure legalizing the action of the Territorial Legislature permitting counties to vote bonds, although specifically declaring the special session invalid.

[1] Kingsbury, *History of Dakota Territory*, I, 623.

Congress also required railroad companies to issue stock certificates for the full value of bonds they might receive from any county or local unit of government.

The railroad interests expected the voters of Clay and Union counties to follow the example set by the public-spirited citizens of Yankton in voting bonds. Since construction was to begin on the Big Sioux, they concentrated first on Union County, and after several months of parleying, made it clear that Elk Point Township was to raise $15,000, and the town of Elk Point an additional $5,000 toward a depot. Sentiment against aid was so strong that the corporation did not care to risk a vote by the entire county; in fact, a court order was necessary to compel the county commissioners to call an election in Elk Point Township. The Dakota Southern announced flatly that unless bonds were voted, the railroad would follow the Big Sioux north for some fifteen or twenty miles before making a turn westward toward Yankton. The results of the two special elections held in May, 1872, were favorable, assuring Elk Point of railroad connections.

When Clay County had its opportunity to vote bonds a few months later, only 63 voters were in favor, compared to 763 opposed. Clay County did not have the same stake as the other two counties at the time the decision had to be made. The railroad was already under construction, and was certain to run through Vermillion. Moreover, many Clay County voters were opposed in principle to any bond issue, remembering eastern railway bond swindles in days gone by. Vermillion businessmen furnished some help by raising $4,000 for a depot.

The opening of the Dakota Southern to traffic between Sioux City and Yankton in February, 1873, was an occasion for great rejoicing in the Dakota settlements. The improved marketing facilities were a tremendous stimulus to agricultural production, and helped greatly in attracting new settlers. Yankton especially was benefited. The railway made the town a prominent river port on the Upper Missouri for nearly a decade, a position to which it clung until subsequent railroad building finished the river traffic. The railroad facilities at Yankton were directly responsible for the large volume of traffic that passed through the Dakota capital during the Black Hills gold rush.

Nonetheless, Yankton County paid a high price for its railroad. Whether a railway corporation would have been willing to build without aid is impossible to say. The settlements along the Missouri did not extend much beyond Yankton, and local traffic was hardly sufficient to attract speculative enterprise. Without local aid it seems likely that railway building into the southern part of Dakota Territory would have been delayed. The Panic of 1873, which hit the country shortly after the Dakota Southern began operations, temporarily suspended all railway construction. Not until 1878, when railroads from the Mississippi Valley finally reached its eastern border, did southern Dakota secure more railroad facilities. And even then the corporations undertaking construction demanded special tax privileges before they would agree to build in advance of settlement.

The action taken by Yankton County in tendering bonds bearing a face value of $200,000 to the Dakota Southern had a long-drawn-out and costly sequel. In the beginning all went smoothly. The construction company disposed of the securities to a New York banking firm, realizing about $140,000 from the transaction. The bankers, in turn, sold the bonds in small lots to the public at a big profit. Most of the bondholders lived in Maine, a few in England. After the bonds were issued, some Yankton citizens objected to the special two per cent railroad tax. The Legislature during its 1874–1875 session actually passed a bill repealing the original aid measure of April 21, 1871, but Governor Pennington vetoed the repeal bill. After three annual payments of the special railroad levy, a Yankton taxpayer secured a court order restraining the county treasurer from collecting the tax.

From September, 1875, until 1883 no railroad tax was collected and no interest paid on the bonds. The Territorial Supreme Court in a split decision had held that the proceedings under which the bonds had been issued were invalid. Following this decision, the First National Bank of Brunswick, Maine, owner of a large block of bonds, promptly brought suit for the collection of defaulted interest. Refused judgment by the territorial courts, the plaintiff appealed to the Supreme Court of the United States, which, after a four-year delay, reversed the decision of the Supreme Court of Dakota Territory and directed judgment for the bondholder.

The people of Yankton County, however, were determined to secure favorable terms from the bondholders, and in 1881 the Territorial Legislature came to their assistance with several measures designed to block enforcement of the judgment against the county. When the bondholders, now organized into a protective association, obtained a writ of mandamus against the county commissioners, the latter availed themselves of the legislation enacted for their benefit and resorted to a hide-and-seek routine. By meeting in secret and resigning upon the conclusion of official business, reactivating themselves when new business accumulated and then resigning again, the county commissioners managed to evade the officers of the law from August, 1881, to April, 1883.

The bondholders finally won settlement on their own terms. Fearing complete repudiation should Congress relinquish control over Dakota before the litigation was ended, they campaigned vigorously against a statehood bill pending in Congress until they gained their objective. Under a new arrangement approved by the voters on April 25, 1883, Yankton County funded the original eight per cent bonds into a new issue of thirty-year bonds bearing a lower rate of interest. By this time the total obligations, representing the face value of the bonds plus accrued interest, amounted to approximately $340,000. The Chicago, Milwaukee, and St. Paul Railroad, which had purchased the Dakota Southern, paid the county about $16,000 for its railway stock. The final chapter in the bond case was not written until 1919 when the last bonds were redeemed.

With the opening of the Dakota Southern in 1873, the settlements along the Missouri entered a new state of development. Many lumberyards and implement stores sprang up almost overnight in the railway towns along the Missouri. The assurance of a wider market led to expanded farming operations. Farms close to the railroad doubled in value. Dakota wheat commanded a favorable market in the Mississippi Valley, as did the flour processed by commercial mills located at Elk Point, Vermillion, and Yankton. The railroad also performed a notable service in transporting new settlers into the Territory.

FOREIGN COLONIES IN DAKOTA

Several nationalities were represented in the migration of the early 1870's. The Norwegians, who constituted a large segment of the population along the Missouri, remained the dominant Scandinavian element, playing an especially important role in the advance of settlement up the Big Sioux Valley into Lincoln and Minnehaha counties. The arrival in Clay County of several settlers from Sweden in 1868 marked the beginnings of an extensive Swedish community frequently referred to as "Swedefield" by contemporary writers. Within a period of five years over two hundred claims were occupied within a small area reaching from the Vermillion River in the central part of Clay County to the southwestern corner of Lincoln County.

In the same period, a large Danish colony was formed in Turner County in the vicinity of Swan Lake. Its social center was Daneville until replaced by Viborg two decades later. The Turner County community with its several hundred families was characterized by a visiting clergyman as "the most Danish settlement in America."

During the summer of 1869 the vanguard of a fairly heavy Bohemian immigration arrived in the locality of Lakeport seven miles west of Yankton along the Fort Randall military road. These settlers were identified with a colonization society formed in Chicago and eastern cities to establish Czech colonies in western states and territories. They were soon joined by compatriots who began to occupy claims from Lakeport west into Bon Homme County. The first trading center was Ziskov, established in 1870. Tabor, established two years later, eventually became the center of the Czech settlement.

In 1873 began a migration of Germans from Russia that brought several thousand to Bon Homme, Hutchinson, Turner, and Yankton counties. Generally referred to as German-Russians, these settlers were the descendants of Germans who settled in large groups in southern Russia during the eighteenth century. Under special concessions granted them, they were able to preserve their cultural and social identity, retaining their own language, worshipping in their own faith, administering their own educational system, and selecting their own local and district officials. In a spirit of reaction, the Russian government in June, 1871, decreed the abolition of these special privileges, giving the German colonists what amounted to a choice between leaving Russia within ten years or becoming completely Russianized. Many decided to migrate to Canada and the United States. Among them were members of the Mennonite and kindred faiths who particularly objected to their loss of exemption from compulsory military service.

The first German-Russians to come to Dakota Territory arrived at Yankton in the spring of 1873 over the recently constructed Dakota Southern. The mission of this advance party of four was to find a favorable location for a group then en route to the United States. Escorted by territorial officials, they toured the vicinage of Yankton and the counties west and north, finally selecting several townships in the northern part of Yankton County as a favorable location for their countrymen. This was a Lutheran group. Influenced by these early arrivals, related groups soon followed. Altogether, about five hundred German-Russians settled in Yankton County during 1873.

The first Mennonite settlers came in the fall of 1873, a small group led by Daniel Unruh, which settled in Childstown Township, Turner County. The following year at least two hundred Mennonite families totaling probably one thousand souls reached southern Dakota. Many others followed during the next few years.

The Hutterian Brethren, or Hutterites, also migrated from Russia to the Dakota prairies. This sect, closely related to the Mennonite in some of its religious beliefs, practiced a form of religious communism, living in colonies and holding all goods and property in common in accordance with a strict interpretation of early Christian teachings. A group of forty families established the first colony, or *Bruderhof,* in Bon Homme County in 1874. In the same year a second group established a colony at Wolf Creek in the southern part of Hutchinson County. In 1877 the Elm Spring colony was organized. From these three original communities, through a process of natural growth and branch colonization, the Hutterites expanded within the course of half a century to a total of seventeen colonies, all of them except for the mother colony at Bon Homme located along the James River or its tributaries. In their search for unimproved lands where they might form compact communities with minimum infiltration by other nationalities, the Mennonites advanced beyond the line of settlement along the Missouri and the Big Sioux. The course taken by the Mennonite settlers usually led up the James River Valley into Hutchinson and Turner counties, with the heaviest concentration in the vicinity of Freeman.

Before 1875, the citizens of Yankton assumed the greater part of the burden of directing the German-Russian immigrants to Dakota. They provided for the temporary care of the newcomers upon their arrival over the Dakota Southern and subsidized the activities of private immigration agents. Merchants on business trips to the East frequently met incoming steamships, hoping to induce immigrants from Russia to settle in Dakota Territory.

These activities supplemented the work of the immigration bureau established by the Legislature in January, 1871. James S. Foster, who had been designated as an official immigration agent as early as 1869, was the first Commissioner of Immigration. Serving without salary and limited by scanty appropriations, Foster published immigration pamphlets and took occasional journeys to the Atlantic seaboard where he tried to organize emigration societies.

The heavy influx of German-Russians during 1873 and 1874 evoked a popular demand that the Territory make a greater effort to draw European immigrants to Dakota. Other western states and territories maintained immigration bureaus and competed with each other as well as with the several land-grant railroads of Minnesota, Nebraska, and Kansas for new settlers. The citizens at Yankton considered it essential to maintain agents at the seaports. Immigrants from Russia were met at Chicago to keep them out of the toils of unscrupulous railway agents.

Responding to the demand for a reorganization of the immigration office, the Legislature in December, 1875, created an immigration bureau of five members, and both the territorial government and the town of Yankton took steps to construct immigrant houses to shelter the European newcomers.

The immigration bureau proved cumbersome and expensive, and its work was considered unsatisfactory. Two of the members did make several trips to the seaboard and intermediate points to direct migration to Dakota. One, a German, watched over the German immigration, checking trains at Chicago and steamboat arrivals at New York and Philadelphia; the other, a Norwegian, took as his assignment the Scandinavians. He met steamships at Montreal and Quebec, and made frequent journeys to the Upper Mississippi Valley, another important recruiting ground for prospective settlers. Most of the Scandinavians escorted by the immigration agent settled in the northern part of the Territory near Fargo. The bureau ceased to exist in 1877 when the Legislature refused to provide for its continuance.

By this time there was no longer so urgent a need for a governmental agency to advertise the Territory to the outside world. The statistics which showed mounting crop production in the older counties seemed to refute the earlier slanders concerning the Territory. Particularly welcome services were rendered by the Bohemian and German-Russian settlers who, pushing west and north beyond Yankton County, once and for all dispelled the myth about the unsuitability of that region for agriculture. There were no protracted droughts such as those of the sixties. Aside from a few localities in

1874, rainfall was generally adequate for farming operations during the entire period of the seventies.

Nevertheless, the conditions of life in the newly settled areas during the seventies were harsh and rigorous. As the soil usually required cultivation for several seasons to put it in proper condition for maximum yields, crops on virgin land were light. Many of the settlers were unaccustomed to farming and reaped poorly for several years. The German-Russians were a notable exception in this respect; they were expert in the art of agriculture and put their skill to good use on their Dakota farms. All, however, had to adjust themselves to the new country and learn proper tillage methods from bitter experience. Short crops spelled discouragement and failure for the homesteaders, and at times even rendered them destitute.

GRASSHOPPER RAIDS

The swarms of grasshoppers to which the Great Plains were periodically subject were a major cause of hardship for the Dakota settlers during the seventies. After a respite of several years following the devastating plagues of the sixties, the migratory grassland insects, or red-legged Rocky Mountain locusts, as they were termed by entomologists, reappeared during the summers of 1873 and 1874 to leave behind them "a scene of desolation, broken hopes, and saddened homes." Few appeared in Dakota in 1875, but there was a destructive visitation the following year.

The raids, as a rule, came during the latter part of July while the wheat harvest was in progress. Borne by moderate northwest winds and appearing like the clouds of dust that often darkened the sky, the grasshoppers fell upon the country like local showers, apparently descending on a particular spot under the influence of some peculiar weather condition. Since they did not always alight as they swarmed over the countryside, the damage varied between communities. A whole county, or the greater portion of it, might escape entirely, while a nearby locality would be nearly stripped of vegetation. The length of their stay was likewise variable; usually it lasted six or eight days, but if the breeze was just right, the insects might make the southward journey within a day.

Regardless of the duration of the visit, a field of ripening grain could be completely destroyed as the heavy mass of grasshoppers crushed the weak stems to the ground. In addition to destroying the crop, the insects usually left behind a multitudinous number of tiny eggs deposited in small holes in cornfields or some other bare spot. Although the young hoppers that hatched the following spring were sure to migrate, they could be equally destructive to the sprouted grain before their wings had fully developed.

Because of the localized character of the grasshopper raids, the full extent of the devastation cannot be measured. The appearance of the hoppers during the wheat harvest usually left a partial grain crop even in the fields that were attacked. Contemporary newspaper accounts testify to extensive wheat shipments over the Dakota Southern even during the most destructive raids. Garden crops and potatoes were very vulnerable; corn invariably suffered the greatest damage. During the severe plague of 1874 the entire corn crop within a sixty-mile stretch from Yankton to Sioux City was practically destroyed, yet within the same area there was a good crop of wheat and potatoes. The newly settled parts of the Territory were the chief distress areas. Here the destruction left the settlers with extremely limited resources. The northern parts of Clay and Union counties and the areas settled by the Bohemians and German-Russians were particularly hard hit by the grasshopper raids of 1874.

There was so much destitution in 1874 that relief work went on in every organized county within the Territory. An unusually severe winter aggravated the situation resulting from crop losses. To help alleviate the suffering and to provide seed grain to the needy, the Legislature in January, 1875, authorized the issuance of $25,000 in bonds running for ten years at eight per cent. Washington officials questioned the legality of such a step and advised Governor John L. Pennington to veto the bill. In his veto message, the Governor suggested a direct appropriation for relief purposes. The Legislature promptly re-enacted the bond measure, but no effort was made to put it into effect. While the Governor and other territorial leaders at first opposed all relief proposals in the desire to avoid adverse publicity for the Territory, sober second thought compelled them to recognize the critical need for assistance in the rural communities and led to the creation of a Territorial relief committee. The relief agency collected more than four thousand dollars in eastern communities, expending the contributions for food, clothing, and seed wheat. There was an especially great need for the latter.

Congress also appropriated $150,000 worth of food for distribution by the War Department to needy settlers in the frontier areas.

During March and April of 1875 General Alfred Terry distributed approximately 75,000 pounds of flour and 25,000 pounds of bacon to nearly 4,000 persons in Dakota Territory, each individual receiving what was considered a twenty-five day supply. In December, 1874, Congress passed a law permitting settlers in grasshopper-stricken regions to be absent from their homestead and pre-emption claims until the following July so that they could find employment in other parts of the country. Congress also extended the time for making proof. Two years later it granted a further extension of time for final proof on pre-emptions.

The Territory had a respite from the grasshoppers in 1875, and a bumper crop was harvested. The following season started auspiciously, but the pests once again made their appearance, wreaking destruction upon corn, potatoes, and garden crops; fortunately, much of the wheat crop had been harvested.

The recurrence of the plague in 1876 bred fears that distressed communities would fail to draw new settlers and might even face depopulation. The situation was considered to be so serious that a four-day convention was held at Omaha on October 26, 1876, to consider control measures. It was attended by the governors of Iowa, Nebraska, Missouri, and Dakota Territory. The convention discussed various methods for fighting the insects, and before adjourning adopted a resolution suggesting a public day of prayer. Dakota Territory observed such a day of fasting and prayer on May 4, 1877.

The settlers stepped up their efforts to destroy the unfledged insects, for there was no practical defense against the hoppers in the flying stage. Grasshopper-eradication conventions were held that spring in a number of townships, and local committees were appointed to watch the hatching process and decide on the proper time for burning the prairies. But the plague had run its course by this time, and crops sustained little damage.

Notwithstanding all the ills that can be charged against the grasshoppers, there were some beneficial results. The efforts to alleviate crop damage led to marked improvement in farming practices. Better preparation and earlier seeding advanced the wheat harvest sufficiently to escape the midsummer raids. The settlers began to diversify their farming operations, and experimented with locust-resistant crops like flax and rye. These experiences speeded the adaptation of agriculture to the Dakota environment.

The grasshopper ravages coincided with an unfavorable economic situation induced by the Panic of 1873. The subsequent depression affected agriculture adversely throughout the country. In Dakota Territory it ended the boom which had begun a few years earlier, and made credit even harder to obtain. The numerous notices of farm foreclosures and sheriff sales that appear in Dakota newspapers for 1875 and 1876 testify to the hard times.

THE CREDIT SYSTEM

The most serious single problem confronting the early Dakota settler was his need for credit. He generally moved into the region with very little—usually with just enough to enable him to take a claim and plant a few acres. For a season or two he often sought employment at sawmills, or at military posts and Indian agencies, and sometimes on the steamboats plying the Missouri River. Earnings from such work could tide the family over until a crop was harvested, or could provide money to buy more livestock and equipment.

For the Dakota homesteader, as was generally true on the frontier, the main sources of credit were the local banker or loan broker, the farm implement dealer, and the local storekeeper. The banker or loan broker was the professional money-lender, and he protected himself with either a real estate or a chattel mortgage. The implement companies as a rule held time notes, secured by chattels. Store credit usually remained unsecured, although in some instances chattel mortgages were required. The settler had to depend upon the local store for his supplies. In the absence of ready cash, there was a great deal of bartering, but even in barter, credit often had to be granted in anticipation of the harvest.

During the early seventies Dakota Territory was cursed with high interest rates. The prevailing rate for chattel mortgages was ten per cent. Real estate mortgages, however, commanded whatever rates the traffic could bear. The maximum legal rate under legislation enacted in 1871 was two per cent a month or 24 per cent a year. In 1873 the maximum rate was fixed at 18 per cent. These high rates were sanctioned in order to attract capital to the Territory; in fact, official immigration pamphlets issued in 1870 and 1872 called special attention to the advantages of high interest rates.

Approximately one-half of the real estate mortgages recorded in Clay County during 1872 stipulated interest at 24 per cent. The principals generally ranged from $50 to $500. A few mortgages bore a low rate of seven per cent. During 1873 and 1874 a number commanded the maximum rate of 18 per cent, although rates of 15, 12, and 10 per cent were becoming more common. In Union County relatively few mortgages were taken at maximum interest.

The Legislature in 1875 complied with the popular demand for a revision of the usury law by fixing 12 per cent as the legal rate, but this reduction only mitigated some of the worst features of the credit system. As grasshopper infestations recurred, foreclosures again became numerous. A typical mortgage sale notice appeared in the *Dakota Republican* for January 18, 1877, announcing the sale of a tract of land near Vermillion to satisfy a mortgage placed in 1872 for $275 at 24 per cent interest.

THE GRANGE

This credit situation was only one of the problems in an agricultural society still in its first stage of development. Pioneers were concerned when the larger part of their profits seemed to go to eastern capitalists in the form of interest. Consequently, the Patrons of Husbandry or the National Grange, as it was commonly called, met a warm welcome in Dakota Territory. Moreover, many of the native-born settlers came from the Upper Mississippi Valley where they had become familiar with the various farmers' clubs and their programs of cooperative buying and selling.

The first grange was organized near Vermillion on December 4, 1872, and received a national charter the following May. Later in the year a territorial grange was organized with twenty-five subordinate granges. By September, 1874, the Grange had reached its fullest growth in Dakota Territory with fifty-six local lodges and a probable membership of two thousand.

The Grange drew most of its members from the older counties along the Missouri, although Lincoln County in the Big Sioux Valley also boasted a fairly large membership. The members were chiefly of native American stock. The Scandinavians, except for the Norwegian settlers in Lincoln County, were averse to affiliation. The German-Russian settlements were unaffected, as were the Bohemians. Unfamiliarity with American ways and an inbred antipathy for secret organizations made these groups unresponsive.

As the Grange grew in prestige and power, persons not directly engaged in farming, notably politicians and newspaper editors, began to identify themselves with the organization. The appearance of the movement in Union County motivated the founding of the *Dakota Gleaner* at Elk Point in February, 1874. Although Grange officials disclaimed it as an official organ, this journal, during its brief existence, served as a forceful spokesman for the Grange.

By the end of 1875 the Grange's influence was on the wane. The grasshopper raids of 1874, together with the organization's failure to bestow promised material benefits, caused a decline in interest. Many of the clubs had discontinued their meetings and in spite of attempts to revive and expand the Grange, by 1877 most of the clubs were defunct. A few new granges appeared several years later in newer settlements, but these also became inactive within a short time.

The handicaps under which the farmers on the Dakota frontier were struggling militated against the success of the Grange. The scarcity of capital rendered the plans for cooperative activities ineffectual. There was no escape from the credit system, despite admonitions of Grange officials against buying machinery and running into debt. The main benefits derived from the Order were the opportunities for a fuller community and social life. Grange meetings also served as fruitful occasions for discussing problems of common interest and making plans for community action as, for example, against the grasshopper plagues.

CHAPTER 10

Opening the Black Hills

IN AUGUST, 1874, came the electrifying news that gold had been discovered in the Black Hills. The attention of the entire country was immediately focused upon the region. For the older settlements of Dakota Territory the economic developments of the gold rush were particularly opportune, counterbalancing in large measure the adverse conditions of the period.

The Laramie Treaty of 1868 had merely postponed the occupation of the Black Hills. The existence of mineral wealth was taken for granted, and the government's action in sealing off the region through the creation of the Great Sioux Reservation simply whetted the desires of the whites. The insistent and increasing agitation for the exploration of the Black Hills finally prompted a warning from the military authorities in March, 1872, that strict measures would be taken to prevent trespassing on Indian lands.

The guiding spirit in the movement to colonize the Black Hills was Charles Collins, eccentric Irish-American editor of the *Sioux City Times*. Following collapse of a scheme to plant a colony of fellow Fenians in Dakota Territory near the present site of Chamberlain in 1869, Collins had turned his attention to the Black Hills. He was instrumental in organizing the Black Hills Mining and Exploring Association at Sioux City in February, 1872, and began to publish highly colored, sensational stories about the prospects for gold. With his Sioux City associates, Collins openly solicited recruits throughout the Missouri Valley for the express purpose of entering the Black Hills. But the projected expedition was given up when General W. S. Hancock, then commanding the Department of Dakota with headquarters at Fort Snelling, ordered its immediate abandonment.

Notwithstanding military orders against trespassing by the whites, officials at Washington appeared favorable to an early opening of the Black Hills. Early in 1872 Secretary of the Interior Delano expressed his opinion that the Black Hills were not necessary to the happiness and prosperity of the Indians. According to George W. Kingsbury, pioneer journalist and historian of Dakota Territory, ". . . assurances from high authority were given Dakota's representatives, that as soon as the disposition of troops would permit, a military expedition, under an experienced officer, would be sent to the Black Hills for the purpose of exploring the country."[1]

For the military authorities, the Black Hills question had wider implications. Less than half of the Teton Sioux had settled down to agency life after the signing of the Laramie Treaty of 1868; the rest, including most of the northern bands, continued to roam through the Powder River country, ignoring the provisions of the treaty to which they had refused to affix their signatures. When the Northern Pacific in 1871 decided to follow the south bank of the Yellowstone, there were open hostilities as wild bands of nontreaty Sioux tried to drive railroad surveyors from their hunting grounds. Extensive military operations in the Powder River country during 1872 and 1873 failed to subdue the Indians.

The disposition of the Tetons to make trouble was by no means confined to the region of the Yellowstone. Many nonagency Sioux appeared during the winter months at the Oglala and Brûlé agencies near the Platte, and while they availed themselves of rations and annuity goods, they bred all kinds of mischief among the agency Indians, even instigating occasional raids upon whites.

THE CUSTER EXPEDITION OF 1874

General Philip H. Sheridan, commanding the military department of the Missouri, believed that the solution to the problem posed by these wild bands lay in the establishment of a large military post in the Black Hills. With his superiors' approval, he ordered General Terry of the Dakota military district to organize an expedition for a reconnaissance of the Black Hills region. Fort Abraham

[1] Kingsbury, *History of Dakota Territory*, I, 876.

Map courtesy Rand McNally

DAKOTA TERRITORY, 1875

Lincoln, located on the Missouri River opposite Bismarck, which
was then the terminus of the Northern Pacific Railroad, was the
starting point. Brevet Major General George A. Custer, Lieutenant
Colonel of the Seventh Cavalry on duty at Fort Abraham Lincoln,
was assigned to command the expedition. The military orders
issued on June 8, 1874, were explicit with respect to the purpose
of the reconnaissance. Custer was to proceed to Bear Butte or to
some other point on or near the Belle Fourche River, and from

there proceed so as to obtain maximum information about the region.

The historic Custer expedition, comprising over a thousand men, left Fort Abraham Lincoln on July 2, 1874. The cavalcade consisted of ten companies of the Seventh Cavalry, two companies of infantry, a detachment of Indian scouts, and a corps of scientists, together with newspaper correspondents, a photographer, a few miners, and numerous civilian employees. There were 110 wagons, each drawn by six mules, and some ambulances. In addition, a herd of 300 beef cattle was taken along for fresh meat. The cavalry horses numbered a thousand. This was one of the largest, most complete, and best equipped expeditions ever launched on the frontier in a time of peace. There was even a band.

A southwesterly course from Fort Abraham Lincoln brought Custer and his command within eighteen days to the Belle Fourche at the northern edge of the Black Hills where the trail made by Captain Raynolds in 1859 was still plainly discernible. Passing along the northern foothills, the expedition turned south on the Wyoming side to enter the main part of the Black Hills in the vicinity of Harney Peak. Several surveying parties made reconnaissance trips in various directions from the main camp, which was set up on French Creek about seven miles due south of Harney Peak.

The official reports, which incorporate notes of the several scientists who accompanied the expedition as well as the observations of General Custer, consist largely of effusions over the natural beauty of the region with its jagged granite peaks overlooking beautiful parks and valleys and of remarks on the great potentialities of the Black Hills in terms of timber, mineral wealth, and farming. One looks in vain for comments about strategic lines of communications and likely sites for military posts. In its preoccupation with geological matters, the expedition seemed to have lost sight of the widely publicized military objective. While the scientists were searching for scientific data, the miners in the party were exploring the streams with pan and shovel for evidence of gold.

Horatio N. Ross and Willis W. T. McKay found the first trace of gold in the sands of French Creek on July 30 a few miles below the present city of Custer. Great excitement prevailed in the camp following the report of the discovery to General Custer; for a short time even the soldiers joined the teamsters and Indian scouts in panning the stream's gravels. During the next few days the pans continued to yield flakes of gold, and a few of the more enthusiastic members of the expedition met around a campfire to form a mining company, granting the discovery claim to Ross.

In his dispatches of August 2 and 12 Custer reported the finding of gold in small but paying quantities at several places. He was not ready to venture an opinion on the richness of the deposits because of a lack of opportunity for more thorough examination. Gold, however, did occur in the streams and among the roots of the grass, and it took no experts to find it. The first official news of the discovery was released by military headquarters at St. Paul on August 12.

Custer returned to Fort Abraham Lincoln after sixty days. He had scarcely left the scene of the discoveries before prospectors were laying plans for an invasion of the region. General Sheridan sternly repeated his earlier injunctions and issued orders to commanders of frontier posts for summary action against all white trespassers. But the gold-seekers were not to be deterred.

GOLD-SEEKERS AT FRENCH CREEK

Despite the vigilance of army patrols from Fort Randall and Fort Laramie, a party of twenty-six Sioux City residents organized by Charles Collins and his associates, and including a woman and a nine-year-old boy, stole their way into the Black Hills, reaching French Creek near Custer on December 23. Immediately upon reaching their destination, the men hurried to the site of the Custer diggings, where they quickly found gold. For protection against marauding Indians, they constructed a formidable stockade from the heavy pine timber, and inside this fortress they built seven crude log cabins. Here they spent the remaining days of an inhospitable winter, breaking the monotony by hunting and occasionally prospecting for gold.

After failing in two previous efforts, finally, in early April, the government caught up with the squatters on French Creek where they had organized a mining district and laid out a townsite, named Harney City. The small band, now reduced to eighteen, was compelled to abandon everything, including their mining equipment and supplies. A cavalry troop from Fort Laramie escorted the party to Cheyenne whence the majority returned to Sioux City by rail.

The military forces, by this time fully alerted, took energetic action against a second expedition organized at Sioux City. Near present-day Gordon, Nebraska, a strong military detachment intercepted the wagon train, burning most of the twenty-nine wagons with their heavy freight of provisions and merchandise. The leader of the expedition was kept in military custody for a few months, and the rest were marched under military escort to Yankton and released.

The well-intentioned efforts of the military failed to discourage the whites from entering the Indian country. They came from all directions, from the remotest corners of the nation as well as the nearby settlements on the edge of the Great Sioux Reservation. The scouting duties of the garrisons at Fort Randall and Fort Sully left those posts nearly deserted during the daytime. Yet by the summer of 1875 some eight hundred miners had eluded the military patrols. In fairness to the military it should be pointed out that most of the miners had made their way from Cheyenne and other points on the Union Pacific through a region not so energetically patrolled as was the stretch of Indian lands bordering the Missouri River.

The stampede of prospectors to the new El Dorado placed the federal government in an awkward position. Peaceful relations with the agency bands were endangered; and the Sioux, openly resentful of the disregard of the Laramie Treaty, threatened reprisals. In the meantime, while the soldiers were scouring the plains for trespassers, mass meetings were held at Yankton and other points to pass resolutions demanding that the Hills be opened. From the point of view of the whites, it did not seem unreasonable to expect that the Indians would agree to relinquish the region: after all, the Black Hills were of little use to the Sioux except as a source of lodgepoles and for an occasional hunt in the foothills. But to the Indians the Black Hills were sacred, and keeping them undefiled had deep spiritual significance.

NEGOTIATIONS WITH THE INDIANS

High officials in Washington, confident that the Sioux could be persuaded to part with their rights to the Black Hills, arranged for a delegation of chiefs from the various agencies to come to the capital in May of 1875. Preparatory to the formal discussions, the Sioux leaders were presented to President Grant, who hinted at the impossibility of keeping the whites out of their domain and advised his guests to consider removal to Indian Territory. The

Dakota governor, John L. Pennington, was present at the meetings with the Indians. The chiefs were unwilling to assume responsibility for a cession and asked for permission to return home and confer with their tribesmen.

While these discussions were taking place in Washington, a scientific expedition headed by Walter P. Jenney, a professional mineralogist and geologist, was on its way from Fort Laramie to make a topographical and geological survey of the Black Hills. In the face of conflicting reports concerning the presence of gold, more exact information was essential in order to arrive at a fair purchase price. Persons close to the Indian Office, and prominent army officers also, had been deploring and even questioning the reports given out by the Custer Expedition. Many seriously questioned the wisdom of forcing an issue with the Teton Sioux.

Jenney's party included prospectors, laborers, and miners. There was also a military escort of about four hundred men under the command of Lieutenant Colonel Richard I. Dodge. In March the expedition was fitted out at Cheyenne, Wyoming, in accordance with instructions received from the Indian Office. The work of exploration went on without interruption from early June until October, beginning at French Creek near Custer. Prospectors filtering through the military cordon usually headed for this point, and the whole bottom of the valley for six miles was pocked with prospecting pits. Soldiers and teamsters attached to the expedition tried their luck alongside the miners already working their claims in the area. When Jenney moved his operations to Spring and Rapid creeks and their tributaries and located richer placer deposits, there was a stampede to the newer diggings. The miners fraternized with the soldiers, and Jenney and his corps of surveyors obtained invaluable scientific data from them. As the season advanced, Jenney's dispatches, transmitted to Washington by telegraph from Fort Laramie, became increasingly favorable, though more restrained in tone than the reports made by the Custer Expedition. The Jenney party did not penetrate the northern part of the Black Hills, so had no opportunity to examine the richer deposits of that region.

While Jenney was making his survey, preparations were under way for the negotiations with the Sioux. A formal commission, headed by Senator William B. Allison of Iowa, was appointed in June, and soon after a subcommittee visited the various agencies to prepare for the grand council. Accompanied by Spotted Tail and several of his headmen, the subcommittee also visited the Black Hills where they saw Jenney and his geologists at work. In case the Indians should regard the presence of so many prospectors an act of bad faith, it seemed wise to remove all trespassers before the commission began its bargaining.

General George Crook, to whom had been assigned the unpleasant task of removing the whites, arrived with a cavalry force. On July 29, after visiting with the miners, he issued a proclamation ordering all miners or other unauthorized persons to leave by the middle of August. He expressed the hope that the trespassers would leave voluntarily, and suggested a miners' meeting on August 10 for the protection of their claims. Assembling at the stockade on French Creek, the prospectors organized a townsite company and laid out Custer City. With the consent of General Crook, eight men remained to look after the property of the group; all the others left the French Creek area.

When other miners in other localities learned of the action taken at Custer City, many of them left during the next few days. But a number remained behind, and were joined by a constant stream of newcomers, despite the prohibitory orders of the military.

The grand council convened on September 20, 1875, on White River in northwestern Nebraska, eight miles from the Red Cloud Agency. The Sioux had gathered in force for the occasion—one eyewitness account places the number at twenty thousand—and they were in a quarrelsome mood. From earlier conversations with the chiefs, the commissioners already had grave misgivings about the outcome of the negotiations, and what they now saw did not dispel their doubts. Realizing that the Indians might be unwilling to sell the Black Hills, the commissioners asked only for mining rights, offering an annual rental of $400,000, and reserving for the government the right to terminate the lease on two years' notice. As an alternative, they offered to buy the Black Hills outright for $6,000,-000. The commissioners also asked that the Indians cede the Wyoming Big Horn country over which the northern nontreaty bands were roaming.

When the Indians refused to accept these terms and negotiations collapsed, the government removed the cavalry force from the Black Hills. This tacitly permitted entry into the region without revoking the orders against trespassing. At the same time, the government refused military protection within the bounds of the reservation.

Provision trains carrying food and supplies to the mining camps were advised to arm themselves for defense against hostile Indians, and all others were warned to travel in large groups. At the Sioux agencies, the officials received word to keep their wards close by so that they would not become involved in any disturbances.

THE SIOUX WAR OF 1876

In November, 1875, an Indian inspector filed a special complaint on the subject of the wild bands of Sioux in the Big Horn and Powder River country, who victimized friendly Indians as well as whites in their marauding activities. According to report, only a few hundred warriors were involved, and the government decided to compel these nonagency Sioux to join their kinsmen at the agencies maintained for them. It was assumed that a thousand troops under an experienced officer could easily handle the situation, if force became necessary. During the first week of December the Indian Office issued an order to the effect that if the bands in question had not moved to their respective reservations by January 31, and if they did not remain there, they would be deemed hostile and treated accordingly.

Couriers who went out from the agencies during the Christmas season to communicate the order could not locate all the bands because of severe weather conditions; those who were reached found ready excuses for not coming in by the appointed time. On February 1 the Indian Office was satisfied that the Indians had been fully advised and turned the problem over to the army which, in anticipation of just such a development, had already decided upon a quick winter campaign.

The Indian Office had estimated the hostile population at about three thousand, and the army did not look for much opposition. A display of force, the military leaders assumed, would bring most hostiles to the agencies, and the rest could easily be coerced. On March 1 General George Crook of the Department of the Platte initiated the campaign from Fort Fetterman, a post on the North Platte west of Fort Laramie. Crook headed for the Powder River country with a force of less than nine hundred men. After an indecisive attack upon a camp of Cheyennes and a band of Oglalas under Crazy Horse, severe winter weather and a shortage of supplies compelled their return to Fort Fetterman.

The military authorities decided to wait until spring, and then to converge upon the Sioux with three columns: one under General Crook from the south; a second from Fort Abraham Lincoln in General Alfred Terry's Department of Dakota; and third under Colonel John Gibbon, which was to move down the Yellowstone from Montana to cooperate with Terry's cavalry force. Serving under Terry was General George A. Custer in command of the Seventh Cavalry.

The fierce resistance offered by the Sioux bands rudely shattered the complacency of the campaign's planners; the hostile forces had been greatly underestimated. Instead of the estimated 500 to 800 warriors, the combined fighting strength of the various bands encountered was probably closer to 3,000 braves. The three columns of troops detailed to subdue the Indians totalled about 2,500 men. According to the army officers, the hostile ranks were swelled by large numbers of agency Sioux who had slipped away from their reservation quarters upon hearing of the military movement into the Powder River country. Agency officials, however, stoutly disputed this contention.

The Sioux War of 1876 was fought mainly in the region south of the Yellowstone between the Big Horn and Powder rivers in Montana and Wyoming. Augmented by fresh arrivals from the agencies, the several bands of Sioux and Cheyenne, who passed the winter in the sheltered valleys of the Tongue and Powder, by early summer had become the most formidable concentration of Indians ever faced by the army. The tribes had merged their camps for better protection from the soldiers. Because they had been attacked earlier from the south, they traveled in a northerly direction toward the Yellowstone, moving camp constantly to find grass and water.

After numerous delays, the military columns were on the move by May. Colonel Gibbon had been ordered to take his command down the Yellowstone from Montana in a maneuver to cut off escape to the north while Terry was moving westward from the Little Missouri. General Crook, leaving Fort Fetterman a second time, went northward over the old Bozeman Trail in the direction of the Rosebud River where he expected to find the hostile camp. When Crook's column of about thirteen hundred troops reached the head of the Rosebud, it was detected by scouting parties from the hostiles, whose camp now was located in the valley of the Little Big Horn.

Not Crook but the Indians made the surprise attack in the Battle of Rosebud, waged on June 17, 1876. The hostiles under Crazy Horse had halted Crook's offensive, immobilizing the troops for over a month and preventing a juncture with Terry's column.

On June 21 General Terry met with Gibbon and Custer at the mouth of the Rosebud to work out strategy. Gibbon's Montana column and the forces commanded by General Terry were to proceed up the Big Horn to the mouth of the Little Big Horn, while Custer with the Seventh Cavalry was to follow the Rosebud to its headwaters, then cut across to the Little Big Horn and come downstream. The Indians, assumed to be hunting and making leisurely short marches, would be taken by surprise.

General Custer at once prepared for his march up the Rosebud, taking fifteen days' rations. In his command were 31 officers and 585 enlisted men, Indian scouts, an interpreter, and several civilians, including a newspaperman from the *Bismarck Tribune*. The evening of the third day out, Custer arrived at the trail across the divide toward the Little Big Horn and immediately decided upon a night march. In the early hours of the morning, the column went into camp between two high ridges. Scouts soon located the camp of the hostiles strung out along the west bank of the Little Big Horn about twenty miles away.

On the morning of June 25, Custer decided to move at once to the attack. He had made no effort to learn the exact position of the enemy or to determine their numerical strength. Overweeningly confident that he could overcome the enemy and apparently obsessed by the idea that the Sioux would be trying to escape, he ordered his scouts to steal or stampede the Indian pony herd. Several miles east of the river, he divided his small command into three groups preparatory to attacking a camp of at least two to three thousand warriors. His orders were that Captain Benteen with one battalion of three troops was to ride across the valley to prevent escape to the south and west, and Major Reno with another battalion and a few Arikara scouts was to attack the upper end of the camp. One troop would accompany the pack train. Custer himself, with the remaining force of 223 men, intended to move along the bluffs seeking a ford at the lower end of the camp.

Reno's attack upon the upper end of the camp was repulsed by a large force of warriors, and the troops were forced to retreat to a position on the higher ground east of the river. Although Benteen's command later joined him at this point, Reno was unable to go to the support of Custer, who had moved downstream and was heavily engaged at the lower end of the camp. Custer's command was quickly and completely annihilated by a swarming mass of Indians, including many who were returning from the fight with Reno. The pressure on Reno's and Benteen's commands continued until the next day when the Indians, learning of the approach of Terry's forces, suddenly moved up the valley and headed for the Big Horn Mountains to the south.

General Custer's course of action at the Battle of the Little Big Horn has aroused much speculation. Without a doubt he was smarting under the disfavor of President Grant which he had incurred by his damaging testimony against the Secretary of War and members of the President's family before a Senate investigating committee the previous spring. Grant had shown his displeasure by ordering him to remain in Washington and placing General Terry in charge of the troops Custer had expected to lead against the hostiles in Montana. Finally, after Terry interceded, Custer was permitted to join the expedition at the head of the Seventh Cavalry, his regular command, but in a subordinate capacity to Terry. It is plausible that Custer was determined to vindicate his honor, and it was quite in keeping with his character not to obey orders implicitly. At any rate, he was a day ahead of schedule in attacking the Indian camp, and he made no effort to await the arrival of the Terry-Gibbon column. Custer's greed for glory may have been his undoing.

Many myths have grown up over the years about the Battle of the Little Big Horn, tending to magnify not only the many errors made by the army, but also the fighting strength and prowess of the Teton Sioux. After a sifting of the voluminous accounts and discounting of the fanciful claims, the story of the tragic incident assumes a simpler form.

The conditions under which Custer was defeated did not require that the Indians have forces of the size ascribed to them in so many accounts, nor was it possible for the full enemy strength of probably twenty-five hundred warriors to be concentrated at one time against any single unit of Custer's command. Moreover, it is quite certain that no more than half the Indians had guns of any kind at all, let alone the latest improved Winchester rifles, as claimed by army spokesmen desperately seeking excuses after the battle. The Indians' guns were a haphazard assortment of many makes and models, and their supply of ammunition was small. About half of them fought with bows and arrows.

The combined forces of Terry and Gibbon reached the Custer battlefield on June 27 and rescued Benteen and Reno, who were still ignorant of Custer's fate. Terry then withdrew to the Yellowstone at the mouth of the Big Horn to await reinforcements. The wounded from Reno's command were transported by litter to the mouth of the Little Big Horn and from that point by steamboat to Bismarck, where on July 5 the public received the first full account of the Custer disaster.

By the time offensive operations were resumed in August, the hostiles' huge camp on the Tongue River had been broken up into a number of small ones, as each separate band set out on its own in search of food. Their trails led toward the Little Missouri in the general direction of the Black Hills. The Indians' familiarity with the terrain helped them avoid General Crook's men, who followed the scattering trails southeastward to furnish protection to the settlements in the Black Hills.[2] By September 1 the bands of hostiles had entered the region along the South Fork of the Grand River near Slim Buttes in present-day Harding County. Here they again formed a single camp of perhaps seven or eight hundred lodges. Many of the bands intended to go to the agencies for the winter. Some already had returned, and others were leaving the big camp daily.

On the evening of September 8, at Slim Buttes some ten miles east of the main body of Indians, an advance column of the Crook command surprised one of these small groups under American Horse and destroyed its camp. During the night the rest of the troops reached the scene and when morning came were able to repulse a strong counterattack under the leadership of Crazy Horse. After the skirmishes at Slim Buttes, the Sioux moved their camp closer to the Little Missouri, while some of the warriors followed the soldiers who continued their slow progress toward Crook City in the Black Hills.

The last stage of Crook's campaign is known as the "Starvation March" because a shortage of rations forced the troops to subsist on horsemeat and wild berries. Almost incessant rainfall during the last week of the march further aggravated the hardships. After crossing

[2] Harry H. Anderson, "A Sioux Pictorial Account of General Terry's Council at Fort Walsh, October 17, 1877," *North Dakota History*, XXII (July, 1955), 93–116, covers thoroughly the movements of the hostiles after the Battle of the Little Big Horn, and the manner in which the camps broke up.

the swollen Belle Fourche, the expedition finally received relief on September 13 when a small herd of beef cattle and several wagon-loads of supplies arrived from Deadwood.

The army, having taken over the main agencies, proceeded to disarm and dismount the Indians. At Cheyenne River and Standing Rock all the friendly Sioux were so treated as a precautionary measure, and at Red Cloud Agency two bands of friendlies were relieved of their guns and ponies, but the friendlies at the Spotted Tail Agency were not molested. Although many of the hostiles had planned to return to the agencies, they were generally not disposed to surrender without an assurance of good treatment. The knowledge that the army had attacked one of their bands on its way back to an agency and planned to relieve them of arms and ponies kept many from returning. Some of those who had gone back to Cheyenne River Agency became disaffected and slipped off to the hostile camp.

Led by Crazy Horse, fully two-thirds of the Sioux who had taken part in the engagement on the Little Big Horn spent the winter of 1876–1877 in the Powder River country. After alternately parleying and skirmishing with them, the military finally enlisted the aid of Spotted Tail. With 250 picked men, he set out for the hostile camps in February, 1877, and persuaded many to surrender. Some 200 lodges under the leadership of Gall and Sitting Bull crossed the international boundary line into Canada, where they remained until 1881. The rest yielded under further military pressure. By May, 1877, nearly 4,500 had come in, going mostly to the Spotted Tail and Red Cloud agencies. The last to return were Crazy Horse and his band, who went to the Red Cloud Agency.

The tragic events in the Powder River country during the summer of 1876 brought a quick conclusion to the negotiations for the Black Hills. On August 15 Congress passed a Sioux appropriation bill with a proviso that no further appropriations would be made for the Tetons unless they agreed to relinquish the Black Hills. With the terms of the treaty fully outlined by Congress, the commission's work became mere routine.

Mindful of the hectic moments spent by the Allison Commission in a great council, the new commission decided to consult only the chiefs and headmen of the separate Indian groups. It took the position that the new agreement was a supplement to the Laramie Treaty of 1868, hence the treaty provision requiring signatures of three-fourths of the adult males for any future cession of Sioux lands was inapplicable. Carrying an agreement prepared in advance, the commissioners proceeded to the several agencies of the Teton Sioux during the latter part of September, going first to the Red Cloud Agency and ending at the agencies located on the Missouri. Dispossessed of their arms and ponies and faced with the threat of starvation, the chiefs acquiesced and signed the agreement.

Under its terms the Indians gave up the Black Hills and hunting rights in Montana and Wyoming. The Oglalas and Brûlés at the Red Cloud and Spotted Tail agencies were given a choice between removal to Indian Territory and new agency sites along the Missouri. The western boundary for the Great Sioux Reservation was placed at the 103rd meridian from the Nebraska line to the Cannonball River except for the Black Hills enclave formed by the two forks of the Cheyenne. The Indians agreed that "wagon and other roads, not exceeding three in number" might be constructed and maintained across the reservation to link the mining region with the Dakota settlements east of the Missouri. In lieu of any monetary payments for the land cession, the government committed itself to providing specified rations until the Indians were able to support themselves. The signing was completed in October, 1876, and Congress ratified the agreement on February 28, 1877.

The Oglalas and Brûlés refused to consider moving to Indian Territory after a delegation under Spotted Tail had visited the region. New agency sites were selected for them on the Missouri River, but the Indians still found many excuses for refusing to move to the river. After Crazy Horse was killed at Fort Robinson in September, 1877, by soldiers attempting to place him under arrest, nearly all the surrendered hostiles, including those who had returned in May, broke away and fled northward to join Sitting Bull in Canada. The Indians who remained were finally placated. The chiefs were taken to Washington, and President Hayes gave them his promise that if they would move to the Missouri for the winter they might later relocate anywhere they wished on the reservation. In the spring of 1878 Spotted Tail's bands of Brûlé finally settled down on Rosebud Creek; the Oglalas picked a site at Pine Ridge a few miles from the Nebraska border.

CHAPTER 11

The Black Hills Gold Rush

AT THE PEAK of the gold rush, towns sprang up in the Black Hills as if by magic. Within three months after the lifting of the military ban upon travel into the region, Custer became a community of some six thousand. A Black Hills pioneer who reached the town on March 25, 1876, recorded the following observations:

At that time Custer City was made up of a conglomerate mass of people. . . . There were but few houses completed, but many under construction. The people were camped all around, up and down French creek, in wagons, tents, and temporary brush houses or wickiups. The principal business houses were saloons, gambling houses and dance halls, two or three so-called stores with very small stocks of general merchandise and little provisions. Most of the business was being done in tents. . . .[1]

An estimated ten thousand people were drawn to the Black Hills between November 15, 1875, and March 1, 1876. From Custer the miners fanned out to explore the streams in the Harney Peak area. Favorable prospects in the gulches along Spring Creek led in February, 1876, to the establishment of a second mining camp at Hill City. Within a short time the townsite was covered with a number of tents and hastily built log cabins.

Prospectors reached Deadwood Gulch in the northern part of the Black Hills as early as August, 1875, but it was not until the end

[1] Based on Diary of George V. Ayres in Agnes Wright Spring, *The Cheyenne and Black Hills Stage and Express Routes* (Glendale: The Arthur H. Clark Co., 1949), p. 363.

of the year that they located rich deposits. Further activities during the winter confirmed the favorable indications. When news of the rich discoveries reached the southern camps in May, there was a stampede that almost depopulated Custer City. The Spring Creek diggings were so completely abandoned that Hill City was left for a time with a population of one.

Mining in the northern region was concentrated mostly within a ten-mile radius of Deadwood. By the end of 1876 probably twenty thousand people had been drawn to this area, staking out the several gulches and setting up mining camps around each promising discovery of placer deposits. Deadwood City was organized on April 26, 1876, in the narrow valley below the junction of Deadwood and Whitewood creeks, and building began as soon as the site was cleared of the underbrush and dead timbers that gave the gulch its name.

The settlement began as a string of little mining camps—South Deadwood, North Deadwood, Ingleside, Chinatown, Cleveland, Fountain City, Elizabethtown, and Montana City—sprawling along the gulch so close together that it was hard to tell where one left off and the other began. A few years later, these were all incorporated into the town of Deadwood. The narrowness of the gulch compressed the town into a single street following a ravine flanked by high wooded hills. Where the ground permitted, buildings went up on both sides of the street; elsewhere, only one side was built up, chiefly with log buildings and shanties of rough lumber. The peculiarity of this topography forced Deadwood later to take to the mountainsides, with its residential streets forming so many terraces.

A few miles up the gulch southwest of Deadwood was another string of towns forming a continuous settlement. Gayville was started first, followed by Central and several others. Of these camps, only Central has survived. Another town laid out in 1876, and for a short time challenging the supremacy of Deadwood, was Crook City on Whitewood Creek some seven miles northeast of Deadwood Gulch. Lead City was founded in the spring of 1876 after the discovery of placer gold in the surrounding gulches and hills. While prospectors in the first flurry of excitement were establishing the many little camps in the Deadwood region, the scenic Spearfish Valley attracted others who laid out the townsite of Spearfish during May, 1876, and located ranches down the valley.

On the eastern edge of the Black Hills, a group of prospectors gave up a fruitless search for gold in favor of exploiting the natural advantages of the Rapid Valley for a townsite, and Rapid City was laid out on February 25, 1876. After a few years during which its future was uncertain, the town finally began to take on an air of permanence. As the only community located on the eastern edge of the Hills, it became the eastern gateway to the mining region and an important station on the transportation routes from south and east. To the men in the mining camps it was known as "Hay Camp" or "Hay Town." The extension of the railroad from Chadron, Nebraska, in 1886 assured it of maintaining its pre-eminence over the other Black Hills towns.

In the stampede to the northern camps, it was a case of first come, first served. Finding the most valuable ground already taken, many prospectors drifted back to diggings they had previously worked in such locations as Custer and Hill City. Other late-comers began to prospect farther out from Deadwood and Lead, and discovered gold-bearing gravels and veins in new locales.

Thanks to the wide publicity given the gold discoveries, enterprising individuals who offered their services to conduct parties to the mines had no difficulty finding customers. Every part of the country was represented in the mad rush to the Black Hills. Business was still in the doldrums, not yet recovered from the Panic of 1873, and the prospect of striking it rich in the Black Hills seemed even brighter by contrast. Prominent in the ranks of the gold-rushers were veteran prospectors from the older mining regions of the Rockies. Habitual migrants, these men wandered from one camp to another responding as if by reflex to every real or rumored gold strike. Close on their heels came the hangers-on and parasites characteristic of a mining society: the gamblers and dance-hall girls and sharp operators. The 1876 migration drew many from the mining camps of Colorado and Montana which no doubt accounts for the numerous news items about the older gold fields in the early issues of the *Black Hills Weekly Pioneer,* established at Deadwood in June, 1876.

The peak of the rush appears to have been reached in the spring of 1877, at which time local editors estimated a population of twenty-five thousand. Probably these figures were much too high. There was a constant exodus from the region; at times during the summer of 1876 departures equaled arrivals. Many men who had expected to make fortunes overnight soon found living conditions too primitive and mining too much like work. Most of these "ten-day miners" were tenderfeet from farming and industrial areas; veteran prospectors were more inclined to stay and give the country a try.

The deterioration of Indian relations and the subsequent hostilities also had a retarding effect on the gold rush. Parties bound for the Black Hills and prospectors already on the grounds had to look to their own protection after the removal of troops in December, 1875. During the early months of 1876, when the nonagency Sioux moved northwards along the Black Hills to join Sitting Bull and Crazy Horse in the Power River country, many small expeditions were exposed to attack. The Indians at this time were particularly given to running off horses belonging to the whites.

The only organization then existing for the enforcement of law and order in the area was a small military group known as "Custer's Minute Men." The Minute Men gave some protection against the raids on routes of travel in the southern foothills during April and May. At this time outbound travel was unusually heavy, the Indian danger proving the last straw for many a disappointed gold-seeker. In one mining camp, as a precautionary measure against the Sioux many of the cabins were fitted with loopholes.

Even greater peril faced the mining settlements when the Sioux returned from the battle on the Little Big Horn in the summer and early fall of 1876. Emboldened by their victory over Custer, they made continual raids on outlying settlements in the northern part of the Black Hills. Spearfish and Crook City frequently were targets, and Rapid City by virtue of its location suffered more severely from Indian depredations than any other community. Most of the casualties from Indian attacks occurred during this period. There was widespread fear of a concentrated assault on the Black Hills, and loud cries went up for military protection. Governor Pennington appealed for troops, but President Grant was reported to be more in favor of protection for those trying to leave than for those determined to stay on forbidden ground. At last, in September General Crook and his men brought relief when they established a temporary camp near Bear Butte.

Although the agreement whereby the Indians ceded the Black Hills was ratified in February, 1877, the settlements were still exposed to raids from hostile bands which had not surrendered. Governor Pennington repeated the request for troops and was again

politely refused by the military authorities who were then engaged
in final operations against the hostiles along the Yellowstone River.
In this situation the county commissioners of newly organized
Lawrence County offered a bounty of $250 "for the body of each
and every Indian, dead or alive, killed or captured," within the
boundaries of the county.[2] (One bounty is said to have been collected when a Mexican "cashed in" an Indian who had been killed
by a posse of miners near Deadwood.) After all the Sioux were
subjugated, a permanent garrison was placed on the south side of
Bear Butte Creek near Sturgis in August, 1878, the site of the Fort
Meade military reservation.

PLACER MINING

Placer mines not only contributed heavily to the gold output during 1876 and 1877, but also played an important part in the occupation and settlement of the Black Hills. The prospectors first took
out the gold found in the gravel bars of streams and along the
gulches. The gold occurred in the form of small flakes or colors, as
small grainlike particles, and occasionally, as in the case of extraordinarily rich deposits, in the form of nuggets. Because of the easy
accessibility of the gold, placer mining required little capital, but
the requirements for water seriously limited the scope of operations.

Pick, shovel, and pan constituted the tools in the prospecting
stage, and the panning method was employed by many a miner
working the gold gravels of French Creek and other streams of the
southern Hills. Sluicing, the method most widely used in placer
mining in the Black Hills, required inclined wooden troughs, or
sluice boxes, ten to twelve feet long and two feet wide, with nailed
cleats, or riffles, at the bottom. A steady flow of water was sent
through the sluices, and the riffles caught and retained the gold
which settled to the bottom. Sluicing operations called for skill and
dexterity, and required the services of several men. At regular intervals the water was turned off for a cleanup, during which the accu-
mulations of gold, black sand, and gravel were scraped from the
cleats into a pan. The gravel and other substances were then washed
off the ore in a nearby stream.

Where the water supply was inadequate for sluicing, the miners
used the primitive rocker. This was a boxlike contrivance mounted

[2] Text of resolution incorporating the proclamation in *The Black Hills
Weekly Times,* July 29, 1877.

on a pair of rockers; there were a succession of sieves and tiny riffles on the bottom. The rocker was easily transported to any place where there was pay gravel and sufficient water; two men could operate it, one shoveling the gravel, the other rocking the cradlelike device with one hand and pouring water on the gravel with the other. It was most extensively used in Rockerville Gulch, some thirteen miles southwest of Rapid City. Here in an area about six miles square were deposits exceeded in richness only by the placers of the Deadwood region; but water was so scarce that operations were generally limited to the rocking process and had to be undertaken mostly in the spring when melting snow supplied the mountain streams. It has been estimated that more than half a million dollars in gold was reclaimed from Rockerville Gulch by the several hundred rockers operated there over a period of two or three years.

There was an ambitious attempt to utilize hydraulic power in mining Rockerville's rich dry placer beds by bringing water from a dam on Spring Creek near Sheridan. The Black Hills Placer Mining Company, a $10,000,000 corporation formed in New York City in 1879, undertook to build a huge wooden flume over a winding seventeen-mile course to Rockerville, along the sides of steep mountains and on lofty trestles across deep gorges.[3] The flume was constructed at a cost of from $250,000 to $300,000, and was in operation for several years. Strong streams of water were forced through nozzles which broke down the great chunks of gold-laden material preparatory to sluicing. But the gigantic hydraulic enterprise was a financial failure, and after a brief period of excitement during which Rockerville had visions of rivaling Deadwood, it lapsed into a humdrum existence. A few other hydraulic operations, carried on in other parts of the Black Hills and involving big outlays of capital for equipment and labor, also ended in failure.

It is impossible to state how much gold was taken from the placer deposits. The amount extracted from the gulches in the vicinity of Deadwood has been variously estimated at from $3,000,000 to $4,000,000. At best, placer mining was a wasteful method; even under the most favorable conditions only about 65 per cent of the gold was recoverable under sluicing. It was, however, a poor man's

[3] For the story of the ill-fated Black Hills Placer Mining Company, see Paul Fatout, *Ambrose Bierce and the Black Hills* (Norman: University of Oklahoma Press, 1956). Bierce served as the company's general agent at Rockerville during 1880.

way of making a living and, after the disillusionment that followed the original stampede to Deadwood Gulch, many a miner was content to return to the southern Hills to work the "ten-dollar diggings" he had scorned earlier.

The search for the rich ore bodies or lodes from which the placer gold was derived began with the first prospectors. Many of the men from the older Rocky Mountain mining camps, more interested in lode mining, were constantly on the lookout for promising gold-bearing ledges while working their placer claims. In the Deadwood area the hillsides overlooking the gulch were vigorously prospected as early as April, 1876.

QUARTZ MINING

The claim that became the famous Homestake mine was located by Moses Manuel, a prospector who had come to the Black Hills from Alaska by way of Montana. Manuel and his partners began at once to sink a discovery shaft. They built on Whitewood Creek an arrastra (a crude device for crushing quartz by dragging a block of granite around on a circular stone bed), and made a roadway to transport the ore. During the winter of 1876–1877 the original Homestake claim produced about $5,000 in gold.

By the end of 1876 there were more than 150 quartz mines within a radius of five miles of Deadwood. Promising discoveries had also been made in the central and southern parts of the Black Hills.

In 1878 quartz mining began to supersede the impermanent placer diggings which were already showing signs of becoming exhausted. By the summer of 1879 over 4,700 locations of quartz mines were recorded. Mining in the Black Hills was on its way to becoming a business requiring large capital investment and skilled engineers, and the mining settlements became more stable as the transient miners were replaced by a more permanent population.

The prospecting for gold-bearing rocks led to what has been called the "mortar and pestle era"—a reference to the principle on which the stamp mill operates. During this period the sound of little one-stamp mills could be heard day and night from every quarter of the mining camps. In the next stage came "the clinking of picks and shovels, the creaking of many windlasses, and the roar of dynamite, that tore the rocks asunder. . . ."[4]

[4] Annie D. Tallent, *The Black Hills* or *The Last Hunting Ground of the Dakotahs* (St. Louis: Nixon-Jones Printing Co., 1899), p. 342.

The first quartz mill brought into the Black Hills began to operate near Gayville in September, 1876. The ore was pulverized by the action of steel balls tumbling from side to side in a revolving hollow cylinder; by the end of the year about $20,000 in gold had been extracted. Improved machinery in the form of a ten-stamp mill was introduced later in the year. It pulverized and ground the quartz into a wet pulp, its heavy steel stampers rising and falling on the lumps of ore fed through the battery—a narrow iron box which also contained water and mercury. The crushed ore was further reduced and the gold particles separated out; then the soft, puttylike mass was placed in a fire retort in molds from which it finally emerged in the form of gold bars.

This first mill, which began to drop its stamps on December 30, 1876, proved a profitable investment. The ores of the Deadwood-Lead region were admirably adapted to stamp-milling. By the early part of 1878, at least twenty stamp mills were in operation, dropping about 500 stamps. In 1880 there were thirty-eight paying quartz mines, but the richer deposits soon became exhausted and much of the free milling ore was of too low a grade for economical processing. Moreover, large bodies of ore were so refractory in nature that they could not be processed by the stamp mills. Their development had to await the introduction of smelters and still later improvements in the form of chlorination and cyanide processes.

The total output of gold for the Black Hills in 1878 and 1879 has been estimated at about $3,000,000 a year, increasing to $5,000,000 by 1880. Subsequently, there was a drop to a figure slightly above $3,000,000, reflecting a stabilization of the industry by the several companies whose properties were bringing profitable returns. The gold found in the narrow gulches of the northern Hills originated from the extensive Homestake ore bodies, and was richer than that taken from the placers of the southern Black Hills region which were supplied by much smaller veins and lodes and were therefore more diffused.

The backbone of the mining industry in South Dakota has been the Homestake mine which produced gold bullion to the value of $301,000,000 out of the total of $358,000,000 for the entire Black Hills region between the years 1876 and 1935. The original Homestake claim was purchased from Moses Manuel and his partners in the fall of 1877 by George Hearst, prominent California mining capitalist, for the sum of $70,000. Hearst had sent a miner to examiñe the rich gold-bearing region in the vicinity of Lead. The Homestake lode, which covers an area about a mile and a half long and half a mile wide, particularly attracted the California interests. After a short visit to the region to complete the purchase arrangements, Hearst returned to San Francisco, where on November 5, 1877, he incorporated the Homestake Mining Company. Machinery was rushed to Lead City, and an eighty-stamp mill began to crush ore on July 12, 1878.

Most of the early quartz mining operations had a brief existence. Others gradually went out of business or were absorbed by larger mining groups commanding greater financial resources. By 1899, in addition to the Homestake, there were only two reduction mills operating in the Deadwood-Lead area. Deserted shafts, abandoned tunnels, remnants of expensive machinery, and ghost towns all over the Black Hills were reminders of the great gamble for gold.

The ventures in quartz mining were by no means confined to the Deadwood-Lead district. Around Hill City and Custer in the central part of the Black Hills, several mines continued in operation to the end of the century. In the southern Hills, in the Keystone mining settlement southwest of Rockerville, the Holy Terror and Keystone mines showed great promise during the 1890's. The resurgence of mining activities at the turn of the century ended during World War I when increased milling costs forced suspension of many mining companies.

Other minerals than gold attracted the early prospectors. Early in March, 1876, during the search for gold along Bear Butte Creek southeast of Deadwood rich silver deposits were discovered. A mining camp, named Galena after a vein of almost pure galena, became a center of activity, climaxed in 1883 by the erection of a completely equipped smelting plant, said to have been the first of its kind in the Black Hills. Litigation closed the plant after a year's operation. The silver mining industry revived shortly before 1900 and was undertaken in conjunction with the mining of lead in the Galena area and at Keystone. In later years silver was chiefly a byproduct of gold mining.

Mica, although not mined intensively in the Custer region until after 1900, was discovered in 1879 and mined on a small scale until about 1884, when production declined because of competition from cheaper mica produced in the East Indies.

Tin ore was discovered accidently in 1883 near Harney Peak in the Etta Mine which was being worked for mica. As a result of the wide publicity given the discovery, a group of Englishmen formed the Harney Peak Consolidated Tin Company and began to buy up all the potential tin-bearing locations. A large reduction plant, erected near Hill City, was put in operation in November, 1892, ran for two months, and then was permanently shut down, after estimated expenditures of $2,000,000.

MINING DISTRICTS

In the absence of any legal authority before February, 1877, the residents of the Black Hills had to depend on themselves for the protection of their interests and the maintenance of order. In the mining camps these objectives were attained through mining districts in which rules and regulations were set up governing such matters as water rights and the size of mineral claims as well as the related problems of law and order.

A group of persons who had taken claims on French Creek near Custer held the first miners' meeting in the Black Hills in June, 1875; they formed the Cheyenne Mining District and drew up a mining code. The Lost Mining District was formed at Deadwood and a mining code agreed to in December, 1876, shortly after the discovery of the rich placers in Deadwood Gulch. Provisional governments, supplementing the mining district, were set up in the various towns for the purpose of selecting town officials, assigning lots, laying out streets, and administering routine matters of concern to the community. Miners' meetings, as a rule, proved more effective in settling property disputes than provisional local governments, and also were invariably convened in cases of homicide and horse-stealing.

Despite the general acceptance of the codes, disputes were not always amicably resolved. Arguments over claims were usually settled on the spot on the basis of might-makes-right. Claim-jumping was prevalent in the early years and frequently resulted in violence which might even be carried to the extremes of pitched battle and occasionally murder. In the early part of 1877 the situation became tense when veteran miners, drifting in from the older mining camps of Montana and other parts of the Rockies, found most of the choice ground in Deadwood Gulch already taken. They threatened to force a reduction of the frontage allowed by the mining district from three hundred to one hundred feet, but finally conceded that smaller holdings could not be worked to advantage and a battle was averted.

A dispute of a different character occurred in the Hidden Treasure Gulch near Central City in November, 1877. A group of workers staging a sitdown strike in protest against unpaid wages moved their household belongings into the mine tunnel, determined to stay there until their employer made good his vague promises to pay. A cavalry detachment from Camp Sturgis near Bear Butte failed to evict them, but the miners finally were driven out by the fumes from burning sulphur dropped down an air shaft.

When Congress legalized the gold rush by ratifying the Sioux agreement in February, 1877, the brief heyday of placer mining was nearly ended. More stable and productive years followed the establishment of law and order, but it is this early, raffish, and ephemeral phase of Black Hills history that has commanded the lion's share of the attention.

DEADWOOD

Deadwood itself has become a tradition. It is usually characterized as the wildest, the wickedest, and the most flamboyant mining town on the American frontier. Its heterogeneous population at the peak of the gold rush has been represented as typifying the mining society of the entire Black Hills region. Its early days have been romanticized and exploited in dime novels and Wild West shows and on movie and television screens. Moreover, characters of such dubious repute as Wild Bill Hickok and Calamity Jane have been transformed into legends.

The years 1876 and 1877 were certainly flush times for Deadwood. The objective point of nearly all travel into the Black Hills at the time, the town mushroomed from a few log cabins into a community of some seven thousand people within seven months. As the newcomers continued to crowd into the gulch, business establishments went up as fast as the supply of lumber permitted. Both sides of the main street were crowded with structures of all sizes and shapes, the majority of them saloons and gambling houses. Construction could not be pushed fast enough to serve the needs of the rapidly increasing population. Hotels and eating places in particular reaped a rich harvest, as well as the innumerable saloons and gambling places. By the first of June, 1877, three dance halls were in full swing, and before long two variety shows and a theater were giving regular performances. Deadwood had become a seething cauldron of restless, reckless humanity; and life there was characterized by much lawlessness and the usual pandering to man's frailties. The most notorious of the many acts of violence perpetrated on this frenetic scene was the murder of Wild Bill Hickok by Jack McCall in a Deadwood gambling saloon on August 2, 1876.

Not everything was vicious and disreputable, nonetheless, even amidst all the turbulence of the rough and undisciplined mining society, and popular accounts probably are greatly overdrawn. According to Richard B. Hughes, a reliable eyewitness of much that transpired in Deadwood during 1876:

> The reason that Deadwood acquired a worse reputation than any of the surrounding towns and camps was because it was the first established and offered the first field of operations for the vicious; this centering of the worst classes of the population worked to the advantage of other communities nearby in giving them a degree of immunity. Not that other places in and about the Hills were free from such contamination; that could not be expected; but there vice and crime did not flaunt themselves as brazenly as in the metropolis of the Hills, where strength of numbers made the lawless element defiant of restraint. Writers for eastern publications vied with one another in their wild, weird stories of the vice and corruption, and painted the picture in darker colors than even the bad conditions warranted.[5]

Deadwood owed many of its business activities to its position as the only distributing point for supplies in the northern Hills. Thousands of dollars were paid out weekly to wage-earners who drew from five to seven dollars per day and this money, received in the form of gold dust at a rate ranging from eighteen to twenty dollars per ounce, passed freely into circulation.

Sunday was by all odds the busiest time because on this day the mines were generally shut down and the miners collected their weekly earnings of dust. Prospectors and miners from the outlying gulches joined the regular weekday crowd in Deadwood to get their supply of provisions for the next week, pick up their mail, and spend their earnings in the various pleasure domes. On any Sunday nearly the entire population of the northern Hills is said to have been concentrated on Deadwood's Main Street.[6]

With the introduction of quartz mining, settlements grew up near

---

[5] Richard B. Hughes, *Pioneer Years in the Black Hills,* ed. Agnes Wright Spring (Glendale: Arthur H. Clark Co., 1957), pp. 199–200.
[6] Hughes, *Pioneer Years in the Black Hills,* p. 110.

the mills and drew much of the jobbing business away from Dead-wood. Most of the floater population had disappeared by the end of 1877, and as more stable influences began to assert themselves in the community, Deadwood emerged from its wild and wooly stage. Yet it retained many characteristics of the mining frontier and for years enjoyed a dubious distinction as a wide-open town.

Because gold dust from the placers was practically the only me-dium of exchange, every businessman in the Black Hills was equipped with a pair of gold scales and a blower to separate the dross or sand from the gold; miners carried their gold in a small bottle or buckskin sack; at the gaming table the play was for gold dust; and in commercial transactions, accounts were settled with a pinch of dust taken by the tradesman from the gold sack. When banks were established later, there was active trading in gold dust, a business that slowly vanished as placer operations came to an end. Gold coins then began to replace gold dust and nuggets, but for years paper currency was looked upon with suspicion in Black Hills communities and was in limited circulation.

Isolated from the outside world as the mining camps were in the beginning, they suffered seriously from a shortage of supplies. Many of the early outfits making their way into the Black Hills tried to carry enough stores for a year. The demand for provisions far ex-ceeded the supply until the Indian danger subsided and regular lines of communication were established. The difficulties and exces-sive costs of transportation were other factors which kept prices outrageously high.

In times of greatest scarcity, the price of flour might shoot up to $60 a hundred pounds; at other times, quotations ranged from $9 to $30, bringing ruin to speculators whenever the market became glutted. During the winter of 1875–1876, at a time when forage was not available in the immediate vicinity of Deadwood, hay was shipped in and retailed at twenty cents a pound.[7] Occasionally, if roads were impassable or travel was cut off by the Indians, the set-tlers actually went hungry.

FREIGHTING AND STAGE LINES

The movement of supplies into the Black Hills started with the very beginnings of the gold rush. Nearby railway towns were quick

[7] Hughes, *Pioneer Years in the Black Hills,* pp. 91, 92.

to sense the tremendous benefits from the traffic in provisions and supplies which would accrue to points through which flowed the main lines of travel into the mining region. In guidebooks, local newspaper articles, and editorials, each of the contending towns extolled its own advantages and painted a disparaging picture of all competing routes. The rivalry between Sioux City and Yankton was particularly keen.

Two other contenders for a share of the business created by the gold rush were Cheyenne, Wyoming, and Sidney, Nebraska, both located on the Union Pacific. Although considerable traffic came for a year or two from the more distant Sidney, Cheyenne found itself in a favorable situation at the outset. Since the mining camp at Custer was located close to the Wyoming line, most of the travel over the Cheyenne route was outside the Sioux reservation and therefore under full military protection—this at a time when travel over the Missouri River routes was either proscribed or left without military escort.

Supplies were freighted from Cheyenne as soon as the troops left the Black Hills to go into winter quarters at Fort Laramie in November, 1875, and it was soon planned to open a stage line to Custer by way of the Red Cloud and Spotted Tail agencies. The Cheyenne and Black Hills Stage, Mail and Express Line left Cheyenne on a semiweekly schedule, beginning on February 3, 1876. The trip to Custer took five days. The firm of Gilmer, Salisbury, and Patrick bought the stage line and made immediate plans for a direct connection with Custer from Fort Laramie, but Indian hostilities delayed carrying out the plans until June 24. Three months later stage service was extended to Deadwood; in the meantime, a military patrol between Fort Laramie and Custer assured protection for the station-keepers and the stock along the route as well as for the Concord coaches plying the regular run.

The new owners of the Cheyenne line were widely known operators of stage lines in Utah, Idaho, and Montana. Gilmer, the senior partner, had been connected with the famous firm of Russell, Majors, and Waddell and had driven coaches for Wells, Fargo and Company. The Cheyenne firm also operated a freighting department which carried huge consignments, including most of the heavy mining machinery shipped from California over the Union Pacific. The entire bullion output of the Homestake mine up to

1881 and most of the other gold produced in the Black Hills during the early years were carried by the Cheyenne and Black Hills Stage Company.

Yankton and Sioux City interests used the overland route from Fort Pierre to various points in the Black Hills. Sioux City merchants, who organized a transportation company in the spring of of 1876, sent their wagon trains directly to the Black Hills through the sandhills country of northwestern Nebraska until August, when they started shipping their cargoes by steamboat to Fort Pierre. These activities led to the formation of the Fred T. Evans Transportation Company.

Yankton residents organized both stage and freight lines in the same spring. A stage line of four Concord coaches, organized by Charles T. Campbell and John Dillon, followed a route up the James River Valley by way of Scotland, Rockport, and Firesteel, thence to Fort Thompson and Fort Pierre. When the company went out of business, another line was organized, operating out of Fort Pierre.

Bramble, Miner and Company, which operated a flour mill and wholesale mercantile establishment at Yankton, formed the Merchants Transportation Company in April and carried freight and passengers to the mining country from Fort Pierre. After a brief interruption in service in June when a temporary military ban was placed on the Fort Pierre route, the Bramble and Miner firm soon became one of the heaviest shippers and a major rival of the Evans Company. In 1880 it employed 300 men and 2000 yoke of oxen in its freighting business. The goods transported over the Fort Pierre route were carried by steamboat from Sioux City and Yankton.

In the northern part of the Territory, Northern Pacific Railroad interests and Minnesota mail contractors joined forces in February, 1877, to form the Northwestern Express and Transportation Company. Bismarck, then the nearest railway point to Deadwood, became the eastern terminus of one of the three wagon roads permitted to cross the Sioux reservation under the Black Hills Treaty. As soon as the road was laid out, service began over the 210-mile route; the first stages left Bismarck on April 11, 1877. The monotony of the thirty-six-hour trip was broken only by seventeen stations placed at intervals of from six to twenty-two miles. In addition to the passenger and express business, the firm established a freight department which used mule and ox teams. Mail contracts were an important source of income for the Bismarck company.

When the Chicago and North Western Railroad reached the Missouri River at Pierre in the summer of 1880, Bismarck lost its privileged position to Fort Pierre. The Northwest Express and Transportation Company accordingly transferred its business to the new railway terminal; most of the business over the Sidney and Cheyenne routes shifted to Fort Pierre, and the river traffic in Black Hills freight from Sioux City and Yankton also ceased. In this same year Chamberlain became the point of departure for a third wagon road across the reservation when the Chicago, Milwaukee and St. Paul Railroad reached the Missouri. The Chamberlain route was used for a short time by several freighters, particularly the Evans line, but it lost out to the Fort Pierre route.

Supplementing the activities of the several major companies were a number of independent freighters operating between various points and competing at times with the larger freight lines. Moreover, during the early days of the gold rush when provisions in the mining camps were still in short supply, local businessmen and farmers in the Dakota settlements along the Missouri frequently loaded their wagons with flour and other provisions and set out for the mining camps.

The arrival of the first railway train in Rapid City on July 4, 1886, marked the passing of the freighting era. This important event, moreover, symbolized the economic, political, and social stability attained by the Black Hills settlements. As early as 1880, visitors were commenting on the changes that were taking place. The population had grown to about sixteen thousand. Banditry and stage holdups by road agents were rarer occurrences. Civil authority had become firmly established, following the organization of county governments in 1877. The mining camps were losing their frontier look, and the constructive forces of religion and education were everywhere in evidence. A higher degree of economic diversification prevailed through the development of agriculture in the fertile valleys and the growth of industry in the larger towns.

BEGINNINGS OF THE RANGE CATTLE INDUSTRY

The Black Hills agreement with the Teton Sioux in 1877 not only opened up the mining region of western South Dakota, but also made accessible the rich grazing lands of the surrounding area. Ever since 1867, when Texas herds first were driven north to Abilene for shipment, the cattleman's domain had been spreading northward. The range cattle industry had its origins in Texas, where ranching was first practiced on a large scale and where an extensive herding industry had developed. At the end of the Civil War, the Texas plains were literally swarming with large herds, many of them wild, which were of little value at home but commanded a high price in eastern markets. The westward advance of the rails into Kansas led to the northern drive, first to Abilene and then tó Dodge City and other "cow towns," as the shipping points were called. When the Union Pacific began to draw some of the trade to its main line in Nebraska, Ogallala also became a prominent shipping point.

The reduction of the buffalo herds and the confinement of the Indians to the reservations opened the way for the incoming herds. Government freighters and army officers, moreover, had discovered from experience that cattle on the Northern Plains not only could survive severe winters without feed, but actually grew larger and fatter than did those in Texas. The drive to Dodge City and Ogallala, consequently, became the first stage in a longer drive that ended on the distant feeding ranges of the north.

By 1878 the cattlemen were entering the range lands of Dakota Territory. The influx of miners and tradesmen into the Black Hills created a heavy demand for meat and dairy products which numerous small farms or ranches along the several streams in the foothills sought to supply. The opportunity for a local market that could supplement the beef contracts of the Sioux agencies soon brought large herds of Texas cattle into the region. Among the first cattlemen to arrive were Erasmus and John Deffebach who, during 1876 and 1877, brought several herds from Wyoming and Nebraska which they disposed of to local butchers at lucrative prices. In the fall of 1878 they located a ranch near the mouth of the Belle Fourche River. Other herds were driven into the area during that same year for fattening on the ranges surrounding the Black Hills.

By 1880 the cattlemen had occupied most of the range between the eastern foothills and the confluence of the Belle Fourche and Cheyenne rivers and also the area comprising present-day Fall River County. Many of the herds came from the overstocked ranges of Wyoming and Nebraska.

The economy of the Black Hills, nevertheless, continued to be geared to the mining industry, thus setting the region apart from the rest of Dakota Territory. Moreover, in a physical sense, the Black Hills were still cut off from the eastern settlements by the wide expanse of Indian country. At the same time, the emergent mining society promoted a political sectionalism in the Territory that was to become further accentuated by the end of the 1870's as the Great Dakota Boom got under way east of the Missouri River.

CHAPTER 12

The Great Dakota Boom, 1878–1887

UNTIL 1878 agricultural settlement was still generally confined to the region south and east of a line running from the Yankton Reservation and the western part of Hutchinson County to the Minnesota border east of Brookings. A small vanguard had already gone beyond the line of settlement, following the Big Sioux, Vermillion, and James valleys or drifting into the vicinity of Big Stone Lake. On the military trails along the Missouri between Fort Randall and Fort Yates and on those that connected Fort Sisseton with the river posts there was an occasional roadhouse or ranch to break the monotony of travel. Elsewhere in the central and northern counties of South Dakota the vast expanse of prairie was still uninhabited. All this was changed within a few years' time as an unprecedented movement of people led to the occupation of virtually all available lands east of the Missouri. By the middle 1880's settlers' shacks and little towns and villages had sprouted throughout the entire region.

Statistics of the public land offices reveal the rush for land that ran its course during the ten-year period from 1878 to 1887. The total annual land entries for the southern section of the Territory soared from 163,739 acres in 1877 to 941,800 acres for 1878, the initial year of the Great Dakota Boom. The total annual filings, including both original and final entries, for the southern counties east of the Missouri River were as follows:

1878— 941,802 acres	1883—5,410,687 acres
1879—1,075,560 acres	1884—4,169,384 acres
1880—1,271,271 acres	1885—2,257,114 acres
1881—1,455,136 acres	1886—1,688,881 acres
1882—3,082,417 acres	1887—1,123,233 acres

The aggregate acreage for the period was slightly more than 24,000,000. Dakota land had proved itself a stronger lodestone than even Black Hills gold. Although the northern part of Dakota Territory was equally affected by the boom, the greater proportion of the public lands brought into the market lay in the southern counties. Only in 1884 was the volume of business for the northern section greater. In the year 1883 about 23 per cent of the land filings for the entire nation was accredited to the region east of the Missouri and south of the 46th parallel.

The progress of the boom is even more accurately reflected in the population figures for the period. During the decade from 1870 to 1880 the population of southeastern South Dakota grew from about 10,000 to 81,781. By 1885 the number had risen to 248,569 for the same region. Since the peak of the land rush was probably reached about 1887, the 1890 census returns of 328,808 for South Dakota, inclusive of the Black Hills, fail to record the topmost figure for the boom period. The population of the Black Hills increased from 16,487 in 1880 to 32,559 in 1890, while that for North Dakota stood at 34,909 and 182,719 for the two respective census years.

Foremost among the several factors contributing to the outbreak of "Dakota fever" was the railroad. Railroad capitalists were now willing to risk construction beyond the western borders of Minnesota and Iowa where it had halted when the Panic of 1873 hit the nation. By 1878 economic conditions had improved enough to make capital venturesome again and to forecast a general revival of the westward movement.

The new railroad construction coincided with the return of more favorable weather conditions to the Northern Plains. The grasshopper plague which had given the entire region such an unsavory reputation a few years earlier had passed. The combination of favorable rainfall, excellent soil, and adequate marketing facilities seemed to refute the idea that successful agriculture was impossible in the central part of Dakota, even though so eminent a person as the Minnesota-born United States Commissioner of Agriculture still adhered to that view as late as 1878.

Further impetus to the Dakota boom came from the improvements in farm machinery. The numerous plow factories, already established in the Middle West, were turning out products with better wearing and scouring qualities and with improved moldboards designed to cope better with the tough prairie sod. The harvesting of grain had been revolutionized by the development of self-binding reapers. By 1882 twine was rapidly replacing wire in the binding attachment. There were significant developments, too, in flour milling: the introduction of the middlings purifier and the metallic roller process of grinding made it possible to process hard spring wheat into flour markedly superior to the product of the softer kerneled varieties.

It was natural that spring wheat became the cash crop of the new settlements, especially in the central part of the James Valley. The plant was well suited to the soil and climate, it required little skill and knowledge to raise, and its product always commanded a good market. Wheat farming, moreover, was less complicated than mixed husbandry. The initial reports of success, even as a sod crop, led to a craze for wheat culture that made the central and northern regions of Dakota Territory an integral part of the spring wheat empire. The abundant supply of wheat from Dakota fields and the convenient facilities for transport were important factors in establishing Minneapolis as the world's milling center.

The promotional activities of railroad corporations, townsite interests, and real estate agents also were a significant factor in accelerating settlement. It was not enough to have free or cheap public lands available; their attractions had to be called to the attention of prospective settlers. The railroads, which had the greatest need for settlers if their investments were to prove profitable, were particularly active in publicizing Dakota. Through their passenger and immigration departments they distributed pamphlets and brochures and inspired newspaper stories spreading the word of bumper crops and favorable conditions. Displays of Dakota products in exhibition cars at agricultural fairs supplemented printed propaganda. Homesteaders' excursions at special reduced rates were run into localities where the boom was still in its initial stage.

Townsite companies and local boards of trade vied with each other in concocting glowing accounts of the rich endowments and natural advantages of their localities, and in publicizing their own areas drew attention to the Territory as a whole. There was no territorial immigration office from 1877 until 1885, at which time the Legislature again provided for a commissioner of immigration. His duties were primarily to act as territorial statistician and to compile and disseminate information, much of which was distributed through the railroad companies.

THE RAILROAD BOOM

While the first outward manifestation of the Great Dakota Boom was a heavy influx of settlers out of Minnesota into the Big Sioux Valley, perhaps its real beginning—and certainly its main impetus —may be traced to the decision of the Chicago and North Western and the Chicago, Milwaukee, and St. Paul railroads to extend their lines westward into Dakota.

After personal inspection of the Dakota prairie in 1877, Marvin Hughitt, the manager of the Chicago and North Western Railway Company, transmitted some of his own enthusiasm for the new country to the board of directors, and planning began immediately on the building of the Dakota Central division from Tracy, Minnesota, to Pierre on the Missouri River. The Chicago, Milwaukee, and St. Paul, also in the mood for expansion, was quick to accept the challenge and projected a westward extension from Canton so as to parallel the North Western tracks.

A move by the Milwaukee company to build from Ortonville on Big Stone Lake across the Sisseton Reservation into the Upper James Valley at Aberdeen was matched by an extension of the North Western from Lake Kampeska to a crossing of the James River at Redfield, some forty miles to the south of the rival line at Aberdeen. The same rivalry led to the construction of competing lines running north and south. Although other companies participated in the scramble for the patronage of the new settlers, most of the approximately 2,500 miles constructed in the state by 1890 was claimed by the more active companies, the Milwaukee being credited with 1,096 and the Chicago and North Western with 744 miles.

The Dakota Central division of the Chicago and North Western became a leading highway into the Territory. Even before its rails crossed the Minnesota border during the summer of 1878, settlers began to stream into Brookings County and the eastern part of Kingsbury from the railway terminus at Canby, Minnesota. The railway surveyors arrived the following spring, and by autumn of 1879 the railroad was graded and ironed as far as Volga. Traffic

started across the state line to Aurora in early October and reached
Volga by the middle of November. The towns of Elkton and Brookings also made their appearance during the same year. Volga was the
terminus during the winter of 1879–1880 and served as construction camp while grading and track-laying was continued in the direction of Huron. Three hotels and a railroad boarding house provided accommodations for the town's transient population which
included some 300 railway workers as well as the settlers who were
flocking into the region in ever-increasing numbers.

Huron was plotted a mile west of the James River the following
May and sprang up as a construction camp and division point for
the Chicago and North Western. Marvin Hughitt had selected its
site in person two years earlier while scouting the country in a buck-
board. The materials for the first buildings were hauled from Volga.
The railroad reached the town in the latter part of June, and the
roundhouse and shops soon were constructed.

The region served by the Dakota Central division between the
Big Sioux and the James was rapidly populated as settlers spread
out from the several railroad towns platted along the way, including
Nordland (now Arlington), Lake Preston, De Smet, and Iroquois.
Building westward from Huron proceeded at a fast pace, uncom-
plicated by any serious engineering problems. The construction
crews laid many miles of track across the level stretches of prairie
by merely placing crossties on the sod, leaving the work of ballasting
the roadbed for a later time.

Since the North Western was expected to build across the Great
Sioux Reservation into the Black Hills, there was much speculation
about the point at which it would cross the Missouri. The company's surveyors seemed to be headed for a site on Medicine Creek,
but other railroad agents turned up in a covered wagon on the east
bank of the Missouri opposite Fort Pierre. Pretending to locate a big
cattle ranch, they quietly bought out the claims of the squatters
occupying the area. After acquiring title through the use of scrip,
the railroad company surveyed the land, laid out the town of Pierre,
and placed its lots on sale. The first train reached the new townsite
on November 4, 1880, and it at once became the center of freighting
activities for the Black Hills, as most of the traffic to the mining
country was diverted to the Fort Pierre route. Passengers and freight
destined for the Black Hills moved over the Chicago and North
Western line to Pierre where they were transported by ferry across

the Missouri to Fort Pierre. Pierre remained the freighting center until another division of the Chicago and North Western reached Rapid City from Nebraska in 1886.

Settlement lagged for a few years in the country between Huron and Pierre. In lieu of the usual railroad townsites, the Chicago and North Western marked off progressively numbered sidings at regular intervals in anticipation of local traffic. By 1883 a number of towns were laid out, including Wolsey at Siding No. 1, Wessington at Siding No. 2, and St. Lawrence, Miller, Ree Heights, and Highmore at the next four sidings. Harrold and Blunt began as sidings in Hughes County. St. Lawrence, to its everlasting regret, met with unexpected rivalry when in 1881 settlers from Illinois platted the Miller townsite less than three miles away and persuaded the railroad company to install a siding at that point.

While the North Western was rushing its operations to the Missouri, the Chicago, Milwaukee, and St. Paul road had crossed the Big Sioux at Canton, pointing its tracks westward toward the James River at Mitchell. From Marion Junction, platted by railway townsite interests in August, 1879, an extension led to Running Water on the Missouri River several miles above Springfield. Such new towns as Lennox and Parker sprang into existence as the railroad passed through the homesteaded parts of Lincoln and Turner counties.

The railway surveyors decided on a crossing of the James near the mouth of Firesteel Creek in preference to one at Rockport. Finding the location of the existing village of Firesteel unsatisfactory because of its low elevation, the railroad in early 1880 laid out Mitchell, named after the company's president, Alexander Mitchell. It became a railroad division point and enjoyed a rapid growth. Westward from Mitchell, the railroad company built down American Creek to the Missouri, where it laid out the town of Chamberlain during the latter part of 1880. Like Pierre, Chamberlain became an important gateway to the trans-Missouri region and envisioned an early extension of the railroad westward across the Indian reservation. For a few years it also benefited from Black Hills freighting.

In the northern part of the state, the course of settlement was shaped by the extension of the Hastings and Dakota division of the Chicago, Milwaukee, and St. Paul railroad from Ortonville, Minnesota. Grading into Grant County started in July, 1880, and continued until the townsite of Aberdeen was reached a year later.

Rumors that the Northern Pacific was setting its sights on the James Valley south of the 46th parallel spurred the Milwaukee Company into activity in this region. A few settlers had entered Grant County before 1878, but the first real rush came after the railroad announced its plans for an extension. Big Stone City was a favored town until the railroad company planted the townsite of Milbank in June, 1880. The usual sidings were constructed at ten-mile intervals in the unsettled region west of Milbank, and the towns of Webster, Bristol, Andover, and Groton appeared in quick succession.

The town of Aberdeen was platted on January 3, 1881. When lots were placed on sale in the spring, settlers flocked to the new town. Building materials came from Bristol, the nearest railway point. While most of the earliest residents followed the course of the railroad from the east, during the summer a large caravan of settlers arrived from the north along the main line of the Northern Pacific. The Hastings and Dakota division, intending to make a connection with the Northern Pacific at Bismarck, had planned at first to run its line northward from Andover through the newly established settlement of Columbia. When the townsite owners balked at the request for a free right of way and ground for a depot, the railway agents proceeded to build the road straight west to Aberdeen. The first train reached the town on July 6, 1881. Here the railroad company halted its construction temporarily, two years later continuing its line to Ipswich.

While the Chicago, Milwaukee, and St. Paul Company was promoting the boom in the northern tier of counties, the Winona and St. Peter division of the Chicago and North Western began an extension westward from Lake Kampeska toward the James Valley. The Winona and St. Peter branch had completed its line from Marshall, Minnesota, to Lake Kampeska as early as 1873 so that it would qualify for a federal land grant given Minnesota Territory in 1857 to aid railway construction, but not until March, 1879, did it maintain regular service west of the Minnesota border at Gary. The line was rebuilt in 1878 and Watertown, which became the railway terminus, was quickly populated with settlers. A few years later the railroad was built to Redfield, where it made a connection with a north and south line of the North Western.

During the early years of the boom, the flow of migration was almost entirely from east to west, following the course of the railroads from the Big Sioux into the James Valley. It was not until the central and northern parts of the state were generally occupied that there were through rail connections with the southeastern section. This region was also affected by the Great Dakota Boom, although most of the public lands in the area had been taken by 1878. The increase in population reflected the dimensions of the boom in the leading towns, especially Sioux Falls and Yankton.

Sioux Falls was reached from the east by the Chicago, St. Paul, Minneapolis and Omaha in June, 1878, and from the south by the Chicago, Milwaukee, and St. Paul in December of the following year. Between 1886 and 1888 the Rock Island, the Illinois Central, and the Great Northern also constructed their lines to the city. By 1890 Sioux Falls had supplanted Yankton as the primary city in South Dakota. Its population of 10,177 in 1890, compared with 2,164 in 1880, was nearly three times that of any other city in the state. Minnehaha County in which the city was located assumed first rank among the counties by 1890.

RAILROAD TOWNS

The northeastern and central parts of the state received the largest accretion of settlers during the boom period. The population statistics of representative counties in that region indicate the rate of growth from 1880 to 1885:

County	1880	1885
Beadle	1,290	10,318
Brown	353	12,241
Codington	2,156	5,648
Hand	154	7,057
Hughes	268	5,268
Spink	477	10,446

Unparalleled activity accompanied the rapid settlement of the region. At times during 1882 as many as eighteen trains arrived daily at Huron, transporting immigrant freight. In the spring of 1883 about 250 cars of immigrants' goods were unloaded in a single month; one week about a thousand passengers were carried to the city. A Congregational clergyman, on the scene eagerly scanning prospects for mission churches, reported in 1883:

The railroads much of the time have had two passenger trains a day each way, with from seven to nine coaches full of new-comers, while there have been nine or ten freight trains a day taking their goods, and yet they have not been able to take them fast enough. At a single public house for weeks in succession from 400 to 500 people a day have been fed as they have passed through in search of land and homes. At almost every station goods have been piled up promiscuously in every direction waiting to be moved out to the future homes of their owners, and settlements have sprung up like magic.[1]

The landseekers rapidly occupied the area within ten or twelve miles of the railway and later comers then crowded into the lands farther from the tracks. The influx of settlers into Jerauld County in the early 1880's is indicative of the astonishing rapidity with which the Dakota prairie become inhabited. The Milwaukee railroad between Mitchell and Kimball "was lined on both sides with people in wagons, in tents and some without any shelter, in camp, getting their moveables ready, as fast as possible to move off into the country."[2] Hundreds of men left the train every day at Plankinton, White Lake, and Kimball, swarmed to the hotels and eating places, and then rushed toward their destinations as fast as teams could be hired.

Similar scenes were enacted along the railroads between Aberdeen and Huron as the settlers descended upon the public lands in Edmunds and Faulk counties. At the peak of the boom vacant lots and back yards in Huron were covered with the camps of transients whose claims were not yet selected or readied for occupancy.

When the Milwaukee extended its tracks from Aberdeen into Edmunds County in 1883, the line of settlement was pushed into McPherson County and the region west of Ipswich. The same intense activity prevailed at Ipswich, which for two years was the jumping-off place to the unoccupied lands beyond. Within a year after the town was platted, it had 700 inhabitants, twelve hotels, three hardware stores, ten dry goods and grocery stores, six lumberyards, and about twenty real estate offices.

While the settlers were rushing over the prairies in a race for the choicest claims, townsite boomers also were strenuously occupied wooing professional and businessmen and nurturing fond hopes for the future. A special correspondent of the *Yankton Press and*

[1] Report of Rev. Stewart Sheldon, Superintendent of the Congregational Church in Dakota Territory, Watertown, September 2–23, 1883, in *Minutes . . . of the General Association of the Congregational Churches of Dakota*, 1883, p. 11.

[2] N. J. Dunham, *A History of Jerauld County, South Dakota* (Wessington Springs, S. Dak.: privately printed, 1910), p. 32.

Dakotaian quipped that such was the mania for getting hold of townsites, it seemed likely the prairies of the Upper James Valley would be surveyed and marked on the maps as embryo cities rather than fertile farms. Woonsocket, formed in 1883 in Sanborn County at the junction of two lines of the Milwaukee railway, grew with such speed that the railroad personnel nicknamed it "Boom-strucket." When the town was only nine months old, it had an estimated population of 1,800 and contained sixty business houses, including eight groceries, three hardware stores, three banks, eight hotels, five lumberyards, and three livery stables.[8]

Few towns realized their dreams for the future; many experienced a rise and decline, finally passing into oblivion. The map of Dakota Territory is dotted with place-names cast into the limbo of ghost towns with the passage of time.

A number of railway towns received their first permanent residents from nearby hamlets that were doomed to extinction when railroad surveyors passed them by. Brookings, for instance, drew from Fountain and Medary, Mitchell from Firesteel, and Watertown from Kampeska City. The villages of Old Madison and Herman compromised by moving to a halfway point where they merged under the name of Madison; and in Edmunds County three infant towns—Edmunds, Freeport, and Georgetown—pulled up stakes and settled at the new railway townsite of Ipswich platted equidistant between them. Cameron, near the present site of Canistota, faded away when Salem and Bridgewater came into being.

The Great Dakota Boom was said to have generated more paper railroads than real ones. Townsite boomers were especially active in promoting new lines. Occasionally a townsite succumbed because its sole reason for being was a railway line that never materialized. Such was the fate of Fairbank, a townsite in Sully County on the east bank of the Missouri River opposite the mouth of the Big Cheyenne, some forty miles northwest of Pierre. It was laid out in 1883 in the expectation that the Chicago and North Western would build an extension to the Pacific coast from Aberdeen and make a river crossing at that point. In its heyday in 1884 it had a population of about 500, a hotel, lumberyards, two newspapers, and even,

[8] S. S. Judy and Will G. Robinson, "Sanborn County History," *South Dakota Historical Collections* (Pierre: South Dakota State Historical Society, 1953), XXVI (1952), 45, 46.

for a short time, a college, but within a decade it had become a ghost town.

WHERE THE SETTLERS CAME FROM

The course of migration followed the usual pattern. The majority of the settlers were of American stock, hailing from nearby states. According to census statistics for 1900, about 60 per cent of the native-born population claiming a birthplace outside the state came from Iowa, Wisconsin, Minnesota, and Illinois. On the basis of evidence available for the period of the 1880's, Wisconsin and Illinois seem to have supplied the greater number of the American-born who settled in the James River Valley. Unquestionably the majority of those seeking permanent homes in Dakota Territory came from communities which were essentially agricultural or rural.

Although conditions in the Dakota country might vary somewhat from those which they had previously known, many of the newcomers were already accustomed to frontier life. The experiences of the family of which the writer Hamlin Garland was a member were typical. In 1881 Richard Garland settled at Ordway, a boom town near the James River twelve miles northeast of Aberdeen; Hamlin, the son, a few years later filed a pre-emption claim in McPherson County. Within the course of two generations the Garland family had moved halfway across the continent from their original home in Maine, homesteading first in Wisconsin, then moving to newer lands in northeastern Iowa, and eventually joining the stampede to Dakota Territory.

When young Hamlin decided to join his father, who operated a store at Ordway while "holding down a claim" on the side, he "felt to its full the compelling power of the swift stream of immigration surging to the west." Recounting his journey, he wrote later:

. . . I bought a ticket for Aberdeen, and entered the train crammed with movers who had found the 'prairie schooner' all too slow. The epoch of the canvas-covered wagon had passed. The era of the locomotive, the day of the chartered car, had arrived. Free land was receding at railroad speed, the borderline could be overtaken only by steam, and every man was in haste to arrive.[4]

[4] Hamlin Garland, *A Son of the Middle Border* (New York: Macmillan Co., 1920), p. 244.

Many of the foreign-born came to the Territory from Iowa, Wisconsin, Minnesota, and Illinois, in particular the Scandinavians whose compact settlements were all along the eastern part of the state. The Hollanders, who during the early part of the 1880's formed other compact communities in the western part of Douglas County, came mostly from the Dutch settlements of northwestern Iowa.

Settlers of many nationalities came directly from the Old World. Of particular importance was a second wave of German-Russians arriving some eleven years after the immigration that had settled in Hutchinson and Turner and portions of Bon Homme and Yankton counties. The new settlements sprang up in the vicinity of Roscoe, Hosmer, and Eureka in 1884. Eureka, established in 1887 and remaining the railroad terminal for a number of years, became the main dispersal point for a heavy immigration that in the late 1880's gave Campbell, McPherson, and Walworth counties their preponderantly German character.

The railroads facilitated settlement by groups or colonies whose members were drawn together by national or neighborhood ties. Special trains were made up at many towns in the upper region of the Mississippi Valley, chartered by people from the same neighborhood so that they could continue to be neighbors in the new country. Land agents, representing both railroad and townsite interests, encouraged the planting of colonies, most of which had no formal organization.

Nearly every county occupied during the boom period had such communities. Place-names like Appomattox and Gettysburg bear witness to colonies established in Potter County by Civil War veterans. So-called Illinois and Michigan colonies were especially numerous. In the vicinity of Doland east of Redfield a group of French-Canadians from Kankakee, Illinois, settled in a body in order to continue their neighborhood associations.

A large colony of Welshmen settled in Powell Township in Edmunds County, brought there by a Welsh immigration agent for the Milwaukee railroad. He had carried on recruitment in Welsh farming communities in Wisconsin. The original group of twenty, mostly bachelors, in 1883 reached the vicinity of Powell, where a big shanty gave them temporary shelter until they could establish themselves on separate claims. Others were attracted to the area, and several years later the Welsh colony numbered more than 150 persons.

LAND LEGISLATION AND ABUSES OF THE SYSTEM

The administrative machinery of the national government was strained to the utmost in meeting the demands made upon it by the settlers. Some railroad land was available in the Upper Sioux Valley under a land grant to the Winona and St. Peter Railroad in 1858. The settlers bought such land at prices averaging four dollars per acre. Title to some of the government land was procured by tendering scrip which sold on the market at quotations ranging from ten to forty dollars per acre. Land scrip was used by townsite owners as well as railroad companies who needed quick title to choice tracts.

Most of the public lands, however, passed into private ownership under the basic land legislation then in operation: the pre-emption, homestead, and timber culture laws. Each of the laws limited the size of the holding to 160 acres or a quarter section. To accommodate the landseekers in the newer sections, the government opened additional land offices, and either closed down or removed the older ones in the southeastern counties where little or no public land was left. The bulk of the land business during the boom period was transacted at offices located in Aberdeen, Huron, Mitchell, and Watertown. The greatest activity experienced at any land office in Dakota Territory occurred on October 9, 1882, the opening date of the Huron office, when 690 original entries were made, contests instituted on 163 claims, and about 1,200 applications for final proof received.

The movement of landseekers into the region beyond the James River Valley was so heavy by 1883 that vast tracts were taken as fast as they could be surveyed, and whole townships were being occupied by squatters in advance of the survey. One township fifty miles west of Huron was said to have been occupied by squatters in a body, one for each quarter section; when the survey was completed, the settlers marched to the land office as a battalion to file.[5] In an unsurveyed area some squatters employed private surveyors to extend the lines from surveyed townships, while others would measure

[5] Sioux Falls *Argus*, February 26, 1887.

from an established corner stake with a marked buggy or wagon wheel, or merely pace off the required distance.

It was possible for a settler to acquire possession of two and even, in some instances, three quarter sections. The most common method was to file first on a pre-emption claim, acquire title upon the payment of $1.25 an acre at the end of a minimum period of six months, and then exercise the homestead privilege. If the homestead right was used first, five years of residence had to elapse before a pre-emption filing could be made, unless the homestead claim was commuted to a cash payment, payable after six months. The minimum period for a commutation was extended in 1891 to fourteen months' residence. When the timber culture privilege began to be exercised after 1878, many settlers used it to acquire a second quarter section, whether pre-emption or homestead rights were used for the first claim. In some cases, a settler might resort to all three laws. Usually, however, the third claim was defaulted. According to a story related by a Danish traveler, a Miner County couple accumulated holdings of 960 acres by getting a legal separation and then remarrying after each had secured three claims, but this lacks plausibility.

The individuals who filed on the public domain during the boom period fall in two categories: those who hoped to establish permanent homes on the land, and those (like Hamlin Garland) who merely intended to hold the claims long enough to obtain title and convert them into cash, and then move out of the country. It was the second group which was responsible for the many flagrant abuses of the land laws.

There was a mania for land, and even high railroad officials entered timber culture claims, driven by the urge to profit off a government believed rich enough to provide everybody a farm. Many townspeople such as businessmen, clerks, and mechanics filed on two quarter sections, complying with the law sufficiently to get title, and selling the land on a brisk market or holding it for an advance in price, meanwhile allowing the tracts to remain unimproved and lie idle. Timber culture in Dakota, one observer sarcastically remarked, was more profitable than raising wheat.

Stories are legion of fraud and manipulations in government land during the boom period. A packing box or a chicken coop might be called a house, and a weed patch with a few straggling sprouts would represent a cultivated tree claim. Sworn affidavits from "witnesses" amounted to wholesale perjury, while lawyers who specialized in land cases availed themselves of every loophole to evade the law.

Although the commutation option of the homestead law was abused too, the pre-emption and timber culture laws were the special delight of speculators and for that reason finally were repealed in 1891. The pre-emption law, which then required only six days' residence for the entire six-month period, was particularly subject to exploitation by younger people. Pioneer accounts are studded with references to young bachelors taking their departure after they had converted their claims into a goodly profit. So many young women, most of them maintaining temporary residence, filed in one section of Sully County southwest of Clifton that the community was locally known as Girltown.

Loan companies played a key part in this speculative process. A pre-emptor could easily secure a several-hundred-dollar loan on a mortgage, pay the purchase price, interest, and commission, pocket the balance, and then leave the country after turning the title over to the loan company. The company would market the mortgage in the East and make the proceeds available for similar transactions.

The timber culture law was originally enacted in 1873 with provisions that were impossible of fulfillment, but in 1878 Congress reduced the required acreage of trees from forty to ten. Intended "to encourage the growth of timber on the western prairies," the law provided that any person who would plant, protect, and keep in a healthy growing condition ten acres of timber, might secure title to a quarter section. The patent would be issued if there were 675 living thrifty trees at the end of an eight-year period of cultivation. Only one timber claim was allowed to a section. The qualifications for entry were the same as for the homestead act, except that the law did not require actual residence. The planting could include seeds, nuts, or cuttings, and the claimant could make final proof at the end of eight years or any time within fourteen years.

Most timber claims were located through the services of land agents. There were many instances, according to the surveyor general, in which unscrupulous land agents made entries in newly surveyed townships for all the timber claims that the law allowed, using fictitious names and false affidavits. Later they would make the claims available for relinquishments at whatever price the traffic would bear. The timber culture act was all too often employed as a means of withdrawing land from the market, with little or no intention of making final proof. Only about 25 per cent of the timber claims east of the Missouri River were actually patented under the timber culture act.

Relinquishments, which merely gave a settler the opportunity to file on claims released by earlier entrymen, generally commanded prices ranging from $50 to $400. Evidence indicates that in some areas there were times when one-half of all the land entries, including homesteads, were relinquished to bona fide settlers at an average cost of $100 per relinquishment.

On completing a journey through the central part of Dakota Territory shortly after his arrival during the summer of 1880, Governor N. G. Ordway called official attention to frauds perpetrated upon the government. Since it employed no special agents, the Dakota Governor suggested that the Interior Department detail a few "bullet-proof clerks" and send them along the new railroad lines to "ferret out and bring to justice perjurers and swindlers now so successfully plying their vocation."[6] In time the Interior Department became more vigilant and instituted numerous prosecutions, especially in the Huron and Mitchell land districts during 1883. When President Grover Cleveland took office in 1885, he frankly took the attitude that unscrupulous land-grabbers were looting the public lands, and his new appointee in the land office, William A. J. Sparks, was in full agreement.

Sparks, an Illinois lawyer noted for his great firmness of character and stubborn honesty, was convinced that fully half the land patents were fraudulent. His special inspectors had scoured the West and their reports showed, among other infractions, that nearly one-fourth of the land in central Dakota had been taken under the timber culture act with few bona fide attempts to comply with legal requirements. On April 3, 1885, he suspended final action on all land entries, excepting private cash and scrip, in the western states and territories.

The suspension order was impractical and certain to cause hardship to bona fide settlers. For a time Sparks created havoc among the boomers, and especially perturbed the agents of mortgage com-

---

[6] Governor N. G. Ordway to Secretary of the Interior Carl Schurz, July 8, 1880, Official Letter Book, Executive Office, Dakota Territory, pp. 148–159, Territorial Papers (North Dakota State Historical Society, Bismarck, N. Dak.)

panies, but the force of inspectors was inadequate to investigate each of the thousands of entries ready for final patent. Although the suspension order was revoked and Sparks was forced to resign, his successor continued to turn up abundant evidence of fraud in both land entries and surveys. The increased vigilance on the part of the land inspectors resulted in more cancellations of entries for failure to fulfill the requirements for final patents.

The outcry against Sparks that arose in Dakota Territory came mainly from vested interests in the towns. Genuine settlers, exercised over claim-jumping and the bold activities of speculators, were inclined to sympathize with the efforts at reform. An indignation meeting in Huron to protest Sparks' actions was attended by land locators, real estate dealers, loan agents, nurserymen, newspaper publishers who reaped a harvest from land patent notices, and, of course, representatives of the thirty-seven law firms doing business in the budding city.

An analysis of land-office statistics indicates that the homestead law was definitely not the chief medium for converting the public lands into private ownership. The traditional picture of the 160-acre homestead earned by five years of faithful toil does not square with the facts. Title to the greater part of the land deeded by the government during the period of the boom was procured by direct purchase through the pre-emption law and the commuted homestead. The final homestead patents represented only about 15 per cent of the total area originally filed upon, and considerably less than half of the original homestead entries. Many of these homesteaders, however, undoubtedly secured a second quarter section under one of the other two laws.

Generally speaking, the actual settler who put permanent improvements upon his land and made it his home was a second- or even a third-comer, obliged to buy his farm on the market at a premium. The primary benefits from a government policy of free or cheap land thus accrued to the speculator. This was a perversion, if not an actual violation, of the spirit of the original homestead law.

Moreover, the speculative mania, fostered by a lax administration of the public land laws, not only served to keep land out of cultivation, but actually retarded social progress. Without question the abuses of the public land system contributed to the growth of farm tenancy; some of the counties in central Dakota showed a rate of 16 per cent of tenancy in 1890.

CHAPTER 13

Pioneer Life

WHILE THE STORY of pioneering on the Dakota prairie has many variations, pioneering essentially is a process of adjustment and adaptation, and the pioneer experience followed a pattern that we have come to think of as typical. Settlers usually traveled out in the autumn to select their land, returning to their old homes for the winter. In their search for choice claims, they often engaged the services of professional land locators, whose charges ranged from ten to twenty-five dollars. When a claim had been located it was marked with some evidence of occupancy—four posts to indicate the corners of a shack, or a three-foot hole to represent a well—as protection against rival claimants until a filing could be made at the land office. Hamlin Garland marked his claim with a "straddlebug," a tripod made of boards on which the landseeker placed his name.

In the years before the railroad, settlers typically brought their possessions in covered wagons; most of the families who moved into the Upper Big Sioux Valley before 1879 trekked all the way by oxteam from eastern Minnesota or Wisconsin. Later settlers generally followed the railroad, some of them even riding on the construction-train caboose into the hinterland. If they had chartered an emigrant car to transport their possessions, one member of the party was allowed to ride in the car to look after livestock.

Most pioneering families literally had to count pennies; and even though there were special rates for settlers, the list of chattels to be freighted to the new country was kept to essentials. Perhaps there

175

were a few pieces of light furniture, a stove, possibly a sewing machine, a barrel or two of kitchen utensils, dishes, clothes, and personal possessions, but priority was given to farm implements, tools, and lumber for the new home. There might be a few head of livestock, including a cow to provide milk for the younger children. Occasionally a melodeon or a treasured piano would be carefully fitted into the crammed allotment of space.

On reaching his claim, the settler's first concern was to have a roof over his head. Some families lived under tents; for others the wagon which brought them from the railway point provided shelter until a dwelling place could be built. The commonest types of habitation for newcomers on the prairie were shanties and sod houses. Whichever type was chosen, construction work was always expedited by the irritating attentions of the fleas infesting the prairie grass.

A typical frame shanty measured at least nine feet by twelve, and was built of pine boards; a tar-paper covering helped to make it weatherproof. Sod houses required no lumber except for windows, roof, and door frame; they were constructed of sod strips cut from the prairie. In some locales, dugouts served as temporary dwellings. Livestock could be sheltered in a sod stable, a hay-covered frame, or even a lean-to. (When a settler graduated from a soddy to a frame house, the soddy invariably was inherited by the livestock.) Sod houses were more comfortable than wooden houses during periods of extreme heat or cold and, if floored, could be made passably attractive. But they were prone to be damp, and in rainy weather might leak or even cave in. Even though intended for temporary occupation, many of the larger shacks and sod houses did service for years. The construction of more substantial houses had to wait until the time when the settlers were well established.

After his home had been built, the settler began the task of converting virgin prairie into farm land. A specially designed breaking plow was used to cut through the tough, fibrous prairie sod. A team of four oxen or horses pulling a fourteen-inch plow could break from one to two acres a day. By the terms of the homestead act, it was required to break five acres during the first year, but most settlers broke more than that; at the peak of the boom it was not unusual for thirty acres to be broken on a single claim. Settlers who did not own a team had the breaking done by more fortunate neighbors.

The breaking season lasted from early June until the midsummer droughts set in, usually in July. Sod broken before or after this time

might make poor producing land for several years. In the fall the
sod was either backset or cross-plowed in preparation for spring
planting. Sometimes the ground was not backset but was pulverized
with disc harrows. The plow was set an inch or two lower for the second operation.

The summer that the land was broken, there was little raised except sod corn and a few potatoes and vegetables. When weather conditions were unusually favorable—as was the case during the early
eighties—many settlers successfully raised flax and even wheat on
new breaking. Indeed, at times it was possible to raise a fair sod crop
of corn from seed-dropped in holes chopped in the sod with an axe.

Most of the settlers, as has been noted, had very little money, especially those who recently had come from Europe. Their farming
operations necessarily were limited by their working capital, and
had to be confined to modest plantings until they could afford better
equipment and more livestock.

For the settlers of the seventies and early eighties, during their
first years on the claim the main motive power and means of transportation was supplied by oxen. Horses were scarce, higher priced
than oxen, more expensive to keep, less docile, and more likely to be
stolen. There was no longer the risk of their being driven off by Indians, but organized bands of horse thieves were still active while
the line of settlement was advancing to the Missouri slope. In a virgin land which did not yet produce its own cultivated feed, the ox
which could support itself from the prairie grasses seemed to possess
every virtue of practicality. However, beginning in 1881 ox teams
gradually began to disappear.

So long as his claim could not support the settler's family, it was
imperative to find other sources of income. In the Big Sioux Valley
many a settler turned fur-trapper during the winter months. Those
who owned teams hired out their services to neighbors with land to
be broken. Others found employment in the towns, where there was
an especially heavy demand for carpenters and blacksmiths. While
the boom lasted, the railroads offered the best chance to find work;
they were constantly in need of both laborers and teams to build
grades and roadbeds. In 1883, for example, the Chicago and North
Western provided steady employment for more than seven hundred
men and several hundred teams while building the line between
Hurley and Centerville in Turner County.

In many cases, a settler's first earnings came from collecting the buffalo bones which littered the prairie and also were found in the low places along the James River. Often the first outward-bound freight from a new town would have aboard a load of bones and horns; many tons of them were shipped out of Dakota Territory and found a ready market in Chicago and elsewhere for processing into fertilizer.

WATER AND WOOD

Obtaining an adequate water supply was one of the settlers' most difficult problems. The water lay from forty to sixty feet below the sod, and most lacked the equipment to reach that depth. Mostly they dug surface wells from fifteen to twenty feet deep. Because of the heavy snows that fell during the winter of 1880–1881, and which saturated the subsoil with moisture, the problem was not so serious for a year or so. But more normal moisture conditions had returned by the time the tide of migration had moved out of the James Valley onto the higher prairie lands.

Many wells turned out to be merely dry holes in the ground. On claims and even in towns it frequently was necessary to dig down in several sites before water came in. For years, open well holes scattered over the prairie created a serious hazard on abandoned claims. Communities which had easy access to an abundant water supply made much of it in advertising their advantages.

In the mid-eighties localized droughts dried up many shallow wells, forcing the settlers to spend much time digging new ones. If their efforts were vain, they had to haul water to their claims from the deeper wells in the neighborhood. Improvements in well drilling and the discovery of artesian waters underlying the glacial drift in central South Dakota eventually relieved the situation.

Fuel was scarce on the treeless prairies, and the price of coal made its use almost prohibitive. The "coal of the prairie" was buffalo chips; cow chips collected from corrals also were utilized. For cooking purposes the pioneers commonly used twisted hay. The lush prairie grasses provided the hay, and the whole family usually was drafted to twist it into "cats." The place-name of Hayti (originally "Hay-tie") in Hamlin County is said to have originated at a meeting of pioneers who were twisting hay for fuel while discussing a name for their town. Stoves specially devised for hay-burning were available on the market. In the simplest type, a drum packed with hay or straw was placed upside down on the cook stove over the open fire-box. A tightly packed drum would keep a good fire going for an hour or two.

Since most of the settlers came from wooded areas, one of their first projects was planting trees around their homes for beautification as well as to serve as windbreaks. Various varieties of fruit trees were set out to test their hardiness and adaptability to the Dakota climate, and the timber culture act was meant to encourage the planting of wood lots and groves.

The success of tree planting varied in different regions. Results were better in the east and southeast than in the area between the James and the Missouri, where there usually was less rainfall. A succession of drought years killed or damaged many of the seedlings on the Missouri plateau and in the James River Valley.

In spite of adverse growing conditions, many groves were successfully maintained in the eastern section. West of the James River, tree claims did less well, even though the settlers made backbreaking attempts to satisfy the provisions of a law that was unrealistic for the Great Plains environment. Yet even in this region there are a few groves whose beginnings can be traced to a tree claim.

Lax administration of the timber culture act and its widespread abuse have obscured the well-intentioned and honest use made of it in South Dakota. Many settlers received their final patents to tree claims only after complying fully with the law. In the early 1900's a questionnaire was sent to some sixty pioneer settlers who had held tree claims in Spink County thirty years before; at least half of them indicated they had raised the required number of trees. Several of the tracts still had a good stand of timber. Nonetheless, the law patently failed to accomplish its general objective, as was finally recognized by Congress in 1893. It then enacted a law sponsored by Congressman J. A. Pickler of South Dakota, which enabled all claimants to make final proof on tree claims upon evidence of honest efforts at compliance with the requirements even though not a single tree had survived.

Many varieties of trees were found unsuited to the Dakota environment. The ash, the box elder, and the cottonwood were considered the most desirable. Although nursery stock from other regions was available, most of the planting material was native to South Dakota. Some of the stock came from gulches along the eastern border, but most of the tree seedlings came from the bottom lands and sandbars along the Missouri River. For a number of years a large crop of such seedlings was gathered annually during the early spring months and sold either to nurserymen or directly to farmers for planting windbreaks and for use on timber culture claims. At Yankton on one day in the spring of 1885, 40,000 cottonwood trees from two to six feet in height were gathered, sorted, and bound up in bundles of a hundred each. The sale of 200,000 trees within a single week by a Redfield dealer is indicative of the demand at the time.

BLIZZARDS

The blizzard—a combination of extreme temperatures, winds of high velocity, and swirling dustlike particles of snow—was a phenomenon peculiar to the Northern Plains. Even when there were no blizzards, the winters were extremely severe, and not infrequently settlers, unprepared for the rigorous Dakota climate, were found frozen to death in their claim shacks.

During a blizzard the fine particles of whirling snow would entirely obscure the landscape, making it impossible for a settler to find his way from building to building without a guideline. The intensity of the cold and the wind-driven snow which sifted inside clothing made survival impossible for those caught out in the open during such a storm. The winter storms were also the bane of cattlemen; losses to the herds were especially heavy in the open range country of the western plains in 1886 and 1887.

Three blizzards in particular are remembered for their severity: these occurred during the winters of 1873, 1880–1881, and 1888. The great storm which visited the Upper Sioux Valley during the early months of 1873 was the settlers' first real initiation into the eccentricities of a Dakota blizzard. A belated snowstorm sweeping across the central plains into southern Dakota during April of the same year brought great hardship and suffering to the Seventh Cavalry under the command of General Custer in camp at Yankton en route to Fort Abraham Lincoln.

The winter of 1880–1881 often has been called "the hard winter." A blizzard occurred as early as October, and although most of this early snow disappeared, heavy precipitation throughout the winter resulted in an accumulation of more than eleven feet of snow in many communities. Hardships were due not so much to low temperatures as to the privations caused by the snow blockade. Food and fuel grew scarce as connections with the outside world were cut off. Some of the newly settled areas along the Upper Sioux and in the

James Valley were snowbound for as long as from October to March.

The unprecedented snowfall had a catastrophic aftermath in the devastating spring floods which deluged the Big Sioux and Missouri valleys. Dams were demolished and the gristmills they served were damaged. At Yankton the flood swept away the entire town of Green Island on the Nebraska side, scattered the steamboats in dock for the winter, and inundated the low plains to Sioux City. At Vermillion where the main part of the town lay below the bluff, practically everything was carried away. The raging torrent cut a new channel along the Nebraska bluff, straightening out the river's course and eliminating some seventeen miles of meandering passage for the steamboats. When the waters receded, Vermillion was completely bypassed by the Missouri. The business district was rebuilt on the higher ground where most of the town is located today.

The heavy snowfall of 1880–1881 was not without its compensations. The large volume of moisture released by the spring thaw transformed the sloughs and low places into temporary lakes and thoroughly saturated the subsoil, insuring bumper crops for a few years.

Probably the worst blizzard experienced by Dakota settlers occurred in January, 1888: the so-called "school children's storm" because in many areas the storm broke without warning and school children were among the victims. They had been dismissed early in the hope they could get home before the storm reached its peak. Many tales of heroism are told of teachers who kept vigil with their pupils in flimsily constructed schoolhouses until relief came the next day.

The discomforts and perils of the old-fashioned blizzard are largely things of the past. Settlement and windbreaks check the storm's sweep in many localities. More important, however, is the effective protection against the weather provided by better built homes, more adequate clothing, and improved communications which give ample warning of the storm's approach. The Dakota blizzard of today, although still a menace to rancher and stockman, has lost much of its ferocity and deadliness.

The publicity about the loss of life and the intense suffering endured during the early blizzards gave the Dakota climate an unenviable reputation that has persisted to the present day. To outsiders South Dakota is still known as a land of blizzards and heavy snows, in spite of the weather records which show low annual precipitation for the region.

PRAIRIE FIRES

Equally dreaded and more calamitous than blizzards were prairie fires, a source of danger in the fall and the spring when the grass was dry and highly combustible. They occasionally swept over large areas, covering several townships, consuming haystacks, fields of grain, and even inhabited dwellings.

When a prairie fire got under way, sometimes racing over the country at thirty miles an hour, only concerted action on the part of the settlers in throwing up firebreaks and setting a backfire could stay its destructive course. Towns as well as farming communities were menaced by the conflagrations. In April, 1889, the six-year-old booming town of Leola with a population of about 300 was almost reduced to ashes by a fierce prairie fire driven by a strong wind. The fire covered an area of 400 square miles. Only a few buildings survived in Leola, but fortunately no lives were lost.

As a protection against prairie fires, settlers placed firebreaks around their homes or around their whole claims. The fireguards usually consisted of two sets of furrows plowed a few rods apart with the grass on the intervening ground burned off. For many years such fireguards were maintained around all the townships in Hand County. In some instances when disaster struck, public relief was made available. In April, 1889, the board of commissioners of Jerauld County furnished lumber and seed grain to residents victimized by devastating prairie fires.

Prairie fires were less common after more land was broken up and graded roads constructed, but they by no means disappeared. Some of the worst came after the country was well settled. A most destructive fire occurred in Edmunds County in April, 1909, when a small fire near Roscoe got out of control and fanned out to a fifteen-mile width, traveling some thirty miles before it was brought under control near Cresbard in Faulk County. In September, 1947, the northern half of Hyde and sections of four adjoining counties on the north and west were the scene of a conflagration which swept over an area of more than 300,000 acres along an irregular strip from twenty to thirty-five miles wide and about twenty-seven miles long. The loss of livestock was negligible, but a number of farm homes were destroyed. The total damages were estimated at $2,000,000.

The primitive conditions of pioneer life could be endured because the settlers were confident that they were transitory, and that better times were coming. It was this vision of the future that gave them the fortitude and patience to live through the hardships and privations of early days. Life was particularly austere and unnerving for the women as they faced the monotonous solitude of the prairie, the continual dread of sickness and disease, and the poverty attending crop failures and other misfortunes. Life on the frontier was, nevertheless, not much different from that which prevailed in rural communities in the older sections of the country, and its drab and dull features can be easily exaggerated when measured by the present-day mode of living with all its gadgets, comforts, and diversions.

SOCIAL LIFE

Despite its hardships, pioneer life was not without its bright spots and rewards. The spirit of cooperation and neighborliness brought the settlers into frequent communication with each other and promoted sociability. Symbolic of the helpful spirit that prevailed on the Dakota frontier was the lighted lantern hung on a pole in front of the settler's shack to guide benighted travelers across the uncharted prairie. The guidepost was a great boon, especially during storms. The display of a red light, or no light at all, was a distress signal and a call for help.

When there were too few children for a school district, a subscription school frequently was maintained in a private home. Sometimes schools were organized in sod houses and claim shanties. These cooperative efforts to provide children with an education made it simpler to organize formal school districts later on. The first textbooks came from families who had brought to Dakota the schoolbooks used by their older children.

After the school districts were organized, the schoolhouses became centers of community social life. Concerts, plays, spelling bees, singing schools, literary societies, and meetings of various sorts served to bring the settlers together. The school building was also used at times for church services and Sunday school.

The same spirit of cooperation and neighborliness was manifest in the mutual help rendered in the building of homes, breaking the sod, and harvesting crops. The exchange of labor, or "changing work" in pioneer parlance, afforded further opportunity for sociability.

Dancing was a popular diversion in private homes and community halls, and usually climaxed an Independence Day celebration or some other special occasion. Music for public gatherings was supplied by local orchestral groups and brass bands. The universal interest in sports and games inspired the formation of local athletic clubs, and virtually every town and township had its baseball team in the summer. When the roller-skating craze swept the nation during the middle eighties, skating rinks were built in various localities. There were race tracks in many communities to accommodate the activities of local driving associations.

Fraternal and social organizations, local improvement societies and other civic organizations, local units of temperance unions, and reading circles played an important part in promoting the social and cultural aspects of pioneer life. They supplemented the activities of local religious organizations. The common interest in farming led to the organization of county agricultural societies and fairs which were held in most counties in the eastern part of the state and occasionally in a Black Hills county.

As in earlier days, the zestful game of politics continued to be a leading interest of the settlers, bringing them together at party caucuses in local schoolhouses or in the nearby town. Other political gatherings might consider a movement to divide the county or to move the county seat. Whatever the purpose of the assemblage, it afforded excellent opportunity for a sharing of experiences and the discussion of matters of mutual interest. It also brought the farmer into closer association with the townsman.

In localities that did not have rail connections, communication with the outside world was maintained through the rural post offices. The first post offices were usually set up in private homes located along the stage routes that radiated from the nearest railway points. They became community centers for patrons who were often scattered over several neighborhoods. A neighborhood store often was found alongside the rural post office, if not under the same roof, and frequently was the nucleus of a hamlet or small village.

Towns and Their Services

The town rather than the surrounding farms dominated the scene in the new country. It supplied a variety of services to the nearby settlers and in turn commanded their loyalty if it became involved in a county-seat contest or in some other form of rivalry. The trade area served by the town was limited by the distance that could be conveniently traversed by the farmers. For this reason, the country was well dotted with villages and towns, all serving important economic, social, and cultural functions. Many of these towns outlived their usefulness, and disappeared or declined, victims of the technological advances of modern society. More fortunate were the towns that became county seats or attained some other position of importance. They were destined to become more urban in their outlook with their more diversified business, industrial, and professional interests. Nonetheless, the larger towns and cities retained much of their earlier rural character and remained in a close affinity with the rural sections because of their community of interests.

The services provided by hotels and livery stables were especially important during the boom. The hotel was not infrequently the earliest business establishment in a new town. A large circus tent, soon replaced by a sod structure, first served Aberdeen as a hotel. At times the demand for lodging was so great in new settlements that patrons crowded into unfinished hotel buildings, rolling themselves up in blankets and sleeping on the rough wooden floors. Some of the first hotels were partitioned off into rooms with army blankets. The public celebration which frequently accompanied a hotel's official opening is an indication of its important role. A town's growth during the boom period was measured by the number of its crowded hostelries.

Lodging facilities were taxed to the utmost when signs of an impending storm brought settlers flocking from their claims for shelter. The hotels also furnished opportunity for employment, especially for young women who were holding pre-emption claims on the side. In such instances, hotel managers allowed employees enough time off to spend the required number of nights in their claim shacks.

Although most hotels had stables, the livery stable formed the major link between the town and the countryside. The livery barn was where the settlers put up their teams on their occasional trips to town, and it maintained rigs and teams for hire. It also frequently supplied a driver. Landseekers used livery rigs to locate land, or even to transport their families and belongings to their claims, and land agents, drummers, and representatives of loan agencies hired them when making the rounds of rural settlements.

The blacksmith and the harness-maker were indispensable craftsmen in the horse-and-buggy era. Although the blacksmith was kept busy shoeing horses and oxen, there were so many demands for repairing broken machinery or improvising equipment that he also operated the equivalent of a local machine shop. In a few towns the blacksmith shop actually evolved into a machine shop or small foundry. In some communities, the demand for carriages and wagons and for repairs also led to wagon-making as a side line for the blacksmith shop. Every community had its local harness-maker and saddlery. The harness-maker also made and repaired shoes, and had a large assortment of harness and buggy whips for the trade.

Equally prominent in their services to the settlers were the general stores, the drug stores, the implement houses, the gristmills, and the numerous lumberyards which sprang up almost overnight with the arrival of the first freight train. Lumber was usually aboard the first inbound freight in newly settled communities and was hauled out in all directions for use on homesteads and in villages.

Important as doctors were for their professional services, they were no more indispensable than the lawyers, who seem to have been more numerous in the boom towns than members of any other profession. Much of the early legal work was connected with proving up or settling disputes over claims. A second source of business concerned the generous pensions granted Civil War veterans, many of whom had settled in Dakota Territory. Most of the lawyers specialized in land-office and pension matters. The land-office business also was responsible for the origin of many newspapers that were first published during the boom. Newspapers were frequently established to promote townsites and to advance a town's claim to county-seat honors. The *Pierre Free Press,* for instance, was established by a townsite company. In many communities the first newspapers were subsidized, usually in the form of a deeded lot and building, although sometimes the main consideration was a small cash bonus. However, the income derived from legal printing required under the homestead law was sufficient motivation for most of the newspapers that came into being during the Great Dakota Boom. After 1879 every occupant of a homestead was required to run a final-proof notice in five consecutive issues of the newspaper nearest his claim. Contest notices also had to be published. During the boom period, the usual fee for a patent or final proof notice was $6.50, and $5.00 for a contest notice.

Newspaper plants rushed into new communities so as to be on the spot when the first patent notices appeared. The first issue was often printed under a tent. Most of the papers carried the so-called patent insides, or patent outsides, which were printed in some distant city and shipped to the country newspaper plant where the rest of the issue was made up from local materials. It was not unusual in Aberdeen, Huron, and Watertown for a newspaper to carry as many as a hundred land notices an issue during the boom years. An Ipswich paper in 1883 contained 211 such notices in a single issue. The newspaper population ran high in the newer counties during the early eighties: twelve, for instance, in Spink, nine in Sully, eight in Hughes, and seven in Hand and Sanborn. When final proof notices became less plentiful, many of the papers disappeared.

Another intimate relationship between rural settlers and town or urban communities was in the realm of banking and finance. The private bank was usually among the first business institutions in a new town, often opening as an adjunct to some other business enterprise. The first bank in Alpena, for example, began its operations as a private business conducted in the rear of a drug store until it became a chartered corporation a few years later. Local banks and private lending agencies were the main source of small loans which were generally secured by chattel mortgages. Outside investment and mortgage companies usually supplied land credit. Although some moneylending corporations maintained their own official agencies, they also employed local lawyers, real estate firms, and even local banks as their agents. Mortgage companies, as well as the other lending agencies, enjoyed a brisk business during the boom.

Loans made by mortgage companies fell into two classes with respect to the purposes served. There were, first, the speculative loans made to bogus settlers who merely wished to borrow in order to prove up on their claims and then leave. Although some mortgage companies refused to negotiate such loans, this speculative activity represented a heavy volume of business. The second class constituted loans obtained by bona fide settlers in need of funds. It has been estimated that a thousand dollars represented the minimum required to bring a homestead into production at the time of the Dakota boom.[1]

Until he secured a patent to his claim, the homesteader was relieved of any tax except on his improvements and personal property. Moreover, final proof might be deferred until the end of the

[1] Allan G. Bogue, *Money at Interest—the Farm Mortgage on the Middle Border* (Ithaca, N. Y.: Cornell University Press, 1955), pp. 4, 5.

seventh year. This pecuniary advantage was offset, however, by the settler's inability to offer his homestead as security prior to final proof.

The buoyance and optimism which characterized the Dakota boom made the settlers highly susceptible to the blandishments of the many agents making their rounds through the country selling farm machinery and equipment. Land mortgages often seemed preferable and more desirable than time notes and chattel mortgages. Many a homesteader undoubtedly commuted his claim to a cash entry after a year or two of residence in order to borrow on the land.

The credit situation during the boom period showed little improvement over conditions during the early seventies. As in the earlier period, chattel mortgages generally ran from ten to twelve per cent. Small loans on time notes commanded usurious rates up to two and three per cent per month. In sharp contrast, however, with the high rates so prevalent in the southeastern counties a decade earlier, land mortgages were generally placed at seven per cent during the 1880's. Most of the loans ranged from $350 to $500 per quarter section.

Interest charges naturally ran higher in newly settled regions because of their more unstable population and the few improvements on the land. The higher rates reflected the greater risks incurred by the lenders. Even though mortgage rates had declined, they were still considered exorbitant by the settlers. The feeling against mortgage companies ran especially high when reverses set in. Many claims were lost on $200 to $400 mortgages in the James River Valley and the prairie settlements to the west.

A particular target for criticism were the extra charges—commissions, special bonuses, and inspection fees—that were added to the mortgage principal. A $300 loan, running for five years, often became a mortgage for $400, bearing seven per cent interest on the accumulated amount. Whatever the validity of the contemporary outcry against farm mortgages, the credit situation was a potent factor in the agrarian protest which loomed large on the political horizon by the end of the boom period.[2]

[2] The files of the *Dakota Farmer,* which began publication in 1882, reveal the settlers' concern over the debtor-creditor relationship. Sharply critical comments appear in published accounts by such pioneers as N. J. Dunham, *A History of Jerauld County, South Dakota* (Wessington Springs: privately printed, 1910); Elbert W. Smith, *Pioneering in Dakota* (Laconnor, Wash., 1929); and John H. Bingham and Nora K. Peters, "A Short History of Brule County," *South Dakota Historical Collections,* XXIII (1947), 1–184.

CHAPTER 14

Politics in the Seventies

THE PHYSICAL AND ECONOMIC GROWTH of the seventies was accompanied by greater stability in the political and governmental sphere. As it emerged from the hand-to-mouth phase of its existence, the Territory was no longer so dependent upon federal expenditures for the support of its settlers. Government contracts for military supplies and for the support of the Indians were still an important source of income, but the economy had attained to a higher degree of self-sufficiency.

As for the factionalism that had characterized Dakota politics during the sixties, it was to persist a few years longer. When Governor Burbank came into office, the Republican intraparty feuds were exacerbated by his flagrant meddling in political affairs and by the way in which he exploited the Territory to his own advantage.

After the change of administration at Washington on March 4, 1869, there were many new names on the official roster of Dakota Territory. The factional quarrels at Yankton afforded President Grant a convenient excuse for giving appointments to nonresidents; and to the dismay of the local leaders, he turned most of the patronage over to party spoilsmen. The major territorial offices went for the most part to outsiders. Burbank, the new governor, was a brother-in-law of Senator Oliver P. Morton of Indiana, a powerful figure in Congress and a close friend of the President. Hannibal Hamlin, Senator from Maine and a former Vice President, was influential enough to draw the Dakota secretaryship for his son-in-law, George A. Batchelder, when that office became vacant. The position

189

of surveyor general, which carried with it valuable patronage in the form of surveying contracts, was at the disposal of a particular Congressional district in Wisconsin. William H. H. Beadle, who came to the Territory in April, 1869, was the first appointee under this arrangement which obtained until 1881.

Through their connections with the Grant administration, the new officials crippled the patronage efforts of Delegate S. L. Spink. Few major appointments could be attributed to his influence; in fact, some positions were filled by Dakotans who had opposed his election. With Spink thus handicapped, Burleigh, the stormy petrel of past years, decided to run again for delegate, and secured a controlling interest in the *Union and Dakotaian* to promote his candidacy. During the preliminary skirmishes in the Yankton County precinct caucuses, the Republican party split wide open. Shortly thereafter a new weekly, the *Yankton Press,* began publication as a Spink organ. Burleigh succeeded in controlling the party machinery, forcing the Spink group into the role of bolters. The Democrats, enthusiastic over the prospects for victory, nominated Moses K. Armstrong. Then followed one of the liveliest campaigns in the annals of Dakota Territory. To the delight of the Democrats, charges and countercharges flew back and forth between the two Republican factions, and probably all three groups attempted to bribe the voters. Burleigh, with his usual open-handedness and callous indifference to the political proprieties, was the subject of major complaints about election irregularities.

Although the Democrats elected their territorial ticket and won a majority of the legislative seats, it was a hollow triumph in at least one respect. Congress had amended the Organic Act, substituting biennial for annual sessions, and Washington ruled that the legislators chosen in 1869 should remain in office. The Democrats, consequently, could not gain control of the legislative body. Armstrong, as delegate, championed the Territory's interests in Congress.

THE BURBANK REGIME

With the approach of the 1872 campaign, Republican leaders tried earnestly to heal the party breach. But the rancor remained from the previous contest, and the feuding broke out anew when two party members, Judge W. W. Brookings and Gideon C. Moody, both aspired to the office of delegate. Governor Burbank and most of the territorial officials supported Brookings; Moody was backed by a rabidly anti-Burbank element and the greater part of the old Burleigh wing. While it probably was much exaggerated in local contemporary accounts, the bitterness engendered by rivalries and jealousies between Yankton's Broadway and Capital streets also contributed to the factional feeling. Moody lived in Broadway, or uptown, district, and Brookings zealously promoted business interests on Capital Street.

The campaign of 1872 duplicated the preceding one, this time with Brookings and Moody the chief targets for slander and personal abuse. Because of the Republican split, Armstrong under the Democratic banner again carried the day. He also received the support of a Liberal Republican movement organized as a protest against the brawls within the majority party. According to unofficial returns, Brookings appeared to have won with 3,270 votes as against 3,070 for Armstrong and 2,539 for Moody, but the canvassing board rejected a majority of the votes, paring the totals to 1,549 for Armstrong, 1,241 for Moody, and 948 for Brookings. Overzealous campaign managers had opened up voting precincts along the projected line of the Northern Pacific in the northern counties with fantastic results. In the vicinity of present-day Bismarck, where about fifty railway graders were camped, the precinct "polled" some three thousand votes, more than half of them for Judge Brookings. The official canvass rejected all votes cast along new railway lines in unsettled areas.

The confusion and bitterness arising from the election of 1872 were reflected in the new Legislature in the number of contested seats. The session was "characterized a portion of the time by proceedings bordering on the scandalous" and served to continue the rift in the Republican party for another year.[1]

Growing dissatisfaction with Governor Burbank further aggravated the political factionalism. The Governor had used his political connections to good advantage during the many long absences from Yankton that tried even the patience of his superiors at Washington. Aside from his influence on the patronage, he acquired extensive townsite interests at Springfield in Bon Homme County, obtained a new United States land office for his town, and persuaded Congress to designate his townsite, rather than Yankton, as the terminus of the Dakota Southern Railroad. He aligned himself with the railroad interests at Yankton, and was rewarded with a place

[1] Kingsbury, *History of Dakota Territory*, I, 681.

on the board of directors of the Dakota Southern. It was no wonder that the Dakota Governor had succeeded in getting himself generally disliked, yet in spite of a petition bearing at least 1,200 signatures opposing his retention in office, Burbank received a reappointment in the spring of 1873.

The indignation provoked by his extended tenure was augmented by quarrels between Yankton County and the Dakota Southern management. The county commissioners, representing Yankton County as a stockholder by virtue of the $200,000 subsidy, sought to restrain the railroad from mortgaging itself, and A. H. Barnes, federal judge assigned to the Yankton district, handed down rulings unfavorable to the railway interests. Burbank retaliated by threatening to transfer the jurist from Yankton to the Pembina district in the far north. While attempts to adjudicate the matter were in progress, P. P. Wintermute, a Yankton banker actively identified with the anti-Burbank clique, shot and killed the territorial secretary, Edwin S. McCook, in a barroom brawl. Business rivalries, election animosities, railroad quarrels, and the widespread animus against the Governor and his associates were the background for this crime, which brought feuds and party brawls to a sensational climax.

The rulings of Judge Barnes on both the railway case and the Wintermute trial continued to irk both the Governor and the new territorial secretary, Oscar Whitney, McCook's father-in-law, who had been named to the vacant position out of sympathy for the murdered man's wife. In the absence of Burbank, Secretary Whitney transferred Barnes to the northern district and assigned Chief Justice Peter C. Shannon to Yankton. It was generally believed that the reassignment of the judges had been agreed upon by Burbank and Whitney as a rebuke to Barnes. This action had immediate repercussions in Washington. Under instructions from President Grant, Secretary of the Interior Delano at first requested Whitney to revoke the reassignment, but upon further deliberation reversed himself and upheld the reassignment. The executive office at Yankton, it was decided, possessed full discretionary powers for the transfer of judges.

There were extenuating circumstances which made Judge Barnes' reassignment defensible. In 1871, at his own request Chief Justice French had been assigned to the Pembina district by the Supreme Court, even though he failed to change his residence from Yankton. When Peter C. Shannon replaced French as chief justice in April,

1873, he claimed jurisdiction over the Yankton district "as a matter of law and right," arguing that French had been assigned to Pembina without any authority of law. The claim was disputed by Judge Barnes, who had a specific appointment to replace W. W. Brookings on the bench at Yankton. Since the two new judges could not agree on their districts, Governor Burbank, acting upon the advice of the Attorney General at Washington, officially assigned Shannon to the Pembina district and Barnes to the Yankton district vacated by Brookings. In a letter to the Attorney General, Burbank wrote that although he considered the assignment the best that could be made at the time, he would feel free to change it if the judges should desire it or if, in his opinion, the public interests might require it.[2]

It was the abuse rather than the use of executive power that made the reassignment of Judge Barnes by Secretary Whitney so reprehensible. Clearly Chief Justice Shannon had looked upon his Pembina assignment as temporary, and his claims on the Yankton district affected the decision that the transfer of Barnes could stand. Nevertheless, the furore over the reassignment and all the emotionalism and tension aroused by Wintermute's two trials and his acquittal, indicated a scandalous state of affairs in the Territory.

Governor Burbank's influence finally ran out. His record of political manipulation and financial exploitation had brought the territorial system into disrepute, and official pressure from Washington brought his resignation, effective January 1, 1874. Secretary Whitney was permitted to continue in office until the closing months of the new year.

Burbank's resignation marked the close of a distinct political period for Dakota Territory. The desire to end factional strife and restore party harmony found expression in November, 1873, when Yankton's rival Republican journals consolidated to form the *Press and Dakotaian.* Judge Jefferson P. Kidder of Vermillion was nominated as a compromise candidate for delegate and in the subsequent 1874 election captured the seat from the Democratic incumbent, Armstrong, by a two-to-one margin.

John L. Pennington, the new Governor, took office on the last day of December, 1873. He had been a strong Unionist in his native state of North Carolina during the Civil War, and later had moved to

[2] Governor John A. Burbank to Attorney General George W. Williams, Washington, D. C., April 14, 1873. Records of the Department of Justice, Chronological File of Dakota, 1873, National Archives.

Alabama, where he was prominently associated with the Reconstruction program imposed on the South. At Yankton he studiously avoided involvement in factional strife and participation in nominating conventions. Like most other governors, he felt his interests lay in the Territory and he established permanent residence.

THE BLACK HILLS COUNTIES

The major political problems during Pennington's four-year term grew out of the Black Hills gold rush. Local provisional governments, although they had no legal powers, established some semblance of order in the several mining communities. Their work supplemented that of the miners' districts which handled matters bearing on mineral claims and water rights as well as occasional homicide cases. The only jurisdiction assumed by the federal government concerned the liquor traffic on Indian reservations. The conviction of a Custer saloonkeeper in the district court at Yankton in April, 1876, received wide publicity as the first legal case to come from the Black Hills.

In anticipation of Congressional ratification of the Indian treaty, the Territorial Legislature in February, 1877, enacted a mining code and prescribed machinery for incorporating mining associations. It also created Custer, Lawrence, and Pennington counties in the Black Hills. In providing for new counties, the governor was authorized to name not only the county commissioners, but also all other county officials, without regard to any Black Hills residence. This deviation from the customary practice in organizing new counties seemed justified by the transient character of the mining population, which made it virtually impossible to check residential qualifications.

A wave of claim-jumping in the Deadwood community following ratification of the Indian treaty made the establishment of law and order imperative; all the local provisional governments had ceased to function as soon as the treaty was ratified. Miners who had located claims prior to the extinguishment of the Indian title found their property seized by armed men, and there were no local officials to whom they could appeal for protection.

Responding to the plea for early action, Governor Pennington appointed most of the officials from outside the Black Hills and included a number of Yankton residents. The great outcry that immediately went up was motivated to some extent by sheer partisanship. This was especially so in Lawrence County, which was more populous than the other two. As the majority of its citizens were Democrats, they were highly critical of the Republican appointees. But the main opposition to the appointments came from communities whose county-seat aspirations had been ignored. The selection of Sheridan over Rapid City as county seat for Pennington County evoked heavy criticism and allegations that a Yankton "ring," which included the Governor, was promoting a new townsite. The first term of circuit court was held at Sheridan in October, 1877, when accommodations were still so limited that some lawyers had to sleep on the floor of the log courthouse. The town was also for a short time the designated location for a United States land office. The temporary selection of Crook City as county seat for Lawrence County was extremely objectionable to Deadwood, and the residents of Custer charged collusion in the selection of Hayward City.

The dissatisfaction with Governor Pennington's appointments led to demands that they be replaced by popularly elected officials. When county clerks refused to call special elections, they were over-ruled by Judge Granville G. Bennett, the jurist assigned to the new judicial district. At a special election on November 15, 1877, Custer, Deadwood, and Rapid City were the popular choices for county-seat honors in their respective counties, and new county officials were named by the voters. In Lawrence County, scene of the major contest, most of the Democratic candidates were victorious. By the end of the year elected officials had taken over everywhere except at Custer, where the original appointees succeeded in delaying the induction of new officials for several months.

The uncertain location of the boundary line separating Dakota Territory from Wyoming complicated the task of instituting civil authority. Rumors that Custer and Deadwood lay west of the 104th meridian grew stronger as county treasurers started their tax-collecting rounds. By mid-July the boundary line was established, and there were no further attempts at evasion by Deadwood saloon keepers who had been refusing to pay license fees.

Most of the legal problems in the Black Hills concerned the status of property rights established prior to the extinction of the Indian title. In the fall of 1877 Judge Bennett conceded full legal rights to settlers who had acquired property before the Indian agreement. It was his contention that the treaty of 1868 had merely given the Indians the right of occupancy and did not preclude prospecting and the acquisition of property in the Indian country under the mining laws of the United States. In 1879, when he was no longer on the bench, the territorial Supreme Court reversed Bennett's ruling by a unanimous decision.

The southwestern Dakotans' dissatisfaction with the Yankton government had been pointedly expressed even before Governor Pennington's unpopular county appointments. In July, 1876, Congress received a petition from the Black Hills requesting that a separate territory be formed out of the mineral region, and a bill providing for the establishment of the Territory of the Black Hills was introduced in December. But it was not until Pennington announced his appointments that the separatist movement gained real momentum. Then the separatists charged that "farmer legislators" from the "cow counties" had grossly neglected the mining communities, had inflicted unjust and oppressive enactments on them, and had failed to give the Black Hills a fair legislative apportionment. "We have had about enough corn-growing legislation for the mining regions," a Black Hills editor wrote, "and do not propose to have any more."[3]

The separatist movement was headed mostly by Deadwood men who came from the older mining country and were out of sympathy with those who hailed from eastern Dakota and other nonmining areas. As zealous Democrats they were innately opposed to Republican domination in political matters, and their grievances with the Territorial Legislature were more fancied than real.

A proposal for the creation of Lincoln Territory came before the Congress during the summer of 1877, sponsored by representatives from Nebraska and Colorado. It provided that the eastern parts of Wyoming and Montana territories be combined with the western part of Dakota Territory to form a parallelogram extending 300 miles from east to west and 360 miles from north to south. The measure was vigorously opposed not only in the older settlements of Dakota Territory but also in Montana and Wyoming. Kidder, the Dakota delegate, countered with a proposal to divide the Territory along the 46th parallel. When it became apparent that Congress would not give favorable consideration to either bill, there was a move to redraw the boundary lines, dividing Dakota Territory vertically along the 100th meridian. Bismarck, which had hopes of be-

---

[3] *Black Hills Daily Pioneer* (Deadwood), July 1, 1877.

coming the capital for the western half, strongly supported the new proposal.

The failure of the separatist movement forced the Black Hills communities to reconcile themselves to the existing order at Yankton. The composition of the population, moreover, was altered by an increasing number of settlers from eastern communities. Nevertheless, a strong conviction that they could outvote the rest of the Territory gave the Black Hills residents, regardless of their origin, an exaggerated sense of importance and led to arrogant demands for greater representation in the Legislature and a stronger voice in party councils. Despite local differences, the Black Hills settlements possessed a unity of interest that enabled them to work together and exert a strong sectional influence.

The potential strength of the Black Hills counties was a matter of concern to both political parties as the election of 1878 approached. Less than five thousand votes had been cast in the special county elections held in the fall of 1877, but Black Hills leaders claimed a much larger voting population. Both parties were anxious to placate the Black Hills residents. The Democratic central committee was especially liberal in apportioning thirty convention delegates to the mining section out of a total of ninety-five; in the Republican convention, twenty-nine out of one hundred and thirty-nine delegates were allotted to the Black Hills. The two parties held their nominating conventions at Yankton on the same date during the latter part of August.

When the Republican convention opened, Jefferson P. Kidder, who had been easily re-elected in 1876 and desired a third term, was the favored candidate. Other candidates were Gideon C. Moody of Yankton and Judge Granville G. Bennett, who had the support of the entire Black Hills delegation. The Moody forces exerted themselves to prevent Kidder's nomination, and began shifting their votes to Bennett on the eighth ballot to break a deadlock. A stampede to the Black Hills candidate followed, and Bennett was declared the unanimous choice of the convention. This was bitterly resented by Kidder's supporters, who claimed their candidate had actually commanded a majority at one point during the final minutes of the balloting. Moody was rewarded by an appointment to the judge's bench vacated by Bennett, and the Union County man who started the stampede to Bennett became chairman of the central committee.

Bennett's choice over Kidder showed clearly the change in the complexion of territorial politics which had taken place by the late seventies. The convention manipulations and the combinations formed between sections forecast the political pattern for the next decade.

The Democrats nominated Bartlett Tripp of Yankton. During the campaign influential Republicans in the southeastern counties threw their support to the Democratic candidate, but Bennett won by a comfortable margin, even though he lost a number of counties, including Clay. The Black Hills section, polling somewhat in excess of thirty per cent of the territorial vote, gave a majority to the Democratic party.

Governor Pennington hoped to be reappointed, but he was unpopular in the Black Hills, and at Yankton there were active gubernatorial candidates who did not hesitate to belittle him or even to spread calumnious reports about his character. In the spring of 1878 he was replaced as governor by William A. Howard of Michigan. President Hayes was deeply obligated to Howard for helping to swing the Michigan delegation to his support at the Republican Convention of 1876. Although reluctant to accept any official position because of ill health, Howard finally agreed to take the Dakota appointment. In case he had declined, the President had been ready to reappoint Pennington;[4] instead he was named collector of internal revenue for Dakota Territory as a consolation.

A NEW POLITICAL ERA

Governor Howard, who was old as well as ailing, found the official atmosphere at Yankton congenial. Unlike his predecessors, he had his political career behind him and was less likely to come in serious conflict with Dakota politicians. For advice the new governor leaned heavily upon a small coterie of officials and businessmen who, through marriage ties and close social and professional relationships, were able to wield tremendous influence in Yankton government circles. The group included former governors and other prominent residents who had originally come to the capital city by way of federal patronage. Among them was W. H. H. Beadle, who served for a time as Howard's private secretary, and later became

---

[4] Martha M. Bigelow, *The Political Services of William Alanson Howard* (Ann Arbor: reprint from *Michigan History*, March, 1958), p. 24.

Superintendent of Public Instruction. The influence of the Yankton oligarchy also extended to the Indian Bureau thanks to the policy initiated by President Grant of permitting the Episcopal Church to nominate most of the Indian agents in Dakota Territory.

The concentration of political power in Yankton is indicated by the fact that except for the Governor and the auditor every major territorial official in 1879 was a permanent resident of the town. Heading the political empire was the Secretary of the Territory, George H. Hand. Hand settled in Yankton in 1865 and served in various minor positions until his appointment as Secretary in 1874. He was capable and highly respected, and closely related by marriage to influential families at the capital. His cousin was the publisher of Dakota's leading newspaper, the *Press and Dakotaian.*

As Secretary of the Territory, Hand exerted no small influence over political appointments as well as Indian patronage and contracts. This had been true during the Pennington administration, and when Howard took over the executive office, Hand became even more influential. Because of his familiarity with territorial matters, he was freely consulted by the new governor. More than that, during Howard's frequent illnesses and prolonged absences from Yankton, Secretary Hand assumed all the gubernatorial responsibilities by virtue of his official position.

Governor Howard's tenure was cut short by his death at Washington on April 10, 1880, following an illness that had incapacitated him for nearly six months. He had served long enough, however, to gain an insight into the emergent political problems and to demonstrate his independent spirit and high regard for principle. He was of unimpeachable character and was generally held in high esteem. W. H. H. Beadle, with whose views on education the Governor was in full accord, called him the most unselfish man and public officer he ever knew.[5]

Howard was in the executive office at a time when significant political changes were occurring. The Territory's growth from a cluster of settlements in the southeastern corner into three distinct and diverse sections not only increased the burdens of government, but also drastically altered the relationship between the legislative and executive branches. Although Howard's official relationship with

[5] "Personal Memoirs of William H. H. Beadle," in *South Dakota Historical Collections,* III (1906) , 169.

the Territorial Legislature was more cordial and more harmonious than that of subsequent governors, he did not hesitate to veto legislation he regarded as injurious to the public interest.

The Black Hills section was especially demanding in its requirements. During the summer of 1879 Governor Howard complained that Lawrence County alone was absorbing more than half the revenues of the Territory, although not a single dollar had yet been paid into the territorial treasury by any Black Hills county. Most of the expenditures Howard referred to were for the care of convicts and insane persons from the mining communities; more cases of insanity came out of Lawrence County than all the rest of the Territory.

Since there was no provision for the care and confinement of mental patients and criminals, the facilities of neighboring states were used. In 1873 an arrangement had been made with Minnesota to care for insane persons from Dakota Territory, but because of overcrowded conditions the service could not be continued beyond January, 1879. Facilities in other states were unavailable, and the Territory was thrown upon its own resources.

After a careful search for accommodations in several towns in the older settlements, in September, 1878, Governor Howard on his own responsibility and at his own expense moved two unoccupied immigrant houses from Yankton to a school section two miles north of the town. They had been built at public expense in 1875 for use by German-Russian immigrants before they located on claims. The Legislature officially located the territorial hospital and provided funds for its maintenance in February, 1879. It also reimbursed Governor Howard in part for the money advanced by him in erecting the hospital buildings prior to the legislative session.

There was a move in the legislative session of 1879 to establish a territorial penitentiary, but the need was not as immediate as in the case of the hospital for the insane. Convicts could still be economically cared for under existing arrangements with Michigan and Iowa. Also, it seemed reasonable to expect that the federal government would eventually build a territorial penitentiary, or at least furnish substantial financial assistance. The Legislature made provisions for a penitentiary building at Sioux Falls, but Governor Howard withheld his approval. It was built two years later, the federal government contributing a second wing to the building.

Governor Howard's veto of the penitentiary bills in 1879 and his intimate association with Yankton's leading citizenry made him a target for attack by Richard F. Pettigrew of Sioux Falls. In the advancement of his own political interests, Pettigrew did not hesitate to cross swords with the so-called Yankton "ring." The *Press and Dakotaian*'s monopoly in printing territorial laws became the subject of special investigation by an unfriendly legislative committee headed by Pettigrew. Governor Howard regarded Pettigrew's conduct as motivated entirely by malice against Secretary Hand, who dispensed the printing patronage and who was accused of official misconduct by Pettigrew.

Secretary Hand also was regarded with suspicion by his superior, Secretary Schurz of the Department of the Interior, during the unsuccessful prosecution in federal court at Yankton of former Indian Agent Dr. Henry F. Livingston. Hand was related to Livingston by marriage and, like most members of the Yankton community, was entirely out of sympathy with the prosecution. Pettigrew's attempts to have Hand removed from office all were blocked by Governor Howard.

Upon Howard's death, Secretary Hand became an active candidate for the vacant office, and except for loud dissent from Pettigrew, received nearly universal support throughout the Territory. Within three days following Howard's death, however, Hayes offered the post to a West Virginia attorney, who saw fit to decline. A month later he appointed a New Hampshire resident, Nehemiah G. Ordway, who was duly installed at Yankton the latter part of June. Apparently Hayes had given no serious consideration to Hand's aspirations. Savage attacks made by the *Press and Dakotaian* upon Secretary Schurz and his policy concerning the Sioux agencies could hardly incline Washington toward a friendly feeling for Hand, despite his written disclaimer to Schurz of any personal connection with the Yankton newspaper.

In his decision not to appoint Hand, Hayes may well have been influenced by certain views Governor Howard had formed concerning the Dakota governorship. His experiences at Yankton had convinced him that only a nonresident governor would have sufficient detachment to resist local groups and special interests within the Territory. After Howard's death, his family let his views be known to the President.[6]

[6] William S. Howard, May 1, 1880, letter to Rutherford B. Hayes, in Hayes Papers, Hayes Memorial Library, Fremont, Ohio.

Shortly after Governor Ordway's arrival, Pettigrew announced that he intended to stand for Bennett's seat in Congress. In the pre-convention campaign, he succeeded in capturing nearly all the delegations from the southeastern section except the delegates from Union and Yankton counties, who supported Bennett. John B. Raymond, a United States marshal living at Fargo, shared with Bennett the delegates from the northern and Black Hills sections. Pettigrew appealed to the Republican voters to end political domination by federal officeholders and a knot of politicians at the capital. Bennett and Raymond had both come to the Territory with federal commissions, and both were denounced by Pettigrew as carpetbaggers. For Pettigrew, it was an anti-Yankton as well as an anti-Bennett campaign. As was generally the case during the territorial period, factional divisions within the sections proved to be more significant than any sectional alignment. Pettigrew won the nomination on the seventh ballot.

The Democratic party, hoping to profit from possible disaffection within Republican ranks, named a candidate from the northern section, but Pettigrew won by almost a two-to-one margin. Moreover, the political organization he had built up during the campaign also won control of the lawmaking body. By the end of 1880 the stage was set for a head-on collision between a Pettigrew-dominated legislature and a new governor.

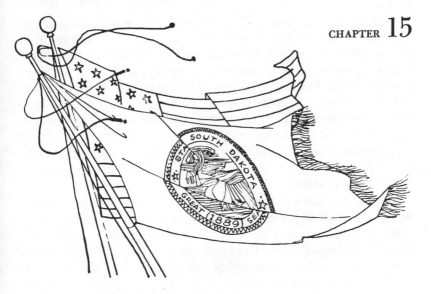

CHAPTER 15

Prelude to Statehood

NEHEMIAH G. ORDWAY served as governor during the peak years of the Great Dakota Boom when virtually every part of the Territory was in a state of change. The speculative activities of townsite interests and the strife over organizing county governments, including intense rivalries over county-seat locations, caused great excitement and confusion. The rapid growth of the central counties in the James Valley foreshadowed plots to relocate the territorial capital, and the general population increase accentuated sectional rivalries, giving momentum to a movement for separate statehood for the southern area. A combination of all these developments, together with the self-assertive character of the Governor, made the four years of the Ordway regime the most turbulent period in the entire span of South Dakota history.

The conflicts over county government were characteristic. After a county was organized and its county seat chosen by popular vote, attempts to relocate the county seat were likely to cause further confusion. County-seat fights were common occurrences, and were accompanied in many instances by the forcible removal of county records. The struggle between Big Stone City and Milbank, in Grant County in 1881, for example, resulted in costly litigation, embittered feelings, and near violence. In Spink County a six-year fight over the county-seat location all but led to armed hostilities in the fall of 1884. Some three hundred settlers marched upon Redfield following the removal of the county records from a farmhouse at Old Ashton by Redfield residents. Two companies of territorial militia were dispatched from Fargo to the scene of the "Spink County War," but order had been restored by the time of their arrival. Governor Ordway described at length the confusing county organization situation in his annual report to the Secretary of the Interior in October, 1883.[1] It was just one of the problems of the boom era with which he was involved.

Ordway was not a political novice. He had been sergeant at arms in the House of Representatives from 1863 to 1875 during a period when political morality at the national capital was at a low level. He was strong-willed and resolute in his ideas and determined, moreover, to exploit opportunities afforded by the Territory for his own political advancement.

THE ORDWAY REGIME

The impressive-looking, gray-bearded executive lost no time in acquainting himself with his bailiwick. Less than a month after his arrival in Yankton in June, 1880, with his family, he set out upon a tour of the Black Hills and the major communities in the northern part of the Territory. Shortly thereafter he left for the East to exhibit Dakota products. No previous governor had displayed so much energy and such seeming devotion to the territorial interests.

Ordway's statesmanlike manner extended to his message to the Legislature when it convened at Yankton the following January. The document covered a wide range of topics, presuming to advise an immature society whose political institutions might require remodeling in preparation for statehood. The master role which the Governor wished to play is apparent from a letter to President Hayes two days after the opening of the session. In referring to his message, Ordway wrote:

. . . I felt constrained to point out what seemed to me the radical defects in the Territorial laws as they now stand.

There has been a systematic effort for several years past in this Territory to ignore the National authority and in some instances to thwart U. S.

[1] "Report of the Governor of Dakota," in *Report of the Secretary of the Interior, House Executive Documents,* 48 Cong., 1 Sess., 1883–1884 (Serial Number 2191), Vol. 2, 536–539.

Officials in the discharge of their duties. I . . . have endeavored to impress upon the Members the importance of rising above local jobbery and act for the interest of all the people of the Territory.

. . . I have some hope that I shall be able to secure legislation which will ultimately place the Territory in a position where a State Government may safely be extended over a part or the whole of the Territory.[2]

Although there was no open clash, the lawmakers did not hesitate to assert their independence. Much of the unprecedentedly large volume of legislation concerned the creation of new counties and the revision of county boundaries. Other measures authorized the construction of county jails and courthouses, the issuance of county bonds, and the refunding of county debts. Ordway interposed a veto against much of this legislation. Several measures he disallowed upon the advice of the attorney general at Washington. The Governor particularly objected to the numerous bills for county buildings and for bonding newly organized counties without submitting the propositions to a popular vote. In only a few instances were his objections sustained.

Ordway also made an effort to resist the scramble for territorial institutions. The legislative body showed a special predilection for normal schools, authorizing institutions at Alexandria, Madison, Spearfish, Springfield, and Watertown without providing any appropriations. Ordway objected to overburdening the Territory with such institutions for the gratification of local interests and unsuccessfully tried to limit the authorization to a single school at Madison. At the same time, he approved a measure locating the agricultural college at Brookings. The university had been located at Vermillion in 1862, and so required no new enactment for its establishment.

To many people throughout the Territory, the Governor's behavior contrasted favorably with the logrolling and other manipulations of the Legislature. The severest stricture against the lawmakers came from a Democratic editor who referred to them as "a howling mob of gangsters and corruptionists, caring nothing for right or law, but led by the nose by one or two tricksters whose whole object was to fill their pockets by schemes of jobbery and plunder."[3]

In spite of the tendency of the legislators to disregard the chief executive, the outward relations between the two branches of government remained cordial for the duration of the session. Ordway

[2] N. G. Ordway, January 13, 1881, letter to Rutherford B. Hayes, in Hayes Papers, Hayes Memorial Library, Fremont, Ohio.
[3] Yankton *Dakota Herald*, February 26, 1881.

was discreet and courteous, and succeeded in having most of his appointments confirmed by the Council. He refrained from criticizing the Legislature until a few weeks after adjournment when, in a Washington interview, he referred to the lawmaking body as a "crude affair" which went off on a tangent and indulged in some harum-scarum legislation.[4] In subsequent interviews he elaborated further on his relations with the Legislature.

In characterizing a majority of the legislators as irresponsible and extravagant, he was furthering a political feud between himself and Richard F. Pettigrew, the territorial delegate. Pettigrew's supporters were in control of the Legislature, and Ordway's attack on them was part and parcel of a campaign to discredit the delegate and elevate himself to a position of political dominance.[5]

Quite obviously Ordway intended to share the Dakota patronage with the delegate. Only through a direct appeal to Senator Platt of New York was Pettigrew able to maintain his patronage prerogatives. There is evidence that Ordway called upon Pettigrew to suggest that they combine their influence and work in harmony throughout the statehood campaign so as to ensure for themselves the two Senate seats, but Ordway's overtures fell upon deaf ears and led to a complete estrangement.[6] In the meantime, Ordway maintained a condescending and patronizing attitude, posing as a champion of the public against "land rings" and unscrupulous politicians trying to despoil the Territory.

In the early part of May, Pettigrew filed charges against the Governor and demanded his removal from office. In September a four-page sheet captioned "Ordway's Record" was printed anonymously on the press of a Sioux Falls newspaper owned by the delegate. The publication made a vicious attack on the Governor, alleging misconduct in his relations with the Territorial Legislature and also charging him with malfeasance while serving as sergeant at arms in Congress. Included in the defamatory materials was a personal letter solicited by Pettigrew from the head of a Congressional committee that had conducted an inquiry into Ordway's conduct. The former

[4] See *Press and Dakotaian,* April 8, 1881.
[5] An excellent account of the Ordway regime appears in Howard R. Lamar, *Dakota Territory, 1861–1889—a Study of Frontier Politics* (New Haven: Yale University Press, 1956), pp. 177–243.
[6] R. F. Pettigrew, "Early Day History of Governor Ordway," unpublished manuscript in File OP, Pettigrew Papers, Pettigrew Museum of Natural History, Sioux Falls. This manuscript forms the basis for the references to Ordway in R. F. Pettigrew, *Imperial Washington* (Chicago: C. H. Kerr and Co., 1922), Chapter 10.

Congressman stated: "I have no hesitancy in giving it as my opinion, in view of all the evidence developed against him that he is one of the most corrupt and unprincipled men that has ever disgraced and degraded the public service of this country."[7]

To many Dakota residents, the quarrel between Pettigrew and Ordway seemed to be a private vendetta. Ordway had generally won their esteem by championing the rights of the people against a "legislative gang," controlled by the territorial delegate. On the other hand, Pettigrew, through his ruthless political methods, had made many enemies. Most territorial officials at Yankton made common cause with the Governor against Pettigrew as did many of the foremost citizens of the community.[8]

During the summer of 1882 the anti-Pettigrew element promoted Secretary Hand for delegate. Governor Ordway gladly joined forces with this group. The preconvention campaign was especially bitter in the southern counties, and many contested delegations appeared at the Republican nominating convention held at Grand Forks early in September. Most of the county delegations from the northern section favored John B. Raymond of Fargo, while the southern counties east of the Missouri were the particular battleground for the Hand and Pettigrew forces.

Although not a delegate to the convention, Ordway accompanied the Yankton delegation and played an important part in directing strategy. Hand controlled a large number of uncontested delegations and, with the help of friendly delegates from the northern section, was in a position to dominate the credentials committee. Perceiving the hopelessness of his cause, Pettigrew entered into a combination with enough northern delegates to assure the seating of his own supporters. As a result, the convention voted down the majority report of the credentials committee and seated most of the Pettigrew delegations. When North Dakota delegations appeared to be voting to seat Pettigrew supporters, Ordway excitedly rushed out upon the floor to keep the delegates in line. At that moment, Pettigrew dramatically stepped forward to withdraw his own candidacy

---

[7] J. M. Glover, letter to R. F. Pettigrew, July 24, 1881, in File OP, Pettigrew Papers. A copy of "Ordway's Record" is found in the same file.

[8] *Press and Dakotaian*, April 24, 1882. Following the publication of "Ordway's Record" and the subsequent attempt to effect Ordway's removal from office, ex-Governors Edmunds, Faulk, and Pennington joined W. H. H. Beadle and other territorial officials in endorsing the Ordway Administration. Copy of endorsement in Territorial Papers, Appointments Division—Dakota, "Papers of N. G. Ordway," File 165, National Archives.

and to place John B. Raymond, the northern counties' favorite, in nomination. As a result, the northern section carried off the main prize while the Pettigrew faction controlled the party organization.

In strange contrast with the preceding session, Governor Ordway was able to work in harmony with a majority of the Legislature when it assembled at Yankton in January, 1883. He disapproved relatively few bills, and in only one or two instances was any attempt made to pass legislation over his veto. An avalanche of special legislation reflected the mood of the boom. The Legislature created forty-one new counties, naming half of them for members; in eighteen others, it redefined or readjusted boundary lines.

Northern communities were favored with three normal schools, an insane asylum at Jamestown, a territorial penitentiary at Bismarck, a university at Grand Forks, and an agricultural college at Fargo. The southern counties secured a reform school at Plankinton and a school for the deaf and dumb at Sioux Falls. Normal schools at Madison, Spearfish, and Springfield were re-established. The only objection raised by the Governor with reference to territorial institutions concerned several proposals for normal schools designed primarily to boom townsites in northern counties. He also vetoed a bill locating a school of mines at Rapid City.

RELOCATING THE TERRITORIAL CAPITAL

The relocation of the territorial capital was the most important piece of legislation enacted in the 1883 session. Hitherto, Yankton had been successful in keeping the capital issue in the background. While conceding the eventual removal of the capital to a more central location, the citizens of Yankton argued plausibly that relocation should await the outcome of the question of division and statehood. However, as the field of potential candidates widened under the impetus of the boom, Yankton could no longer forestall combinations against her.

The parliamentary maneuvers behind the capital removal in 1883 are not altogether clear; moreover, many writers have exaggerated their melodramatic aspects in the effort to cast in villainous roles both Governor Ordway and Alexander McKenzie, Bismarck lobbyist for both the Northern Pacific Railroad and northern townsite interests.

Whether he masterminded the proceedings or not, the Governor certainly participated in a combination against Yankton. He may have desired to place the capital in a location of his own choosing for private gain. His personal interests, however, extended beyond the confines of any particular locality. His major motive may have been a desire to punish Yankton. Although the "Yankton oligarchy" had joined him in common cause against Pettigrew, it was showing signs of resistance toward his haughty manner and dictatorial methods by the time the Legislature convened. In fairness to Ordway, one should note the suggestions for selecting a new capital in his 1881 message.

In the third week of the session, to the surprise of even the representatives of Beadle County, Councilman Walsh of Grand Forks introduced a bill designating Huron as the capital. Twice reported adversely, the bill was referred back to a special committee which sent it to the Council without recommendation. A special committee of five then took over and evolved a bill placing full authority for the selection of a new location in a commission of nine men. The Legislature devised the commission plan because of the difficulty in obtaining a majority vote for any specific site. The representatives from the southern counties divided 8 to 7 on the bill in the House and 4 to 5 in the Council. The solid support of the northern section assured passage of the measure. An amendment requiring popular approval of the commission's selection almost carried in the Council.

The nine members of the commission were named in the bill, out of distrust of the chief executive. Six came from the southern section. Each of the seven Council members favorable to removal named a member of the commission. McKenzie and Governor Ordway chose the other two commissioners. Arriving at Yankton after the removal combination had taken shape, McKenzie played a prominent part in the later stages of the parliamentary maneuvering.

The removal bill not only overshadowed all other legislation, but also bore close relationship to other enactments, including the location of territorial institutions and financial support for the agricultural college at Brookings and the university at Vermillion.[9] The removal group was in full control and worked in close cooperation

[9] For an excellent account of the manipulations and stratagems in the "game of grab" in securing public institutions for the northern section during the 1883 session and their relation to the removal of the capital from Yankton, see Louis G. Geiger, *University of the Northern Plains: A History of the University of North Dakota, 1883–1958* (Grand Forks: University of North Dakota Press, 1958), pp. 14–20.

with the Governor. The latter readily gave his approval to bills sponsored by members favorable to removal and vetoed measures introduced by antiremovalists. To Ordway's critics the Governor appeared
to be indulging in the same tactics of logrolling and jobbery that he
deplored so much in the preceding session.

In accordance with the enactment, the capital commission was to
select "a suitable site for the seat of government . . . , due regard
being had to its accessibility from all portions of the Territory and
its general fitness for a capital." A candidate had to offer at least
$100,000 and provide 160 acres of land.

The opposition immediately initiated injunction proceedings
against the commission so as to prevent its organization at Yankton
as required by law. Undaunted by such legal obstacles, the nine
members secretly proceeded to Sioux City where in the early hours of
April 3, 1883, they boarded a special train consisting of an engine
and a single coach, and set out for the capital. As they reached the
city limits at about six o'clock that morning, they halted the train
briefly while they organized themselves. Then followed a junketing
through the Territory by "The Capital on Wheels," as the commission was nicknamed, to inspect prospective sites and consider inducements. Eight of the eleven contenders lay south of the 46th
parallel, all but one of them in the central section. One candidate
in a central county was actually a paper town, while two others
had only a single building.

Bismarck won the prize on the thirteenth ballot because of the
failure of the southern counties to agree on a common choice. In
the final vote, three commissioners living at Deadwood, Canton, and
Elk Point, respectively, joined McKenzie and another northerner in
giving Bismarck a majority. Alexander Hughes of Elk Point, who
was by this time working in close relationship with the Governor,
cast the deciding vote. Ordway was on hand for the final balloting.
According to Burleigh F. Spaulding of Fargo, one of the northern
members of the commission, few in the beginning took Bismarck's
candidacy seriously. Legislators identified with the removal group
had advised him of a gentleman's agreement to locate the capital below the 46th parallel at some point fairly central to the southern
half if it should be admitted as a separate state, and yet readily accessible to all in the event of organization as a single state. This
understanding presumably explains why Bismarck was the only
prominent North Dakota town in the race. At no time did Spaul-

William Clark

Meriwether Lewis

John C. Frémont

William S. Harney

Henry Leavenworth

Manuel Lisa

Pierre Chouteau, Jr.

Fort Pierre, 1833

Sioux dressing buffalo meat and robes
(Painting by George Catlin)

Sketch of Fort Randall, 1860

Bull boats on the Missouri

The *Yellowstone,* first steamboat on upper Missouri
(*Painting by Charles Bodmer*)

George Crook

George A. Custer

Sitting Bull

Red Cloud

Struck by the Ree

Spotted Tail

Rosebud Agency, 1889

Big Foot's band at Grass Dance, August, 1890
(*Most of band killed later at Wounded Knee*)

Sioux Commission of 1889 at Crow Creek
(*Chairman Crook, second from right, seated*)

Oglala Sioux Delegation in Washington, D. C., 1880
(*Chief Red Cloud seated, center*)

J. B. S. Todd

William Jayne

Walter A. Burleigh

Moses K Armstrong

William H. H. Beadle

Newton Edmunds

N. G. Ordway

John A. Burbank

Deadwood, 1877

National Archi⬩

Custer Expedition approaching the Black Hills, 1874

Steamboats at Yankton landing, 1878

Black Hills stage coach, 1878

Fort Pierre-Deadwood freighting, 1885

Marketing wheat at Eureka, 1892

Arrival of German-Russian immigrants, Eureka, 1898

In the Rosebud country, Bonesteel, 1904

Registering for claims in Gregory County at Yankton, 1904

J. A. Anderson photo

Life on Rosebud Reservation, about 1900

Buffalo horses are hard to break

Coe I. Crawford

Peter Norbeck

Henry L. Loucks

Charles H. Burke

Andrew E. Lee

Arthur C. Mellette

Richard F. Pettigrew

Sod house

Claim shacks, 1904

Breaking sod, 1910

Steam threshing, Edmunds County, about 1892

Courtesy Miss Frances Byers

Horse-power threshing outfit, Perkins County, 1909

The modern combine

Queen Bee mill, 1881

Sioux Falls woolen mill, 1891

Yankton cement plant, 1891–1910

Sheepherder and wagon

Sheep on range

Roundup chuck wagon

Cowboy

Cowboy regalia

Range cattle, 1960

Soil drifts on Beadle County farm, 1935   Stock dam built in 1938

Contour strip-cropping, Sully County, 1958

Sioux Falls, 1872   S. J. Morrow photo

Sioux Falls, 1910   Courtesy Pettigrew Museum

Sioux Falls, 1960   Sioux Falls Chamber of Commerce

Early days in Rapid City, 1886

Rapid City, 1960

Lewis and Clark Lake and Gavins Point Dam

Fort Randall Dam and reservoir

Irrigation in Belle Fourche Valley

Ralph Herseth

Archie M. Gubbrud

Nils A. Boe

E.Y. Berry

Benjamin Reifel

George S. McGovern

William J. Bulow

M.Q. Sharpe

George T. Mickelson

Sigurd Anderson

Joe Foss

Francis H. Case

Karl E. Mundt

Doane Robinson

Niels E. Hansen

Badger Clark

Harvey Dunn

Gutzon Borglum

Oscar Howe

John Morrell Co. meat-packing plant, Sioux Falls

Bentonite mill in Belle Fourche

View of the University of South Dakota

Campus scene at South Dakota State University

Oahe Dam and reservoir

Big Bend Dam and Lake Sharpe

Pathfinder Power Plant in Sioux Falls

State cement plant in Rapid City

In the Black Hills

Mitchell Corn Palace

Mount Rushmore

In the Badlands

Slim Buttes area in Harding County

Platte-Winner bridge across Lake Francis Case

Governor's Pond and state capitol

Interstate 90 and 190 Interchange near Rapid City

Amphitheater of Black Hills Passion Play

Scene in Angostura Irrigation District

ding support Bismarck; the final ballot, in fact, found him voting for Redfield.[10]

Spaulding's version seems to bear out the contention of a Spink County legislator that he gave the removal bill his support under a pledge that the new capital would be located at some point south of the 46th parallel.[11] This promise was sufficient to encourage two Spink County towns—Frankfort and Redfield—to become candidates. At one time during the balloting, Redfield actually commanded three votes.

Governor Ordway bore the brunt of the charges of corruption and illegality directed at the capital commission. Feeling ran so high at Yankton that an attempt on his life was feared. He vehemently denied having taken part in the inception of the removal scheme, and sought to defend himself as well as the Legislature against charges of intimidation and jobbery.

The removal of the capital created a sharp cleavage between the northern and southern sections. Prior to this, division along an east and west line, presumably the 46th parallel, was generally taken for granted. Petitions advocating division had appeared in Congress as early as 1870. In anticipation of division, bonds issued for territorial institutions were by statutory provision made an express obligation of the section in which the institutions were to be located. Before 1883, the northern counties had been favorable to division and immediate statehood for the southern section. With the territorial capital in their midst, they began to shift their ground, opposing division and favoring a single state. In the southern counties, on the other hand, the animosities generated by the removal fight led to a redoubling of efforts for separate statehood.

CAMPAIGN FOR STATEHOOD

The campaign for statehood had started without much fanfare in 1879. In the initial stages, reformers were its major promoters. Foremost among these was William H. H. Beadle, the Territorial Superintendent of Public Instruction. Recalling how the common school

[10] Lewis F. Crawford, *History of North Dakota* (Chicago: American Historical Society, 1931), Chapter XXI, pp. 347–356, contains a lengthy discussion by Spaulding on the removal of the capital. In a letter to Professor O. G. Libby, December 9, 1932, Spaulding gives an account of the balloting based on a memorandum book kept by him during the voting. Letter in possession of North Dakota State Historical Society at Bismarck.

[11] Kingsbury, *History of Dakota Territory*, II, 1306.

lands in Indiana and other frontier states had been frittered away because of inadequate safeguards, Beadle hoped to avert a similar dissipation of the school lands in Dakota. With the support of Governor Howard and Reverend Joseph Ward, founder of Yankton College, Beadle launched a campaign to form a separate state out of the southern part of the Territory. His objective was a minimum price of ten dollars as well as other constitutional restrictions on the sale of school lands. In the meantime, he busied himself with the prosecution of squatters who were crowding onto school sections.

Through statehood clubs and in private discussion, Beadle and his friends sought public support for their movement. Called by a citizens' constitutional association, a convention met at Canton on June 21, 1882. The gathering included prominent clergymen and laymen interested in prohibition as well as in matters of policy that included the school lands question. Other individuals, more politically minded, were equally active and had full support and cooperation from both Beadle and Ward. Bills introduced into Congress called for immediate admission of the southern counties while continuing territorial status under some other name for the less populous northern counties. A school census taken by Beadle during the summer of 1882 substantiated the population claims of the southern section.

Political conditions in Congress seemed favorable for an enabling act during the winter of 1882–1883. The Republicans, in control of both houses of Congress for the first time in eight years, were generally regarded as friendly to the Dakota statehood movement. Moreover, a serious objection to statehood disappeared when Yankton County, under pressure from statehood leaders, made settlement with its creditors relative to the Dakota Southern railway bonds issued in 1871. Congress, however, adjourned on March 3, 1883, without a vote on the proposal. In the next session the Democrats were again in control of the lower house.

The failure of Congress to pass the division and statehood bill in early 1883 coincided with the turbulent scenes enacted in the waning legislative session at Yankton. Moreover, as if to compound his "villainy" against Yankton and the southern section, Governor Ordway vetoed a bill authorizing the southern counties to convene a constitutional convention, and marshalled all the forces at his command to oppose separate statehood.

The anti-Ordway movement and the campaign for separate statehood now coalesced. Political leaders at Yankton, who earlier had avoided close identification with the reform element, joined hands with the group represented by Beadle and Ward and actually took over the leadership in the statehood movement. A mass meeting at Huron in June took steps to form a constitution without legislative sanction and authorized a convention to meet at Sioux Falls the following September.

When the convention met, it accepted Beadle's proposals for placing restrictions on the sale of school lands despite sentiment fostered by speculative interests for a minimum price of $2.50 per acre. At the same time, the convention overwhelmingly rejected a prohibition clause lest its inclusion might jeopardize acceptance of the constitution. Yankton was named as the capital out of deference to outraged feelings in the community over the loss of the territorial capital. The Constitution of 1883 was approved by a vote of 12,336 to 6,814 in a relatively light poll. Several counties made no returns; in others, voting precincts remained closed. Despite energetic efforts to arouse their interest, many citizens considered the movement futile without legal sanction. Heaviest opposition came from Brookings, Clay, Lincoln, and Union counties, whose legislative representatives played such a prominent part in the capital removal. Pettigrew's own county, Minnehaha, also overwhelmingly rejected the constitution. The independent course pursued by the statehood leaders was a cause of resentment above the 46th parallel and strengthened materially the Ordway faction in the southern counties. Moreover, many voters undoubtedly followed the admonition of the Methodist Church and die-hard prohibitionists in voting against the constitution because of the omission of a prohibition clause from the document.

Despite the light vote, the statehood leaders claimed an overwhelming endorsement and descended upon Washington with a formal request for admission. There they found equally articulate delegations, headed by the Dakota governor, actively counterlobbying and imputing a seditious character to the statehood movement. The Republican-controlled Senate gave its approval to the Dakota statehood bill. The Democratic majority in the House, on the other hand, ignored it, denying a legal status to the Sioux Falls convention.

Ordway's intimate identification with the opposition to separate statehood intensified still further the efforts in the southern counties to remove him from office. The Governor's enemies, by now legion, turned with alacrity to the scandals attending the organization of county governments. In the case of a fraudulent organization of Douglas County in 1881, Ordway's conduct had been blameless. Because of the numerous county organizations formed under his authority a few years later, however, the Governor was highly vulnerable to charges of corruption and misconduct. Information came to light that Ordway, if not personally profiting from the appointment of county commissioners, was at least making it possible for close relatives and cronies from the East to do so. He was specifically accused of turning commissions of appointment over to his son for sale to the highest bidder.[12]

Ordway's political enemies continued to gather evidence of irregularities, especially in connection with the organization of Faulk and Hyde counties. An indictment by a grand jury at Yankton for corrupt practices, including acceptance of a bribe, was, however, quashed. A territorial governor, it was held, could be tried only under impeachment procedure. Consequently, the case against Ordway was never brought to trial. In view of the mounting sentiment against Ordway, President Arthur decided not to reappoint him in June, 1884, and replaced him with Gilbert A. Pierce, a Chicago newspaperman and former practicing lawyer.

The territorial government was still in a state of confusion when the new governor arrived. The legality of the capital commission was in question,[13] and some officials, notably Secretary Teller, were refusing to move. Governor Pierce, playing his hand cautiously, had himself sworn into office at Yankton on July 25 before proceeding to the new capital. When the new capitol building became ready for occupancy the following November, all the executive offices were installed at Bismarck.

Chastened by their loss of the capital to the northern section, the Republican leaders below the 46th parallel began to resolve their

[12] James H. Teller, Denver, May 23, 1933, letter to author. Teller, who had become Territorial Secretary in March, 1884, wrote half a century after the event, "As Secretary I signed and sealed the commissions, and I saw enough of the proceedings to know that there was graft in them . . . . Ordway thoroughly disliked me, because he could not use me, and because I defeated some of his county plans . . . ."

[13] Judge A. J. Edgerton at Yankton held the capital commission measure invalid. Upon reversal of his decision by the Territorial Supreme Court, the case was taken under appeal to the United States Supreme Court where it remained on the docket until 1889 when statehood ended the litigation.

factional differences. For the remainder of the territorial period the southern counties were to control the party conventions as well as dominate the legislative branch. No more delegates from the north were elected to Congress. Despite the appearance of harmony during the legislative session of 1885, there was a disposition to retaliate against the old removalist combination and to punish localities that had been favored the preceding session.

Governor Pierce tried to halt a further scramble for spoils in the allocation of public institutions. Bills vetoed by him included a proposal to establish a third territorial university at Ordway. He also vetoed a bill to remove the capital from Bismarck to Pierre. Many residents of the southern section had urged the Governor to veto the removal bill because of its promotion by speculative townsite interests. Bribery charges against Pierre lobbyists may have played a part in Pierce's decision to veto the measure. Like his predecessors, Governor Pierce deprecated the tendency toward special legislation.

The division advocates pressed their campaign and finally succeeded in obtaining legislative sanction for a constitutional convention. The measure empowered the convention not only to draw up a constitution for the new state, but also to provide a full slate of state officials. The Dakota State League replaced citizens' clubs that had been organized by Beadle and his associates in the earlier stages of the statehood movement.

The constitutional convention, representing all but five of the organized counties in the southern section, assembled at Sioux Falls on September 8, 1885, to draft a frame of government for the second time within two years. The controversial prohibition issue was avoided by submitting the question to popular vote as a separate question. The northern boundary for the new state was placed at the 7th standard parallel, a more practical line than the 46th parallel of latitude, which would have required a redrawing of county lines. Aside from a greatly refined and expanded section on corporations, the new Constitution was virtually a replica of the 1883 document.

A significant feature of the 1885 Constitution was a clause denying any powers of government to the Legislature or any other officials "except such as may be authorized by the Congress of the United States." The adoption of such a restrictive clause represented a victory for the moderate element, headed by Judge A. J. Edgerton of Yankton and Gideon C. Moody of Deadwood. This group wished to avoid any clash with Congress. A more radical position was taken by Hugh J. Campbell, also of Yankton, who maintained that the citizens possessed an inherent right to initiate and activate a state government without waiting for an enabling act. In advancing this view, Campbell received support from Joseph Ward and other reform leaders.

Campbell's revolutionary views had received wide circulation following the failure of Congress to enact a statehood measure during the session of 1882–1883 and had furnished the rationale for both constitutional conventions. By adopting the restraining clause, the moderates accepted Campbell's "we are a state" doctrine as a means of exerting pressure upon Congress without putting the doctrine itself to a legal test.

At the general election in November, 1885, the voters overwhelmingly endorsed the new Constitution, adopted the prohibition clause by a small majority, and rejected a provision for minority representation intended to placate the Democratic party. Moreover, they elected two Congressmen and a full slate of state officials headed by Arthur C. Mellette of Watertown as governor. Huron was their choice for capital.

In accordance with plan, the Legislature met at Huron on December 14, organized itself, listened to a spirited address from "Governor" Mellette, and then proceeded to select two United States Senators. Although a strong supporter of the "we are a state" concept, Mellette cautioned against any action that might place the authority of the "State of Dakota" in conflict with the Territory and the national government. As if in response to such advice, the legislative body chose Edgerton, the moderate, for a Senate position over the more radical Campbell, who wished to set the state government in operation even if denied admission by Congress. Moody, also a moderate, was the unanimous choice for the second Senate position.

In Washington Congress divided along party lines, the Republicans supporting a bill for the admission of the "State of Dakota" and the Democrats, under southern leadership, sponsoring a bill for a single state. The result was a stalemate.

Impatient over the dilatory tactics in Congress and fearful lest an apathetic public might agree to a single state, Campbell made strong efforts during 1886 and 1887 to repeal the restraining clause. The moderate view, however, prevailed after sharp warning from Senator Benjamin Harrison of Indiana and other Republican supporters of the statehood bill that any radical action by the Dakotans would result in certain defeat for the entire division movement.[14] Through adjourned sessions of the constitutional convention and its own meetings, the State League tried to keep the statehood issue alive. The Legislature elected in 1885 reassembled the following year to keep the squatter government intact.

The national victory of the Democratic party in 1884 posed a new threat for the statehood proposal. Heretofore most Democratic leaders in the southern counties had supported the division movement. With the national organization committed to the single-state idea, the rank and file in Dakota began to align themselves with the national Democratic leaders, actually boycotting both the convention of 1885 and the referendum on the Constitution. Democratic office-holders, mostly residents, began to replace Republican appointees in the Territory. However, President Cleveland, exhibiting a genuine interest in civil service reform, permitted Governor Pierce, a Republican, to stay in office until February, 1887, even though Pierce had offered to resign earlier.

Pierce's continuance as governor was not looked on with favor by the Dakota Democrats. With the prestige of a national administration behind them, the party leaders had been hopeful of cutting down the Republican strength. A number of Dakota newspapers, noting that Democratic appointees were in the land offices, were shifting their party allegiance, and there were other indications of a Democratic resurgence. Delegate Gifford's majority for the preceding election was almost halved in 1886. Had a Democratic governor been in full control of the patronage, including the various territorial boards and public institutions, the party leaders argued, the Democratic party might actually have carried the election.

During the closing days of 1886 Cleveland finally yielded to partisan pressure and appointed as governor his close friend, Louis K. Church, a native of New York. Church had located at Huron the preceding year as associate justice of the Territorial Supreme Court. Church was one of a score of applicants for the office of governor and received wide support from the central counties. When it became apparent that the President was reluctant to name any prominent Dakotan, most of the active candidates withdrew their applications. Church was fairly popular and considered free from any

[14] O. S. Gifford, May 17, 1886, letter to A. C. Mellette, May 17, 1886, Mellette Papers, South Dakota State Historical Society, Pierre. Gifford was the territorial delegate to Congress at the time.

factional alignment or sectional bias. Many prominent Republicans, including Campbell and Mellette, joined in congratulating Cleveland upon his choice.[15]

The Legislature was already in session when Church took office on February 21, 1887. He exercised his veto powers freely in his efforts to restrain the lawmakers from making excessive appropriations. Among the vetoed bills was a proposal for a territorial university at Aberdeen. A measure locating a soldiers' home at Hot Springs became law over his veto. Legal training and an innate conservatism prompted Church to scrutinize each bill for technical flaws or improprieties. Despite his vigilance, appropriations for new buildings and other improvements at the various institutions raised the territorial debt to nearly $650,000.

Governor Church soon indicated his preference for a single state. This led to a quarrel within Democratic ranks in the southern section, dividing the party into "home-rule" and "carpetbag" factions, with the former generally favoring division. The anti-Church feeling among the Democrats became so bitter that an attempt was actually made to impeach the Governor.

The year 1887 was a crucial one for the divisionist forces. A referendum held in June, 1887, led to rather inconclusive results: a two-to-one vote favorable to division in the southern counties and a slightly larger margin of unfavorable sentiment in the northern section. The combined vote gave the divisionists a majority of approximately 5,000 votes. Despite energetic campaigning by the Dakota State League, a disappointingly light vote was cast in the southern counties on the question of division. Fourteen counties registered adverse majorities. The opposition was by no means confined to the border counties along the 7th standard parallel where Aberdeen had hopes for the capital in the event of organization as a single state, but extended to the Black Hills and to Clay, Moody, and Lincoln counties in the southeastern corner where many voters apparently favored a single state. The divisionist strength definitely lay in the central counties where the leading cities were all harboring capital ambitions. With the exception of Campbell and Edgerton, the most aggressive leaders in the statehood movement by this time came from the central part of South Dakota.

[15] Endorsements and correspondence in Territorial Papers, Appointments Division, Governor Dakota, File 235, National Archives.

Encouraged by the strong opposition to division as well as by apparent apathy on the part of the public, the single-state faction called a territorial convention at Aberdeen in December, 1887, to promote its cause. Governor Church and other notable Democrats participated in the convention. A number of prominent Republicans from the southern section, including ex-Governor John L. Pennington and former Delegate Granville Bennett, also gave active support to the single-state movement.

When it was seen that statehood would have to await the outcome of the approaching presidential election, the leaders of the Dakota State League took steps to reconcile the sectional differences. The southern section now offered to share with the northern counties the distinctive name of Dakota instead of monopolizing it for itself. It also agreed to the 7th standard parallel as the boundary line. The spokesmen for the State League, furthermore, pledged support to a movement for immediate admission of the northern section. Much of the northern antidivision sentiment in 1887 was rooted in the fear that statehood for the southern half alone might doom the north to indefinite territorial status. The mutual understanding thus reached between the two sections served to clear the way for the admission of twin states.

THE THIRTY-NINTH AND FORTIETH STATES

The Republican party made the admission of South Dakota a campaign issue in the presidential election of 1888. Republican successes consequently made the Democrats more conciliatory, and a quick switch by their leaders in Congress assured passage of an enabling act during the lame-duck session of 1888–1889. On February 22, 1889, President Cleveland affixed his signature to the Omnibus Bill creating four new states—North Dakota, South Dakota, Montana, and Washington.

The shifting political situation placed the Church Administration in an unenviable position at Bismarck. Although successful in maintaining his hold on the party machinery, the Governor had alienated many of his own party. When the last Territorial Legislature convened in January, 1889, he found himself at loggerheads with virtually the entire membership. The Republican-controlled body, anticipating the appointment of Mellette as governor as well as early passage of the Omnibus Bill, ignored the Democratic chief executive, refusing to confirm even a single appointment. Resigning himself to the turn of events and without any display of bitterness, Church submitted his resignation to President Harrison on March 9. Fourteen days later, Mellette was sworn into office. Extending his congratulations to the new governor after the ceremony, "Church threw his spring overcoat over his arm and left the capitol building with a pleasant salute to the republicans present."[16]

The departure of Governor Church symbolized the passing of the territorial system. His Republican antagonists, mellowed by the years, were to attest later to his personal integrity and devotion to duty. Their stubborn opposition to him was basically a reflection of their aversion to the external authority of the federal government.

Much of the dissatisfaction with the territorial governors had its source in the dissent over special legislation and the establishment of public institutions. Until Congress in 1886 placed limitations on territories with respect to special legislation and the indebtedness of governmental units, the legislatures were under constant temptation to enact special laws on almost any subject and to disregard sound principles of public finance. Paradoxically, the constitution-makers at Sioux Falls in 1883 accepted the position of the territorial governors by imposing various restrictions on the legislative branch. These placed limitations on public indebtedness at both state and local levels and prohibited private or special laws, including the locating or changing of county seats.

The governors were, generally, high-minded individuals who identified themselves closely with their constituency. In view of the small remuneration from office, it was natural for them, as well as for other federal appointees, to exploit opportunities afforded by a new country for political and financial gain. Their exploitative interests differed little in this respect from those of local political leaders who seemed to resent so much the part played by federal officeholders. Aside from Howard, who died in office, only three governors—Jayne, Burbank, and Church—left the Territory when their terms ended.

The statehood campaign in 1883, demanding complete separation from the northern section, was characterized by high feelings and vituperation because of sectional animosities and an intense

16 Kingsbury, *History of Dakota Territory*, II, 1569.

distrust of Governor Ordway.[17] Not until the statehood efforts
had been stalemated by national politics in 1885 was the territorial
system brought under attack. The denial of statehood and the continuance of territorial tutelage then began to appear as a dangerous
usurpation of government by Congress. To men like Hugh Campbell and Joseph Ward, this indicated a trend which, unless checked,
would inevitably lead to further dictation by the national government in local and state government everywhere. Jeffersonian
principles were invoked in defense of the separatist activities under
the Constitution of 1885.

Irrespective of the division issue, the prolongation of territorial
status beyond the middle of the eighties was not to the best public
.interest. The national contribution toward territorial expenses,
hardly exceeding a tenth of the amount raised by territorial and
local taxes, was small compensation for the national control inherent in the territorial system. Moreover, the appointive process as applied under the spoils system at Washington was a poor substitute
for popular election, and was all too frequently a serious deterrent
to administrative efficiency. Of greater moment was the inability
under territorial administration to utilize or even conserve the resources represented by the school lands. Squatters were occupying
and cultivating thousands of acres, exhausting the soil and paying
nothing for its use. There was no territorial authority to take possession of the school lands, and the legal steps taken to prevent trespassing generally proved ineffective.

Despite the disadvantages of territorialism, the territorial framework permitted the high degree of self-government which made a
smooth transition to statehood possible. The men who made up the
delegations to the constitutional conventions were able to draw
heavily upon their earlier experiences in government.

The Enabling Act of 1889 required a new constitutional convention for South Dakota. The decision as to whether the convention
was merely to readopt the Constitution of 1885 or draft a new document was left to the choice of the voters. In an election held in May,

---

[17] The embittered feelings toward Ordway explain the section in the South
Dakota Constitution subjecting the chief executive to penalties for seeking to influence legislators by means of veto threats, political promises, or removals from
political office. These extraordinary clauses were retained from the first constitution drafted in 1883.

1889, the frame of government drawn up in 1885 was overwhelmingly endorsed. Consequently, the delegates to the convention of 1889, sixteen of whom had served in either one or the other of the preceding conventions, considered themselves without authority to make any fundamental revisions or additions.[18]

The convention which met at Sioux Falls in September thus confined its work to specific changes required by Congress. These included an equitable division of the territorial debt and records, a change of the name to South Dakota, the delineation of the boundary between the two Dakotas, and the reapportionment of the legislative and judicial districts. Congress accepted the ten-dollar-minimum price restriction on the school lands and made it mandatory upon all the states admitted in 1889 as well as Idaho and Wyoming upon their admission a year later.

On October 1, 1889, the voters approved the Constitution, accepted prohibition, and elected Mellette as the first governor. Pierre was chosen temporary capital from a field of six contenders. The territorial government ceased to exist on November 2, 1889, when President Harrison formally proclaimed the admission of the twin states. The elected officials of South Dakota had been duly installed two weeks earlier and so were able to enter upon the discharge of their duties at once. The North Dakota officials did not qualify until November 4.[19]

[18] The clause limiting the state indebtedness to $500,000, inherited from the 1883 and 1885 constitutions, presented a dilemma to the 1889 convention in view of the large territorial indebtedness. The limitation was finally placed at $100,000 exclusive of the indebtedness acquired from the Territory.

[19] Governor Arthur C. Mellette to Secretary of Interior John W. Noble, November 4, 1889, Mellette Papers. Neither state can claim priority over the other, as President Harrison purposely shuffled the admission documents so that none might know which came first. By common agreement reached in later years, North Dakota holds thirty-ninth and South Dakota fortieth rank among the states of the Union.

CHAPTER 16

The Farmers' Alliance and the Populist Party

BY THE END OF THE 1880's new issues, basically economic, were thrusting themselves on the political scene. Although the excitement over statehood had somewhat obscured it, a feeling of protest was in the air, challenging the complacency of the Republican leaders and breeding a spirit of political independence. It was a feeling which found expression in the Farmers' Alliance and in its later political manifestation, the Populist party.

The economic unrest, which was by no means confined to South Dakota, had its origins in the deflation that accompanied the resumption of specie payments in 1879. A declining price level, induced in part by increased production, not only narrowed the margin of profit for the Dakota wheat farmers, but also made it difficult for them to meet the heavy financial obligations assumed so lightly during the boom.

As prices for their crops fell, the Dakota farmers became acutely conscious of what seemed to them discrimination and extortionate practices on the part of monopolistic marketing agencies, inadequate credit facilities, high interest rates, monopolistic prices for farm machinery and other necessities, and an inequitable system of taxation. To add to their distress, a succession of devastating drought years beginning in 1887 and running to the mid-nineties

223

cut down their crops and left them at the mercy of the moneylenders.

The first undercurrents of unrest appeared among wheat-growers in the central and northern regions of the Territory during the early eighties. When the farmers realized that transporting their wheat to the large commercial mills was costing them half the value of the product, their earlier patronizing attitude toward the railroads quickly turned into resentment. In addition to high freight rates for short hauls, a special grievance in the spring wheat region was the railroad companies' practice of charging "transit" or through rates to Milwaukee or Chicago even though the flour was usually processed in Minneapolis. The railroads also frequently refused to furnish cars to small shippers or farmers who wished to ship their wheat directly to market. Unfair practices charged up against the local elevators included arbitrary methods of grading and weighing as well as outright frauds.

THE FARMERS' ALLIANCE

The absence of a free market for their produce together with a declining income made the farmers receptive to organization. Milton George, editor of the *Western Rural* in Chicago, had been waging a campaign against monopoly, particularly denouncing the railroads as discriminatory and a menace to the nation. In April, 1880, as a means of aiding the farmers, he organized what became known as the Northern Farmers' Alliance. Within a year he was supplying charters for Alliance chapters throughout the entire Middle West.

The Alliance first appeared in Dakota Territory in February, 1881, when a group of Yankton County farmers received a charter. During the following year other clubs appeared in Bon Homme and Moody counties. In 1884 the movement caught fire in the central counties of the Territory where the farmers were relying mostly on wheat culture for their living. A drop in the price of wheat below the dollar mark, actually going as low as eighty cents a bushel in 1884, lent point to a growing list of grievances against the railroads and elevator companies. From mass meetings of farmers at such points as Clark, Huron, Mellette, and Redfield came resolutions denouncing the marketing agencies for unjust and monopolistic practices and demands for regulatory legislation.

On February 4, 1885, delegates representing Alliances and farmers' clubs from eleven counties located mostly in the wheat belt met at Huron to form the Dakota Territorial Alliance. During the next six months the number of Alliance chapters tripled. While most of them were organized south of the 46th parallel, the new farm order appealed to groups in the northern section as well, especially in the Red River Valley, where embittered small wheat farmers also were seeking relief from excessive transportation charges and unfair grading practices. Farmers' elevators began to appear simultaneously in a number of railway towns in the wheat region, most of them operated by the Farmers' Alliance.

In order to expand the cooperative activities of the local clubs, the territorial organization in July, 1887, incorporated as a joint stock company with a capitalization of $200,000. Watertown was the headquarters for its business branch, which at first had been briefly located at Huron. The Alliance supplied its membership with such commodities as binder twine, coal, farm machinery, and household goods at low prices; it also entered the insurance field, underwriting protection against fire and hail as well as loss of life. The Dakota Alliance was a pioneer in the field of cooperative insurance and saw its system of life insurance copied by other state Alliances. A National Alliance Aid Association, based on the Dakota plan, ultimately absorbed the state aid organizations. The business ventures of the Dakota Alliance were unable to weather the financial storms of the period, and failed during the early nineties.

More important than its campaign against middlemen were the Alliance's political activities. Farmers' tickets made their appearance in 1884 at the same time as the farmers' clubs, bearing an independent label whenever local Republican machines rejected demands that they run farmer candidates. When the Territorial Legislature convened at Bismarck in January, 1885, a strong antirailroad and antimonopoly bloc made it certain that some kind of regulatory legislation would be enacted. The lawmakers created a railway commission, but the railroad corporations were able in the final days of the session to weaken its powers so that the commission had no effective control over freight rates. Two years later a stronger farmers' bloc pushed the enactment of a warehouse law, which provided for the regulation of grain warehouses and elevators and the establishment of rules and regulations by the railway commission for the weighing and grading of grain.

The Alliance kept alive the spirit of discontent for the remainder of the territorial period. Its influence was evident in a revision of the section on corporations in the Constitution drafted at Sioux Falls in September, 1885. The Alliance also focused attention on such side issues as prohibition and women's suffrage. Its potentialities as a political force could be seen in the final session of the Territorial Legislature which convened at Bismarck in January, 1889. Although they did not pass Alliance proposals, a majority of the lawmakers were regarded as Alliance men or "friends of the farmer."

The Dakota Alliance reorganized in 1889. Led by its president, Henry L. Loucks, and its business manager, Alonzo Wardall, the Dakota organization severed its connection with the National (Northern Farmers') Alliance to join the Southern Alliance. This was a secret organization that had made great headway in the cotton states of the South; subsequently Loucks became national president of the order. When it was replaced by the Farmers' Alliance and Industrial Union, there was a further reorganization along secret lines in the two Dakotas.

The Alliance was at first nonpartisan, seeking nominations within the framework of the majority party and claiming a share of the patronage. In some counties it was strong enough to control both Republican and Democratic conventions. In 1888 the Democratic candidate for delegate to Congress, an Alliance man who had the active support of Loucks, made inroads on the Republican vote. As the order continued to prosper, Republican leaders became more solicitous of Alliance favor, posing as friends of the farmers and even incorporating Alliance resolutions in Republican platforms.

After the Enabling Act was passed in 1889, Loucks called the Alliance into special session in each section to decide on the course of action in setting up the state governments. In North Dakota, where a brand-new constitution had to be drafted, the farmers exerted considerable influence. Alliance men at the convention took up the cause of reform ideas and wrote in a number of Alliance principles. A member of the Alliance became the first governor. In South Dakota the Alliance wholeheartedly advocated the readoption of the Constitution written at Sioux Falls in 1885, which they called a farmers' constitution. The local chapters responded with unanimous endorsements. A number of delegates to the South Dakota constitutional convention were chosen from Alliance ranks.

Many Alliance supporters in South Dakota were delegates to the Republican state convention. With Alliance leaders seeking to control the Legislature and to name the leading candidates for state office, an intraparty fight developed. Loucks and Wardall particularly wished to oust Governor Arthur C. Mellette from office, seeing him as too friendly to the railroad corporations, but they were unable to form a combination against him. However, the convention named a farmer for lieutenant governor and wrote a platform that the *Dakota Ruralist*, official paper of the Farmers' Alliance, found praiseworthy. The Republicans won an easy victory over the Democrats in the September election.

When the first State Legislature met in special session at Pierre a month later to select two United States Senators, the Republican machine had no difficulty in electing R. F. Pettigrew of Sioux Falls and Gideon C. Moody of Deadwood, despite the efforts of an Alliance bloc to name Alonzo Wardall and A. J. Edgerton. Edgerton had an understanding with Mellette, Moody, and Pettigrew over a distribution of the major offices and restrained his supporters from dictating his selection over Moody in the Republican caucus. The insistence of Black Hills Republicans upon a Senate seat caused Edgerton to be sidetracked. In accordance with the pact, he received a federal judgeship despite his advanced age. Since Moody, as the candidate of the Homestake interests, was not too popular with the rank and file, the Alliance bloc had hoped to draw enough support to Wardall in the Legislature to defeat both Moody and Pettigrew. When, instead, both men won, the bloc was greatly chagrined, and charged that Edgerton had betrayed the Alliance forces by becoming a party to a "corrupt bargain."

THE INDEPENDENT PARTY

Having failed to achieve its objectives, the Alliance chose to abandon its role as a pressure group within the Republican party. A proposal to launch an Independent party carried by a vote of 413 to 83 at its convention at Huron on June 6, 1890. A month later the new party met in Huron again to nominate its ticket and write a platform. Henry L. Loucks, president of the Alliance, was the unanimous choice for governor. The platform embraced ideas held by the national Alliance organization and called for the abolition of national banks and the substitution of legal tender notes for national bank notes, the free and unlimited coinage of silver, a national income tax, government ownership and operation of railroads, a tax on real estate, and the Australian ballot. South Dakota may be regarded as the birthplace of the Populist party since it was the first state in which it became an independent political organization.

Republican leaders did not underestimate the Independent movement. In a number of counties east of the Missouri, the new party could be expected to exploit the spirit of revolt engendered by local Republican bossism. This was also true in the Black Hills where an anti-Homestake faction stood ready to support any candidates who seemed likely to break the power of the dominant Republican machine. There was, moreover, a real danger of fusion between Independents and Democrats on local tickets, thus jeopardizing control of the State Legislature.

Despite some coolness between Edgerton and Mellette on the one hand and Moody and Pettigrew on the other, the combination between the "big four" remained intact during 1890. The state ticket, headed by Mellette, carried the election, but the Independents got a good share of the Republican vote. Mellette received only 34,000 votes, nearly 20,000 less than the year before. Loucks carried thirteen counties and polled nearly 24,000 votes. Maris Taylor, the Democrat, ran third with 18,480 votes as compared with 23,840 polled in 1889. Heavy defections from Republican ranks occurred among Scandinavian voters in the central counties.

The spirited contest between Pierre and Huron for the permanent location of the state capital was a melodramatic diversion from the political campaign of 1890. Pierre won by a vote of 41,969 to 34,-610. The towns' dubious fund-raising methods and their questionable electioneering tactics prompted legislation in the following session providing for the Australian ballot and a stricter regulation of elections.

When the Legislature convened in January, 1891, the Republicans had a majority of one over the combined strength of Independents and Democrats in the upper house. In the lower house, they lacked control by the same margin. The Independents gained most of the contested seats, including four from Lawrence County where their local ticket had shown surprising strength. Early in the order of legislative business was the election of a United States Senator. Moody, who had drawn the short term, was the unanimous choice of the Republican caucus. The Independents, the next largest bloc, caucused night after night attempting to narrow their field of candidates to a single choice. A Democratic bloc of twenty-four supported Bartlett Tripp. At his maximum strength Moody remained nine votes short of victory, and other Republicans, proposed as compromise candidates, were unable to draw the required number. After nearly four weeks of maneuvering, on the fortieth ballot the Independents succeeded in electing James H. Kyle, a state senator from Brown County, with the help of a solid Democratic bloc. It is said that the Democratic support was given in return for Independent support in the election of a Democratic United States Senator in Illinois.

Kyle, a Congregational minister from Aberdeen, was a relative newcomer to the state. Independent in politics and a public speaker of some note, he had commended himself to the Alliance of Brown County as orator of the day at a Fourth of July gathering the previous summer. Kyle's attacks on corporate wealth and monopolies were still a subject of favorable comment when the time came to pick candidates for the county ticket. The Independents concluded that the man whom they originally had settled on as candidate for the state senate was too radical, prevailed upon him to resign, and then proceeded to name Kyle. In Washington he joined Senator William A. Peffer, who had been elected as an Independent from Kansas. The Independents had elected eight Congressmen from the West and could also command the support of some forty Alliance members elected from the South on the Democratic ticket. Kyle preferred to call himself an "Indecrat." Refusing favors from the Republican majority in the Senate, he took a seat with the Democrats and received several minor committee assignments from them.

The Alliance members in the West were jubilant over their local successes and pressed for a third-party organization on a national basis. Despite opposition from Southerners who wished to achieve Alliance objectives within the framework of the Democratic party, the movement toward a new party continued to make headway.

THE PEOPLE'S PARTY

Alliance members, chiefly from the western states, met with various reform and labor groups at Cincinnati in May, 1891, to launch the People's party. Other meetings followed, preparatory to a national nominating convention at Omaha in July, 1892. The principles endorsed included the major reforms advocated by the Farmers' Alliance. Monetary problems received major attention, with demands for free and unlimited coinage of silver, the issuance of greenbacks, and the abolition of national banks and national bank notes. The convention also endorsed the subtreasury scheme promoted by the Southern Alliance as a measure of farm relief.

The subtreasury plan anticipated the crop-loan features of the New Deal farm program of the 1930's. In a general way, the Farmers' Alliance proposed government loans on basic nonperishable farm commodities in the form of negotiable certificates comparable to legal tender notes. Designed to improve the marketing process and provide a means for rural credit as well as a fluctuating currency, the subtreasury scheme attracted wide attention outside Alliance circles during the early 1890's. The Alliance in South Dakota supported it wholeheartedly and persuaded Congressman John A. Pickler to sponsor a bill embodying its main features. Many objections, however, developed against the subtreasury plan, and the several bills introduced into Congress died in committee.

When the Farmers' Alliance in South Dakota decided to engage in partisan politics, it began to lose ground as a farm order. It held its last important state convention in Sioux Falls in June, 1895. For many of its members, party ties proved stronger than the Alliance connection. But the People's (Populist) party had a broader base than its Alliance origins implied. Recruits came from other quarters, especially from the Knights of Labor which had local assemblies throughout the entire state. The Populists also found converts for their cause among the proponents of women's suffrage and prohibition. Single-taxers, socialists, and professional reformers as well were drawn to the Populist banner in South Dakota.

The Independents showed surprising strength at a special election held in November, 1891, to fill the vacancy created by the death of Congressman John R. Gamble. The Republican candidate, John L. Jolley, a Vermillion lawyer, won with 17,614 votes, but Henry W. Smith, Minnehaha County farmer, polled 14,687 votes and carried sixteen counties. The Democratic candidate received only 7,299 votes.

While the Independent movement was gaining momentum, a feud between Governor Mellette and Senator Pettigrew threatened additional trouble for the Republicans. Pettigrew, looking ahead to his own re-election in 1895, sought to eliminate Mellette as a possible rival. As a close friend of President Harrison, Mellette enjoyed occasional patronage favors, especially from the Interior Department. He also led a campaign to commit the South Dakota delegation to Harrison's renomination. Pettigrew resented Mellette's activities and threw himself into the preconvention contest with the avowed purpose of building up a combination that would give him full control of the party machinery and also withstand the onslaught of the Independents. The Pettigrew forces named a majority of the delegates to the national nominating convention, and dictated the composition of the state ticket. Mellette's only consolation was a resolution instructing the state delegation to support the Harrison candidacy; however, on Pettigrew's advice, the resolution was not honored by the South Dakota delegates until Harrison's renomination became a certainty.

In an attempt to draw votes away from the Independents, the Republican platform favored the direct election of railroad commissioners, a postal savings system, and bimetallism. The Republican nominee for governor was Charles H. Sheldon, a Day County farmer who had served in the Territorial Legislature while a member of the Farmers' Alliance. Congressman Pickler, seeking a second term, was active in the temperance movement and expected to attract support from the prohibitionists.

The Independents met in their state convention in June with more than 500 delegates in attendance. According to an eyewitness, it was an inspired gathering resembling an old-fashioned revival meeting in its display of enthusiasm and confidence.[1] The convention followed the lead of Loucks, who took a strong stand against fusion with Democrats at the state level; however, in some thirty counties efforts to form fusion tickets at the local level were partially successful. Fusion sentiment was especially strong in Brown, Pennington, and Yankton counties. A. E. Van Osdel, pioneer Yankton County farmer, became the Independent candidate for governor.

Loucks led the South Dakota delegation to the Populist national convention at Omaha in July and became its permanent chairman. James B. Weaver of Des Moines, a veteran reformer and presidential candidate on the Greenback ticket in 1880, emerged as the logical nominee for president. A minority group identified with the Alliance element sought a younger candidate and supported Senator Kyle of South Dakota. Weaver won the nomination over Kyle by a vote of 995 to 275.

The Republicans achieved an easy victory on the state ticket in 1892, polling as many votes as in 1890. The Independent vote for governor declined by two thousand and the support for the Demo-

[1] See John D. Hicks, *The Populist Revolt* (Minneapolis: University of Minnesota Press, 1931) , pp. 257–258, for a brief account of the South Dakota convention.

cratic state ticket showed a drop of about four thousand. On the national ticket, Weaver drew heavy support away from Cleveland, the Democratic candidate, and ran ahead of the Independent state ticket by some four thousand votes. The Independents elected only six members to the state senate and eleven to the lower house.

Goaded by their loss of ground in the state contest, the Independents immediately set about to strengthen the county alliances and to effect a closer union with the Knights of Labor in preparation for the next election. They also extended their reform program, including women's suffrage and the initiative and referendum in their platform. Pettigrew, whose Senate seat was in jeopardy, directed Republican strategy in the 1894 campaign. He announced his candidacy for re-election privately as early as July, 1893, ostensibly to nip budding ambitions. Pettigrew had Congressman Pickler's written pledge that he would not try for a Senate seat until Kyle's term expired. Since the Independents were making a major issue of the money question, the Republicans under Pettigrew's direction formed nonpartisan bimetallic leagues. They also included a silver plank in their platform.

Governor Sheldon was re-elected in 1894, receiving approximately 40,000 votes, an increase of about 6,000. The Independents polled 26,568 compared with 22,524 cast for their state ticket in 1892. They had steered clear of the controversial prohibition issue and may have lost some ground to the Prohibitionists, who polled about a thousand votes on a separate ticket. The Independents won twenty-four seats in the State Legislature, ten of them in the senate. The Democrats took only a single legislative seat and saw their total vote cut almost in half. The Republicans had an impressive majority in the Legislature, assuring Pettigrew's re-election to the United States Senate.

When the Legislature convened, the Independents, seeking to exploit the railroad question which still loomed large in the public mind, pressed for a statute that would give the railroad commission effective authority to regulate both passenger and freight rates, patterning their bill after Populist legislation in neighboring states. Less stringent proposals were introduced by Republican members, but the lawmaking body adjourned without any regulatory enactment. The callous indifference of the legislative majority to a rate bill seemed reprehensible even in Republican circles and particularly brought down the wrath of Pettigrew, who had pledged his support to a rate law.

Equally damaging to the prestige of the Republican Administration was the embezzlement of $367,000 by W. W. Taylor, retiring State Treasurer. Unaware of the defalcation at the time of his inauguration, Governor Sheldon had paid high tribute to Taylor, a Redfield banker, for efficient handling of state funds. The Treasurer had absconded to South America, but returned a few months later to stand trial. He served two years in prison for his official misdeeds. To reimburse the various funds affected by the embezzlement, the state issued special bonds which were redeemed with income accruing from the various Taylor assets. The eventual loss to the state was about $98,000.[2]

The question of fusion was a leading topic of discussion in Independent circles during the summer of 1895. Many of the Independents were disaffected Republicans who could see little difference between the leadership of the major political parties aside from opposing tariff views. Democratic leaders were innately conservative and generally unsympathetic toward reformers, including the devotees of prohibition and women's suffrage. Moreover, prejudices inherited from Civil War days were still strong enough to make the Democratic party suspect. Republican orators were particularly given to exploiting the close connection between Independents and the Southern Alliance, and pictured Loucks and his associates as Democratic tools seeking to destroy the Republican party.

Fusion between Independents and Democrats seemed illogical under the circumstances. The editor of the *Dakota Ruralist* expressed the prevailing mood:

In South Dakota we have fought fusion from the start. . . . In our judgment we never will succeed in this state until we can assure the dissatisfied Republican voters that Populist success does not mean semi-democratic victory.[3]

Far more alluring to Independents than fusion with the Democratic party was the prospect of drawing Senator Pettigrew into their camp. Pettigrew had publicly advocated unlimited coinage of silver as early as June, 1890. As the country began to feel the full impact of the Panic of 1893 with its resultant business failures, monetary stringency, and widespread unemployment, Pettigrew, whose own extensive business interests were hard hit, blamed the country's ills on an inflexible currency system. He was dedicated to the cause of

[2] Sioux Falls *Argus Leader*, June 22, 1942.
[3] *Dakota Ruralist*, May 16, 1895.

free silver, and was not unwilling to assist in forming a new party in order to promote it.[4]

At the time of his re-election Pettigrew found himself more and more in disagreement with other Republican leaders on both the silver question and the regulation of railway rates. His critics within the party also recalled his open hostility to President Harrison and active opposition to Hawaiian annexation. Aware of the growing rift within the Republican party, the reform journals, as Independents called their newspapers, were freely predicting by the end of 1895 that Pettigrew would soon be joining the Populist ranks.[5]

THE ELECTION OF 1896

Political developments during the summer of 1896 resolved both the question of fusion and the future role of Pettigrew. The capture of the national Democratic party by the western Democrats under the leadership of William Jennings Bryan and the defection of a free-silver faction from the Republican banner led to a triple alliance in South Dakota dedicated primarily to free silver and effective control over railway rates.

The sequence of events began with the Republican state convention which met at Huron in March to elect eight delegates to the national nominating convention. Anti-Pettigrew forces, determined to sidetrack the Senator, were in full control. By adroitly making railroad regulation a major issue before the convention, Pettigrew outmaneuvered his opposition and forced it to give him a place on the delegation to the St. Louis convention. His opponents thought they had extracted his pledge to support the national ticket and platform, whatever the outcome of the national convention, but Pettigrew had merely said that the will of the Republican party was law to him. In no wise did he consider this an obligation to accept a gold plank. Less than half the convention delegates at Huron favored free silver.

---

[4] As early as September 13, 1893, Pettigrew was anticipating a new party committed entirely to the issue of unlimited coinage of silver. In a letter to A. B. Kittredge of Sioux Falls, he wrote, "The leaders from the silver states and the brightest men of the southern states are seriously discussing the question of forming a new party and while I want to go through next year's campaign as a republican in South Dakota, I am convinced it will be the last fight we will make for the republican party. Of course this is strictly confidential. It must not be known to any one yet I am sure such is the drift of affairs that the republican party will never elect another President and never control again either house of congress." Pettigrew Papers.

[5] *Dakota Ruralist,* December 5, 12, 1895.

When the Republican national convention in June committed it-self to the gold standard, thirty-four delegates left the convention hall, headed by Henry M. Teller, Senator from Colorado and brother to a former territorial secretary of Dakota. The bolters in-cluded Pettigrew. The Republican convention qualified its financial plank with an endorsement of the bimetallic standard under inter-national agreement, but even this concession failed to satisfy the more ardent advocates of free silver. The seceding group organized a Free Silver Republican party with Senator Teller as its standard-bearer, but later decided to endorse Bryan and the free-silver plank of the Democrats.

At Chicago a month later, the action of the Democratic party un-der western leadership in repudiating the Cleveland Administration and making free silver the key campaign issue, left the Populists with little choice in their decision. Although they refused to accept Arthur M. Sewall, the Democratic choice for vice president, naming instead Thomas E. Watson of Georgia, the Populists endorsed Bryan by a vote of 1,042 to 321 in their national convention the lat-ter part of July.

The Republican state convention met in Aberdeen on July 10. Soon after its organization, a Pettigrew follower from Sioux Falls introduced a resolution favoring free silver. When it was defeated by a vote of 103 to 499, twenty delegates withdrew. Most of them were from Minnehaha County. The Republicans then nominated an Elk Point merchant, A. O. Ringsrud, for governor, and adopted a plat-form that expressed opposition to trusts and monopolies and fa-vored stricter regulation of railroads.

By mutual agreement the Populists, as the Independents were generally called by now, met with the Silver Republicans at Huron on July 14 to work out a common course of action on the free-silver issue. Pettigrew publicly declared himself a Populist and worked closely with the Populist organization. The Populists selected dele-gates to the national convention and instructed them to endorse Bryan, the Democratic candidate. After heated argument on the part of antifusionists who were reluctant to sacrifice long-range re-form principles to political expediency, a resolution favoring fusion with the Democrats carried by a vote of 499 to 71. The Silver Re-publicans generally deferred to the Populists in the selection of can-didates for state office. A concession to the Silver Republican group was the nomination for railroad commissioner of William T. La Fol-lette, Chamberlain editor and brother of Robert M. La Follette of

Wisconsin. Andrew E. Lee, Vermillion businessman, whose views on monopolies and free silver and activities as a reform mayor had attracted favorable attention throughout the state, was named by the Populists for governor. Lee's nomination was highly acceptable to Pettigrew.

The Democratic party next fell in line, calling off its state convention and endorsing the Populist ticket through its central committee. A small group of gold Democrats, mostly representing old-line party members in the southeastern corner of the state and federal officeholders loyal to President Cleveland, threw their support to McKinley. A major defection to the Republicans was the Sioux Falls *Argus Leader* which hitherto had supported the Democratic party.

As the campaign got under way, each side predicted disaster for the nation in the event of its defeat. The Republicans pointed to their support of bimetallism under international agreement, made passing reference to the tariff, and warned against the "visionary and socialistic schemes of the Popocrats." The Fusionists, on the other hand, viewed the contest as a struggle of the masses against entrenched privilege, a choice between free institutions of a democratic society and domination by corporate interests. The Fusion campaign took on the nature of a holy crusade for free silver as campaign orators harangued enthusiastic audiences, earnestly endeavoring to trace the cause of all the nation's ills to an inadequate currency system.

Bryan included South Dakota on his itinerary when he traveled through the Middle West, often addressing as many as a dozen audiences a day. Several hundred men pulled his carriage through the streets of Sioux Falls to the accompaniment of a tremendous ovation. After a slow journey northward, with his train falling more and more behind schedule amidst disagreeable weather, he received a thunderous reception at Aberdeen, where he addressed three different audiences after midnight. A large crowd in Aberdeen's Exposition Hall had patiently waited from seven in the evening until one o'clock in the morning for a chance to see and hear their idol.[6]

Nearly ninety per cent of the qualified voters cast their ballots on election day, a turnout unparalleled in the political annals of South Dakota. Bryan carried the state over McKinley by the scant majority of 183 votes. Lee, the Fusion candidate for governor, received 41,187

[6] William Jennings Bryan, *The First Battle* (Chicago: W. B. Conkey Co., 1898), pp. 534–535.

votes as against 40,868 for Ringsrud. The Fusionists elected by small margins the railroad commissioners and the attorney general; they also gained control of the State Legislature and won the two seats in Congress. The other state offices went to the Republicans by equally slender margins. Large majorities for the Fusion ticket in the depression-ridden Black Hills counties were a determining factor in the election's outcome.

Governor Lee fully understood the difficulties facing his administration. The Republicans were a disciplined group supporting well-defined political principles. The Populists and their allies, on the other hand, were a diverse body held together only by a common faith in bimetallism. The task of building a reform party out of the disparate elements called for tactful handling of the patronage and a faithful fulfillment of campaign pledges.

The Lee Administration received its first major setback when Kyle was re-elected to the United States Senate by a combination of fifty-four Republicans, ten Populists, and three Democrats. Kyle had alienated Lee and Loucks as well as other Populist leaders; Pettigrew, moreover, had never warmed up to him. The Populists, unable to agree upon a single choice in their caucus, divided their strength among four candidates. The Republicans, having failed to elect John A. Pickler, took advantage of the disunity among the Fusionists after a month of monotonous balloting and supported Kyle on the strength of his promise that he would support the Republican national administration. Previously he had repudiated radical and socialistic elements among the Populists, and his defection caused little surprise.

In accordance with campaign pledges for a maximum rate law, the Populists enacted the Palmer-Wheeler Bill, incorporating provisions they had supported during the session of 1895. The new legislation placed all railroads in the state under the general supervision of the railroad commission and empowered that body to set maximum rate schedules. In addition, the law provided for the assessment of railroad property by the State Board of Equalization.

When the Populist-dominated commission set up a schedule lowering passenger rates from four to three cents per mile, the Chicago, Milwaukee and St. Paul Company refused to accept the action. The courts granted an injunction staying the enforcement of the law, and finally in August, 1901, declared the rate-fixing powers of state commissions unconstitutional. Thus the Populist attempt to force a reduction of railroad rates met with failure. Governor Lee too failed in his repeated efforts to raise assessments on railroad property.

In 1897 the Legislature also dealt with the question of liquor sales. After five years of parliamentary maneuvering, the antiprohibitionists had resubmitted to the electorate the constitutional provision for prohibition adopted in 1889. The voters registered their dissatisfaction with the measure, repealing it by a vote of 31,901 to 24,910. The Legislature, with Lee's approval, provided for a licensing system pending acceptance of a state dispensary plan by the voters. Although two years later the electorate accepted a proposal for local distribution of alcoholic beverages by public dispensaries, the plan was never put in operation.

In accordance with the Populist platform, the Legislature overwhelmingly endorsed a constitutional amendment providing for the initiative and referendum. The amendment was accepted by the voters at the next election and implemented with requisite legislation on March 3, 1899.

Governor Lee encountered determined resistance in his efforts to bring the various administrative boards and commissions under Populist control. It required a court order to unsnarl a tangle in the reorganization of the Board of Regents when the old board controlled by Republicans refused to relinquish its authority to the new.

Much of the energy of the Populist Administration was expended on official investigations of Republican officials or Republican-controlled boards. The Legislature provided for a three-man investigating commission and a public examiner whose duty it was to expose all irregularities whether in state offices or in public institutions. The commission failed to function, but the public examiner undertook numerous investigations. Some irregularities were uncovered and one official was removed on charges of corruption as a result of his activities.

Governor Lee exhibited his high standards of responsibility in public office when he subjected his own appointees to official investigation on charges of inefficiency and mismanagement. Recalling the Taylor defalcation, Lee suggested that the Legislature require Kirk S. Phillips, newly elected state treasurer and a Republican, to submit all state funds in cash for an accounting prior to approval of his bond. The Populist majority responded favorably to the Governor's recommendation. In the latter part of January, 1897, at the

Legislature's request nearly three hundred thousand dollars was brought to Pierre by train protected by armed bank messengers and a company of national guardsmen. After a legislative committee had counted the state's funds, they were returned to the depository institutions. Lee also accused Phillips of illegally receiving interest payments on state funds, but was unable to secure sufficient evidence for legal action. The Treasurer's denial to the contrary, such was common procedure in various states at the time; legislation after 1900 banned the practice in South Dakota.

Lee was re-elected in 1898 by the slim margin of 370 votes over his Republican opponent, Phillips, but it was an empty victory. The Republicans had close to a two-thirds majority in the Legislature and won all the other state offices by margins which ranged from 2,000 to 4,000 votes. Lee found himself in constant disagreement with a hostile Legislature. The lawmakers ignored most of his recommendations, and he vetoed a number of measures passed by the Republican majority. The Governor received little cooperation from other state officials.

When the Spanish-American War broke out on April 19, 1898, the War Department called on the state to furnish volunteer infantry out of the National Guard organization. Instead of convening the Legislature in special session to provide funds, Governor Lee decided to raise the money privately to mobilize the troops, and personally advanced nearly $4,000 out of $15,000 needed. The federal government later refunded the money.

Twelve companies totaling more than a thousand men were mustered into the national service as the First Volunteer Regiment, commanded by Col. Alfred S. Frost. Their participation in the Philippine campaign soon became a subject of political controversy. Although the Fusionists had favored the liberation of Cuba from Spanish rule, they criticized the McKinley Administration for involving the country in the Filipino insurrection. Governor Lee in April, 1899, demanded the return of the South Dakota volunteers from the Philippines, claiming that their term of enlistment had expired upon the signing of the peace treaty the preceding December. The continued exposure of the troops to hardships and sickness in the Philippine jungles led to further criticism of the conduct of the war. When the men finally returned to the United States in September, 1899, they were left stranded in San Francisco after receiving their discharge papers. To bring them back home, money again had to be advanced by private individuals until the Legislature could appropriate the requisite funds at its next session. Further bickering developed between Fusionists and Republicans as each group sought to exploit the public receptions held for the returning veterans.

THE ELECTION OF 1900: DECLINE OF THE POPULIST PARTY

Shortly after the return of the troops, the 1900 political campaign got under way. The Populist party held its national convention at Sioux Falls on May 9 and 10, 1900. Delegates were present from twenty-eight states. Governor Lee gave the opening address to a crowd of about fifteen hundred in a tent designed to accommodate twelve thousand. Bryan was nominated for the presidency by acclamation. Through the influence of Pettigrew, Charles A. Towne, a Silver Republican from Minnesota, became the vice-presidential nominee. The convention took a strong stand against "the imperialism of the McKinley administration" and incorporated in the platform a plank opposing expansion. Towne withdrew from the race when the Democratic national convention refused to accept him as Bryan's running mate and nominated Adlai E. Stevenson of Illinois.

When the Populist state convention met at Yankton on July 4, the Democrats were again on hand, but fewer Silver Republicans attended. The Fusion platform included the usual planks advocating free silver, tariff reform, antitrust legislation, and strict regulation of railroads. Lee was nominated for Congress against his wishes. B. H. Lien, a Pettigrew follower from Sioux Falls, was the convention choice for governor. At the Republican state convention held at Sioux Falls in May Charles N. Herreid of Leola was nominated for governor and Charles H. Burke of Pierre and Eben W. Martin of Deadwood for Congress. The Republicans emphatically endorsed the gold standard and approved the course of the McKinley Administration in the Spanish-American War.

The Republicans were confident of electing their state ticket and concentrated upon the legislative contest to ensure Pettigrew's defeat and retirement from public life. A number of nationally known figures came to South Dakota to make the renegade Senator their special target. Among them were Theodore Roosevelt, the Republican nominee for vice president, and Marcus A. Hanna, chairman of the Republican National Committee, both of whom had been subjected to personal abuse in the Senate by Pettigrew.[7] The Republicans swept the state, defeating the Fusionists by margins averaging about thirteen thousand votes. Improved economic conditions had robbed the Populists of an effective issue, and the Republican "full dinner pail" campaign under Hanna's leadership wrought its magic in both agricultural and mining regions of the state. Fusionist hopes of cutting into the virtually solid Republican bloc of German-Russian voters on the anti-imperialism issue also proved futile.

The election marked the end of the Populist party in South Dakota. The Populist administration had failed to distinguish itself with any noteworthy achievements. Frustrated in its efforts to control the railroad corporations, it remained content for the most part to play politics. The initiative and referendum were the only reform measures to which it could rightly claim credit. The party lacked cohesion from the outset. Pettigrew, with the support of Lee, wished to fashion it into a free-silver party. The reformists among the Populists, on the other hand, had little interest in the monetary issue, and became more and more impatient as they watched the party organization falling under the shadow of the Democratic party.

As the Fusion movement disintegrated, most of the Populists and Silver Republicans returned to the Republican fold. Henry L. Loucks and Hugh Campbell led the way during the 1898 campaign, and others followed. Doctrinaire Populists, including former Congressman Freeman Knowles, Father Robert W. Haire, popular Aberdeen priest who also headed the Knights of Labor, and William E. Kidd, who had succeeded Loucks as editor of the *Dakota Ruralist,* turned to the newly formed Socialist party. Such leaders as Lee, La Follette, and Pettigrew had become too involved in the political struggle to turn back to their former party allegiance and identified themselves with the Democratic party for the future.

Even though the Populist party did not survive, many of its ideas were eventually accepted by American society.[8] Reforms that were to be championed by new leaders within the framework of the major parties in later decades at both state and national levels had their ideological roots in the farmers' revolt of the nineties.

[7] Herbert Croly, *Marcus Alonzo Hanna* (New York: Macmillan Co., 1912), pp. 335–338.
[8] See Hicks, *The Populist Revolt,* pp. 404–423.

CHAPTER 17

The End of the Open Range

THE FIRST YEARS of the new century saw the close of one of the most colorful and best-remembered chapters in American history, the chronicle of cattle-raising on the open range. The cattle industry, spreading north from Texas, by the early seventies had reached eastern Colorado and the North Platte country of Wyoming and western Nebraska; there, as has been told, it had to await the removal of the Indian barrier before penetrating the rich heartland of the northern short-grass country.

The Northern Plains area, of which the Sioux lands were an integral part, afforded natural advantages for stock-raising by virtue of its dry climate, terrain characterized by many sheltering coulees and breaks, and its highly nutritious grasses. The native grama and buffalo grass have a higher fattening value than introduced grasses and retain their nutrient qualities when cured on the stem. Since rains would leach out the nutriments and reduce the value of the cured grass for winter storage, the semiarid climate is an asset.

After the signing of the treaty with the Teton Sioux, the trail drives from Texas no longer ended at rail points in Kansas and Nebraska. Fat, mature animals still were shipped east to Kansas City and Chicago slaughterhouses, but the young steers were removed from the herds and headed for a two- or three-year fattening period on the northern range. While some cattle were driven in from Idaho, Oregon, and Washington, or shipped in as "pilgrims" from the farmlands of the Upper Mississippi Valley, most of the herds on the Northern Plains were made up of Texas longhorns, a type resulting from the crossing of long-horned Spanish cattle imported from the Iberian peninsula in colonial times and northern European breeds brought to Texas by the first Anglo-American settlers during the 1820's.

The Black Hills Live Stock Association was organized in the spring of 1880, little more than two years after such early-comers as Erasmus and John Deffebach located in the area roughly bounded by the Belle Fourche and Cheyenne rivers and the eastern foothills of the Black Hills, and in the extreme southwestern corner of the present state. During the winter of 1881–1882, the combined cattle holdings of the Association's sixty members were estimated at 264,000 head. The firm of Sturgis and Goodell on the Cheyenne River and N. R. Davis on Hat Creek had 45,000 and 30,000 head, respectively; twenty members owned 5,000 or more.

By the early eighties several large organizations were utilizing the public domain north of the Black Hills along the Belle Fourche, the Little Missouri, and the tributaries of the Grand and Moreau rivers west of the 103rd meridian in present-day Butte and Harding counties. This region, particularly noted for the luxuriant forage offered by the native grama and western wheat grass, formed a part of the extensive range that included portions of North Dakota, Montana, and Wyoming.

Here the cattlemen had to await the extermination of the buffalo, which was completed by 1886. By 1880 the professional hunters were concentrating upon the northern buffalo range which extended into the northwestern corner of South Dakota. At least 5,000 white hunters and skinners participated in the ruthless slaughter of animals whose hides were the principal freight for the Northern Pacific, which had extended its main line westward from Bismarck into the Powder River country during 1881 and 1882. Dickinson became the main outfitting and shipping point for the hunters in Dakota Territory. Harding County was first settled in 1884 by buffalo hunters who saw the county's potentialities while in drying camps along the Little Missouri and Grand rivers.

CATTLE COMPANIES

The lure of big profits in the range cattle industry led to a bonanza period dominated by large companies, some of which operated several "spreads" scattered over the northern range. The larger part of their capital came from England and Scotland, and most of the larger companies maintained their headquarters elsewhere, although a number of prominent cattlemen made their homes in Deadwood, Spearfish, and Sturgis. By 1884 the range in western South Dakota was pasturing between 700,000 and 800,000 head of cattle.

Among the leading organizations were the Dominion Cattle Company, the Continental Land and Cattle Company (better known as the Hash Knife outfit from its brand), and Western Ranches, Limited (using the VVV brand). South of the Cheyenne River the Anglo-American Cattle Company and the Keystone Land and Cattle Company absorbed several smaller ranches and became the dominant outfits in Fall River County during the eighties.

The Anglo-American Cattle Company was organized in 1882 by a group of New York and English financiers who wished to build up a large ranching business on the Wyoming range. Harry Oelrichs, its president and general manager, went to Cheyenne to look over the field, and in 1882 consolidated the holdings of three large ranches in Fall River County. Owning 34,000 head of cattle, the Anglo-American Cattle Company was the largest firm to operate entirely within the confines of South Dakota at the time. In 1885 it moved headquarters from Cheyenne to the new railroad town of Oelrichs where feeding pens were built for fattening cattle before shipment. During 1888–1889 the company also operated a modern packing plant at Oelrichs.

The era of bonanza ranching ended with the severe winter of 1886–1887 which took a heavy toll among the herds on the northern range. The storms struck early in the fall of 1886 and were accompanied by subzero temperatures that continued for days. Herds recently driven in from the southern Great Plains states and Texas suffered heaviest losses. Animals which had spent an earlier winter on the northern range were better able to withstand the cold. The disaster drove many of the cattle companies out of business or forced them to reduce their scale of operations. The Turkey Track, one of the few large companies to survive, rebuilt its herds from the depleted stock of retiring firms, and continued its operations until 1901 when it sold out to the Franklin Cattle Company. The losses from the disastrous winter ran from ten to ninety per cent, depending on where the cattle ranged. Generally speaking, the cattlemen of South Dakota suffered lighter losses than those using the rangelands in Montana, North Dakota, and Wyoming. Some ranchers in the Belle Fourche region, however, lost more than half their stock. In Custer and Fall River counties, where the storms were less severe and the foothills afforded better shelter, the losses were negligible.

The experiences of 1886–1887 made reorganization of the range cattle industry imperative. The lure of big profits had led to over-extended operations and overstocking. The disastrous winter also indicated clearly that year-round grazing was impractical on the northern range; it needed to be supplemented with feeding at sheltered corrals. The shortage of pasturage and the necessity of retiring their debts compelled the cattlemen to retrench as well as to change their methods of operation. They began to store hay for winter feeding and to give more attention to the improvement of breed herds. They also had to resolve the many new problems connected with the influx of homesteaders and cowmen with small herds who were running barbed-wire fences around their lands and the water holes.

The first encroachment by homesteaders was in Fall River County when the Chicago and North Western line from Chadron, Nebraska, was extended to Rapid City during 1885–1886; this was followed by the building of the Burlington line through the western part of the county between 1888 and 1890. The railroad that they had so eagerly awaited proved to be the cattlemen's undoing. The homesteaders soon forced the large cattle companies to cut down their herds or even to retire from business altogether.

The Anglo-American Company liquidated its holdings in 1888. The Keystone Land and Cattle Company, known as the Z Bell ranch, held on a little longer. When the homesteaders took up so much land along the Cheyenne as to cut off access to water and pasture, the company moved part of its Z Bell herd to the eastern part of the county near the Pine Ridge Reservation. But profits continued to dwindle and the stockholders in the fall of 1893 decided to dispose of the company's entire holdings.[1]

The sheep industry also moved in on the western range at an early date. John D. Hale located a band of 3,000 in the vicinity of Bear Butte in 1878. During the next few years a number of sheep ranches were in operation in the surrounding area. The industry

[1] A. H. Schatz, *Opening a Cow Country* (Ann Arbor: Edwards Brothers, 1939), gives a good account of the range cattle industry in Fall River County.

soon became so important that the sheepmen formed the Sheep
Breeders and Wool Growers Association at Sturgis in May, 1884.
About 85,000 sheep grazed in the Black Hills region at the time.
Several successful sheep ranches were operating in the rough country west of Edgemont in Fall River County by 1890, prompting the
Burlington Railroad to construct a large shearing pen at Marietta,
nine miles northwest of Edgemont. By 1900 the number of sheep in
the Black Hills area had increased to over half a million. However,
it was not until after 1910 that the sheep industry became prominent
in western South Dakota.

INDIAN RESERVATIONS, 1889

Horse-raising on the western range developed as a side line to
the cattle industry. All the larger cattle ranches raised horses for
their own needs, selling the surplus. There were enough on the
range by 1887 to require a separate roundup. In Fall River County
the Anglo-American Cattle Company owned nearly a thousand head
of horses, and a few other large outfits were running several hundred. There were also a few horse ranches along the eastern edge
of the Black Hills. The horse ranchers met at Rapid City in May,
1887, to plan the first roundup. The area covered extended from
the Belle Fourche Valley southward into Fall River County along

the Cheyenne. Even though horses wintered better than cattle, the market for them was so limited that few ranchers entered the business of raising horses to the exclusion of other stock.

The constant search by the cattle industry for new pasturage was an important factor in the agitation for reduction of the Great Sioux Reservation during the eighties. The agreement finally consummated in 1889 made available to the whites approximately 9,000,000 acres. The cession included virtually the entire area of present-day Perkins County, the northern part of Meade County above the Cheyenne, and the region between the Cheyenne and White rivers, except the lands comprising the Lower Brûlé Reservation. It also included two small areas along the Missouri south of the White River in Lyman and Gregory counties.

The official opening of the reservation lands in February, 1890, failed to draw many homesteaders. Townsite boomers, operating out of Pierre and Chamberlain, tried to conjure up a land rush, but the drought conditions of the period militated against a stampede. The boom was confined to Fort Pierre and to Oacoma, which, almost overnight, became a thriving town across the river from Chamberlain. Most of the homesteaders soon left, abandoning their claims to the government. Those who remained settled chiefly along streams where the soil was rich, fuel handy, and rough land available for stock-raising. Here they were joined by owners of small outfits, cattlemen and sheepmen who also located close to water. The north side of the White River Valley and the valley of the Bad River were especially favored by small ranchers operating on a free-range basis, who frequently lived thirty miles apart. Most of the inland trading posts such as Hayes, Hotch City (present-day Kennebec), Interior, Midland, Presho, and Westover, which served as post offices, were located on stage routes operating between Rapid City and the Missouri River at Pierre and Chamberlain. The majority of the settlers, including the cattlemen, were squatters who postponed making entry on their lands until a decade later.

Among the prominent cattlemen on the range along the Bad River was James ("Scotty") Philip, a Scottish immigrant active in western South Dakota after 1875, first as mining prospector in the Black Hills, next as scout and dispatch rider for the military, then as Black Hills freighter from Fort Pierre and points in Nebraska, and finally as cowboy and rancher. In 1881 he established a ranch about a mile from what is now the town of Powell in present-day Haakon

County where he lived until 1890. He then moved to the Fort Pierre community and directed his extensive ranching interests from there until his death in 1911. A buffalo herd maintained by him on a large pasture along the Missouri above Fort Pierre at one time numbered over nine hundred animals, and was for years a great tourist attraction.

The newly opened area on the western edge of the Cheyenne River and Standing Rock reservations drew few settlers before 1900 because of its distance from railway points and its general inaccessibility. Small cattle ranches were established along the Moreau and Grand rivers, sharing the range with cattlemen who had extended their operations into the region from the Slim Buttes and Cave Hills region on the west.

The area comprising present-day Harding County also remained relatively unsettled until the turn of the century. Its earliest occupants were cowboys running line camps for the large cattle outfits, a few professional buffalo-hunters, and migrants from Black Hills mining camps who settled during the middle eighties in the vicinity of Camp Crook along the Little Missouri. Others located during the same period along a stream in the vicinity of Harding near the Short Pine Hills. By 1890 there were also scattered ranches in the butte country that lies between the Grand and Moreau rivers.

STOCKMEN'S ASSOCIATIONS

The range industry of South Dakota reached its heyday during the 1890's when as many as fifty cattle outfits were running moderate-sized herds on the public domain. The common use of the public lands required close cooperation. Stockmen's associations were local at first, formed by ranchmen in a given area for mutual protection. A range code was developed to define the limits of each rancher's grazing grounds, and to deal with innumerable other problems of mutual concern. The local associations in time were absorbed by a larger organization exercising jurisdiction over a wider area. The general association formulated the rules for working the range and provided various safeguards for the interests of its members. It insured the cooperative action needed for protection against rustlers and predatory animals as well as for the inspection of cattle shipments at railway points. It also promoted legislation and governmental policies designed to benefit the industry. The Western South

Dakota Stock Growers Association, formed in 1892 with thirteen charter members, is one of the oldest stockmen's organizations in the country.

The roundup was the major association activity of South Dakota cattlemen from 1881 to about 1905. There were usually a spring roundup to cut out the calves for branding, and one in the fall to prepare for the shipment of matured animals to market. Each detail was worked out in advance at a general meeting, usually held in March at Rapid City and attended by a representative of every cattleman on the range. During the early period the cattlemen on the upper range along the Belle Fourche frequently planned their roundups at Spearfish.

The roundup program scheduled by the Western South Dakota Stock Growers Association in the spring of 1904 suggests the scope of operations at that time. In order to cover every part of the range in as short a time as possible, the association organized sixteen different roundup outfits. This was one of the last large general roundups to be staged in South Dakota. The homesteaders were about to converge upon the cattlemen's domain and disrupt the range industry. Perkins County saw its last roundup in 1906. The last one in the region between the White and the Cheyenne occurred in the fall of 1908.

Another major problem facing the cattle industry was the protection of the various brands or marks used to designate ownership. Most of the early cattlemen chose brands that were easy to apply and difficult to alter. Legislation concerning brands and branding goes back to 1881, the date of the first roundup in Dakota Territory. The counties held jurisdiction over brands until 1897 when a revised brand law placed the responsibility in the hands of a state brand commission under the supervision of the secretary of state. In 1925 a state brand board assumed jurisdiction. The brand law requires all brands for marking cattle or other animals to be registered. The same symbol may be used by different ranchers, but cannot be applied to the same part of the animal. There were over 21,000 different livestock brands in use in the state in 1968.

Other early legislation designed to protect the cattle industry included a quarantine law enacted in 1887 to check the spread of Texas fever caused by ticks carried by Texas cattle. A hide law, passed in 1891, was aimed in part at checking the cattle rustling then so prevalent in Lyman County and adjoining areas along the Missouri River. This legislation required meat dealers to keep a complete record of animals purchased.

Until approximately 1887 the main trail for the steady stream of cattle from Texas onto the Dakota range ran northward from Ogallala, Nebraska, along the western edge of the Great Sioux Reservation. Commonly called the Black Hills and Canadian trail, it entered the state east of Oelrichs and crossed the upper reaches of the streams feeding into the Cheyenne and Belle Fourche rivers. It continued northward from near the mouth of the Belle Fourche to the east of the Slim Buttes country, and then led northwest into the Little Missouri Valley. The Belle Fourche trail branched off from the main trail to supply Dakota and Wyoming stockmen in the Belle Fourche Valley north and west of the Black Hills. The herds driven north from Texas varied in size, but usually did not exceed three thousand head.

The extension of railroad facilities into the range country gradually eliminated the long drive. When Buffalo Gap, Oelrichs, and Smithwick came into existence along the North Western line from Chadron, Nebraska, to Rapid City during 1885 and 1886, much stock was shipped to these points and then trailed northward into the Belle Fourche Valley. A few years later, in 1890, an extension of the North Western reached Belle Fourche.

Among the several railroad towns that served the range industry during its heyday, Belle Fourche occupied a strategic position. It served the entire Belle Fourche Valley into western Wyoming and shared the trade of the Little Missouri and Grand River ranges with Dickinson in North Dakota. For a few years during the early nineties Belle Fourche was the world's largest primary cattle-shipping center. In 1894 alone its outbound shipments totaled 4,700 carloads. For the southern Cheyenne and badlands area, Smithwick became the major shipping point, while Chamberlain and Pierre were the outlets for the small cattlemen whose herds grazed the region between the Cheyenne and the White. The Milwaukee Railroad during the early 1890's constructed stock-watering dams at intervals of twenty-five miles across Lyman County to the inland village of Westover as a means of drawing traffic to its river terminal at Chamberlain.

During the eighties, prior to the Sioux cession, Pierre had already become an important port of entry and the distributing station for

Iowa and Minnesota-bred cattle supplied to the range west of the Indian reservation. Thousands of cattle were also trailed east along the reservation right-of-way to Pierre for shipment to market.

Shortly after 1900 two new railroad towns—Evarts and LeBeau—appeared on the Missouri on the eastern edge of the Cheyenne River Reservation. Evarts was the first to become prominent. It was founded when the Milwaukee Railroad continued its Aberdeen line westward in anticipation of an extension across the Indian lands.

To avail themselves of this direct and shorter route to the Chicago market, the cattlemen on the upper reaches of the Grand and Moreau made an agreement with the railroad officials whereby the former secured from the Indians a six-mile right-of-way along the northern edge of the Cheyenne River Reservation while the railroad company provided stockyards and dipping pens on the Missouri's west bank. The Indians received a toll of twenty-five cents per head for all cattle and horses driven over the eighty-seven mile stretch across the reservation. Sheep were excluded from the trail. The railroad maintained a pontoon bridge for a year and then provided ferry service. It also placed several stock dams at regular intervals across the strip.

In 1902 the Indian Service was leasing on five-year contracts nearly one and a half million acres in the western half of the Cheyenne River Reservation to four nationally known cattle companies. Both the Matador, headed by Murdo McKenzie, and the Diamond A, managed by Burton C. Mossman, were Texas outfits. G. E. Lemmon, representing the Lake, Tomb, and Lemmon syndicate, secured a lease to 865,000 acres on the Standing Rock Reservation. Under the conditions of this lease, the area had to be enclosed with a three-wire fence. In 1904 the remainder of the Cheyenne River Reservation was leased to owners of large herds.

G. E. Lemmon, commonly known as "Ed," was a veteran South Dakota cowman who arrived from Texas in the summer of 1880 as straw boss for the Sheidley Cattle Company, which operated for a few years along the Cheyenne near French Creek before moving to the Moreau River. The syndicate with which Lemmon was connected had extensive cattle interests in Texas as well as in the Dakotas. Its main range was on the north fork of the Grand River. "Ed" Lemmon and "Scotty" Philip share the honor of being the first South Dakotans named to the National Cowboy Hall of Fame and Museum, established at Oklahoma City in 1958.

The decision of the Milwaukee Railroad to cross the Missouri at a point eight miles to the north meant the end of Evarts. Mobridge came into existence in October, 1906, after the bridging of the river, and immediately fell heir to the cattle shipments that had flowed through Evarts. In the meantime, the Minneapolis and St. Louis Railroad was building to the Missouri River, extending its line from Watertown to a point twelve miles below Evarts. By the end of 1907 the railroad had its trains running to the new town of LeBeau and by the middle of 1908 had the cattle pens ready for shipments from the Cheyenne Reservation. A ferry carried the livestock across the river. As at Evarts, heavy shipments of Texas cattle arrived during the spring for the short drive to the range, and later in the year there was equally heavy traffic to eastern markets.

LeBeau throve as a boisterous cow town for about three years and then went into a rapid decline. Most of the traffic in the trans-Missouri region was by this time passing into the hands of the Milwaukee Railroad which had followed the homesteaders into the reservations with extensions to Faith and Isabel. Its own dreams for a bridge and westward extension remaining unfulfilled, LeBeau clung to existence until 1924 when the Minneapolis and St. Louis tore up the tracks from Akaska to the river.

HOMESTEADERS ON THE RANGE

The operations of the big cattle syndicates on the Cheyenne River and Standing Rock reservations were the final phase of the open-range cattle industry. The end of this colorful era was linked with South Dakota's last land boom, which brought thousands of homesteaders onto reservations and Indian lands ceded in 1889. These settlers cut up the range into small holdings as they sought to transform the short-grass country into a farming region. The nation's recovery from the depression of the nineties, the renewal of railroad construction, and the return of favorable weather conditions all helped push the agricultural frontier into the normally semiarid short-grass region.

By 1900 new settlers were already entering the badlands region of eastern Pennington County and crossing the Missouri in search of homesteads in Lyman and Stanley counties. They also occupied the ceded lands in Gregory County east of the 99th meridian in sufficient numbers so that in 1902 the Chicago and North Western Railroad built a line out of Nebraska to the ten-year-old village of

Bonesteel. The abandonment of the Fort Randall military reservation in 1893 had made additional lands available in this area.

The construction of railroad connections between Rapid City and the Missouri River at Pierre and Chamberlain during 1905–1907 set off a heavy migration into the entire area between the Cheyenne and White rivers. The public domain in Harding and Perkins counties became accessible to the homesteaders when the Milwaukee Railroad projected a transcontinental line west of Mobridge, reaching Lemmon in October, 1907. Most of the settlers in this region arrived during 1907, 1908, and 1909. While the agreement of 1889 with the Teton Sioux called for a graduated price for these lands, the provision for payment was repealed in a "free homestead" law passed in 1900. The legislation, however, was not made applicable to the surplus Indian lands.

The surplus lands on the Indian reservations supplied the principal stimulus for the intense activity in the trans-Missouri region. Between 1904 and 1913 the government negotiated a series of agreements with the Teton subtribes on the Rosebud, Lower Brûlé, Pine Ridge, Cheyenne River, and Standing Rock reservations whereby over half the reservation lands, a total of over four million acres, were made available for purchase by white settlers.

The government followed a new procedure in placing the surplus Indian lands on the market. In order to avoid a stampede, it resorted to a lottery. Prospective settlers registered at designated points, after which lots were drawn for the claims. The price paid for the surplus lands generally ranged from a maximum of $6.00 an acre (less on some reservations) to a minimum of $2.50, depending upon the filing period. All land entered or filed upon within three months after the official opening commanded the maximum price. An intermediate price prevailed for the subsequent three-month period, after which the minimum was charged. After four years all unentered lands were generally sold for cash at public auction or under some other procedure prescribed by the Secretary of the Interior, the sale limited to 640 acres to any one purchaser.

Although at first the government negotiated specific agreements with each Indian group whose surplus lands were to be sold, this procedure was abandoned following a court ruling that the Indian reservations were a part of the public domain and fully subject to the authority of the national government. The income derived from the sales was placed in a trust fund.

At the first sale of Indian lands, which occurred in 1904 in Gregory County in the eastern part of the Rosebud Reservation, 2,412 claims of approximately 160 acres each were made available. One hundred six thousand persons registered at Bonesteel, Chamberlain, Fairfax, and Yankton from July 5 to July 23, more than half of them at Yankton, where there was great excitement when nearly seven thousand registered in a single day. Vendors did a real "land-office business" serving the blocklong queues of eager land-seekers, some of whom stood in line all night long awaiting the opening of the registration office. Food was rushed to the registration point by railroad from Sioux City.

Large crowds also assembled at Bonesteel, the eastern gateway to the coveted lands. Here there was a carnival atmosphere: swarms of gamblers and sharpers and other questionable characters had been drawn to the town, and there was disorder and rioting when they got out of hand. Before order was restored by an armed guard of law-abiding citizens, one gambler had been killed and two others severely wounded in a shooting affray July 20, 1904, which has been called the "Battle of Bonesteel."

Chamberlain was the scene of the public drawing five days after the registration closed. The successful applicants made entry for their homesteads first at Bonesteel, later at Chamberlain. At the end of a sixty-day period, no regard was given to the order in which the numbers had been drawn.

A second drawing for Indian lands took place in 1907 when nearly three hundred fifty homesteads became available in the western part of the Lower Brûlé Reservation north of Presho. In this case the price of the land was based on its appraised value regardless of the time of entry.

The following year additional surplus lands in the Rosebud Reservation were thrown open to settlement in Tripp County, the price ranging from $6.00 to $2.50 per acre in accordance with the time of entry. Six registration points—Chamberlain, Dallas, Gregory, and Presho in South Dakota and O'Neill and Valentine in Nebraska—drew 114,768 persons to participate in the great gamble for four thousand homesteads. The registration was accompanied by the usual excitement and uproar as huge crowds taxed the limited facilities for lodging and food. At both Chamberlain and Dallas crammed trains pulled in and out during the peak period, while registration officials worked around the clock in four-hour shifts. In Dallas the registrants for a single day totaled nearly fifteen thousand persons, transported by fifteen trains making daily runs to the frontier village.

In 1909 some ten thousand claims became available on the Cheyenne River and Standing Rock reservations, opening to settlement Corson, Dewey, and Ziebach counties in South Dakota and the southern portion of Morton County in North Dakota. The registration was conducted during October at Aberdeen, Bismarck, LeBeau, Lemmon, Mobridge, and Pierre. There were 81,456 applications for claims, 55,364 of which were registered at Aberdeen, 10,106 at Bismarck, and 8,293 at Pierre. The drawings were made at Aberdeen. Six years later more than six hundred additional homesteads on the Standing Rock Reservation in South Dakota, representing approximately one hundred thousand acres, were placed on the market.

A million and a half acres of remaining surplus and unallotted lands on the Rosebud and Pine Ridge reservations in Bennett, Mellette, and Washabaugh counties were opened in the fall of 1911. There were a total of 53,728 registrations at Chamberlain, Dallas, Gregory, and Rapid City for approximately ten thousand homesteads. The drawing was held at Gregory. Severe drought during 1910 and 1911 lessened enthusiasm for these lands so that there were fewer registrations. The region, moreover, was less accessible than the areas opened through earlier drawings.

In the course of a decade the entire short-grass country had taken on a new look. As the homesteaders or "honyockers" began to dot the wide, open spaces with their soddies and black tar-papered shacks, to break up the range with their plows, and to enclose their claims with barbed-wire fences, the cattlemen were forced to reduce their herds, or, as in the case of the larger operators, to liquidate their entire holdings. Many small ranchers, however, procured additional pasturage by leasing Indian allotments and by grazing unoccupied or abandoned claims.

Among the first to see the handwriting on the wall was the Franklin Cattle Company of Deadwood. Beginning in the spring of 1885 in the Belle Fourche Valley with a few head on Alkali Creek, this family firm had built up one of the largest businesses in the state. It had absorbed both the Hash Knife and Turkey Track outfits as well as others adjoining. Its annual shipments of some 10,000 cattle from a herd of at least 45,000 head had contributed greatly to Belle

Fourche's reputation as a cow town. Faced with a rapidly shrinking range, the Franklin Cattle Company disposed of all its livestock holdings to outside interests in 1907.

The census figures indicate the dimensions of the boom in the trans-Missouri region. According to the federal census, the population for the western half of the state rose from 43,782 in 1900 to 137,687 in 1910, an increase of 214 per cent. Most of the newcomers must have arrived between 1905 and 1910, as the state census for 1905 showed a population of only 57,575 for the area.

Except for the modern innovations of automobile and steam and gasoline tractors, the movement of settlers into the short-grass country was, generally speaking, a miniature of the boom experienced a few decades earlier in the eastern counties. Land locators plied their business in almost every town, and there was the usual traffic in relinquishments. Similarly, the fourteen-month commutation privilege was freely invoked by speculators in securing early title to their claims.

Along the course of each new railway line appeared new towns, spaced at regular intervals and usually platted as railway townsites. Faith on the Milwaukee and Winner on the North Western enjoyed special advantages as terminal points in Meade and Tripp counties, while Lemmon on the Milwaukee's newly constructed transcontinental line at the northern edge of Perkins County also served a large clientele. There were the usual disappointments for inland villages left without rail connections when on sober second thought railroad corporations decided against extending lines into sparsely settled areas. Bennett and Harding counties never acquired railway facilities, nor did Buffalo County east of the Missouri River. Nevertheless, numerous small communities sprang up in the interior as trading centers and postal stations to serve the homesteaders and small ranchers.

An interesting feature of the "west-river" homesteading period was the mushroom crop of newspapers which exploited the final-proof notices. Lyman County alone, within the course of a decade, boasted fifteen different newspapers as compared with the two that serve the county today. A publishing firm organized by E. L. Senn at one time or another operated as many as thirty-five different newspapers, most of them serving as "proof sheets." When the last proof notices were printed in one locality, Senn moved the equipment to a newer community. Another publisher ran a chain of

seven in Meade County. Many of the newspapers bore such eupho-
nious names as *Brushie Blade, Highland Herald, Prairie Sun*
(Lyman), *Presho Post, Reservation Wand* (Ammons), *Seoneville
Star, Westover Wave,* and *White Owl Oracle.*

In their political activities, the new communities ran true to
form, with the usual spirited contests over county-seat locations.
There were also occasional quarrels about county divisions. The
conflict of interest between rancher and homesteader further en-
livened the political scene. The cattlemen exerted themselves to
postpone as long as possible the organization of county government, and vigorously opposed the application of the herd, or fence,
law which made owners of livestock fully responsible for damages
to crops. But superiority in numbers soon enabled the homesteaders, or "nesters," to gain the upper hand. At first applied to
western counties only on a local-option basis, the herd law was made
applicable everywhere in 1911, which ended the open range.

The physical aspects of the short-grass country presented serious
problems for homesteaders as well as ranchers. As if to prove the
cattlemen's contention that the environment was hostile to farming, severe droughts hit the area in 1910 and 1911, forcing a retreat
from many farmsteads. Contrasting with the westward procession a
few years earlier, lines of covered wagons moved out of the White
River Valley through Chamberlain during the late summer of 1911.
The state census of 1915 listed only 120,151 persons in the region
west of the Missouri.

Attempting to halt the exodus, the railroad companies carried
hay, feed, and coal into the distressed communities at no charge and
other supplies at half rate; and county commissioners pushed construction work on roads and bridges to furnish employment for
homesteaders whose crops had failed for two successive years. Congress also passed relief measures, permitting homesteaders to leave
their claims temporarily and granting an extension of time on their
payments. The homesteaders who stayed learned to adapt themselves to the region, and at the same time forced the cattlemen to
modify their operations. The result was a combination of ranch
and farm economies, a development which will be treated in a later
chapter.

CHAPTER 18

The Progressive Era, 1903–1924

ALTHOUGH the decisive victory of the Republicans in 1900 had extinguished the Fusion organization in South Dakota, it could not kill out the spirit of reform engendered by the Populist Movement. Economic recovery had lessened free silver's appeal as a monetary issue and quieted the outcry against trusts; the railway problem, with all its political implications, was to continue as a cause of unrest. Other aspects of the reform movement were merely dormant for the moment.

Shortly after Governor Herreid took office in January, 1901, Republican leaders executed what was considered a master stroke of strategy on the rate question. At about the same time that the courts invalidated the Populist-sponsored maximum rate measure of 1897, they persuaded the railway corporations doing business in the state to reduce freight and passenger rates voluntarily. A small coterie headed by Alfred B. Kittredge, formerly Republican national committeeman and chief dispenser of patronage for the McKinley Administration, took credit for the reduction of rates. Associated with Kittredge, who was then general counsel for the Chicago, Milwaukee, and St. Paul Railroad Company, were general agents of the North Western and Milwaukee railroads, the Standard Oil Company, and other persons connected with corporate interests. "The story freely circulated in these early years of the state's history that these men made the laws in the Locke Hotel in Pierre and the legislators ratified them."[1]

Although the railroad corporations, exultant over the legal victory, had benevolently lowered the rates, they failed to overcome the unfriendly sentiments still held in many quarters. Moreover, their close identification with the Republican organization made them a natural target for antimachine elements in intraparty contests. The hostile feeling toward railroad interests became the basis for an organized rebellion within the Republican party.

The Progressive Movement in South Dakota began in a revolt launched by Coe I. Crawford against the Kittredge leadership in December, 1903. Crawford, who had served as attorney general during the Sheldon Administration and had run unsuccessfully for Congress in 1896, had moved from Pierre to Huron in 1897 when he became general counsel for the Chicago and North Western Railroad Company. After his hopes for a Senate seat upon Kyle's death in 1901 were dashed by Governor Herreid's appointment of Kittredge, Crawford laid plans to run for governor.

There were various signs of dissatisfaction with the party leadership, which he was quick to exploit. At a big rally in Huron in early December, 1903, a full six months before the state convention, he dramatically announced his candidacy in a speech that made pointed reference to the usurpation of political power by a few for the purpose of controlling nominations for "selfish and special purposes." At the same time, he announced his resignation as legal agent for the North Western Railroad. Two months later, in a general letter addressed to the state's Republican voters, he accused the railroad corporations, the Standard Oil Company, and telegraph, express, and insurance companies of allying themselves against him with machine politicians, and urged the enactment of a primary election law and other political reforms to "shake off from the state the incubus of corporate dominion and to wrest [it from] the control of the party bosses."[2]

---

[1] Calvin Perry Armin, "Coe I. Crawford and the Progressive Movement in South Dakota" in *South Dakota Historical Collections*, XXXII (1964), p. 58.

[2] Letter of Coe I. Crawford, February 1, 1904, Pettigrew Papers.

Despite Crawford's energetic campaign, the Kittredge machine remained intact at the state convention and succeeded in nominating Samuel H. Elrod of Clark over the Huron insurgent by a vote of 778 to 226. Although Crawford gave full support to the state ticket at the November election, he had laid the foundations of a movement that was soon to sweep Kittredge and most of his cohorts out of power.

The men associated with Crawford represented varying degrees of liberalism. Some were merely disgruntled office-seekers who had run afoul of local machines, but the greater number were probably actuated by loftier motives. Like Crawford, they understood how railroad influence, through passes and retainers to local attorneys, had permeated to the lower levels of government, the idea being to control the selection of legislators and of local officials entrusted with decisions concerning corporate taxation. Some of Crawford's group already were infected with the spirit of progressivism manifesting itself under Governors Albert B. Cummins and Robert M. La Follette in Iowa and Wisconsin. A few had flirted with Populism and kept their reformist views when they returned to the Republican fold.

In planning their strategy the Crawford supporters decided to promote a direct primary law. Under the direction of Richard O. Richards of Huron, an enthusiastic advocate of the direct-primary principle, they organized the Republican State Primary League during the summer of 1904. Being well aware that chances were remote for the enactment of such a law in a machine-dominated Legislature, the proponents of the reform drafted and submitted a bill under the initiative and referendum law of 1899.

But when the Legislature met in January, 1905, it refused to accept the initiated bill in spite of the list of 8,884 signatures it carried. Instead, the Legislature enacted an "Honest Caucus Law" designed to regulate party caucuses. Under the substitute measure, the nominating machinery would remain safely in the hands of the existing organization. As anticipated, the Legislature's refusal to honor the initiated bill played into the hands of the insurgents.

Additional support for the Crawford candidacy came by way of the Chautauqua circuit, on which Governor La Follette of Wisconsin was entertaining large and enthusiastic audiences with his discussion of progressive principles. During a South Dakota lecture tour in June, 1905, the Wisconsin liberal met privately with Crawford and other insurgents and gave them welcome counsel. The

Crawford forces, who could now claim a connection with the "Wisconsin Idea," also sought to link their cause with the administrative policies of President Theodore Roosevelt. They formed "Roosevelt Clubs," and followed up with a statewide "Roosevelt League" in November, 1905. In addition, an estrangement between Senators Gamble and Kittredge brought Gamble and a following of conservatives, or Stalwarts, into the Crawford camp by the time the preconvention campaign got under way.

The Progressive forces won an overwhelming victory in the state convention in June, 1906, garnering 893 votes for Crawford against 476 for Elrod, and naming most of the candidates for state office. The Progressive tide also swept away the Stalwart Congressmen, E. W. Martin and Charles H. Burke, replacing them with Progressive nominees. The Stalwarts took defeat with a good grace and raised little objection to the party platform which called explicitly for electoral reform and regulatory legislation.

It was quite apparent that Senator Gamble had endorsed the Crawford candidacy out of political expediency, not because of any devotion to progressive principles. His defection from the party leadership came when Kittredge, looking ahead to his own re-election in 1908, attempted to replace Gamble with Congressman Martin, a resident of the western part of the state. The breach between Gamble and Kittredge had grown so wide by the summer of 1906 that President Roosevelt had the two Senators draw straws or toss a coin in settling patronage matters. The Progressives, even though many found the whole affair distasteful, remained faithful to their political commitments and re-elected the Yankton man when the Legislature convened.

PROGRESSIVE LEGISLATION

In response to the "progressivism" expressed in the Republican platform, the Progressive majority during the legislative session of 1907 enacted antipass and antilobbying legislation, a direct primary law, and laws prohibiting corporations from making contributions for political purposes and requiring a public accounting of campaign funds.

The Legislature also passed measures setting maximum railroad passenger rates at two and one-half cents per mile, creating a food and drug commission and a telephone commission, and providing for free textbooks in public schools. A law requiring a bona fide residence of one year to obtain a divorce brought to an end the laxity in divorce proceedings which had long made the state a mecca for individuals seeking release from marriage vows. At the next election the voters to whom the divorce law was referred over-whelmingly endorsed the measure.

The railroad corporations challenged the validity of the maximum rate law and secured a restraining order against the Railroad Commission so that the courts might determine the reasonableness of the rates. They obtained a similar injunction against a measure enacted by the Legislature in 1909, reducing the maximum rates to two cents a mile. The rate cases continued in litigation until 1914 when a court decree held the two-and-one-half-cent rate reasonable, but adjudged the two-cent rate confiscatory and therefore invalid.

The Progressives also succeeded in raising assessments of corporate property. In 1904 the tax payments made by railroads in South Dakota had averaged $105 per mile in contrast with payments of $218 in Iowa, $300 in Nebraska, and $234 in North Dakota. The Progressives worked diligently to correct the situation, and in spite of the difficulties in arriving at a valuation of railway property, finally were able to exact larger levies. By 1913 the average tax levy per mile had risen to $191.

Although the Progressives remained in the ascendancy, it was usually by a narrow margin. The Progressives, having 266 delegates against 223 Stalwarts, held a slight edge in the state convention in April, 1908, and named the major candidates. The leading contest in the primary was between Crawford and Kittredge for the Senate seat. Crawford won by the close vote of 35,151 to 33,086. Both Charles H. Burke and E. W. Martin, Stalwarts who were defeated two years before, were again nominated. Robert S. Vessey, a Progressive, received the nomination for governor. Winning the primary contest was tantamount to election.

Crawford began his Senatorial duties on March 15, 1909, when Congress met in special session to revise the outmoded Dingley Tariff Law of 1897. When the Senate Finance Committee, under the dictatorial leadership of the reactionary Nelson W. Aldrich of Rhode Island, virtually rewrote the House bill with hundreds of amendments revising rates upward, Crawford joined the Democrats and a small group of Middle Western insurgents to vote against the measure. Although he voted for the Payne-Aldrich bill in its final form when it came out of conference committee, he generally aligned himself with Progressives in the Senate as they stepped up their assaults upon the Aldrich leadership.

The Progressives continued to dominate the political scene in South Dakota in 1910 despite a serious threat posed by George W. Egan, an independent candidate for governor. Egan was a discredited Sioux Falls attorney who for some inexplicable reason was able for several years to maintain a large personal following among the voters. In the Republican primary Vessey won renomination with 26,372 votes, while Egan received 21,446 and Elrod 20,335.

With the approach of the presidential campaign of 1912, the rift between Progressives and Stalwarts began to widen. A state branch of the National Progressive Republican League, organized at Washington to promote the candidacy of Senator La Follette, was established at Pierre in February, 1911, as the Progressives sought to capitalize on the growing unpopularity of the Taft Administration throughout the country. Richard O. Richards, who by this time had severed relations with both Crawford and Vessey, confused the issue by setting up a rival organization and acting as La Follette's campaign manager with the Wisconsin Senator's authorization.

The rival Progressive groups submitted separate sets of convention delegates to the Republican primary in June, 1912, and the Stalwarts named a third slate. Rising sentiment for Theodore Roosevelt, who had visited the state during the summer of 1910, prompted the Crawford-Vessey group to associate Roosevelt's name with that of La Follette. This was done in accordance with the amended primary election law of 1909 permitting delegations to national conventions to proclaim their principles in mottoes of five words or less. The chosen motto read, "La Follette Roosevelt Progressive Principles." The delegates who subscribed to this legend won an easy victory over the other two tickets in the primary and went to the Chicago convention, where they divided their ballots evenly between La Follette and Roosevelt.

After Taft's nomination, instead of bolting the Republican organization and forming a third party as did Progressives elsewhere, the Progressives in South Dakota followed the more practical expedient of retaining control of the regular party machinery. Although a few Stalwarts won places on the state ticket, the Progressives dominated the state convention to an extent that permitted them to name presidential electors pledged to Roosevelt. Stalwart attempts to thwart the Progressives through court action were vain. The Progressive ruse in denying them an opportunity to vote for their presidential candidate led many Stalwarts to support Wilson. The Progressives, nevertheless, carried the state for Roosevelt by about ten thousand votes. Frank M. Byrne, their candidate for governor, won by a scant margin of 3,310 over his Democratic opponent. There was a significant crossing of party lines in the gubernatorial contest, as Byrne drew support from disgruntled Democrats, at the same time losing Stalwart votes to his opponent.

Disaffection had developed among the Democrats prior to the meeting of the national convention. There were two factions, one representing the older party leaders who favored the candidacy of Champ Clark, the other consisting of a rebellious younger group, led by Edwin S. Johnson, which supported Woodrow Wilson. Unable to compose the intraparty differences, the Democrats sent two delegations to the Baltimore convention, where the pro-Wilson group was seated. Johnson, who won the nomination for governor, also received the party's support for the United States Senate when Pettigrew, the official candidate, renounced Wilson in favor of Roosevelt during the campaign.

The Democrats, elated over their national victory, succeeded in patching up their quarrels, but the Republicans remained out of harmony a while longer. The bitterness of the campaign of 1912 was not easily forgotten. During the subsequent legislative session the Stalwarts were unable to prevent the election of Thomas Sterling, who had resigned as Dean of the School of Law at the state university and had defeated Gamble in the Senatorial preferential primary during the summer of 1912.

Two years later the Stalwarts avenged themselves on Crawford when he lost the primary battle for the Senate seat to Congressman Burke by nearly six thousand votes. Burke, who had served continuously in Congress since 1899 except for his defeat by a Progressive in 1906, lost at the general election to Edwin S. Johnson, the Democratic candidate, by a margin of nearly four thousand votes. The Democrats also gained a seat in Congress. The rest of the Republican ticket won by handsome majorities. An attitude of rule or ruin within the party was the undoing of both Burke and Crawford.

After ten years of incessant feuding, the Republicans finally were reunified by the election of Peter Norbeck as governor. Norbeck, a successful Redfield businessman, aligned himself with the Progressive cause at an early date and was soon one of the inner circle. He served in the state senate and took an active part in the promotion of the National Progressive Republican League, serving for some time as state chairman. In 1914 he became lieutenant governor. Aspiring to the governorship in 1916, he won the primary contest with a clear majority over two other opponents. In the general election he defeated the Democratic candidate by a vote of 72,789 to 50,545, running far ahead of the national ticket. The state was carried for Charles Evans Hughes, the presidential candidate, by the slender margin of about five thousand votes.

PROGRESSIVISM IN THE SECOND PHASE

Following Norbeck's election, the Progressive Movement in South Dakota advanced to its second and more positive phase. Governors Crawford and Vessey were concerned mainly with the popular control of government by means of a direct primary law and related enactments. The measures taken against the railroad corporations were closely related to this political objective. The moderate policy followed by Crawford and Vessey and a fairly even division of strength between the contending factions kept the advocates of more radical positions in restraint. However, in March, 1915, a bank depositors' guaranty law was enacted with Governor Byrne's full support after several years of agitation.

After the election of 1916, the Republican party followed more advanced reform concepts and supported a broad program of governmental action designed to promote the public social and economic welfare. Governor Norbeck's mastery of the political scene and the overwhelming votes of confidence registered for his policies at election time left the conservative, or Stalwart, element with no choice but to fall in line, even though reluctantly at times.

True to his campaign pledges, Norbeck unfolded a far-reaching program of action to the Legislature in January, 1917. Foremost among his proposals was the enactment of a rural credits plan whereby the state would go into the lending business, extending loans to farmers. A constitutional amendment adopted at the November election had granted authority for such legislation. The Governor further recommended that the Legislature consider the advisability and feasibility of a system of state hail insurance on farm crops, a state coal mine, state-owned and state-controlled terminal grain elevators, and the desirability of acquiring and developing water-power sites on the Missouri. He also urged an extensive road-building program, a workmen's compensation law, and conservation measures for the protection of wild-life resources.

The Legislature responded in short order with a rural credits law and set up committees to investigate the practicality of the public enterprises suggested by the Governor. It also created the office of marketing commissioner under a law which declared the business of marketing farm products was in the public interest and subject to control by the state. Other enactments included workmen's compensation, mothers' pension, and prohibition laws. A constitutional amendment prohibiting the manufacturing and sale of intoxicating liquors had been accepted by the voters at the preceding election.

The session of 1917 was a busy one for the South Dakota lawmakers; they enacted a total of 376 laws out of 545 bills brought before them for consideration. Five new departments were created, among them an industrial commission and a state highway department, the latter set up partly for the purpose of securing federal aid on a dollar-matching basis under the Federal Highway Act of 1916. The Legislature also adopted resolutions submitting twelve constitutional amendments to the voters. Three of them provided for state hail insurance, a cement plant, and a state-owned hydroelectric project. Still another would permit the state to construct and operate grain elevators, warehouses, flour mills, and packing houses. The most sweeping proposal was an amendment permitting the state to engage in internal improvements and enter any business enterprise considered proper by the Legislature within specified financial limitations.

THE NONPARTISAN LEAGUE

The legislative session had scarcely ended before the Norbeck Administration found its leadership threatened by the Nonpartisan League. This organization took shape in North Dakota in 1915 through the efforts of Arthur C. Townley, a former Socialist who sought to weld the farmers of the Northwest, particularly the wheat growers, into an effective political body which would promote a program of state socialism. The League's demands included the exemption of farm improvements from taxation, the operation of rural credit banks at cost, state inspection of grain, state hail insurance, and state ownership of terminal elevators, warehouses, flour mills, packing houses, and stockyards.

Organizers in "flivvers" owned by the League began entering the state from North Dakota in December, 1916. Their object was to exploit economic discontent among the farmers and extract from them sixteen-dollar membership dues for a two-year period. Within three months the League was claiming a membership of 20,000, including most of the farmers in Brookings, Brown, and Moody counties. By July there were forty-two organizers maintaining headquarters at Sioux Falls, and the South Dakota branch of the League continued to spread despite strenuous opposition from the professional men and businessmen in the towns. "Whenever the League gained a foothold in a community, a cleavage followed in the relations between farmers and businessmen."[3]

Although the Legislature did not contain any League members, organizers appeared at Pierre during the session, working especially to promote the constitutional amendment which would permit the state to engage in internal improvements. Publicly they expressed themselves as "highly pleased" with the work of the Legislature. The close similarity between the demands of the League and the socialistic character of some of the Norbeck recommendations later brought charges from the Nonpartisan League that the Republican party had deliberately appropriated League principles to forestall it. While the investigative work of legislative committees might be said to indicate League influences, Norbeck and other Progressives had been advocating the major enactments of the 1917 session before the League was born.

Norbeck's strategy against the Nonpartisan League began to take shape by early 1918. The Governor and his close associates emphasized legislative achievements and pledged support to the proposed constitutional amendments which would permit the state to enter into business enterprises if the public so desired. Thus a free choice would be given the voters without expressly committing the Norbeck Administration. At the same time, the Governor and his lieutenants attempted to discredit the League leaders, charging radicalism and disloyalty.

[3] Carl J. Hofland, "The Nonpartisan League in South Dakota" (unpublished Master's thesis, Department of History, University of South Dakota, 1940), p. 21.

In a lengthy campaign document "Norbeck argued that the state already had more progressive legislation than North Dakota and that it would be folly to overthrow an administration characterized by performance in order to accept the Nonpartisan League program of promises."[4] He favored the permissive amendments, but advised horse sense in setting up state enterprises.

The Norbeck Administration had to battle it out with the League forces in the general election, since Townley's followers decided not to enter the Republican primary. Conservative Republicans, and even Democrats whose party platform also endorsed the constitutional amendments, flocked to the Governor's support. The results were a crushing defeat for the Nonpartisan League. Norbeck received 51,175 votes against 25,118 for the League candidate and 17,585 for the Democrat. All the amendments permitting the state to engage in business carried by majorities ranging from 7,000 to 17,000.

In no way related to the contest with the Nonpartisan League but of great import to the women of the state was the adoption of a constitutional amendment granting equal suffrage rights. This was the seventh attempt since 1890 to secure for South Dakota women the voting privilege. The final chapter in the history of the women's suffrage movement was written in December, 1919, when the Legislature, called into special session for the purpose, ratified the women's suffrage amendment to the United States Constitution.

Although a majority of the voters had seemingly subscribed to a state-ownership philosophy, it was a question how far the Republican administration at Pierre would go in fulfilling campaign promises. As Norbeck entered upon his second term, he again urged a state hail insurance law and advocated steps toward a state-owned coal mine, cement plant, and state-owned stockyards. He also recommended an appropriation for surveying dam sites for hydroelectric development. The lawmakers readily enacted these recommendations into law, except for the stockyards proposal. With reference to the operation of terminal elevators, flour mills, and packing plants, the Governor advocated caution, expressing some doubt as to their feasibility. The Legislature was in agree-

[4] Gilbert C. Fite, "Peter Norbeck and the Defeat of the Non-Partisan League in South Dakota," *Mississippi Valley Historical Review*, XXXIII (Sept., 1946), 223.

ment with him: bills designed to carry out the intent of the amendment were reported adversely out of committee.

Defending his proposals to put the state in business, Norbeck denied that he was a Socialist. In retrospect his program must be viewed as a part of the Progressives' campaign against monopolistic prices. There was, moreover, the fervent desire to make the services of the state government available to agriculture in the search for cheaper credit and the elimination of marketing abuses. These were basic tenets of the Progressive philosophy of government. Another motive was the desire to develop the state's natural resources. Although their economic soundness was called in question by many individuals at the time of their adoption, the business activities were considered justifiable. In the words of the constitutional amendments, the projects were "works of public necessity and importance in which the state may engage."

According to Norbeck and his adherents, the public was to derive a twofold advantage: first, through lower costs resulting from the elimination of middleman charges and unnecessary long freight hauls, as in the case of coal and cement; and, secondly, through the re-establishment of competitive prices which would force down the general price level. With reference to the alleged monopolistic price of cement, Norbeck declared, "The state can well afford to operate such a plant at cost in order to re-establish competition and reduce the price to the consumer."[5] The arguments in support of state-owned business enterprises seemed especially cogent during the years from 1917 to 1920 in view of the soaring living costs and highly inflated prices induced by World War I.

The expansion of governmental activities brought into existence additional boards and commissions, including a state cement commission, a coal-mining commission, and a hydroelectric commission. The Legislature also established a state bonding department. Moreover, in accordance with the Governor's urgent recommendation, it created a state park board to supervise the development of Custer State Park. Norbeck had interested himself in this project as early as 1905. As chairman of the park board, he was in a position to give his personal attention to the detailed work which was to make Custer State Park one of the largest in the nation.

[5] Quoted in Gilbert C. Fite, *Peter Norbeck: Prairie Statesman* (Columbia: University of Missouri, 1948), p. 87.

WORLD WAR I

The United States' entry into World War I in April, 1917, imposed upon the state administration various duties and responsibilities related to the war activities. In response to a request from the National Council of Defense at Washington, Governor Norbeck appointed a State Council of Defense a month after the war declaration. Although without legal authority until the following year, the Council was to assist in every way possible in the prosecution of the war, taking all necessary steps for the full utilization of the military, industrial, and civil resources of the state. Under its direction county councils were set up to coordinate whatever work needed to be done in organizing local defense units, assisting local draft boards, conserving food and fuel, promoting bond drives, conducting campaigns for funds for the Red Cross and welfare organizations, and fostering loyalty and patriotism in general.

South Dakotans responded well to the call for increased food production and exceeded the state quotas in the drives for funds for the Red Cross and other national welfare organizations. Over $3,-300,000 was raised, two-thirds of which went to the Red Cross. Five bond drives netted a total of $109,000,000 for the purchase of war bonds.

The only troops available in South Dakota for immediate service upon the declaration of war were a National Guard infantry regiment which had just returned to the state after a seven-month period of guard duty on the Mexican border. After the regiment was recruited to full strength, it was broken up and assigned to the United States army under a new policy whereby all the armed forces were placed under the direct control of the federal government. Several companies were transferred to the 147th Regiment of Field Artillery; the rest were assigned to various other units, as were the draftees. More than 32,000 South Dakotans, nearly 22,000 of them selected under the draft, served in the war, many of them taking part in heavy fighting in France from May to November 11, 1918. Altogether, 210 were killed in battle and about 100 died from wounds.

The State Council of Defense did not assume any importance until it was given legal recognition by the Legislature during the spring of 1918. The Council was empowered "to do all acts and things not inconsistent with the constitution or laws of the State of

South Dakota . . . which are necessary and proper for the public safety . . . ."[6] Any persons violating, refusing, or failing to obey the orders or rules of the Council were subject to heavy penalties.

In addition to creating the State Council of Defense, the lawmakers, in a special session convened in May, 1918, responded with statutes relating to criminal syndicalism, enforcing compulsory labor by idle and unemployed persons, requiring instruction in patriotism in educational institutions, and prohibiting instruction in any foreign language in the common schools. The Legislature also made legal provision for the home guards organized earlier on a volunteer basis without any public support.

Local defense councils, with general backing from the state organization, did not hesitate to use heavy pressure in the sale of war bonds and war thrift stamps. Not infrequently individuals were intimidated by local councils into subscribing for prescribed amounts. The Hutterite sect, which was maintaining seventeen communities or colonies at the time, was made the object of special attention for its refusal to support the war activities. In two different counties the local defense council resorted to extreme measures, actually seizing and selling at public auction cattle owned by the Hutterites and turning the proceeds over to the pacifist organization after deducting specified amounts for contributions to the Red Cross and investment in war bonds. Dismayed by the treatment accorded them by their neighbors, all but one of the Hutterite colonies disposed of their lands and moved to Canada. While in the process of selling their properties, the Hutterite corporations were forced to invest a certain percentage of the proceeds in war bonds and to make prescribed contributions to the Red Cross. An effort to vacate and cancel the articles of incorporation under which the Hutterites maintained their communities was unsuccessful.

The action taken against Hutterites and other conscientious objectors was mild when compared with the repressive measures against the Industrial Workers of the World and members of the Socialist party who openly expressed their opposition to the war on politico-economic grounds. In the latter category were many organizers for the Nonpartisan League, who were actively recruiting members during the war period.

The "wobblies," as I.W.W. members were called, came into the

[6] *Report of South Dakota State Council of Defense, 1917–1919* (Pierre, S. Dak., 1919) , p. 172.

state during the wheat harvest and were suspect whenever acts of violence or cases of arson occurred. The criminal syndicalism measure of 1918 was devised to cope with I.W.W. saboteurs, committed to the violent overthrow of the government. Local vigilantes at Aberdeen, normally the headquarters for the I.W.W., gave rough treatment on occasion to harvest hands found with I.W.W. membership cards in their possession, literally "spanking" them out of the state. One serious fire in the state during the period was of proven incendiary origin. Members of the home guard frequently were posted at wheat elevators and railroad bridges to prevent possible attempts at sabotage by the I.W.W.

A number of Socialists, including the candidate for governor in 1918, were arrested under the federal Sedition Law of 1917 for denunciatory statements against the war and, more particularly, for opposing the draft. As a result of vigorous action against German-language newspapers in Aberdeen and Sioux Falls, the editors were convicted and sent to the federal prison at Leavenworth, Kansas. In November, 1917, twenty-nine Socialists, mostly farmers of German descent in Hutchinson County, were judged guilty of attempted interference with the draft on the strength of an alleged threatening letter to Governor Norbeck, and given heavy fines and jail sentences ranging from one to five years. This was generally referred to in the press as a "spy case"; the convictions were later annulled.

During the 1918 campaign when the patriotism of League leaders was challenged, local defense councils in several counties broke up political meetings and ran League organizers out of town. At one time Governor Norbeck hurriedly traveled the 150 miles from Pierre to Bonesteel to make certain that his League opponent would not be disturbed at a political gathering. An indictment which had been obtained against former Senator Pettigrew under the Sedition Law for having said among other things that there was no excuse for war, was dismissed after the signing of the Armistice.[7]

The concern over the loyalty of the large German element in the population led to wartime efforts to ban the German language. After a law was passed in April, 1918, which prohibited instruction in any foreign language in the common schools, the State Council

[7] H. C. Peterson and Gilbert C. Fite, *Opponents of War, 1917–1918* (Madison: University of Wisconsin Press, 1957), p. 154. Pettigrew had engaged Clarence S. Darrow, famous Chicago attorney, to defend him, but the case never came to trial.

of Defense explicitly ordered all instruction in the German language to cease, except in classes of religious instruction already organized. This was followed by an order "prohibiting the use of the enemy's language in public conversation and over the telephone, except in cases of extreme emergency," and there were a few arrests and fines of persons who had violated the latter provision. The storm of protest against the language ban for religious services resulted in a concession permitting a fifteen-minute résumé of the sermon in German at the end of the services.

The evils resulting from wartime hysteria were not peculiar to South Dakota. Although the State Council cannot be held officially accountable for all the excesses committed in the name of patriotism, the Council's illiberal course of action in matters involving freedom of speech and personal liberty tended to promote a spirit of intolerance which made a mockery of the very principles the nation was seeking to preserve. The activities of the Council and the work of local groups in dumping German textbooks into the Missouri River, daubing private property with yellow paint, and subjecting respectable citizens to personal indignities marred an otherwise commendable record for South Dakota during World War I.

POSTWAR POLITICS AND LEGISLATION

In 1920 Governor Norbeck was elected to the seat in the United States Senate previously held by the Democrat, Edwin S. Johnson. He won an easy victory in the Republican primary, and in the general election he held a slight majority over the combined votes of four opponents, including two independents. The overwhelming victory of Lieutenant Governor William H. McMaster over Nonpartisan League and Democratic opponents in the race for governor assured the continuation of the Norbeck policies in the Statehouse. In the reaction against the Wilson Administration at Washington, the South Dakota Republicans recaptured the Congressional seat in the western district which they had lost to the Democrats in 1914.

The uniqueness of the campaigning prescribed by South Dakota's primary law drew national attention to the state in 1920. The original primary law of 1907, modeled closely on the Wisconsin law, retained features of the convention system and did not satisfy the proponents of more radical features. An initiated measure sponsored by Richard O. Richards, a Progressive best known for his perennial agitation for a complicated primary system as well as for his political independence, was finally adopted in 1912. Although repeatedly modified and even repealed for a time, the Richards Primary Law was again placed on the statute book in 1918 in the form of an initiated measure thirty-nine pages long. Among its novel features were "the party indorsement to appointive offices," the "postmaster primary," the "party recall" whereby elected and appointed officials might be made to resign, an "official party state publicity pamphlet," and a provision making candidates choose "paramount issues" and engage in "public joint debates." The law required at least one presidential and sixteen gubernatorial joint debates between presidential candidates and candidates for governor within the party, and a joint debate between the two leading nominees for governor preceding the general election.[8]

In accordance with the provisions of the Richards Primary Law, McMaster debated his opponent Richard O. Richards sixteen times during the primary and William W. Howes, the Democratic nominee, twelve times during the regular campaign. There were also two joint debates in the presidential primary, one between James O. Monroe, Independent, and James W. Gerard, Democrat, and another between the Republicans Senator Miles Poindexter of Washington and General Leonard Wood. The more unusual features of the Richards Primary Law regarding appointments to office and joint debates were dropped shortly after the election, and the remaining provisions replaced in 1929 by the more traditional form of the primary under the Slocum Law, the basic features of which have continued.

Of the several business enterprises inaugurated during the Norbeck Administration, the farm loan plan under the Rural Credits Law was in full operation when Governor McMaster took office, the coal mine was in partial operation, and the hail insurance department was making a satisfactory showing. The state in 1919 had also entered the business of bonding county officials as well as its own officers and employees. Two years later the Legislature enlarged the scope of the bonding department to include officials and employees of towns, municipalities, and school districts. Construction of a cement plant began in 1921 in Rapid City. After a careful study

[8] Joseph Brannon Laine, "Public Joint Debates under the Richards Primary Law" (unpublished Master's thesis, Department of Speech, University of South Dakota, Vermillion, 1952), is a good discussion of the complexities of the Richards Primary Law as it operated in its most complete form during the 1920 campaign.

of the cement industry, the cement commission, appointed by Mc-Master, decided to sell the product at market price instead of at cost as had been proposed by Norbeck and other advocates of the project. Production of cement was under way by December, 1924.

In August, 1923, Governor McMaster made headline news by putting the state into the retail gasoline business. Contending that the prevailing price of 26.6 cents per gallon was excessive, he ordered the supply stations of the Highway Department to sell motor fuel to the public at sixteen cents. After an agreement on a base price of sixteen cents was reached by the major oil companies in a series of conferences with the Governor, the state ceased its sales. The "gasoline war" continued intermittently for more than two years. Whenever the gasoline dealers raised the price to a point the Governor considered too high, the Highway Department started selling from the several filling stations operated throughout the state for the express purpose of holding prices in line.

McMaster claimed public savings of $150,000 for the consumers throughout the Middle West through the price reductions he forced on the oil companies. The 1925 Legislature signified its approval of McMaster's actions by granting statutory authority to the Highway Department to engage in the sale of gasoline, oil, and lubricants whenever the Governor or other designated state officials considered retail prices "unreasonable and excessive." Governor Carl Gunderson, successor to McMaster, stood ready to continue the "gasoline war" with the private dealers, but an adverse Supreme Court decision on October 28, 1925, ended the state's venture in the retail gasoline business.

Although the voters in 1918 had adopted a constitutional amendment permitting the state to establish a hydroelectric project, four years later they reversed their earlier position by an overwhelming vote, rejecting a plan to harness the waters of the Missouri for public power. An initiated measure providing for the construction of a hydroelectric plant at Mobridge was defeated by a vote of 55,563 for and 106,409 against. While there was some opposition on sectional grounds because of the selection of a site in the north central part of the state, the heavy negative vote reflected a growing reaction against public ownership principles that had found so much favor a few years earlier. In the same election the voters overwhelmingly rejected a Nonpartisan League–sponsored measure for a state-owned bank by a vote of 33,032 for and 122,807 against.

The Republicans had no difficulty in carrying the election of 1924. Carl Gunderson, the Lieutenant Governor, moved into the governor's office, and McMaster won a seat to the United States Senate after defeating Senator Sterling in the primary. In the presidential contest, President Coolidge received the support of 50 per cent of the voters. The presidential electors pledged to La Follette, the third party candidate, polled about 37 per cent, while the votes cast for the Democratic presidential ticket dropped to 13 per cent of the total votes cast.

The election of 1924 marked the end of the Progressive era in the state. Dissension among its leaders had weakened the Progressive element. There was, moreover, considerable questioning of the economic soundness of rural credits and the rest of the business ventures that had saddled South Dakota with the highest per-capita state debt in the nation. By the mid-twenties the growing reaction against the socialistic policies of the Progressives had led to a resurgence of conservatism within the Republican party.

CHAPTER 19

The Twenties and Thirties—Hard Times and the New Deal

THE POSTWAR DEFLATION which began during the latter part of 1920 made its impact upon the South Dakota economy throughout the decade of the twenties. The sharp decline in farm income and a shrinkage of property values made it difficult for farmers to fulfill obligations assumed during a period of high prices, and a bank crisis was in the making by the end of the McMaster Administration. Although there was only one bank failure during 1921, nine state banks closed their doors in 1922, and thirty-six in 1923. The federal government provided temporary relief to state banks through short-term loans from the Agricultural Credit Corporation organized under the Intermediate Credits Act of 1923, but the procession of bank failures continued. The economic strain soon depleted the depositors' guaranty fund, and the commission which administered it had to issue certificates of indebtedness to cover deposits in insolvent banks.

By the time of Governor Gunderson's inauguration, 175 state banks had closed their doors, and the guaranty fund was running a deficit of $30,000,000 covered by certificates of indebtedness. At first the failures affected only small banks, but larger institutions were soon forced into insolvency as the financial structure continued to sag. The crisis left many communities without banking facilities.

The bank situation overshadowed all other problems when the Legislature convened on January 6, 1925. Faced with the impossible task of redeeming depositors' claims out of the insurance fund, a majority of the lawmakers reacted favorably to recommendations of the South Dakota Bankers Association for a repeal of the Guaranty Law. The Legislature, however, expressed no opinion on the state's moral or legal obligations for redeeming the certificates of indebtedness. These continued to mount until, by the end of 1926, they had reached a total of $43,000,000.

The repeal of the Guaranty Law became a major issue in the election of 1926. The Republican platform definitely upheld the course followed by the Legislature, while the Democratic and Farmer-Labor parties were critical of repeal. All three political groups favored a popular expression on the question of the state's financial responsibility to depositors of closed banks. The repeal measure was referred to the voters, who rejected it by a vote of 79,-823 for and 95,830 against.

The 1927 Legislature took the final step in liquidating the bank deposit insurance system. Rejecting the view of the new governor that the state had a moral obligation to reimburse depositors, the lawmakers rewrote the old measure to provide for a separate guaranty fund set up for each state bank, each individual fund to be administered by a depositors' guaranty fund commission. The Legislature abandoned the insurance features of the original enactment, but required the assets of the old guaranty fund to be disbursed.

Shortly after the new measure was passed, the Supreme Court of South Dakota declared the guaranty fund insolvent. The popular agitation for redemption by the taxpayers of the certificates of indebtedness, consequently, began to subside. Although it is difficult to determine with exactness the losses sustained by depositors, it has been estimated that approximately $39,000,000 of certificates of indebtedness issued against the guaranty fund remained unpaid.

RURAL CREDIT

While the legislators were attempting to resolve the difficulties arising from the Depositors' Guaranty Law, there were ugly rumors that all was not well with the rural credits department. The handling of rural credit funds had been under fire during the 1925 session, when a special investigative committee accused the rural credit board of selling bonds for the express purpose of bolstering up weakened state banks. As charges of mismanagement continued, the Legislature provided for a full-scale investigation.

Although considerably hampered in its work by a lack of cooperation on the part of A. W. Ewert, the treasurer of the rural credit board, the select committee in charge of the investigation had no difficulty in unearthing irregularities and other evidences of mismanagement. The state had issued over $47,500,000 of rural credit bonds, entailing annual interest charges of more than $2,258,000, and the rural credit department had approved 11,693 farm loans for a total of $45,000,000. The investigation revealed further that nearly $800,000 of rural credit monies was in closed banks, about one-half of that amount on deposit in Ewert's own bank. When handed a subpoena ordering him to produce certain rural credit accounts, Ewert hurriedly closed the bank he managed in Pierre.

Although the findings of the committee were limited, the Legislature prohibited the sale of any additional rural credit bonds except for the purpose of redeeming outstanding indebtedness. This legislative action terminated the state's moneylending business after nearly eleven years of operation; it also provided for its liquidation through the sale or leasing of property acquired through foreclosure. At the same time the lawmakers set up an interim commission for a more extensive study of the way the rural credit department had been administered.

The steps taken by the Legislature were not without political overtones. Conservatives, inexorably opposed in principle to the state's several business ventures, were biding their time for an opportunity to close out the rural credit experiment. Other members of the majority party, originally favorable to the program, were unfriendly to Norbeck because he had backed McMaster against Sterling for the Senate seat. The anti-Norbeck faction now joined hands with the conservative element. Governor Gunderson identified himself with the former group, which did not hesitate to exploit the unsatisfactory conditions revealed by the investigation and to place the blame upon the two preceding governors.

As a result of the investigation, Ewert was convicted in February, 1926, on charges of embezzling more than $211,000 of rural credit funds and was sentenced to eleven years in the state penitentiary. Upon receiving the interim commission's report in January, 1927, the Legislature took further steps for salvaging the assets of the

rural credit department. The rural credit system was not fully liquidated for more than twenty-five years. Special tax levies were required from time to time. Ultimately, the state acquired nearly
two million acres through foreclosure proceedings. At one time
the taxes alone on the acquired lands amounted to $1,500,000 a
year. In some counties, where loans had averaged $26 an acre, fore-
closed lands were ultimately disposed of for less than $7. When the
last tract was sold and final payment made on rural credit bonds, the
rural credit venture had cost the state approximately $57,000,000.[1]

The effort to discredit Norbeck by exploiting the rural credit de-
bacle proved unsuccessful. The senior Senator won renomination
in June, 1926, by the largest majority attained in any senatorial primary up to that time. In the general election he won an equally impressive victory, topping all other candidates on the ballot. The rest
of the Republican candidates were elected, with the exception of
Governor Gunderson, who went down in defeat to his Democratic
opponent, William J. Bulow of Beresford, by a margin of some thirteen thousand votes. The Republicans retained control of both
branches of the Legislature. The banking issue may have contributed
to Gunderson's defeat, but the factional quarreling in which he became involved was the major factor.

In addition to the vexing problems posed by the adverse banking
situation and the serious state of affairs relative to rural credits,
budgetary and revenue matters were a major concern of the state
government during the 1927 session. During the preceding administration when legislative appropriations exceeded the budgetary recommendation by nearly a million and a half dollars, Governor Gunderson had yielded to the lawmakers. Subsequently he undertook
to curtail expenditures by requiring heads of state departments and
institutions to revert at least eight per cent of their appropriations.
This action resulted in a saving to the general fund of about a million dollars.

When the Democratic governor faced a similar situation during
the 1927 session, he met the issue head on. Adamant in his demands
for a balanced budget, he insisted that the lawmakers either reduce
appropriations or provide for additional revenue. When the appropriations bill provided for expenditures in excess of anticipated in-

[1] Gilbert C. Fite, "South Dakota's Rural Credit System," *Agricultural History*,
21 (October, 1947), 247. In 1925 the Supreme Court of South Dakota had ruled
that the state must pay taxes on the rural credit lands it acquired.

come by over a million dollars, Bulow interposed a veto, and there were enough Democratic members in the Senate to defeat Republican efforts to override it. Challenging the veto, the Republican majority refused to pass a new appropriations measure. When the State Supreme Court unanimously upheld the veto powers of the chief executive a few weeks later, Bulow called the Legislature into special session, and a satisfactory appropriations bill was finally enacted.

Aside from the wrangle over the general appropriations measure, Governor Bulow maintained an air of cordiality with the majority party which he found rewarding in subsequent bids for office. Many Republican appointees remained undisturbed in their positions. Although the state gave Herbert Hoover an overwhelming majority over Alfred E. Smith, his Democratic opponent for the presidency, and elected fewer Democrats to the Legislature in 1928, Bulow won re-election by twice his previous majority. His second administration he regarded as "a sort of an era of good feeling."[2] As his second term drew to a close in 1930, he sought McMaster's seat in the United States Senate and again came off an easy victor. The Republicans regained the governorship in 1930 through the election of Warren E. Green of Hamlin County and continued in control of the Legislature, although with a reduced majority. Green, the second "dirt farmer" to be elected governor, received his party's nomination over four other candidates in the state convention after an inconclusive primary contest in which he had polled slightly less than eight per cent of the total vote cast.

THE GREAT DEPRESSION

The smaller margin of victory for Republican state candidates in 1930 and an increase in the number of Democratic legislators clearly portended unrest among the voters. Although at the time of the election there was not yet any real comprehension of the adverse situation caused by the stock market collapse in October, 1929, by the end of the Green Administration the economic slump was deepening into the worst depression the nation had ever experienced.

The watchword of Governor Green's Administration was economy. His budgetary recommendations were half a million dollars under the figures suggested by the outgoing governor. The proposed

[2] "William John Bulow: An Autobiography" in Charles J. Dalthorp (ed.), *South Dakota's Governors* (Sioux Falls: Midwest-Beach Co., 1953), p. 46.

reductions in expenditures were mostly at the expense of the state's educational institutions. A special item of nearly three hundred thousand dollars for a new office annex to the capitol building, however, brought the total legislative appropriations to about the same amount that had been authorized by the preceding Legislature. Faced by extraordinarily heavy expenditures, including the interest payments on approximately $45,000,000 of rural credits debt, Green sought to cut down the operational costs of the state government. A sizeable sum reverted to the general fund when he enforced a ten per cent salary reduction at the educational institutions.

Chief public interest in the Green Administration derived from an investigation by Attorney General M. Q. Sharpe of the banking, finance, highway, insurance, and rural credit departments. Disclosures of misappropriation of funds by Fred R. Smith, Superintendent of Banks, led to his arrest; he later confessed to embezzling about $1,200,000 collected from the assets of closed state banks placed on deposit in a state bank operated by members of his family at Platte. The shortcomings of the rural credits venture also drew Sharpe's censure, the Norbeck and McMaster administrations receiving most of the blame for the dissipation of rural credit funds.

The public excitement over the investigations conducted by Sharpe had scarcely died down when a combination of disasters, including grasshopper infestations, drought, crop failures, and an unduly severe winter season, harassed the state. These adverse conditions weakened still further the state's economy, which had remained in the doldrums following the deflationary crisis of the early twenties, thus making it highly vulnerable to the impact of the national depression by the summer of 1932. A decade of heavy debts, relatively low prices, expanding production, and shrinking export markets had left South Dakota agriculture in particular unprepared for the depression of the thirties. Prevailing low prices of farm commodities accentuated the distress. Especially hard hit were the counties in the south-central and western parts of the state.

Seed and feed loans from the federal government, supplemented by private donations used exclusively for the purchase of livestock feed, relieved to some extent the critical situation faced by disaster-stricken communities during the summer of 1931 and winter of 1931–1932. The Red Cross rendered notable services in the distribution of food, clothing, and livestock feed.

The Democratic tide which swept the Republicans out of power at Washington in November, 1932, also engulfed the party in South Dakota. Senator Norbeck, who had discreetly refrained from any reference to President Hoover during the campaign, was re-elected by a margin of more than 25,000 votes over his Democratic opponent; at the same time, Governor Green went down in defeat to Tom Berry, Belvidere rancher, by a vote of 158,058 to 120,473. For the first time in South Dakota's history the Republicans had lost every state office. With the exception of Norbeck, M. Q. Sharpe made the best showing for the Republicans, losing his bid for re-election as attorney general by fewer than 7,000 votes. The Democrats also won overwhelming control of both houses of the Legislature. Franklin D. Roosevelt carried the state by a record vote of 183,515, against 99,212 for President Hoover.

The economic crisis in South Dakota was all but overwhelming by the time the Berry Administration took office. Signs of economic trouble were everywhere. Real estate values had decreased 58 per cent between 1920 and 1930. The average value of farm land had fallen from $71.39 an acre in 1921 to $35.24 in 1930, and dropped to a low of $18.65 per acre within the next five years. The price of wheat on June 1, 1932, ranged from fifty to fifty-five cents a bushel, while oats and corn were selling at twenty-two and twenty-nine cents, respectively. Hogs commanded a price of $2.68 a hundredweight on the Sioux Falls market. The low prices underlined the fact that the farmers' share of the national income had dropped from 18 per cent in 1919 to 7 per cent in 1932, while no corresponding reductions had taken place in the farmers' fixed charges, including debts and taxes. The average net farm income for the nation as a whole fell sharply from $962 in 1929 to $288 in 1932. The cash income from South Dakota crops decreased from $17,000,000 in 1929 to $6,000,000 in 1932, while the income from livestock declined from more than $150,000,000 to less than $45,000,000 for the same years.

The sharp drop in income increased the farmers' debt burden. Farm foreclosures which had reached a high rate during 1924 and 1925 were again on the increase by 1932. During the period from 1921 to 1932 a total of 34,419 farm foreclosures were instituted, involving 7,192,000 acres or 19.6 per cent of the farm acreage on the assessment rolls. Nearly a third of these foreclosures occurred during 1931 and 1932. Farm tenancy had risen from 34.9 per cent in 1920 to 44.6 per cent in 1930.

Although not all bank failures can be attributed directly to the financial plight of the farmers, the instability in agriculture had definitely weakened the banking structure, resulting in a high mortality rate among the banking institutions. Between 1920 and 1934 about 71 per cent of all the state banks had failed, with an estimated loss of about $39,000,000 to depositors. The state banks decreased from 557 to 148 while the national banks dropped from 135 to 64.

A concomitant of the hard times was a high incidence of tax delinquency. In 1935 nearly 19 per cent of the land was tax delinquent. By the time the depression had run its course the tax delinquency rate was ranging from 25 to 50 per cent in a number of counties, and title to large acreages had changed hands through tax deeds. In 1938 four counties in the northwestern section of the state had possession of over a million acres, title to which was acquired through county tax deeds.

As the economic situation got progressively worse during the early 1930's without any immediate relief in sight, more and more farmers in the Middle West began to support the Farm Holiday movement, which advocated direct action. This movement grew out of resistance to a program of testing cattle for tuberculosis in Iowa in 1931. Although the majority of the Iowa farmers were not in sympathy with the violence that broke out in several communities, the spirit of protest struck a responsive chord. The farmers were in a despondent mood and receptive to suggestions that they make common cause against the adverse conditions. Especially appealing to them were proposals for a farm strike or "holiday" whereby they would withhold their products from the market if prices fell below the cost of production.

THE FARM HOLIDAY ASSOCIATION

By March, 1933, representatives from more than a dozen states participated in a national convention of the Farm Holiday Association at Des Moines and adopted resolutions calling for an extensive remedial program as well as for steps to implement a marketing strike. Although the association was loosely organized and lacked cohesion, it took an aggressive stand on matters of farm policy and worked in close cooperation with the Farmers Union and other farm groups.

The Farm Holiday was first organized in South Dakota during the summer of 1932. Theoretically it was controlled by a board of directors representing five separate organizations, including the

South Dakota Chamber of Commerce, the South Dakota Bankers Association, and the three major farm organizations. The Farmers Union generally dominated the movement. A rival group, more aggressive and more radical than the Farm Holiday and frequently confused with it, was the United Farmers Organization. Its membership was mostly limited to the northeastern corner of the state.

The farming interests were heavily represented in the Legislature which convened on January 3, 1933. The membership included a number of persons actively identified with the Farm Holiday movement as well as the Farm Bureau, Farmers Union, and the Grange. Under the leadership of the Farm Holiday Association, these lawmakers formed an aggressive farm bloc which gave support to a legislative program made up of fourteen points on which common agreement could be reached. The objectives included a drastic curtailment of public expenditures, tax reduction, prevention of farm foreclosures, reduction of interest rates on delinquent taxes, and lengthening the time in which tax deeds could be acquired.

Upon assuming his duties of office, Governor Berry called for a return to a simpler and less expensive government. After pointing out that the state administration was expected to set an example for local subdivisions in the practice of economy, he recommended a reduction in state expenditures by at least $2,000,000. The state, he contended, had been trying too long to operate on a prosperity scale. The lawmakers readily responded to the call for economy. The general appropriations measure provided for a 25 per cent reduction over the amount available during the preceding biennium. Most of the educational institutions sustained cuts of 40 per cent.

The search for new sources of revenue to ease what was universally regarded as an inequitable burden upon real property prompted various proposals, including the net income tax and the sales tax. A plan for a two per cent levy on all transactions, including salaries, wages, retail sales, and the sale of farm products, as a substitute for real estate taxes, particularly drew widespread attention. The major farm groups pressed vigorously for a net income tax. Out of the dozens of revenue bills that were introduced a gross income tax measure finally emerged. The law was limited to a two-year period and the proceeds were to be apportioned as follows: 50 per cent to the general fund, 45 per cent to the common school fund; and 5 per cent for the use of embarrassed school districts.

The gross income tax evoked intense opposition in certain business quarters as well as among the membership of the Farmers Union and Grange, and efforts were made to prevent the law from going into effect on July 1. The State Supreme Court on June 30 disposed of a referendum petition bearing some 23,000 signatures by denying its legality by a three to two decision. An effort to secure the tax measure's repeal a month later in a special session of the Legislature also failed. During the 1935 session, the lawmakers replaced the gross income tax with a tax on net income and a two per cent retail sales tax. Two years later the Legislature increased the sales tax to three per cent and set aside the additional revenue for old age assistance, old age pensions, child welfare, and other purposes as provided for under the recently enacted federal Social Security Law.

Other measures enacted by the Legislature in 1933 and designed to bring relief to harassed taxpayers and debtors alike, included a tax delinquency law and a moratorium law. The first allowed taxpayers to spread out delinquent taxes without penalty over a ten-year period; the latter provided an additional year for redeeming foreclosed property. The moratorium measure was amended two years later, lengthening the redemption period to two years. Steps were also taken to reduce assessments on property. To ease the strain on the state treasury, the Legislature diverted half of the four-cent state gasoline tax from the highway department to the rural credit department in order to meet bond repayment and interest charges.

In view of the unfavorable financial conditions as well as the mounting reaction against the state's business ventures, the Legislature of 1933 found it easy to take the state out of the coal-mining business. There had, moreover, been inefficient management, and the supply of coal was nearly depleted. The coal mine was sold in early 1934 for $5,500 with an estimated loss of nearly $175,000 for its fourteen years of operation. The 1933 Legislature also liquidated the state bonding department and the state hail insurance project. The total loss to the taxpayers from the latter venture was approximately $265,000.

Unlike the other business ventures, the cement plant had proved a success. Its earning record was favorable from the beginning. There was, consequently, no disposition on the part of the lawmakers to support any of the proposals made periodically after 1925 for its liquidation.

While legislative bodies throughout the nation were pondering remedial measures during the early part of 1933 in order to combat the hard times, the Farm Holiday Association was drawing attention to its efforts at halting foreclosure sales. Working through local committees, the organization usually sought to bring mortgagor and mortgagee together so that they might work out a satisfactory arrangement for either an extension of time or reduction in principal, or both. Whenever such intercessory activities failed, interferences with foreclosure sales might follow.

Shortly after taking office, Governor Berry appealed to holders of farm mortgages to refrain from foreclosures whenever possible, especially where delinquencies had occurred during the preceding two-year period of crop failures and low income. However, he refused the request of the Farm Holiday leadership for a moratorium on foreclosures, and urged citizens to refrain from illegal activities. Later in the year, in conjunction with the federal government, he appointed an advisory council of seventeen to supervise the work of mediation in the various counties between mortgagors and mortgagees under a voluntary program of farm debt adjustment.

Interference with foreclosure sales occurred in relatively few instances, although threats of mob action caused frequent postponements and even cancellations of advertised sales during the first half of the year. A local sheriff postponed one sale indefinitely at the Governor's suggestion to avert possible violence. At times assemblages of angry farmers made forced sales ineffective by intimidating prospective bidders or buying back mortgaged property for a few cents. When by the end of 1933 federal agencies began to make available more liberal credit facilities, the violent phase of the movement for debt relief had passed.

The Farm Holiday is better remembered nationally for its efforts to withhold crops from market. The farm strike movement spread to South Dakota by the fall of 1932.[3] As the result of a strike in Sioux Falls in October, thirteen roads leading into the city were blockaded and cattle shipments reduced to a trickle; but the strike was poorly organized, and was called off by the farmers after three days.

The South Dakota unit of the Farm Holiday refused to heed the

[3] The most violent phases of the farm strike occurred in Iowa. Sioux City especially was a focal point for Farm Holiday activities in September, 1932, and February, 1933. Pickets identified with the Iowa organization and armed with spiked planks and shotguns blocked all roads into the city, including Highway 77 on the South Dakota side of the Big Sioux. An exchange of gunfire near Jefferson, South Dakota, on February 4, 1933, killed an Elk Point milk producer who tried to run the blockade.

request of the national organization for a farm strike in May, 1933, but the following November fell in line with an attempt to stop the marketing of all farm products. The Brown County organization, however, did not participate. Although he refused to proclaim an embargo from the executive office, Governor Berry expressed sympathy with the objectives of the movement. Compliance with the strike was put on a voluntary basis, but pickets were on hand on the several highways leading into Watertown and Sioux Falls to hold down livestock receipts. Within a week business was back to normal. The federal policies of farm relief under Franklin D. Roosevelt's New Deal administration were diverting attention from the Farm Holiday program of direct action. Benefit payments were reaching the farmers by this time.

NEW DEAL FARM LEGISLATION

The New Deal farm policy was based on the Agricultural Adjustment Act of May, 1933, and the Farm Credit Act, enacted the following month. The major objectives of the legislation were to raise farm prices through a program of production controls and to establish a farm credit program that would include the refinancing of farm mortgages.

The Agricultural Adjustment Act sought to raise farm prices to the same level of purchasing power that farm commodities commanded during the period from 1909 to 1914 in relation to nonfarm commodities. This was the principle of parity price, based on the assumption that agriculture, prior to World War I, had enjoyed a position of equality with industry in the national economy. The law originally applied to seven basic products, including wheat, corn, and hogs.

Farmers who agreed to curtail production were to receive benefit payments, the revenue for which was to come from a special tax levied against processors of farm products who would pass the burden along to consumers. There was no attempt to reduce wheat and corn plantings during 1933. When they accepted reduction contracts for the next two years, wheat-growers were, however, given adjustment payments of about 29 cents a bushel, amounting to the difference between market price and the desired parity price. Under the restriction program the same benefit payments were to continue with acreage reductions of 15 and 10 per cent, respectively, for 1934 and 1935.

The corn-hog program included a hog-killing program in August, 1933, in order to effect an immediate reduction of from 10 to 15 per cent of the supply. The smaller pigs were converted into fertilizer, while the older animals were processed at Huron, Sioux Falls, and Yankton. The meat was distributed among the needy in order to get the product out of marketing channels. Hog contracts for the curtailment of production during 1934 and 1935 carried benefit payments of five dollars per head. Corn acreage was to be cut by 20 per cent with benefit payments fixed at twenty cents per bushel. As a price-boosting device, the Commodity Credit Corporation also provided loans of forty-five cents a bushel on properly stored corn. The loan value in the beginning was set considerably higher than the market price.

While the crop-adjustment program undoubtedly was a factor in the price advance between 1933 and 1935—wheat, for instance, jumping from thirty-eight to ninety cents a bushel, corn from thirty-one to fifty-seven cents, and hogs from $3.50 to $8.35 per hundredweight—a devasting drought in the western states during 1934 also figured importantly in the improved price situation. The drought was especially acute in the western half of South Dakota where pasturage was scarce and water holes had generally gone dry. Certain sections east of the Missouri were also hard hit. At least 10,000 head of cattle were said to have died from the ravages of the drought. Edmunds County especially sustained large losses.

In June, 1934, the federal government through the Agricultural Adjustment Administration began an emergency cattle-buying program whereby a total of 915,039 head from about 67,000 farms and representing nearly 42 per cent of the state's estimated cattle population were purchased at an average price of less than $10 per head. The maximum allowance for healthy animals was $20. Approximately 87,000 animals were condemned and destroyed as unfit for human food. Some of the rest were processed at Aberdeen, Huron, Madison, Mitchell, and Rapid City where canneries were set up for use by relief agencies. A large supply of fresh meat was also distributed directly to relief clients. The drought-relief program was likewise applied to sheep. The federal government purchased nearly 150,000 ewes between September, 1934, and February, 1935.

In February, 1936, the Soil Conservation and Domestic Allotment Act replaced the Agricultural Adjustment Act of 1933 which had been declared invalid because of the processing tax. The new legis-

lation emphasized soil conservation rather than production adjustments, offering "soil-conserving" benefit payments for shifting
acreage from soil-depleting crops as well as "soil-building" payments
for the planting of soil-renovating crops and for soil conservation
practices. In 1936 about 89,500 farmers participated in "soil-conserving" and "soil-building" practices, receiving approximately
$15,000,000 in conservation payments.⁴ About 88 per cent of the
state's cropland was covered by applications for benefit payments at
the time.

Two years later a new Agricultural Adjustment Act retained the
soil conservation features of the 1936 law and re-established the
principle of acreage allotments as a means of adjusting crop production. The Secretary of Agriculture was given authority to establish marketing quotas under specified conditions for certain major
crops, including corn and wheat, provided two-thirds of the produc-
ers approved in a public vote; he was also empowered to grant commodity loans to encourage the systematic storage of farm surpluses
under a so-called "ever-normal granary" plan. The law further provided for parity payments under conditions prescribed by Congress,
and established a system of crop insurance for wheat, beginning
with the crop harvested in 1939.

Whatever the merits of the New Deal farm program with its efforts to reduce surpluses and attain parity price, the government
payments received by South Dakota farmers during the 1930's represented a substantial portion of their income. During 1934 and
1936 the A.A.A. benefit payments virtually amounted to crop insurance for many who had suffered complete crop losses from drought
and grasshopper infestations. The following statistics show clearly
the importance of government payments for South Dakota agriculture from 1933 to 1940:⁵

Year	Total Cash Farm Income (including gov't payments)	Government Benefit Payments
1933	$ 70,800,000	$ 5,100,000
1934	80,400,000	19,400,000
1935	103,200,000	15,600,000
1936	116,900,000	9,800,000
1937	102,600,000	15,000,000
1938	107,800,000	17,500,000
1939	128,100,000	23,100,000
1940	140,000,000	20,000,000

⁴ See pages 352–353.
⁵ Based on *Statistical Abstracts of the United States,* 1935–1940.

A second important phase of the New Deal farm policy was the farm credit program. A few weeks after his inauguration President Roosevelt by executive order consolidated all federal agencies dealing with farm credit into the Farm Credit Administration. Then came passage of the Emergency Farm Mortgage Act and the Farm Credit Act. This legislation provided farm-mortgage relief to thousands of farmers who stood in danger of losing their equities through foreclosure. The refinancing program enabled them to liquidate old mortgages and renew loans at lower interest rates. In addition to the emergency refinancing, a permanent system of farm credit was developed for both long-term and short-term purposes. From May, 1933, to July, 1938, the Farm Credit Administration loaned a total of $83,378,000 to South Dakota farmers. This figure included long-term amortized loans from the Federal Land Bank, seed and feed loans, crop and livestock loans, and drought relief loans.

Urban homeowners also were considered by the federal government in its efforts to ease the credit problem. The critical banking situation, reflected by the suspension of 151 South Dakota banks from 1930 to 1933, threatened foreclosure for thousands of mortgaged homes, especially where owners were jobless. The Home Owners Loan Corporation stepped in to undertake the work of refinancing the mortgages of those in danger of losing their homes and unable to refinance through private capital. By the time it ceased its lending activities in June, 1936, the H.O.L.C. had refinanced more than 15 per cent of all nonfarm properties occupied by owners at an average loan of $1,770.

The Federal Housing Administration, created in 1934, also provided assistance to homeowners. Designed both to furnish credit relief and to encourage new construction, this agency undertook to insure home mortgages, leaving to private lending institutions the business of supplying the capital.

Another major depression problem concerned relief of individuals. The relief situation had become acute during the final days of the Hoover Administration. The preceding years of drought and depression had exhausted reserve funds. In Minnehaha County where the full force of the unemployment crisis struck in 1932, about 47 per cent of the tax levy was expended on the indigent. In other populous areas of the state, the relief problem was equally burdensome. Loans made by the newly created Reconstruction Finance Corporation to local units of government for construction work provided some measure of relief.

In May, 1933, a Federal Emergency Relief Administration began to extend the relief policies of the Hoover Administration. Instead of loans, it made unreturnable contributions to the states on the basis of one dollar of federal payments for every three dollars provided locally. Large sums were also made available in the form of grants to states for direct relief. To provide local funds for matching the federal contribution, a special session of the state Legislature during the summer of 1933 legalized the sale of beer. The revenue accruing from the so-called Beer Law was apportioned equally between the state and the counties for relief purposes. Supplementing direct relief, both state and local agencies engaged in various activities as a means of providing employment. The state relief administration operated a strip coal mine near Firesteel for a short time, providing lignite coal for the needy and furnishing employment for persons on relief.

The severe droughts of 1933 and 1934 forced many families to seek public assistance. The relief rolls in December, 1934, comprised 39 per cent of the state's population. This was the highest relief load for any state. North Dakota, with comparable problems, was next in rank. More than half of all farmers in South Dakota were receiving emergency relief in December, 1934. At one time more than 80 per cent of the farmers in one county in the central section were on relief rolls. Had it not been for A.A.A. payments, South Dakota would have had more people on relief. The greater proportion of the relief population lived in the central section where drought and dust storms were aggravating serious land-use problems.

In 1935 the federal government began to place more emphasis upon work relief than on direct relief by cash payment. The Works Progress Administration replaced the Federal Emergency Relief Administration. The major objective of the new agency was to provide work for all employables. Supplementing its activities were the Public Works Administration and the Civilian Conservation Corps. Direct relief, involving mostly the care of such unemployables as the aged, the blind, and dependent children, was made the responsibility of the states with whatever federal assistance the Social Security Act of August 14, 1935, made available.

The W.P.A. expended over $35,000,000 in South Dakota from 1935 to 1938. It assisted in the construction of 131 public buildings and the modernization of 250 others, including a number of school buildings. Other useful W.P.A. projects included the construction of bridges, athletic fields, playgrounds, and swimming pools. Through the subsidiary agency of the National Youth Administration, high schools and colleges received grants for the employment of needy students on a part-time noninstructional basis, enabling such individuals to earn an average of about fifteen dollars a month. The major federal expenditures in the state were made under the W.P.A. In addition to assistance in road construction work, the Public Works Administration made loans and grants for educational buildings, waterworks, and sewer projects. Voters approved bond issues in many towns and cities in order to raise necessary funds to qualify for 45 per cent P.W.A. grants from the federal government.

During its period of operation from April, 1933, to July, 1942, the Civilian Conservation Corps maintained an average of nineteen camps in South Dakota, giving employment to 23,409 young men from the state between the ages of seventeen and twenty-four and 2,834 nonenrolled personnel, including camp officers and work supervisors. Most of the camps were located in the Black Hills. The conservation activities included forest protection, reforestation, dam construction, prevention of soil erosion, and the development of recreational facilities. The largest single project was the construction of Sheridan Lake, a water-control dam in Harney National Forest. In other parts of the state, the C.C.C. assisted in the development of the Sand Lake migratory bird refuge near Aberdeen and the improvement of Farm Island at Pierre. It also carried on soil conservation activities at Alcester, Chamberlain, and Huron.

A special program was devised in 1935 through the Resettlement Administration to cope with the problem of rural poverty. It was made applicable to low-income farmers at or near the relief level whose requirements were not met by work and direct relief measures. It represented an effort to restore destitute farmers to self-support. Included in the rehabilitation program was the attempted resettlement of families residing on submarginal lands. The voluntary farm debt adjustment service of the Farm Credit Administration was also made an activity of the Resettlement Administration.

The Farm Security Administration replaced the Resettlement Administration in 1937. The new agency aimed to promote farm ownership as well as rehabilitation. Its major objectives were the promotion of farm-home ownership through long-term amortized farm mortgage loans to selected tenants for the purchase of family-sized farms; the rehabilitation of distressed farm families through supervised short-term loans for equipment, livestock, and supplies such as feed, seed, and fertilizer; and the purchase of tracts considered submarginal for farming as a means of promoting a more efficient land-utilization pattern.

The rehabilitation program was a combination of financial aid and advisory assistance in farm and home management.[6] Upon its inception the program was looked upon as a means of preventing or slowing down the exodus from drought-stricken communities. The rehabilitation loans, which were repayable over a five-year period, averaged approximately $300.

The land-use adjustment and resettlement programs received major emphasis in South Dakota because of alleged improper systems of farm management. The heavy relief needs in the central and western parts of the state were considered an inescapable by-product of maladjustments in land use. Although 850,000 acres of submarginal and rough, uncultivated land were acquired by the federal government in the western part of the state, the idea of moving people from poor land to good land lying within other sections had practical limitations. Consequently, rehabilitation began to receive more and more emphasis as the program continued. The resettlement program was minor in terms of families assisted, but it involved heavy expenditures and so attracted much public attention. Most resettled families were placed on individual, scattered farms purchased by the Farm Security Administration from private owners. Title was also obtained from the state to rural credit tracts for resettlement purposes.

A unique feature of the resettlement program during its operation in South Dakota was a subsistence homestead project established at Sioux Falls in 1936. It was devised as a cooperative community experiment in order to prove that smaller farm units could be profitably operated under a properly supervised system of farm management. The Farm Security Administration acquired title to 4,540 acres of land and divided the tract into fourteen units on which it built dwelling houses and outbuildings. The project repre-

[6] Two excellent studies of the New Deal period with special interest for South Dakota are James G. Maddox, "The Farm Security Administration" (unpublished Doctoral dissertation, Harvard University, 1950) and Olaf F. Larson, "Ten Years of Rural Rehabilitation in the United States" (Washington, D.C.: U.S. Department of Agriculture, Bureau of Agricultural Economics, 1947).

sented a total cost of $218,000, or $15,570 per unit. The subsistence homestead experiment found little public favor in the state and was closed out during the middle of the 1940's.

There was an earlier attempt in 1934 to set up a subsistence homestead project at Jamesville some twenty miles northwest of Yankton on the site of an abandoned Hutterite colony, whose title had been acquired by the rural credit board. Since the seventeen-hundred-acre tract with its large apartment buildings and numerous outbuildings readily lent itself to an agricultural community organization, the state relief administration decided to utilize it as a rehabilitation center for transient relief families especially selected for their farming background. Approximately fifty families took part in the project, which was abandoned in April, 1935, after a year's operation.

In 1946 the Farmers Home Administration was created by Congress to replace the Farm Security Administration. By this time the resettlement projects were in process of liquidation, and rehabilitation was becoming primarily a farm credit activity. Farm ownership remained the major objective of the program, but with greatly reduced appropriations both for loans and funds for supervisory and technical services to clients. The land-utilization program was likewise retained, although administered by a different federal agency.

THE POLITICAL SCENE

The various relief and recovery programs inaugurated in South Dakota during the early thirties proved advantageous to the political party in control. The Democratic candidates won the 1934 election with increased majorities. Governor Berry defeated W. J. Allen, his Republican opponent, by a vote of 172,228 against 119,477.

As the campaign of 1936 got under way, private surveys showed New Deal policies continued to be popular among farmers and relief clients. The summer was hot and dry, and grasshopper infestations were the worst the state had ever experienced. Many counties were declared disaster areas, and relief activities were stepped up. Faced with a denuded range, ranchers begin to ship their herds to neighboring states where pasturing conditions were more favorable. To help alleviate the situation, the federal government instituted another cattle-buying program as well as other relief measures designed to save foundation herds. Whatever political advantages accrued to the Berry Administration from the beneficence of relief and recovery policies were, however, largely offset by anti-third-term sentiment and a strong reaction among Black Hills voters against an ore tax measure which had been piloted through the 1935 legislative session by the Farmers Union.

President Roosevelt carried the state by a handsome majority, but Governor Tom Berry was defeated by Leslie Jensen of Hot Springs, the Republican nominee, by a margin of 9,404 votes. The Republicans also elected the lieutenant governor and a member of the Public Utility Commission in a close contest. The Legislature swung back into the Republican column with control of the upper house held by the margin of a single vote. In the Congressional race, Congressman F. H. Hildebrandt, the Democratic incumbent, successfully met the challenge of Karl E. Mundt of Madison; in the west-river district, however, Theodore E. Werner was forced to relinquish his Congressional seat to Francis H. Case of Custer. Senator Bulow won re-election over Chandler Gurney, the Republican candidate.

With tax delinquency on the increase and income for both farmer and businessman still running low, depression policies remained a major concern of the state government during Governor Jensen's term of office. The relief problem was especially serious, since many counties had reached the legal limit of tax levies for both poor relief and mothers' pensions, and registered county warrants issued for relief purposes were carrying heavy discounts.

The 1937 Legislature created a state department of social security to enable South Dakota to comply with the provisions of the federal Social Security Act. A special legislative session during the closing days of the Berry Administration had already adopted measures for meeting requirements of a state-federal system of unemployment compensation. The social security program required an outlay of over two million dollars annually by the state. Despite this new item of public expenditures for old age assistance, aid to dependent children, and other welfare activities, the Jensen Administration was enabled to wipe out an overdraft of more than twenty years' standing and create a balance in the general fund, at the same time reducing the bonded indebtedness and building up sinking funds for the retirement of cement plant bonds.

The legislative program of the Jensen Administration included the refunding of rural credit bonds at lower rates of interest and the restoration to the highway fund of revenues from the state gasoline tax that had been diverted in 1933. The defection of a Republican state senator resulted in a deadlock in the upper house which remained unbroken until a Democratic member finally threw his support to the Republicans, thus assuring passage of the financial measures advocated by the Governor.

After serving one term in the governor's office, Leslie Jensen in 1938 ran for the Senate seat formerly held by Peter Norbeck, who had passed away in December, 1936, but was defeated by Chandler Gurney in the Republican primary. In the general election Gurney defeated Tom Berry by nearly fourteen thousand votes. Harlan J. Bushfield of Miller, formerly Republican state chairman, won an easy victory for governor over Oscar Fosheim, his Democratic opponent.

Governor Bushfield continued a policy of drastic economy during his two terms (1939–1943) in order to keep the state treasury solvent in the face of heavy fiscal requirements for the refunding of rural credit bonds. The state still held 1,700,000 acres acquired by the rural credit department, while the bonded indebtedness due to the rural credit venture stood at nearly $38,000,000. Taking advantage of an improved economy, the Bushfield Administration began to speed up activities in liquidating the rural credit department. The Legislature provided tax relief in the 1941 session through the elimination of the two-mill state property tax and the reduction of the sales tax to two cents. Bushfield's recommendation for a repeal of the state income tax went unheeded until 1943 after his retirement as governor.

By the end of the 1930's the depression had generally run its course. More favorable economic conditions had resulted in an upsurge in Republican sentiment among the voters, fully restoring the party to power. In the meantime, new problems closely related to a worsening international situation were beginning to take the spotlight away from domestic issues.

CHAPTER 20

World War II and After

WHILE THE UNITED STATES was preoccupied with economic recovery and domestic reform, forces of aggression were at work overseas. A premeditated attack by Japanese soldiers upon Chinese troops in Manchuria in September, 1931, was followed by a series of provocative incidents and military intervention on the part of Germany and Italy as well as Japan. By 1938 the world stood on the brink of a major conflict. The following year the German invasion of Poland precipitated World War II.

Although President Roosevelt showed a deep concern over the dangers of involvement, the American public was sharply divided in its response to the worsening international situation. Disillusionment over the postwar developments of the Treaty of Versailles and a genuine desire to hold aloof from the bickerings of other nations had produced a strong feeling of isolationism. The Congressional delegation from South Dakota supported the so-called neutrality legislation during the years 1935 to 1937, and the majority of their constituents were in accord with them.

The march of events led inexorably to the involvement of the United States in a global war. Four days after Japan's surprise attack on Pearl Harbor, December 7, 1941, Germany and Italy declared war on the United States. President Roosevelt's appeal for unity in his war message of December 8, when he asked Congress to recognize an obvious state of war with Japan, evoked an enthusiastic response throughout the nation.

Fortunately, the entry into World War II found the nation better prepared than had been the case in 1917. The outbreak of European hostilities in September, 1939, had led to various measures designed to strengthen the national defense. These included the enactment of a peacetime Selective Service Act in September, 1940, and the activation of selected National Guard units. In August, 1941, Congress extended the operation of the draft law by a close margin.

THE WAR EFFORT IN SOUTH DAKOTA

As in the First World War, South Dakota played a creditable part in the conflict. It has been estimated that the state furnished 64,560 troops to the armed forces up to September 1, 1945. About two-thirds of this number were inducted under the Selective Service Act. Casualties sustained during the war period included 1,560 killed in combat and 484 who died from other causes.

In accordance with the national policy of "federalizing" the National Guard, the state units were called into active service and integrated into the national defense structure. The 147th Field Artillery Regiment was the first unit to be called. It went into training at Fort Ord, California, in December, 1940, as a part of the Sixth Army and was alerted for overseas service a year later. The troops were in mid-Pacific en route to Manila, when news came of the attack on Pearl Harbor, and they were rerouted to Australia. The personnel originally with the 147th Artillery Regiment saw heavy action in the Pacific sector of the war.

Other National Guard units, including the 109th Engineer Battalion, the 109th Quartermaster Regiment, and the 34th Signal Company, all a part of the 34th Division, as well as the 132nd Engineer Regiment, were called into federal service by executive order in February, 1941. These units trained at Camp Claiborne, Louisiana, until 1942 when they were sent to Fort Dix, New Jersey, and then to northern Ireland. They saw vigorous action in North Africa and Italy as well as on the second front after its establishment in May, 1944.

South Dakota provided facilities for several training establishments during the war. The largest of these was the Sioux Falls Training Base where an estimated 45,000 men received technical instruction. Pierre was also the location of an air base. The Rapid City Air Base, later known as the Ellsworth Air Base, was continued after the war. Subbases of the Sioux City Army Air Base were maintained at Watertown and Mitchell. Another permanent war installation was the Black Hills or Igloo Ordinance Depot, six miles south of Edgemont at Provo.

South Dakota's educational institutions made their contribution to the war effort in various ways. As soon as the war started, the schools were called upon to assist prospective draftees in preparing themselves for army life. The larger high schools offered specific vocational preinduction courses in such subjects as aeronautics, shopwork, electricity, and radio fundamentals, while courses in all the secondary schools were slanted toward preinduction objectives. Courses in mathematics and physics were increased or expanded in response to a greater student demand. The colleges also played a vital role as they directed their resources toward the training of personnel for war industries as well as for the armed forces. Special defense training programs included a civilian pilot training course started during 1939 and 1940 under the sponsorship of the Civil Aeronautics Authority. Five institutions participated in the program up to its termination in 1943. Another program made use of facilities for trade and industrial education to train noncollegiate men for war industries. College training programs were set up in two institutions for special branches of the service, including the training of air cadets and navy pilots. The army also utilized the services of four collegiate institutions under a specialized training program in engineering for enlisted or drafted men.

To meet the demands imposed upon them, the colleges accelerated their schedules, making earlier graduation possible through shorter vacations, longer summer sessions, and, in some instances, a shortening of the semester period. Under the accelerated program, the colleges were able to utilize physical plants on a twelve-month basis. They also found it necessary to revise the curriculum to make room for more scientific and technical courses. All the colleges were adversely affected during the war by serious budgetary difficulties that resulted from declining enrollments. Many highly trained staff members were drawn into either military service or private employment, or were lost to war agencies. Numerous adjustments were necessary as a result, especially in institutions where service programs were in operation.

The war's impact upon the colleges was still felt on the return of peace when veterans flocked in large numbers to the classrooms to continue interrupted programs or to enroll for the first time. The larger enrollments, induced in large part by the financial aid provided for veterans by Congress, taxed facilities with respect to faculties, classrooms, and laboratory space. In many institutions, temporary housing had to be provided, especially for married students who began to appear on college campuses in increasing numbers.

In addition to the work of the schools and colleges, the home front required the performance of a multitude of services by civilians. Individuals representing all walks of life gave unstintingly of their time in administering the duties of draft and rationing boards, serving as air-raid wardens in towns and cities, soliciting funds for the United Service Organizations, and taking part in eight different bond drives. The civilian defense work was carried on in cooperation with the federal government through a state council of defense with the assistance of county and local councils authorized under state legislation enacted in 1943.

Salvage drives, which were generally conducted by the schools, resulted in the collection of vast amounts of metal scrap as well as waste paper, rags, rubber, and tin. An interesting feature of the salvage program was a milkweed pod collection during the summer and fall of 1944. Milkweed seed floss was found to be suitable buoyant material for filling life jackets which formerly had been stuffed with kapok imported from Java. The school children collected 14,-000 bags of floss in thirty-six counties east of the Missouri River.

The war emergency programs received the wholehearted support of the people. Disagreements over foreign policy generally disappeared after the attack on Pearl Harbor so that there was no open criticism of the war such as minority groups had expressed during World War I. There was, moreover, none of the wartime hysteria exhibited in the state in 1917 and 1918. South Dakota exceeded its quotas in the various bond drives with purchases of $328,000,000 in war bonds during the war period. Contributions by South Dakotans to the Red Cross from December, 1941, to the end of 1947 totaled $2,281,000.

In addition to the financial support, the war effort required compliance with numerous regulations that interfered with the normal routine. Restrictions on travel imposed by gasoline and tire rationing and low speed limits necessitated cancellation of numerous public meetings and reduced automobile traffic to a minimum. Rationing stamps were required for the purchase of sugar, butter, meat, coffee, and canned goods. There were also rent controls and price freezes. Such restrictions were deemed necessary in order to serve the needs of war industries, to distribute existing consumer supplies more fairly, and to check inflation.

The major contribution made by South Dakota to World War II lay in the field of agriculture. Increased demand induced by the war needs, higher prevailing prices, and favorable growing conditions brought farm production to a high level. During the war years farmers were especially called upon to grow more flax and soybeans and to increase the production of meat animals, milk, and poultry products. The total number of cattle on farms and ranches on January 1, 1944, was the highest since 1920, a marked contrast with the situation facing the cattle industry a decade earlier in 1934 when the cattle-buying program of the federal government was in progress.

The increased production of grain, including wheat, was achieved with a smaller cropland acreage than had been utilized during the late 1920's. This was made possible through more intensive farming methods and the utilization of cropland that had been lying idle or was in fallow as a result of the A.A.A. crop-reduction program. Relatively little grassland was plowed up during the period of the Second World War.

The wartime agricultural production was attained despite inadequate equipment and a serious shortage of farm labor. Most parts of the state had emerged from the drought and depression period with obsolete or worn-out farm machinery. Repair parts were hard to get during the war, and new machinery was virtually off the market. Blacksmiths and mechanics were consequently in great demand for improvising parts and keeping old machinery in repair. The depletion of the labor supply as a result of draft calls and an exodus of defense workers to industrial centers found farmers especially shorthanded during 1945 and 1946. In Minnehaha County servicemen from the Sioux Falls Training Base helped in harvesting crops, while in other areas nonfarm youths and businessmen from the towns and cities volunteered their services.

POSTWAR PROSPERITY

The prosperous state of agriculture continued after the war.[1] Cash income from crops and livestock, exclusive of government benefit payments, approached the half billion mark in 1946 for the first time in the state's history and continued to exceed it in successive years until 1955. For the South Dakota farmers it was a period of un-

[1] See Chapter 22 for an elaboration of the state's agricultural history.

precedented prosperity. The high point was reached in 1947 with a total cash farm income of $673,000,000, and an average income of $7,600 per farm.

As a result of the improved economic conditions during the war and after, farmers were in a position to reduce or liquidate indebtedness and build up financial reserves. Those who had lost their farms were able to repurchase them. Rising commodity prices created a favorable market for farm land which facilitated the sale of rural credit tracts under the state's liquidation program in progress during the war. Counties that had acquired title to large acreages also profited from the improved situation, as did insurance companies and other corporations as well as federal agencies which had acquired title to agricultural lands through foreclosure. By 1956 most county-owned lands had been sold to private owners and returned to the tax rolls. Farm tenancy, which reached an all-time high of 53 per cent in 1940, had dropped to 29 per cent by 1954. Five years later it reached a low of 26.8 per cent.

The economic improvement experienced by South Dakota agriculture after 1940 is best illustrated by statistics of farm indebtedness. The number of mortgaged farms dropped from 29,700 in 1940 to 19,612 in 1950. During the same period the amount of farm-mortgage debt declined from $127,706,000 to $87,536,000, while the ratio of debt to value fell from 56.5 per cent to 25.1 per cent. Moreover, farm foreclosures, which had reached a peak in 1932 with 3,864 foreclosure proceedings, occurred infrequently in subsequent years. At no time during the period from 1947 to 1960 were there more than eighteen foreclosures in any given year. In 1957 the number dropped to ten.

The favorable economic conditions were also reflected in higher standards of living for the rural areas. Modern modes of communication served to bring countryside and town into closer relationship. Improved roads and motorized transportation not only enabled the farmers to market their produce with greater ease, but also put an end to the isolation that had so long characterized farm life. In 1954 nearly 60 per cent of the farmers in the state were served by telephone facilities and 91 per cent enjoyed the benefits of electricity. By 1960 electricity was available to 96 per cent of all the farms in South Dakota.

The rural electrification program instituted by the federal government in 1935 effected a veritable technological revolution on the farm, making electric power available for farming operations as well as for modern conveniences in the farm home. The Rural Electrification Administration was set up in 1935 in order to aid in the construction of electric lines into rural areas that were without electric facilities. At that time only 3.4 per cent of the farms in South Dakota were served with central station electricity. The R.E.A. became a permanent agency through the Rural Electrification Act of 1936. The first R.E.A.-financed line was put in operation in 1937 by the Clay-Union Electric Corporation. In 1960 thirty-four cooperatives were participating in the self-liquidating projects, serving nine-tenths of the electrified farms.

The construction of power lines into rural areas, accompanied by increased needs in urban communities, has required careful long-term planning. Private utilities have been particularly active in expanding their facilities, supplementary to the hydro-power from Missouri River dams. The formation of power pools and interconnected systems of transmission lines, including those of the Bureau of Reclamation, provide the framework for coordinated planning.

Pioneering efforts were made during the 1960's by Northern States Power Company to develop nuclear energy at its Pathfinder Power Plant near Sioux Falls. Constructed with financial aid from the Atomic Energy Commission and several privately owned middle western firms, it made its initial output in July, 1966. Considered the world's first all-nuclear plant, it was converted to a conventional plant after a year's operation because of technological difficulties. The experimentation, however, provided invaluable experiences, including the training of personnel for nuclear plants erected later in Minnesota.

The increased consumption of electricity in both rural and urban areas of South Dakota was closely related to plans for the comprehensive development of the Missouri River Basin under the Flood Control Act passed by Congress in 1944. This vast program for developing the water resources of the Missouri River anticipated far-reaching benefits for the entire Missouri Basin in the form of flood control, navigation, irrigation, fish and wild-life conservation, and the development of recreational areas as well as the production of hydroelectric power.

THE MISSOURI RIVER BASIN DEVELOPMENT PROJECT

The inauguration of the Missouri Basin development project came after fifty years of agitation and bickering. The Missouri River is a regional body of water and presents problems in its lower reaches vastly different from those facing inhabitants of the Northern Plains states. It is readily navigable below Sioux City. Moreover, in its lower courses it has been subject over the years to destructive floods which have taken heavy toll of life and property. Kansas City, the scene of twenty-nine serious floods within three-quarters of a century, was an especially heavy sufferer. The residents in the lower river basin have consequently desired a reservoir system of small dams sufficient to harness floods and release water as needed for navigation purposes. The inhabitants of the Upper Missouri Valley, on the other hand, have wished to divert the greater part of the water resources for the development of their particular region, seeking large storage dams for irrigation purposes and for the development of hydro-electric power. The Army Corps of Engineers has always represented the flood-control interests; the Bureau of Reclamation has championed the second group.

Plans for the development of the Missouri River by the federal government began to take form during the early 1940's, supplementing earlier studies and reports. Damaging floods in the Lower Missouri Valley during 1942 and 1943 gave further impetus to calls for flood relief. Proposals made to Congress for a comprehensive system of storage reservoirs on the Upper Missouri and the establishment of a nine-foot navigation channel below Sioux City brought on a clash between the United States Army Corps of Engineers and the Bureau of Reclamation.

The Pick Plan, sponsored by General Lewis A. Pick of the Corps of Engineers, called for a system of dams situated where they could do the most good for flood control and navigation. It included five major dams on the main channel between Fort Peck and Sioux City as well as a number of reservoirs on the Missouri's tributaries. The Bureau of Reclamation, under the leadership of Assistant Director W. Glenn Sloan, proposed a number of reservoirs in the headwaters of the Missouri primarily for irrigation and power, locating the dams where they would do the most good for irrigation. Under this proposal, the greater portion of the reservoir capacity was to be on the tributaries, rather than on the main stem of the Missouri. An interagency committee finally reached a compromise agreement under the Pick-Sloan Plan which formed the basis for the Flood Control Act of December, 1944. A few months later Congress authorized a nine-foot channel for the Missouri River below Sioux City.

The Pick-Sloan Plan called for a series of four rolled-earth multiple-purpose dams on the main stem of the Missouri within South Dakota, supplementing the Fort Garrison dam in North Dakota and the Fort Peck dam which was built in Montana during the 1930's. The South Dakota dams, in order of construction, are Fort Randall, Oahe, Gavins Point, and Big Bend.

The Fort Randall dam, located near the site of the old military post, was the first of the main-stem dams to be constructed. After ten years of work, the dam was dedicated in August, 1956. U.S. highways 281 and 18 cross the crest of the 160-foot embankment on a 24-foot paved road. High voltage lines, built and operated by the Bureau of Reclamation, carry the power across the entire state of South Dakota and interconnect with public power districts in Nebraska. The reservoir created by the Fort Randall dam extends a distance of 140 miles to the site of the Big Bend dam above Chamberlain. The first current was released upon an electric signal given by President Dwight D. Eisenhower at the White House on March 15, 1954. The initial power went to R.E.A. cooperatives.

Construction on the Oahe dam six miles northwest of Pierre began in September, 1948. Said to be the largest rolled-earth dam in the world, the 242-foot-high structure was completed in 1964. A 250-mile-long reservoir with an estimated shoreline of 2,500 miles was planned to make available a huge body of water for possible diversion into the James River Valley between Woonsocket and Aberdeen for use by the Bureau of Reclamation for irrigation purposes. This would also, in addition to irrigation, make a greater supply of water available to the area for industrial and municipal use. The Oahe dam is the second largest in the series of main-stem dams, ranking next to the Garrison dam.

The Gavins Point dam, constructed a few miles west of Yankton during the years 1952–1956, provides flood control storage and generates power. It also regulates the flow of water released from the Fort Randall dam. It is the smallest as well as the lowermost of the main-stem dams and offers the greatest potential as a recreation area through Lewis and Clark Lake, the thirty-seven-mile-long reservoir of impounded waters.

The Big Bend dam, designed primarily for power production, is the sixth and final link in the whole chain of main-stem dams. Ground was broken for its construction in May, 1960. The dam was completed in 1966. The regulatory reservoir, officially named Lake Sharpe, forms an eighty-mile lake extending to Pierre.

The Pick-Sloan Plan is of far-reaching significance for the entire Missouri River Basin. For South Dakota the system of dams, reservoirs, and transmission lines signifies a more stable and better balanced economy. The team of main-stem dams with its array of four large lakes should prevent the recurrence of such devastating floods in the state as overwhelmed Pierre and other communities along the main channel in 1952. The problem of floods along the Big Sioux and the Vermillion rivers, however, still remained unresolved in 1968. The transmission lines radiating from the Big Bend, Oahe, and Fort Randall dams furnish cheaper power to municipalities, R.E.A. cooperatives, and private power companies and provide inducements for industrial development. The dams and reservoirs also promote the development of fish and wildlife habitats and afford extensive recreational facilities. According to records maintained by the Army Corps of Engineers, over three and a half million people were drawn to the shores of the new "Great Lakes" region of South Dakota during 1966.

In addition to the formidable engineering tasks, the Pick-Sloan Plan presented three important problems with reference to its administrative and operational aspects. The first major problem concerned the make-up of the agency responsible for the administration of the various projects embraced in the program. The conflict of interest between federal agencies as well as between different localities in the Missouri Basin resulted in the rejection of a proposal for a centralized federal agency comparable to the Tennessee Valley Authority. Instead of a valley authority or a federal commission, an Inter-Agency Committee, composed of representatives of the several federal agencies concerned and the governors of the ten basin states, was finally set up as a coordinating body.

A second problem arose out of the conflict between the upper and lower sections of the Missouri Basin over the respective needs for irrigation and navigation. Although the Pick-Sloan Plan conceded priority to the use of the Missouri River for irrigation purposes, the water requirements of a nine-foot channel for barge lines below Sioux City still remained undetermined in 1975.

A third issue of vital interest to South Dakotans, also remaining unresolved in 1975, concerned the allocation of power. The likelihood that the demand for electric power might exceed supply added to the gravity of the problem. Under federal statute, public bodies in the form of municipalities, R.E.A. cooperatives, and public power districts enjoy preference over private companies in the use of public power.[2] A fear that the greater portion of the electric current might go to public power districts in neighboring states led to strong demands in South Dakota for preferential treatment. The state regarded the Missouri River as its leading natural resource and felt entitled to the major share of the power produced at the main-stem dams. The equitable distribution of Missouri River power was a matter of especial concern for South Dakota communities trying to attract industry.

FINANCING POSTWAR IMPROVEMENTS

The favorable economic conditions that prevailed after World War II led to an improvement in the financial affairs of the state. The bonded indebtedness, consisting entirely of rural credit bonds, still stood at $24,994,000 on June 30, 1945. Nine years later, a mortgage-burning ceremony was held in the capitol rotunda at Pierre. The total receipts of the state treasury had soared from $32,958,000 in 1945 to $76,741,000 in 1954 to enable the state to become free of debt for the first time in forty years.

The attainment of this debt-free status was especially noteworthy in view of the heavy obligations undertaken in 1949 for the payment of a $28,000,000 bonus to veterans of World War II. Following the adoption of a constitutional amendment by the voters in November, 1948, authorizing a veterans bonus, the Legislature decided to appropriate $7,800,000 from the general fund and provide for supplementary revenues through an increase in the sales tax from two to three per cent, a special two-mill state property levy, and a three per cent sales tax on alcoholic beverages and cigarettes. Sufficient funds had accumulated by October, 1951, for the redemption of the bonus bonds, and the special levies were accordingly terminated. In 1955 the Legislature re-enacted self-repealing revenue measures in order to extend bonus benefits to veterans of the Korean War.

[2] The Legislature met in special session in February, 1950, in order to provide authority for the creation of public power districts so that South Dakota might share equally with other states the benefits of Missouri River development. No attempts were made to establish public power districts in South Dakota up to 1975.

The retirement of the state's bonded obligations obviated further needs for sinking funds and released more funds for expanding public services. Particularly pressing were the needs of the highway department and the schools for greater financial support.

The state highway department at the end of the war faced the problem of building up a system of hard-surface roads capable of carrying the heavy traffic of the modern motor age. The diversion of gasoline tax receipts from the highway fund during the early 1930's in order to maintain payments on rural credit bonds as well as the unsatisfactory financial conditions of the period left the highway department with inadequate support during the depression days. Road construction at the time was generally confined to W.P.A. projects. During the war period a shortage of labor and materials not only militated against new construction, but also made it difficult to keep the state's highway system in adequate repair. All road construction was halted for the duration of the war.

Since practically all the revenue available for construction and maintenance came from the gasoline tax and motor vehicle registration fees, each legislative session after the war was confronted with the problem of providing adequate funds. Proposals for the issuance of highway bonds met with little support. Even though the financing of the highway system was left on a pay-as-you-go basis, an increasing volume of revenue derived from the gasoline tax and direct legislative appropriations from the general fund enabled the highway department to keep pace with modern road-building needs as well as to meet the requirements of the federal government for grants on a dollar-matching basis. In 1957 the gasoline tax was raised from five to six cents to provide matching funds for federal superhighways which are to crisscross the state. The total expenditures of the state highway department for maintenance and new construction rose from $25,809,000 in 1953 to a record high of $69,511,000 in 1965. The grants received from the federal government for highway purposes increased from $10,700,000 to $43,518,000 during the same period.

The problem of providing adequate school facilities has been a matter of vital concern since early territorial days. Throughout the years the major part of financial support for public education had come from local sources, chiefly the general property tax. Upon statehood, income became available from the permanent school fund provided by the common school lands. In 1921 the revenue from this source represented one-fifth of the total receipts collected for school purposes. In subsequent years, when operational costs began to mount, the permanent school fund became less important.

The depression of the 1930's made apparent the need for state aid in support of the public schools. In 1933 the gross income tax law allocated 45 per cent of the revenue to schools as a property replacement tax. Two years later the Legislature substituted for the gross income tax a net income and sales tax, apportioning nearly 30 per cent of the revenue among school districts. Special regard was to be given to districts financially depressed. Subsequent to the repeal of the income tax and the reduction of the sales tax, the Legislature began to provide specific appropriations for school purposes. The direct biennial appropriations made for the purpose of equalizing the financial burdens of the state's educational system grew steadily from an initial million-dollar grant for the 1943–1945 biennium until it reached a total of $15,000,000 for the 1965–1967 biennium.

Closely related to the problem of school finance was the need for reorganizing school districts in the interest of greater efficiency and economy. A school district reorganization measure enacted in 1951 provided for a survey of school conditions and the formulation of plans for reorganization. Four years later the Legislature repealed the measure and provided for county boards of education, consisting of seven members. Under the new legislation, each county board was to draw up a master plan for the reorganization of school districts in accordance with standards set up by the state board of education. The work of reorganization was left on a voluntary basis. Aside from the work carried out in a few counties, little reorganization had been accomplished by 1960. A notable exception was Spink County, where forty-two districts were eliminated in accordance with the reorganization law.

School reorganization made slow progress during the next few years. Finally, in the face of strong opposition, especially in the less populous areas west of the Missouri River, the Legislature in 1966 passed a reorganization measure which provided that common school districts not operating for two years must be joined to independent or common school districts by March 1, 1968. At the time the bill was passed, there were 876 non-operating districts. This law was supplemented in 1967 with a stronger measure making mandatory the reorganization of all territory into twelve-grade school districts. The whole question of compulsory reorganization, nevertheless, remained in abeyance until November, 1968, when the citizens of the state approved the reorganization measure by a narrow margin in a referendum vote.

The state's charitable and educational institutions also posed a serious problem. During the early days of the depression, they had sustained serious setbacks as a result of curtailed appropriations and drastic salary cuts. They not only needed greater financial support to get them back to their former standard, but also required additional resources to meet the new demands placed on them after the war. The improved economic situation made more adequate support possible by the middle forties. Despite heavy sinking fund requirements for servicing the public debt, the Legislature authorized an $8,500,000 long-range building program during the administration of Governor George T. Mickelson. Succeeding administrations continued noteworthy efforts for the general improvement of the state's institutions, providing not only larger appropriations for maintenance and new construction but also for long overdue salary increases for personnel.

Although legislative appropriations for new buildings were generously increased in subsequent years, the needs of the state-supported colleges and universities for student centers and new dormitories were met through federal loans on a self-liquidating basis. In recognition of the state's responsibility, the Legislature in 1967 made provision for a state building authority, subject to approval by the voters at the November, 1968, election. According to the measure, the authority, consisting of a commission of seven, would be empowered to sell self-liquidating bonds for the construction of buildings which would then be leased to the particular governmental agency or institution for which the buildings were constructed. Upon retirement of the bonds, title to the buildings would pass from the authority or commission to the state.

To keep pace with the high cost of living that characterized the inflationary forties and fifties, the Legislature from time to time increased the compensation of public employees. In 1951 it also made public employees eligible for participation in the federal old-age and survivors insurance program. At the same time it authorized a flat $600 cost-of-living increase for elective county offices and all elective and appointive state positions. After rejecting similar proposals at least a dozen times, the voters in November, 1946, finally accepted an amendment removing the limitation placed upon the salaries of the governor and other constitutional officers in the Constitution adopted in 1889. During the following session the lawmakers raised the governor's salary from $3,000 to $8,500 and placed the yearly compensation for Supreme Court judges at $7,200. In 1955 the salary of the governor was fixed at $12,000 and other salaries were adjusted accordingly. In 1965 the salaries for Supreme Court judges were raised to $17,500 and, two years later, the governor's salary was fixed at $18,000.

Despite generally favorable economic conditions throughout the fifties, the rapidly rising costs of governmental operations have become a matter of deep concern to the citizens of South Dakota. Legislative appropriations increased from $19,128,000 in 1945 to $119,262,000 in 1967. The amount provided for social welfare soared from $4,750,000 in 1943 to $23,521,000 in 1967. Other state service costs have risen in the same degree. The total disbursements of the state government were $27,486,000 in 1945 as compared with $188,-525,000 in 1966. Even though the total receipts for the same years jumped from $32,900,000 to $185,278,000, the state has been hard pressed to finance the services demanded by its citizens. The hazards inherent in a northern plains environment and an economy that remained basically agricultural were compelling reasons for exercising caution in the formulation of fiscal policy.

The heavy budgetary requirements led to strong demands during the 1960's for a broadening of the tax base in order to raise more revenue. Closely related to the mounting fiscal needs was the popular demand for reform in the tax structure. Particularly under attack were both the general property tax and the personal property tax. In 1965 the Legislature increased the sales tax from 2 to 3 per cent, also at the same time broadening the levy to cover various professional as well as other services. Motel and hotel accommodations had been included in an earlier measure. As a means of procuring sufficient replacement revenue for major tax relief at the local level, more and more individuals by the end of the decade were proposing the re-enactment of a state income tax measure.

THE POLITICAL SCENE SINCE 1942

During the forties and early fifties the Republicans continued to dominate the political scene in South Dakota. Senator William J. Bulow, who had incurred the displeasure of the New Deal administration at Washington, lost the Democratic primary contest in 1942 to Tom Berry, who in turn went down in defeat at the hands of Harlan J. Bushfield at the general election. M. Q. Sharpe was elected governor, receiving the nomination from the Republican state convention after an indecisive primary contest in which four candidates shared the votes.

Governor Sharpe gave the state an energetic administration, serving at a time when the governor's duties were greatly increased under the war powers prescribed by the Civilian Defense Act of 1943. He also played a prominent part in the preliminary planning that culminated in the Pick-Sloan Plan, heading for a time an organization of state governors formed to study the problem. Sharpe lost his bid for renomination for a third term to George T. Mickelson in the primary contest in May, 1946. The Republican victory at the polls was so sweeping that only four legislative seats were won by the minority party. The prevailing sentiment against a third term led to the enactment of a law in 1947, prohibiting a candidate's nomination to a third successive term as governor.

The overwhelming support given in 1946 to a constitutional amendment inserting a "right-to-work" provision in the bill of rights reflected the conservative mood of the electorate. The approval of the amendment was followed by the enactment of three measures in the 1947 legislative session, outlawing the closed shop, making picketing unlawful, and permitting labor unions to sue or be sued. Subsequent efforts by representatives of organized labor in the state failed to effect a repeal of the antilabor statutes.

The bitter presidential primary contest between Robert A. Taft and Dwight D. Eisenhower attracted nationwide attention in 1952. Taft won the state delegation to the national nominating convention by a margin of less than one per cent of the total votes cast. The Republicans won an overwhelming victory in the general election, with Eisenhower carrying every county in the state. Only two Democrats were elected to the Legislature.

Governor Mickelson (1947–1951) was succeeded by Sigurd Anderson (1951–1955). Like his immediate predecessors, Governor Anderson played a prominent part in the many conferences held in conjunction with the planning and operational problems concerning the development of the Missouri River Basin. He served for two years as chairman of the Missouri River States Committee, made up of governors of all the states in the basin area. The creation of the

Legislative Research Council in 1951 was a major achievement of the Anderson Administration. In 1954 Joe Foss, famed Marine pilot in World War II and holder of a Congressional Medal of Honor, was elected governor, becoming the youngest man to hold the position in the state's history.

A strong Democratic trend, reflecting growing dissatisfaction with federal farm policies as well as resentment against a new assessment law passed by the Legislature in 1955, resulted in the election of George S. McGovern to Congress in the first district and greatly reduced majorities for the Republican state ticket in 1956. President Eisenhower carried the state with 57 per cent of the votes, as compared with a 69.3 per cent majority in 1952. Governor Foss and United States Senator Francis H. Case were re-elected by narrow margins. After an eighteen-year struggle against overwhelming odds, the Democrats seemed to be well on their way to making South Dakota a two-party state. They made striking gains in the Legislature, winning eighteen of the thirty-five senate seats and twenty-six of the seventy-five house seats. The Republicans were able, however, to retain control of the senate when Governor Foss appointed a Republican to represent Yankton County in replacement of a Democrat who was unable to serve because of illness.

The trend against the Republicans continued into the election of 1958 when for the first time in twenty years the voters elected a Democratic governor. Ralph Herseth, who had opposed Foss in the preceding election, defeated Phil Saunders by a small margin. Most of the other state offices also went to Democrats. The Republicans, however, were able to retain control of the lower house of the Legislature. The contest which attracted most attention was the unsuccessful effort of Joe Foss, the retiring Governor, to displace Congressman McGovern in the first district. In the second Congressional district, E. Y. Berry, the Republican incumbent, was re-elected by a comfortable margin.

Governor Herseth suffered the usual handicaps of a divided Legislature, with neither house willing to assume responsibility for additional revenues to meet the budgetary requirements. Efforts of the Democratic administration to broaden the sales tax to include motel and hotel accommodations failed through the refusal of the Republican-controlled lower house to accept the measure. Also rejected was a proposal to tax soft drinks. The only tax measures enacted provided for an increase in the excise tax on cigarettes and a levy on cattle brought into the state for grazing purposes. At the end of the legislative session Governor Herseth appointed a citizens' tax committee to make an intensive study of the whole problem of taxation and to recommend tax changes for consideration by the next Legislature.

In 1960 the Republicans gained a sweeping victory at the polls. Despite an acrimonious and lengthy campaign which created much interest, the final returns failed to match the record vote cast in 1940. Vice President Richard M. Nixon received 58.2 per cent of the ballots, winning the state's four electoral votes over the Democratic ticket headed by John F. Kennedy by a vote of 178,017 to 128,070. In the gubernatorial contest, Archie M. Gubbrud, speaker of the house during the preceding legislative session, eked out a narrow victory over Ralph Herseth by a vote of 154,530 to 150,095. In his bid for re-election, Senator Karl E. Mundt by a vote of 160,181 to 145,267 succeeded in turning back the threat posed by the candidacy of Congressman George S. McGovern. Until Mundt's victory, Peter Norbeck had been the only South Dakotan to be honored with a third term in the United States Senate. Benjamin Reifel, a newcomer to politics who had resigned a position as area director of the Bureau of Indian Affairs at Aberdeen earlier in the year to run in the Republican primary, won the Congressional seat vacated by McGovern. Congressman E. Y. Berry won re-election in the second district by an overwhelming majority. The Republicans won all the constitutional offices and gained a clear majority in the Legislature, holding 57 out of 75 seats in the house and 22 out of 35 senate seats.

Although tax discussions dominated the deliberations of the 1961 Legislature, the Republican majority carried out campaign promises not to vote new taxes unless absolutely necessary. After considerable debate, proponents of annual legislative sessions succeeded in referring the question to the voters at the next general election. Under the proposal, the lawmaking body would meet forty-five legislative days during the odd-numbered years and thirty legislative days during the even-numbered years.

The constitutional amendment providing for annual sessions received the support of the electorate by a small majority in November, 1962. The Republicans were easy victors in the election for the state offices and they increased their majority in the Legislature. These gains were, however, largely offset by their loss of the seat in the United States Senate made vacant by the death of Francis H. Case on June 22. Senator Case had served seven terms in the House and was completing his second term in the Senate.

The choice of a candidate on the ballot to replace Case was left to the Republican State Central Committee which, in a protracted and almost deadlocked session, nominated Lieutenant Governor Joe Bottum of Rapid City over several other active contenders including Speaker of the House Nils A. Boe and former governors Sigurd Anderson and Joe Foss. Governor Gubbrud then appointed Bottum to the Senate seat to serve out the unexpired term. Opposing Bottum in the election was George S. McGovern who had been serving as director of the federal agency, Food for Peace, at Washington under the Kennedy Administration. Unofficial returns showed a victory for McGovern by the narrow margin of about two hundred votes. Both parties charged election irregularities. A recount extended McGovern's lead to 597.

When the Legislature convened in January, 1963, Governor Gubbrud called for an increased budget and recommended measures for additional revenues by broadening the 2 per cent sales tax to include the services of hotels and motels as well as increasing the levies on beer, liquors, and cigarettes. The Legislature accepted the revenue proposals and appropriated a record-breaking total of $76,700,000, an amount about three millions under the governor's budgetary recommendations. The legislation enacted at this session included the creation of a budget office and the establishment of a retirement system for the faculties at the state-supported institutions of higher learning. A law was also passed providing for a minimum foundation program under which state aid to the public schools would be distributed on the basis of both a flat grant and an equalization of fiscal needs.

Aside from the excitement over the selection of a Republican nominee to succeed Governor Gubbrud, political activities in the state in 1964 were overshadowed by national politics. In a spirited primary contest, Nils A. Boe defeated Sigurd Anderson who had resigned from the Federal Trade Commission to aspire to an unprecedented third term in the statehouse. Despite a strong bid in the primary by a slate of delegates pledged to the support of Barry M. Goldwater at the Republican national convention, an unstructured delegation, favored by the major party leaders, received the overwhelming approval of the Republican voters.

Although the state polls indicated Goldwater to be the choice of 52 per cent of the voters, President Lyndon B. Johnson carried South Dakota by an impressive count of 163,010 against 130,108, polling 55.6 per cent of the total vote. In addition to the lack of appeal in the Republican candidate, the vice-presidential candidacy of Senator Hubert H. Humphrey, a native of the state, was undoubtedly an asset for the Democratic ticket. At the same time, the Democrats made gains at the county level and succeeded in reducing the Republican majority in the Legislature, winning seven new seats in the senate and thirteen in the house. They also made a serious threat in the contest for lieutenant governor. Frank Farrar, in his bid for re-election as attorney-general, made the strongest showing among the Republican candidates for state office, polling 55.8 per cent of the vote. Congressmen E. Y. Berry and Benjamin Reifel won re-election by slightly higher percentages. Nils A. Boe won the governorship over his Democratic opponent, John F. Lindley, by a vote of 150,151 to 140,419.

The Legislature met in January, 1965, for what proved to be a stormy session. A measure increasing the sales tax from 2 to 3 per cent and broadening its base to include professions and services met the demands for tax revision. Budgetary measures, however, ran afoul of a controversial reapportionment issue. In re-defining the boundaries of the two Congressional districts, the Republican majority merely shifted the dividing line a hundred miles eastward from the Missouri River, the previous demarcation line. Republican plans for legislative reapportionment met with intense opposition from the Democratic members who considered the proposals prejudicial to their cause. There was general agreement that the membership should remain at 75 in the house and 35 in the senate.

Although the Republicans agreed to some modifications in the bill for redistricting, the Democrats remained unsatisfied and interposed a legislative roadblock by blocking passage of special appropriations measures, which required a two-thirds majority. After lending their support to two minor items, the Democratic bloc killed all remaining bills for special appropriations. It also voted down a bill allocating $16,000,000 from the proceeds of the new sales tax measure to the general fund and to local political subdivisions. The Republicans then, in a highly questionable procedure,

attached all special items to the general appropriations measure by
simple majority vote. Following adjournment, the Supreme Court
invalidated all items covering special appropriations. In the next
legislative session, the invalidated items were re-enacted.

The Republicans won a sweeping victory in November, 1966, re-
electing Governor Boe over his Democratic opponent, Robert Chamberlain. The Republicans also gained twenty-six legislative seats
previously held by Democrats. Senator Mundt was elected to an
unprecedented fourth term, while Congressmen Berry and Reifel
retained their seats by impressive majorities.

The Republican ticket, headed by Attorney General Frank L.
Farrar, experienced little difficulty in winning the 1968 election.
The presidential campaign of that year was of special interest to
South Dakota Democrats because of a contest between two native
sons, Vice-president Hubert H. Humphrey and Senator McGovern,
for the presidential nomination. The latter had drawn national
attention to himself through a break with President Johnson over
the conflict in South Vietnam. The South Dakota voters gave their
overwhelming support to Richard M. Nixon in preference to
Humphrey, the Democratic nominee, but, at the same time, favored
Senator McGovern in his bid for a second term against Archie M.
Gubbrud.

The 1969 session of the Legislature was a stormy one. A controversial income tax measure was narrowly defeated in the Senate.
An equally controversial measure, providing for a three-man council for the regulation of gas and electric utilities, was enacted by a
very small margin. During the subsequent session, the consumers'
council law was repealed, rendering a referendum vote unnecessary.

In 1970, Governor Farrar withstood a bitter primary contest but
lost his bid for a second term to Richard M. Kneip. The Democrats
also elected the lieutenant governor and two minor constitutional
officials. Frank E. Denholm and James Abourezk defeated their
Republican opponents to fill the seats vacated by retiring Congressmen Berry and Reifel.

The legislative session of 1971 proved disappointing to Governor
Kneip. Although the Republican-dominated legislature enacted
much legislation of a constructive nature, it spurned his proposals
for tax revision. During this session the House membership was

reduced to seventy. In 1972, the Democrats made further gains, placing their entire state ticket in office with the exception of two statehouse officials. They controlled the Senate by a margin of one and shared an equal number of seats with the Republicans in the House. James Abourezk captured the senatorial seat vacated by Karl Mundt, while Congressman Denholm won election to a second term. James Abdnor, a Republican, however, gained the congressional seat vacated by Abourezk. Despite the strongest Democratic showing at the state level since 1936, Senator McGovern, the Democratic nominee, lost his home state to President Nixon.

The major achievement during the Kneip administration was the reorganization of the state government. Upon the recommendation of a Constitution Revision Commission, a plan was formulated to modernize the governmental structure through the amending process instead of a constitutional convention. The reorganization plan was accepted by the voters in November, 1972, in the form of four key amendments. These provided for a unified court system, broad home-rule powers for local governmental units, and a restructuring of the executive branch under direction of the governor, henceforth elected to a four-year term. Governor Kneip shortly thereafter, by executive order, formed sixteen departments with each department head enjoying cabinet rank.

The problem of tax revision remained unsolved in 1974. Financial history was, however, made by the 1974 legislature when it approved the largest annual appropriations in state history, reaching a total of more than $130,000,000. This included $23,000,000 for aid to education.

In November, 1974, in an election that engendered a 72 per cent voter turnout and broke the anti-third-term tradition, Governor Kneip defeated his Republican opponent, John E. Olson, for the newly authorized four-year term by a 54 per cent majority. The Republicans won three statehouse positions, including the attorney general's office. The Legislature remained divided with a Republican majority of four in the House and a Democratic margin of three in the Senate. Although Senator McGovern overcame his Republican opponent, Leo K. Thorsness, the Republican challenger, Larry Pressler, defeated incumbent Congressman Denholm. Congressman Abdnor won re-election easily over his Democratic opponent, Jack Weiland.

CHAPTER 21

Reappraisal: The Transformation of the Sioux

THE STORY of South Dakota's first hundred years would be incomplete without some account of the progress made by the members of the Sioux nation in their adjustment to the white man's way of life. After two decades of intermittent resistance against the advancing tide of white civilization, the Sioux, once the proudest and most prosperous of all the Plains Indians, were reduced to the status of wards of the federal government and lived under the close supervision of the Indian Bureau. The beginnings of the acculturation process which has transformed the Indian population of South Dakota lie in the reservation system.

While the whites were building a new commonwealth on the Dakota prairie, the Sioux subtribes were trying to adjust themselves to reservation life. The Pine Ridge and Rosebud agencies, created for the Oglala and Brûlé in 1878, were each responsible for some seven thousand tribesmen, while the Lower Brûlé, Cheyenne River, and Standing Rock agencies served about six thousand additional Teton Sioux. All these agencies were located on the Great Sioux Reservation. East of the Missouri River were the Crow Creek, Yankton, and Lake Traverse or Sisseton reservations with populations in 1878 of about 900, 2000, and 1500, respectively.

The change from a nomadic to a sedentary existence was inevitable, induced not so much by military subjugation as by the collapse of the native economy with the extermination of the buffalo. The buffalo had not only provided food, clothing, and shelter, but also occupied an important place in Indian religious ceremonials. With their means of subsistence gone, the Sioux were left with no alternative but to accept the white man's terms.

Buffalo were already declining in numbers by the time permanent settlements appeared in the Dakota country. A major cause of the warfare between Sioux and whites during the sixties and seventies was the desire of the Indians to protect their hunting grounds. Commercial white hunters turned an erstwhile sport into indiscriminate slaughter, and by the late seventies there were few bison left of the

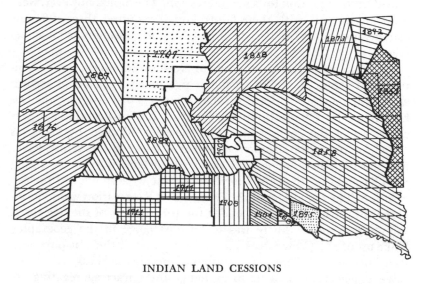

INDIAN LAND CESSIONS

once gigantic northern herd. The Sioux staged their last organized hunts in 1880 and 1882 when fragmentary herds wandered onto the reservation lands of the Cheyenne River and Standing Rock agencies.

The reservation system was conceived to subjugate and assimilate the Indians. Disagreement among the whites was mostly concerned with method; on objectives there was virtual unanimity. The Indian was to be made over in the image of the white man with little regard for his basic cultural traits and traditions. To hasten transition from the tribal or communal manner of living, the native culture was to be broken up as much as possible. Meanwhile, until the Indian could support himself, the government would provide rations of food and clothing. In this acculturation process the Christian missionaries joined their efforts with the schools and government agents.

Despite the liberal land cession under the Black Hills agreement of September 26, 1876, the whites soon began to clamor for a further reduction of the Great Sioux Reservation. Across the lands reserved to the Teton bands lay the travel routes linking the mining communities and the agricultural settlements east of the Missouri. Freighters, townsite boomers, railroad corporations, and cattlemen joined in the agitation for a second cession. The Sioux, however, were reluctant to part with their lands, and it required three different commissions and a full decade of dickering to consummate an agreement.

In 1882 a commission composed of Newton Edmunds, Peter Shannon, and James H. Teller set about procuring a cession in accordance with a measure piloted through Congress by Pettigrew, the Dakota delegate. Edmunds, an old hand at Indian negotiations, was chairman of the commission. The measure adopted by Congress called for the relinquishment of the area between the White River and the Big Cheyenne as well as a strip of land west of the 102nd meridian and north of the Cheyenne on the western edge of the reservation. The remainder of the Great Sioux Reservation was to be divided into five reservations under the jurisdiction of the five corresponding agencies. There was to be no change in the geographic make-up of the Crow Creek reserve lying east of the Missouri with its agency at Fort Thompson. In lieu of money the Sioux were to receive 26,000 head of cattle in exchange for a tract aggregating approximately 11,000,000 acres, a payment of about eight cents per acre.

The commissioners ignored the specific provision of the Laramie Treaty of 1868 requiring the signatures of three-fourths of the adult males in any subsequent agreement. They drove from agency to agency to collect signatures from leading chiefs and headmen, taking with them as interpreter the Reverend Samuel P. Hinman, onetime Episcopal missionary who was thoroughly conversant with Indian customs. The questionable methods employed in securing Indian signatures, including intimidation, threats of removal to Indian Territory, and deliberate misrepresentation of facts, as well as a complete disregard for the three-fourths provision, soon provoked a storm of protest throughout the country. Few of the signers seem to have understood that they were selling tribal lands.

Although the members of the commission denied any improprieties in their negotiations, the United States Senate, in March, 1883, ordered new negotiations. Secretary Teller reappointed the commissioners, who in turn instructed Hinman to collect more signatures. This energetic clergyman soon came up with a sufficient number to satisfy the three-fourths requirement. A subsequent investigation revealed that the signers included 144 Indian boys, ages ranging from three to sixteen, who "touched the pen" while Hinman affixed their names on the register. After a visit to the Sioux agencies by an investigating committee headed by Senator Henry L. Dawes of Massachusetts, the Senate rejected the second agreement also.

It was not until 1888 that Congress authorized a renewal of negotiations. During that year another commission, this one headed by Captain R. H. Pratt of the Carlisle Indian School, visited the Sioux agencies. Except for the price, the terms were substantially the same. The land was to be sold to settlers at the rate of fifty cents an acre, with townsite lands commanding a slightly higher price. The money received for the land was to go into a tribal trust fund.

The Pratt Commission failed to secure the required signatures, so the authorities at Washington decided to bring an Indian delegation to the capital to discuss more favorable terms. The government agreed to a higher price but on a graduated basis. The land was to be placed on the market at $1.25 per acre for the first three years, 75 cents for the next two, and 50 cents for the following five years. All lands not sold at the end of the ten-year period would be purchased by the government at the minimum rate. The agreement called for individual allotments and contained provisions for liberal material support as well as for additional educational facilities.

The success of the third and final Sioux commission during the summer of 1889 may be attributed largely to the confidence inspired among the Sioux by its chairman, General George Crook or "Three Stars," as he was known to the Indians. Crook's reputation for honesty and fair play won the cooperation of the Indians as he and his associates met with influential chiefs and headmen in both formal council and private conference. In gaining his objective, Crook made numerous promises and pledges, giving his personal word that

Congress would reimburse the Sioux for ponies confiscated in 1876. There was much hard feeling later when many of these promises were not fulfilled.

The opposition to the land cession reflected the conservatism of the Sioux and their reluctance to accept change. To the Indian Bureau, the chiefs were a major obstacle in its efforts at reform. While the agents could not ignore the tribal relationship entirely, they sought increasingly to undermine and weaken the chiefs' powers while strengthening their own administrative authority. The establishment of an Indian police system at the several agencies between 1879 and 1881 and the creation of a Court of Indian Offenses in 1883 played an important part in suppressing the power of the chiefs.

Congress further weakened the tribal organization in March, 1885, when it extended the jurisdiction of the United States courts over major crimes committed on the reservation. The case of Crow Dog, who had murdered Chief Spotted Tail near the Brûlé Agency at Rosebud in August, 1881, had focused national attention on the anomaly of employing tribal law for expiating Indian crime. Crow Dog had submitted to arrest and was sentenced to hang following his conviction in 1882 in a Deadwood district court. The Supreme Court of the United States held, however, that the Dakota courts lacked jurisdiction and that, moreover, Crow Dog had made sufficient atonement to the victim's family by paying blood money in the form of ponies. The Crow Dog case, and similar incidents at Rosebud and other agencies, prompted the decision to set up Indian courts and to extend the jurisdiction of the United States government to major offenses.

The acculturation policy of the government produced a division among the Sioux between the conservatives or irreconcilables and the progressives. The members of the first group generally represented the full bloods and former hostiles. Led by the chiefs and medicine men, they longed for a return to the old tribal ways, and tried to hold on to ancient customs and traditional camp life. They were particularly reluctant to abandon the native folkways, including plural marriage and ceremonial dances. The progressives, who usually included the mixed bloods, accepted the course of events as inevitable and willingly cooperated with the agents. Most of the progressives had been in contact with the white world for a longer period of time. A few of the older chiefs were likewise reconciled to the new regime, notably Gall and John Grass of the northern Teton bands.

The Indian opposition was mostly confined to the Teton agencies. At Pine Ridge conditions remained especially turbulent and unsettled for a number of years. Here lived a majority of the Sioux who had been allied with the hostile forces under Sitting Bull and Crazy Horse. Moreover, this agency had become an asylum for dissatisfied and renegade Indians from other jurisdictions.

The ranks of the irreconcilables were swelled by the return of the hostiles who had fled with Sitting Bull to Canada at the end of the Black Hills War. In July, 1881, more than 2,800 surrendering Sioux appeared at the Standing Rock Agency. Sitting Bull was taken with his family to Fort Randall, where the Hunkpapa leader remained confined for nearly two years. Upon his release in 1883, he joined a small band of followers on the Grand River on the Standing Rock reserve. The rest of the returning hostiles were permitted to join their kindred elsewhere. About a thousand went to the Cheyenne River Agency, a large portion of them under Hump settling near Cherry Creek some fifty miles west of the agency quarters. About an equal number of Oglalas and Brûlés moved to the Pine Ridge and Rosebud agencies. These newcomers were of an excitable nature, easily influenced by their chiefs, and the least accustomed to the ways of the whites. They were rabid in their opposition to the Sioux cession and little disposed to cooperate with the agents.

The land cession of 1889 developed feelings of unrest and insecurity at all the agencies west of the Missouri. Hardly was the agreement signed when Congress decided to cut beef rations, this despite Crook's personal assurance to the Sioux signers that the reduction of the reservation would in no wise affect their rations. Although there was some basis for the charge that ration rolls were padded, the cut in the beef ration, coming as it did at a time of crop failure, was most unfortunate. The Sioux were brought to the verge of starvation and suffered an epidemic of diseases attributable in part at least to the food shortage. Many children died, and some adults.

To the Sioux this reduction in rations, together with Congress' failure to reimburse them for their ponies and to expand educational facilities as promised by the Crook Commission, was another proof of the insincerity of the white man's pledges. The situation intensified the resentment of the irreconcilable element against the signers of the land agreement and led to much bickering and feuding among the Indians.

While the Teton Sioux were in this troubled state of mind, rumors reached them of a new religious movement beyond the mountains in Nevada. According to report, a messiah there was holding out the promise of salvation from their plight under white domination and of a return to the old nomadic ways. The new messiah, who was named Wovoka, claimed to have had a vision in which he was taken to the happy hunting ground. In his trance he was made a prophet and instructed to tell his people that if they were good and obedient, they would become reunited with all their friends and relatives in the other world. A feature of the religious movement was the ghost-dance ceremonial taught by Wovoka to his followers. Underlying the ghost dance doctrine was the belief in an Indian millennium, which was to begin in the spring of 1891.

A delegation of Sioux, headed by Kicking Bear of the Cheyenne River Reservation and Short Bull from Rosebud, traveled all the way to Nevada to visit the messiah. After attending a great council held by Wovoka for all the Indians who had come to see him, the Sioux delegates returned to South Dakota to introduce the ghost dance ritual.

Among the Teton Sioux the new religion was an outward manifestation of their dissatisfaction, and was exploited by chiefs and medicine men to bolster up their waning prestige. In South Dakota the ghost dance took on new meaning and a different form: it was made an expression of hostility against the whites, contrary to the precepts of order and peace taught by Wovoka. The Teton Sioux also added the ghost shirt with all its mystic symbols to the ceremonial dance, claiming it gave immunity from the effects of bullets and weapons of war to those who wore it.

Ghost dancing started at Pine Ridge and soon spread to the Rosebud and Cheyenne River agencies. It was not long until Sitting Bull's camp on the Grand River became infected. The most fanatical among the ghost dancers came from the camps of former hostiles. During the summer of 1890, in the midst of efforts to ban the dancing, came another cut in rations, with the result that more and more Sioux, including even some progressive bands, became increasingly defiant of the agents' authority.

Had experienced men remained in charge, the fanaticism among the Teton Sioux might well have run its course without incident. But a change of administration in Washington brought replacement of most agency personnel except at the Standing Rock Agency. The removal of an experienced agent at Pine Ridge, a particularly troublesome spot, was most unfortunate. The new agent, Daniel F. Royer, an Alpena physician-druggist appointed through the influence of Senator Pettigrew, had neither understanding of Indian problems nor personal courage. Within a month he was frantically calling for troops.

When soldiers arrived to take control of the Pine Ridge and Rosebud agencies, the ghost-dancing camps fled across the White River into the badlands country. The situation was critical at the northern agencies in Sitting Bull's camp and in the western part of the Cheyenne River reserve. Word soon reached the Standing Rock Agency at Fort Yates that Sitting Bull, as troublesome as ever since his return, was planning to join the ghost dancers in the south. Agent McLaughlin quickly ordered his arrest. In the early morning hours of December 15, 1890, the Indian police tried to take him in custody; his followers offered resistance, and in a matter of minutes fourteen were killed, including Sitting Bull and six of the policemen.

At the same time, a body of ghost dancers under Big Foot on the Cheyenne River near the mouth of the Belle Fourche were about to move to the agency to surrender. The arrival of fugitives from Grand River with news of Sitting Bull's death threw the entire camp into an uproar, causing most of them to flee into the badlands country. Units of the Seventh Cavalry intercepted the fugitive band and marched it to the cavalry camp on upper Wounded Knee Creek about seventeen miles northeast of the Pine Ridge Agency.

In no mood to humor the frightened Indians, the brash officer in charge proceeded on the morning of December 29 to search the camp for weapons. The cavalry force of 470 men surrounded Big Foot's band of 340, including 106 warriors, training Hotchkiss guns on the camp from high ground. The discovery of contraband arms in the Indian tipis led to a wild haranguing by a medicine man and then a shot, presumably fired from a hidden gun by an excited half-witted warrior. In the ensuing melee some eighty-four Indian warriors, including Big Foot, forty-four women, and eighteen children were killed. Many others died later of wounds or exposure. Most of the women and children were shot down as they tried to escape;

their bodies were scattered over a distance of about two miles. Nearly half the Indians were killed by the first volley from the Hotchkiss guns. The survivors of the cannon barrage escaped to a nearby ravine, where the pursuing troops hunted them down like wild prey. Thirty-one soldiers were killed, most of them in fierce hand-to-hand fighting.

At the time of the unfortunate incident, nearly four thousand ghost dancers were on their way to the Pine Ridge Agency to surrender. Upon hearing of the massacre, they became greatly excited and threatened to destroy the agency. There were several skirmishes, but the danger of a general uprising was averted. General Nelson A. Miles arrived to take personal charge, bringing with him army officers who had had earlier agency experience. From these Miles chose replacements for Royer and the agents on the Rosebud and Cheyenne River reserves. Order was restored, and the ghost dancers returned to their homes.[1]

Public indignation over the Wounded Knee massacre led to an earnest effort to assess the blame. There has been virtual agreement that the ghost dancers were planning no general uprising against the whites. The press had played up the disturbances out of all proportion to the actual conditions. Moreover, there is some evidence that local cattle interests were encouraging the war scare as a means of frightening homesteaders off the newly opened range between the White and the Cheyenne. It was certainly a mistake to dispatch troops to the reservation. Their arrival aggravated the unrest and excitement instead of allaying it, leading many Indians to believe that the army intended to destroy them. The conduct of the soldiers at Wounded Knee seemed to confirm Indian fears that the Seventh Cavalry was out to settle old scores. Unquestionably, however, the outstanding single factor in the crisis precipitated by the messiah movement was the inability of the agent at Pine Ridge to cope with the situation.

The Wounded Knee massacre called attention to shortcomings inherent in methods of managing Indian affairs. Indian policy was basically dependent for its success upon the character, efficiency, and wisdom of the men who administered it upon the reservations.

[1] George E. Hyde treats the ghost-dance craze at full length in *A Sioux Chronicle* (Norman: University of Oklahoma Press, 1956), an excellent account of the Teton Sioux for the period from 1878 to 1892. See also James Mooney, "The Ghost Dance Religion and the Sioux Outbreak of 1890" in *Fourteenth Annual Report of the Bureau of Ethnology*, 1892–1893, Part 2, 641–1136. A more definitive study of the whole movement is Robert M. Utley, *The Last Days of the Sioux Nation* (New Haven: Yale University Press, 1963)."

The reputations earned by corrupt Indian agents during the 1860's and 1870's continued to plague their successors at the Dakota agencies long after the introduction of higher standards of conduct.

Most of the earlier abuses had grown out of the misuse of Indian funds and government property. So long as the agents were in full control of the disbursements, it was easy for contractors to organize dummy companies and put in straw bids or to shortchange both the Indian and the government in the delivery of Texas longhorns. During the early seventies it is said that large cattle contracts at Dakota agencies were sometimes "filled" with four hundred fewer head than bargained for by the simple expedient of checking part of the herd in twice.[2]

Upon becoming Secretary of the Interior, Carl Schurz instituted various reforms and conducted numerous investigations in the effort to uncover wrongdoing. He removed most of the Indian agents in Dakota Territory in 1878 and unsuccessfully prosecuted three of them on charges of financial irregularities and misconduct in office. The Indian Office subsequently required a careful accounting of funds and instituted stricter rules for the inspection of flour and other supplies and the checking of weights in beef and cattle contracts. The zeal with which the Indian Office sought to ferret out dishonesty is reflected in complaints made by subsequent agents over the endless investigations into their conduct. McGillycuddy, a Pine Ridge agent who was both honest and efficient, wrote in 1883 that he felt lonesome unless an inspector or two were camped with him.

Major improvements in the administration of Indian affairs had to await the application of civil service principles in the selection of agency personnel. Low salary schedules, unattractive living conditions, and the uncertainties of tenure reduced efficiency. Many agents failed to understand the Indians and were impatient with them. All too frequently a new agent would appear before his predecessor had sufficient opportunity to acquaint himself with his work. Although by the late eighties Indian agents were appointed for a four-year period, they were still being removed for political reasons upon the expiration of their terms. The minor positions at the agencies were, however, placed under civil service regulations during the nineties.

[2] See Lewis F. Crawford, *Rekindling Camp Fires: The Exploits of Ben Arnold* (Bismarck, N. Dak.: Capital Book Co., 1926), pp. 189–199, for a description of corrupt practices in filling Indian contracts at Dakota agencies.

President Cleveland replaced many Republican incumbents with army officers during his two administrations. Harrison and McKinley, on the other hand, applied the "home-rule system," turning Indian agencies over to local politicians. Violations of civil service rules at Sioux agencies in South Dakota during the campaign of 1892 were the subject of a personal investigation by Theodore Roosevelt, then a member of the civil service commission. When Roosevelt himself reached the White House, he placed the superintendents of the reservation schools in charge of the Indian agencies, thus finally supplying continuity in administration and appointment by the merit system.

The administrative work at the Indian agencies became prodigious as the years passed.[3] Each new turn in policy imposed additional burdens. During the early reservation period the agents were viewed primarily as poormasters doling out rations. As the Indians began to progress, the agents were more and more occupied with multitudinous details that required their constant attention. While some agents were undependable, most were sincere and earnest individuals who applied themselves conscientiously and assiduously to difficult tasks.

The most effective means of assimilating the Indians was through education. Both the Yankton Treaty of 1858 and the Laramie Treaty of 1868 obliged the federal government to provide educational facilities, but little was done to fulfill the commitment before 1879, Indian education being largely entrusted to the missionaries. On the Yankton Reservation, where the government set up a day school as early as 1870, the Reverend John P. Williamson began to establish day schools as well as churches under the jurisdiction of the Presbyterian board of missions. During the early seventies, the Protestant Episcopal Church began to locate both boarding and day schools at the Crow Creek and Cheyenne River agencies as well as on the Yankton Reservation. The missionary bishop of Niobrara, William Hobart Hare, directed these activities. The American Board of Home Missions of the Congregational Church was also active, maintaining two day schools on the Cheyenne River reserve by 1875 under the guidance of the Reverend Thomas L. Riggs. There were also

[3] See *Sixty-Second Annual Report of the Commissioner of Indian Affairs* (1893) in *House Executive Documents*, 53 Cong., 2 Session, 1893–94, vol. 14 (Serial No. 3210), pp. 299–300, for an excellent picture of expanding administrative routine at the Rosebud Agency.

some educational activities on the Sisseton Reservation during the 1870's.

Through the leadership of the Right Reverend Martin Marty, later to become the first Catholic bishop of South Dakota, the Catholics established a number of mission boarding schools before 1900, the first opening on the Standing Rock reserve in 1877. Among the early mission schools were St. Francis near the Rosebud Agency (1885), Immaculate Conception School at Stephan (1886), and Holy Rosary at Pine Ridge (1887), all of which were still in operation in 1961.

Until 1900 mission schools received financial assistance from the government: under "contract," Congress appropriated a fixed sum for each pupil to a religious organization which would provide the staff and physical plant. Growing opposition to such subsidies soon developed, however, and the government gradually reduced the aid and finally withdrew it. For a short time after 1900, rations were even withdrawn from Indian children in mission schools in order to compel them to attend government schools. Most of the mission boarding schools eventually closed. Financial assistance to Holy Rosary and St. Francis was continued from tribal funds until about 1930.

The government maintained three types of schools: the day school, the reservation boarding school, and the nonreservation boarding school. When a boarding school was opened in abandoned cavalry barracks at Carlisle, Pennsylvania, in 1879, with Captain R. H. Pratt as the headmaster, a debate developed over the relative merits of reservation and nonreservation schools. Eastern humanitarians generally agreed with Pratt that to be completely assimilated, Indian children should be enrolled for a period of three or four years in special institutions in centers of white civilization. The advocates of education in the East argued that returning students would accomplish more among their tribesmen than white teachers working in the tribal environment. A prominent feature of the Carlisle School program was the "outing" system whereby the pupils were placed in white homes during the summer months. Among the first pupils at Carlisle were eighty-four boys and girls recruited personally by Captain Pratt from the Pine Ridge and Rosebud agencies. Most of them came from Rosebud where Spotted Tail agreed to send five of his own children. Later in the year, however, he became dissatisfied with the institution and removed the members of his family.

The program of nonreservation institutions did not commend itself to the Indian Bureau, least of all to the Indian agents who insisted on more realistic training for their wards. The life situations to which the Carlisle pupils were exposed did not correspond to reservation life, and the skills in which they were trained were unused after their return to the Indian camps. Moreover, Indian parents were usually unwilling to send their children to distant schools where many contracted tuberculosis or other debilitating diseases. The nonreservation schools, in any case, could serve only a few of the many children in need of instruction.

The day schools, despite their crudeness, low standards, and poor equipment, were generally accepted as the most practical medium for Indian education. In later years the government maintained a number of reservation boarding schools, including one near Mission. It also established boarding schools at Flandreau, Pierre, and Rapid City. The reservation schools emphasized both general and vocational training as preparation for citizenship and the white man's way of life.

Closely related to education was the work of changing or breaking up the nomadic form of Indian life. The first step in curbing the migratory disposition among the Teton bands was taken in 1876 and 1877 when they were deprived of rifles and ponies, thus constraining them to stay at the agencies. At first the Indians tended to camp within a few miles of the agency headquarters, most of them living in tipis and leading idle lives. Breaking up the main body into smaller family groups and settling them in separate localities was an important step toward self-support. Without this social reorganization, the day school could not have functioned.

The Indians' slow progress in adapting themselves to an agricultural economy was disappointing to the whites. Even when they planted a few acres under the watchful eye and constant prodding of the agent, the Indians often neglected their crops and relied upon the regularly distributed rations for their subsistence. Although the agents did not hesitate to withhold rations in order to enforce school attendance or insure compliance with petty social regulations, they came to regard the ration system as a major deterrent to progress on the reservations.

The Black Hills agreement of 1876 had obligated the government to provide the Teton Sioux with specified rations valued at about fifty dollars per person per year "until the Indians are able to support themselves." The Sioux, however, considered the rations as partial payment for the loss of their lands and claimed the full ration as their right. Moreover, the beef ration, which was issued on the hoof every fifteen days, afforded the Indians an opportunity to simulate a buffalo hunt. Groups of thirty mounted men would give chase to each animal, sometimes running it for two or three miles before bringing it down with rifles, the women following to dress the carcass. More humane methods had been adopted by about 1890, and the beef was issued directly from slaughterhouses at substations scattered over the reservations. Because of the enervating effects of distribution of full rations, the Indian Bureau gradually limited full issue to the aged and physically disabled and reduced it for the rest. Able-bodied men had to perform work on agency projects for their share.

A growing conviction that the solution of the Indian problem lay in the substitution of individual holdings for tribal or communal land ownership led to the passage of the Dawes Allotment or Severalty Act in February, 1887. Eastern humanitarians and friends of the Indians were elated over the measure, hailing it as an Emancipation Proclamation under which supervision by the government and the arbitrary rule of the agent might be safely withdrawn.[4] Uniting with the humanitarians in supporting the legislation was a less altruistic group that stood to benefit from the sale of the surplus lands.

The Allotment Act authorized the President of the United States to grant each household head 160 acres with smaller tracts to single men, women, and children. If an Indian failed to take an allotment within four years after its authorization, the Secretary of the Interior might direct the agent to make a selection for him. The allotments were to be held in trust by the government for a period of twenty-five years. All allottees enjoyed the rights of citizenship, including voting privileges, immediately upon receiving the trust patent. Proceeds from the sale of surplus lands were to be placed in a special trust fund.

The work of allotting Indian lands began at the Sisseton and Yankton agencies where the occupants had progressed farther in

[4] *Twenty-second Annual Report of the Board of Indian Commissioners* (Washington: Government Printing Office, 1891), p. 9.

their adjustments to reservation life. In accordance with an agreement negotiated in February, 1889, the government made the surplus lands on the Sisseton Reservation available to white settlers in 1892. The Yankton Reservation was thrown open to settlers in 1895 under the terms of a land agreement made three years earlier. The price at which the surplus acreage became available to the public varied between reservations. The Yanktonnais and related Teton bands at Crow Creek also began to take allotments at an early date.

At the agencies beyond the Missouri where there was less enthusiasm for the new order, the Indians took few allotments before 1900. The Sioux agreement of 1889 authorized allotments of 320 acres to the head of a family and 160 acres for all other members of the household. Moreover, it provided that each Indian taking an allotment was to receive from the proceeds of ceded lands fifty dollars in cash besides a span of horses, farming equipment, and a two-year supply of seed. Although the agents continued to dangle this monetary benefit before the Indians' eyes, the Teton bands preferred to keep their tribal lands, and the Indian Bureau wisely decided not to force the issue. The allotting process finally got under way west of the Missouri River, enabling the white settlers to occupy the surplus lands during the period from 1904 to 1915. The occupants of the Pine Ridge and Standing Rock reservations were the last to take their allotments.

The Dawes Allotment Act of 1887 established the framework of Indian policy for a span of forty-seven years. The allotting process was to be the final step in the destruction of the tribal organization. The Indian families, it was assumed, would settle down on farms and emulate the white neighbors who would infiltrate the reservation through the purchase of the surplus lands. Yet despite the idealism and sincerity under which the reform program was conceived, the achievements under the Dawes Act fell far short of its goals. The allotment policy succeeded neither in making the Indians self-supporting nor in freeing them from the guardianship of the Indian Bureau.

The implementation of the Dawes Act markedly changed the status of the Indian and made the government responsible for watching over his property and financial affairs. Many Indians were physically incapable of cultivating their allotments and became dependents of the Indian Bureau. Difficulties also arose from complex Indian inheritance customs, which multiplied clerical work many times. The allotment program forced the Indian Bureau to become more and more paternalistic toward its charges.

The twenty-five-year trust period posed the first serious administrative problem. Although the allottee was not considered capable of managing his property, he was declared competent to exercise the right of suffrage. The incongruity in granting immediate voting rights on the Sisseton Reservation evoked comment from Theodore Roosevelt during his 1892 investigation of political practices in South Dakota.

The Indian Bureau also had serious difficulty in enforcing the statutory prohibition of liquor traffic on Indian reservations. This problem came to a head in 1905 when the Supreme Court of the United States held that the prohibitory legislation could not apply to Indian allottees who held citizenship rights.[5]

Congress modified provisions regarding the trust period by passing the Burke Act on May 8, 1906. This measure, sponsored by Congressman Charles H. Burke of South Dakota, granted the Secretary of the Interior discretionary power to issue a patent in fee simple whenever he deemed an Indian allottee competent to manage his affairs. The new law postponed the acquisition of citizenship until the granting of such patents. In 1924, however, all Indians were declared citizens irrespective of their reservation status.

The progress made by the Indians under the Dawes Act varied from agency to agency, depending upon their degree of social advancement and the environment in which they lived. Because of the semiarid character of much of their land, the Sioux in the Great Plains region faced greater farming difficulties and more serious problems in adjustment than those occupying reservations east of the Missouri.

Efforts at farming met with indifferent success. The Indians did not value their land as the whites did, and had to overcome a warrior's aversion to tilling the soil. The government was under treaty obligation to train them in agricultural skills, but most of the instructors sent to the agencies were better politicians than teachers. Later, when civil service rules provided more competent personnel, the agency farmers were usually assigned to office work to help handle the growing mass of administrative details.

[5] Francis E. Leupp, *The Indian and His Problem* (New York: Charles Scribner's Sons, 1910) , covers admirably the various administrative problems posed by the Allotment Act.

Stock-raising had been appreciably successful at all the Teton agencies before the reservations were thrown open to settlement. Large tribal herds had shared the reservation lands with private herds run chiefly by mixed bloods or white men who had married into the tribe. During the early 1900's, most of the beef issued by the government was bought from the Indians. Then came the breakup of the reservation, and the land was fenced in small blocks by Indians and whites alike. Because of the high prices during World War I, the Indians were encouraged to sell their herds. They were also permitted for the first time to kill their stock for their own consumption. By 1918 most of the Indian herds had disappeared, and the grazing lands were under lease to white cattlemen.

The years from 1910 to 1934 were the testing period for the allotment policy. During the first half of this period, various tribal funds were paid out to allottees or made available in the form of reimbursable funds for the purpose of making improvements and providing them with farming equipment and seed as well as for the purchase of cattle. Farm management specialists and home extension agents introduced five-year plans to put the Indians on a self-supporting basis.

The reports of the Indian superintendents for the period tell a monotonous story of alternating hope and frustration. Most of the money paid out was squandered or mismanaged by the Indians. Reimbursable funds were all too frequently looked upon as gifts, rather than loans, and were not repaid. Most allotments remained unimproved. A 1925 house-to-house survey of occupied allotments at Pine Ridge showed that a hoe and rake, and occasionally a walking plow, were usually the only farming equipment.[6]

Under these circumstances, most Indians leased their lands. Originally restricted to heirship tracts and allotments belonging to the physically disabled, leasing was extended until at times most of the Indian lands were under leasehold to large cattle-raisers or white farmers. The income from rentals and the distribution of tribal monies seemed to provide greater security for the Indians than their own efforts at farming or cattle-raising.

At the same time, large acreages were passing out of Indian hands. Before the Wilson Administration, the alienation of Indian lands

[6] Annual report of E. W. Jermark, Superintendent of the Pine Ridge Agency, for the year 1928. Unpublished report in Department of Interior files, National Archives.

was mainly limited to heirship tracts and allotments held by handicapped Indians. These lands could be sold by sealed bid. In 1917 a new policy was instituted which was intended to release the Indians from wardship as rapidly as possible.

Enthusiastic Indian superintendents in the Sioux country hailed the new policy as "the beginning of the end of the Indian problem." In conformity with the spirit of the new regime, competency commissions freely adjudged allottees capable of managing their own affairs. The well-intentioned though ill-advised plan to disband the Indian Bureau at an early date and place the Indians entirely on their own was brought to a halt before President Wilson went out of office, but the trend toward alienation continued unchecked during the following decade.

Within a short time fully 80 per cent of the patented allotments, and even more on some reservations, had passed into the hands of land speculators and crop farmers. Most of the Indians who applied for patents in fee simple did so in anticipation of sale. There were especially heavy transactions in Indian lands on the Sioux reservations in 1922.

Most of the Indians felt assured that they would always be able to live on the reservation and that there would always be lands of relatives to which they could move. There was much pressure from agents of land companies and land speculators, and not a little fraud in many of the dealings. An Indian might accept forty dollars and a new suit of clothes, believing it was a down payment, only to find later that he had signed his name or put his mark on a completed deed.[7]

The unsatisfactory conditions existing on the various reserva' during the 1920's led to an economic and social survey of the Am can Indians by the Brookings Institution of Washington, D.C. T Meriam Report, published in 1928, turned the spotlight upon the shortcomings of the allotment policy, placing most of the blame for the Indians' plight upon an inadequate educational program. The survey revealed a yearly per-capita income varying from $86 at Pine Ridge to $247 for the Sissetons on the old Lake Traverse Reservation.[8] Whatever the reason, whether faulty administration or a mis-

[7] Gordon Macgregor, *Warriors Without Weapons: A Study of the Society and Personality Development of the Pine Ridge Sioux* (Chicago: University of Chicago Press, 1946), p. 40. Other allotments were lost through foreclosure and tax-delinquency sales.

[8] Lewis Meriam and Associates, *The Problem of Indian Administration* (Baltimore: Johns Hopkins Press, 1928), p. 449.

conceived philosophy, the allotment policy had proved itself a failure.

A reform program was instituted by President Hoover, who appointed an eastern humanitarian, Charles J. Rhoads, as Commissioner of Indian Affairs in May, 1929. Rhoads replaced the conservative Charles H. Burke, former South Dakota Congressman and author of the Burke Act, who had received his appointment in 1921. The Rhoads regime was the forerunner of the New Deal reform program initiated by John Collier, whom President Franklin D. Roosevelt placed in charge of Indian affairs in 1933.

Collier, who had been actively identified with the Indian Defense Association, blamed the allotment system for the Indians' poverty and the loss of their land. Continuing the work that Rhoads had been carrying on in education, health, and other lines, Collier inaugurated a new policy diametrically opposed to the Dawes policy in its philosophy. The new Indian program sought to encourage, promote, and preserve Indian culture instead of suppressing it. It also proposed the repurchase of lands to increase tribal holdings. As one writer has stated, Collier "set about the job of inaugurating a typically twentieth-century collectivistic reform to replace a typically nineteenth-century individualistic one."[9]

The Indian Reorganization Act of 1934 specifically prohibited further allotting of lands and restored remaining surplus lands to tribal ownership at the discretion of the Secretary of the Interior. Credit facilities were to be provided for the repurchase of land to build up tribal estates and for loans to Indian corporations set up to develop the economic resources of the tribes. The legislation authorized tribal constitutions in order to provide political home rule under a tribal council chosen by secret ballot. Within a year each tribe was to determine whether it wished to organize in accordance with the Indian Reorganization Act.

Despite their earlier approval of the contemplated reforms, the Indians in South Dakota were in sharp disagreement over the acceptance of the Reorganization Act, dividing themselves into so-called "New Deal" and "Old Deal" factions. The only reservations to reject the Act were Crow Creek and Sisseton, and these eventually organized themselves under approved tribal charters or constitutions. The Yankton Sioux accepted the Indian Reorganization Act, but

[9] Randolph C. Downes, "A Crusade for Indian Reform, 1922–1934," *Mississippi Valley Historical Review*, XXXII (December, 1945), 331.

never organized under it; they continued to conduct tribal business in general council. All the other groups, including Flandreau, eventually accepted the Collier program and were organized with approved constitutions, although with some minor variations between the different reservations.

Regardless of the decision to accept or reject the reorganization features of the new policy, the impoverished condition of the Indian population, still further intensified by ravages of drought and depression, called for immediate action. Following a short period of Red Cross and direct relief by federal as well as state agencies, special work-relief projects were set up after 1933, many of them conducted through the Civilian Conservation Corps. On some reservations, particularly Pine Ridge, nearly all the able-bodied men were on the government payroll. As late as 1940 the majority of the Teton Sioux were still deriving most of their income from relief wages and payments and commodities supplied by the government. This dependence upon government support continued until 1942 when the C.C.C. program was terminated.

Supplementing the relief activities was a rehabilitation program which included plans to revive the livestock industry. Although in most cases the alienation of Indian lands had proceeded too far for a consolidation of holdings into large grazing units, steps were taken to regroup land holdings for their more efficient utilization. Privately owned trust lands and heirship lands were bought and placed under tribal management. A unique project to consolidate heirship tracts which was still in operation in 1961 was the Rosebud tribal land enterprise. Through the repurchase provisions of the Indian Reorganization Act, nearly eighty thousand acres of non-Indian lands were put under tribal ownership between 1934 and 1952, most of it on the Cheyenne River, Crow Creek, and Pine Ridge reservations. By 1942 the Cheyenne River tribal council had taken the lead in formulating a code of land management. On the various reservations revolving loan funds made capital available to local cooperative livestock associations, each of which managed several small family herds and pooled the resources of single grazing units.

The Collier policy made an important contribution in permitting Indians greater participation in the management of their own affairs and enabling them to organize along democratic lines. Many of the cooperative activities, however, proved unsuccessful, and other features of the Collier program in subsequent years were discarded as impractical.

Between 1920 and 1950 the Indian population rose from 16,384 to 23,344, an increase of 43 per cent. The federal census of 1970 revealed a further increase to 33,547. Nearly 12,000 of this number lived outside the organized reservations at that time. Full-bloods comprised about a fourth of thetribal rolls. The majority of the Indians lived at poverty level. Numerous programs of federal aid have been made available to tribal governments. Of particular importance have been programs of Indian Community Action bodies.

Health care has been considered the paramount problem facing the Indian population. In 1974 the Indian Health Service was operating hospitals at Rapid City and on all reservations except Crow Creek and Lower Brule. The Indian Service also interested itself in promoting housing and sanitary facilities.

Significant developments in education have included pre-school programs, textbooks stressing Indian cultural values, and activities in adult education. Two-year community college centers were established at Pine Ridge and Rosebud.

Although the tribal governments function under the aegis of the Bureau of Indian Affairs, they have attained greater authority. In actual practice, the Indian Bureau by 1975 was functioning more as an advisory and coordinating body than an administrative agency. The Rosebud Sioux, enjoying greater political stability, could lay claim to greater progress. Factional quarrels and petty bickering on the reservations have made for ineffectual leadership and, all too frequently, jeopardized tribal programs. Pine Ridge, the most populous reservation, has been particularly addicted to frequent changes in leadership.

By the early 1970's the problems of the South Dakota Indian had become a matter of wide concern. Charges of discrimination and a double standard of justice carried greater conviction following incidents along reservation borders. Minor demonstrations led to major ones, particularly in northwestern Nebraska and at Custer. The American Indian Movement, organized at Minneapolis in 1968, appeared on the scene to assume a leading role in promoting the Indian cause. This organization, formed by Indians from urban communities, professed increasing impatience with the slowness of the pace at which the reservation Indians were moving toward autonomy and denounced the elected leaders as mere puppets of the

Indian Bureau. It particularly assailed the federal government for flouting past treaties and pointed to the Fort Laramie Treaty of 1868 as a classic example of a broken treaty.

Following a series of confrontations throughout the entire country, the American Indian Movement directed its attention to South Dakota. After forming a chapter in Rapid City, it began to conduct "grand jury investigations" of alleged abuses and mismanagement on the various reservations. This naturally incurred sharp criticism, especially on the Pine Ridge Reservation, where the organization involved itself in local quarrels. The tribal president, Richard Wilson, actively sought to bar the organization's leaders from the reservation and to outlaw its activities. By this time, the American Indian Movement was beginning to challenge the validity of the elective tribal government, recognizing only the traditional tribal organization based on medicine men and leaders chosen along family lines.

During the night of February 27, 1973, about 250 persons, with a goodly supply of firearms, took possession of the historic village of Wounded Knee. Within a few hours, newsmen and television cameramen joined them to give the occupation nation-wide publicity. Federal marshals and agents of the Federal Bureau of Investigation established roadblocks to seal off the area. This action was taken to forestall an armed clash with the tribal police, who had been reinforced by the tribal president. At times, however, foodstuffs and Red Cross supplies were permitted to enter the area. The confrontation lasted seventy-one days, exacting a toll of two lives and nine wounded besides heavy property damage. After days of seemingly futile negotiations, the militants finally surrendered on May 8.

Russell Means, the leader of the invasion forces and an enrolled member of the Oglala tribe, later decided to contest Wilson's leadership in the tribal election on January 22, 1974. After a bitter campaign, Means led Wilson in a field of thirteen candidates. In the runoff election two weeks later, however, Wilson won by a margin of 200 votes, thus becoming the first tribal president at Pine Ridge to be elected to a successive second term since the first election in 1936. This seemed to assure the continuance of the tribal programs.

CHAPTER 22

Reappraisal: The Growth of the Farm and Ranch Economy

THE DOMINANT FARMING PATTERNS that developed in South Dakota during its first century of growth bear a close relationship to the environmental conditions that characterize the state. The transition area, in which the eastern intensive farming patterns merge into the extensive grazing type of the western half of the state, coincides roughly with the Missouri Hills section where the physical features of the prairie grasslands blend into the Great Plains environment. In the course of time the western half of the state developed an extensive ranch type of livestock production. East of the Missouri River livestock grazing and cash-grain farming were to prevail in the northern part, while a feed-grain and general livestock pattern became predominant in the south. By virtue of the environmental influences, the history of South Dakota agriculture has been essentially a story of adjustments and modifications in farming methods and land use.

The farming pattern that emerged in the southern half of the east-river section had its origins in the diversified or mixed farming practices developed by the early settlers. After a decade of trying experiences at a bare subsistence level, the settlers, when the railroad arrived in the early seventies, eagerly turned to the small grains as their cash crops, with special emphasis on spring wheat. Believing that the growing season was too short for corn, at first they raised it mainly as a sod crop. By 1880 corn and oats had displaced wheat as the main crop. Dairying was also well established by this time. Succeeding years saw larger acreages of corn and oats and a greater number of hogs raised. In this region agriculture was settling into its present-day pattern by 1900.

While the farmers in the southeastern counties were building up a system of diversified or general farming, homesteaders were introducing into the region to the north and west a cash-crop pattern based mostly on the culture of hard spring wheat. After depositing the settlers in the James River Valley, the wave of migration surged westward into the Missouri Hills region to the 100th meridian and even beyond during the early eighties.

Influenced by favorable prices and a propitious supply of rainfall, the settlers looked to wheat for their main source of income. A succession of bumper crops seemed to refute the views of those who still regarded the region between the 98th and 100th meridians as a semihumid land where agriculture could not be "uniformly successful from season to season."[1] The farming conditions seemed to be quite similar to those in the Upper Mississippi Valley, confirming the popular belief that the "rain belt" was keeping pace with the westward push of the agricultural frontier. A cycle of intensely dry years that ran its course from 1886 to 1897 soon dispelled this illusion. The first indications of a diminishing rainfall were noted during the summer of 1889. Drought conditions prevailed for several years in the central counties between the James and Missouri rivers.

The severe droughts of 1889 and 1894 provoked agitation for drought relief in the stricken areas. The federal government responded by repeatedly suspending provisions of public land legislation for the relief of individuals holding homestead and pre-emption claims. State agencies during the winter of 1889–1890 estimated

---

[1] See Paul Meadows, *John Wesley Powell: Frontiersman of Science* (Lincoln: University of Nebraska Studies, July, 1952), p. 53. Powell, who was identified with the United States Geological Survey, contended that subhumid areas required institutions different from those developed in humid areas. In a report on "arid lands" published in 1879, he advocated a classification of the lands west of the twenty-inch line of annual rainfall that would provide for large pasturing units of 2,500 acres and irrigated tracts of smaller size. The land was to be utilized primarily for grazing and for crops raised under irrigation. Powell's views, as well as his proposals for an elaborate system of irrigation in the zone between the arid and humid regions, received little support.

the average yield of wheat in some localities in the James Valley at one bushel to the acre. Following the recommendations of Governor Mellette, the State Legislature in February, 1890, authorized county commissioners to furnish seed grain to drought-stricken farmers. Relief funds and supplies, solicited throughout the Middle West under the direction of Governor Mellette, were distributed through state and local committees. In some counties the distress was so great in 1894 that officials abandoned all efforts to collect taxes. Legislation passed in February, 1895, empowered county and township officials to furnish seed grain.

Many farmers called on the professional rain-maker for assistance. Both quacks and serious-minded scientists held out hopes for precipitation artificially induced through the use of gases and explosives. Numerous rain-making conventions were held during 1892 throughout the James Valley. In 1894 the rain-maker again offered to produce rain for a stipulated price, at the same time selling rain-making materials and advising local committees how to bombard the skies themselves.

The settlers also began to explore the possibilities of the artesian waters underlying the drought-stricken areas as a source of moisture. Because of the use of water from artesian wells for sprinkling lawns and gardens it was widely believed that the underground supply might be made to serve an extensive system of irrigation. By 1889 more than a hundred wells of remarkable pressure and supply were flowing in the James Valley, and during the following year experimentation was under way to determine the feasibility of irrigation.

In response to the urgent request of South Dakota as well as other western states, Congress provided appropriations in 1890 "to investigate the proper location for artesian wells and their use in the semiarid regions between the ninety-seventh degree of west longitude . . . and the eastern foothills of the Rocky Mountains." During the same year the South Dakota Legislature provided for an engineer of irrigation to supervise the development of an irrigation system and to promote the sinking of artesian wells for irrigation purposes. Public wells were sunk in Brule, Beadle, Douglas, Jerauld, Sanborn, and Spink counties for irrigation purposes under legislation enacted in 1891 and 1893. Much of the driving force behind the irrigation movement came from real-estate firms, speculators, and loan companies who found vast acreages in their possession as a result of numerous farm-mortgage foreclosures.

The movement for irrigation with artesian waters failed to make much headway. Boosters of the young state reacted sharply against any adverse publicity, and the proposals for irrigation implied arid conditions which Dakotans were unwilling to admit. Moreover, efforts at irrigation in the James Valley generally proved unsuccessful. Upon the return of favorable rainfall after 1896, interest in well irrigation began to decline.

The State Legislature in 1897, as a result of the waning interest in irrigation east of the Missouri, abolished the office of state engineer of irrigation. At the same time it created a state experiment substation at Highmore in Hyde County "for the purpose of carrying on experiments with drought resisting forage plants suitable for the dry range regions of middle South Dakota." No irrigation was to be employed. The experiment station at the Agricultural College in Brookings gave increasing attention to experiments on the renovation of native pastures and the culture of grasses and forage plants without irrigation. Hardy grasses introduced from Manitoba and Siberia became a special object of experimentation. A new chapter was being written in reclaiming the "semiarid" region of central South Dakota by means of dry farming.[2]

While state and national agencies were trying to help tide the settlers over the disastrous period of the nineties, there was a distinct trend toward diversification in the James Valley and the counties in the Missouri Hills region. The dual handicap of drought and low prices was forcing readjustments in the farm economy. Farmers placed less reliance on wheat as a cash crop. Stock-raising became important. The number of cattle in Hand, Hyde, Hughes, and Sully counties increased from 34,500 to 110,000 between 1890 and 1900, while wheat acreage showed a decline. Highmore became an impor-

[2] A leading advocate of dry farming was Hardy Webster Campbell, who homesteaded in Brown County in 1879. Out of his farming experiences in the James River Valley during a period of abnormal rainfall grew the Campbell system of scientific soil culture which included deep fall plowing, subsurface packing, and summer fallow. Campbell left South Dakota during the 1890's to manage a number of farms in the Northern Plains for the Burlington, Chicago and North Western, Northern Pacific, and Soo railroad companies, at the same time promoting his system through numerous publications. Although his principles of soil culture failed to gain general acceptance among agricultural scientists, Campbell's work has been regarded as the early embodiment of dry-farming propaganda on the Great Plains. See Mary Wilma M. Hargreaves, *Dry Farming in the Northern Great Plains, 1900–1925* (Cambridge: Harvard University Press, 1957), pp. 83–125, and an article by the same author, "Hardy Webster Campbell, 1850–1937," *Agricultural History,* 32 (January, 1958), 62–65.

tant shipping center, by 1895 averaging a carload a day during the shipping season, whereas in 1890 not a single carload had been shipped out.

The advance in sheep-raising in this area was even more marked. During the same period the number of sheep increased from 79,000 to 270,000 within the counties lying between the Missouri River and a line extending from Aberdeen to Woonsocket. A pronounced change in the size of farm holdings accompanied the movement toward diversification. In a number of counties the acreage per farm doubled during the decade. The farms ranged from 400 to 700 acres in size.

In the older settlements in the southeastern part of the state as well as along the Minnesota border, the average size per farm had increased only slightly by 1900. Here a combination of grain and stock farming had become more fixed. The most important new development was a stronger interest in dairying. By 1900 South Dakota was recognized as a leading dairy state, and its butter was widely advertised.[3]

The boom of the post-1900 period, like that of the early eighties, occurred under favorable auspices. There were, indeed, feeble warnings by the United States Department of Agriculture that the favorable conditions west of the 100th meridian were transitory, but caution was thrown to the winds as the land rush gained momentum.[4] Still harboring the delusion that the humid belt was constantly moving westward, railroad companies and real-estate promoters tended to scoff at dry-farming techniques and encouraged the settlers to introduce a cash-crop pattern into the region beyond the Missouri.

The homesteading boom which began so auspiciously after 1900 in the west-river country was cut short by drought. The settlers who did not join the exodus from the area following the droughts of 1910 and 1911 gradually learned to adapt themselves to the region. Since they were mostly of Midwest origin, it was easy for them to follow a production pattern that included corn, hay, cattle, and hogs. For the most part, they ignored such dry-farming techniques as subsoiling and fallowing, preferring less intensive methods of till-

[3] In this discussion of agricultural adjustments, the author drew extensively on his article, "Drought and Agriculture in Eastern South Dakota during the Eighteen Nineties," *Agricultural History*, 5 (October, 1931), 162–180.

[4] *Report of the Secretary of Agriculture, 1906* in *House Documents*, Vol. 21, 59 Cong., 2nd session, 1906–1907, p. 40.

age in a system of diversified farming that included crop rotation. Although wheat had less appeal as a cash crop in the north-central counties, the farmers in that area continued to extend wheat culture whenever favorable seasons coincided with high prices.[5]

Many homesteaders began to raise stock, producing grain primarily as a secondary crop for winter feeding. Others turned to dairying as they acquired abandoned tracts and added milch cows to their herds. By 1915 cooperative creameries had made their appearance in a number of communities along the Milwaukee and the Chicago and North Western lines across the state to Rapid City; a similar venture at Lemmon enjoyed a wide patronage in the northern part of Perkins County.

An important feature of the agricultural adjustments in the trans-Missouri region was the experimentation carried on by government agencies with drought-resistant grasses and forage crops. To supplement the work of the state experiment substation at Highmore, substations were established at Cottonwood, Eureka, and Vivian between 1909 and 1913. The United States Department of Agriculture also established a dry-land experiment station at Ardmore in Fall River County.

The most important single contribution for the period was the introduction and adaptation of a Siberian strain of alfalfa by Professor N. E. Hansen of South Dakota State College.[6] Hansen was a pioneer plant explorer who brought the hardy alfalfa back to the United States from a ten-month exploration trip into Turkestan and Siberia in 1897 under the auspices of the United States Department of Agriculture. On subsequent tours he traced the yellow-flowered Siberian alfalfa to its most northern limits where it grew under severe climatic conditions. Alfalfa studies carried on by Hansen at Highmore and Cottonwood from small quantities of imported seed showed the Siberian strains could survive the rigorous environment of the Northern Plains. The imported varieties especially proved their hardiness during the drought of 1911 when other forage crops, including native varieties of alfalfa, failed.

[5] See Hargreaves, *Dry Farming in the Northern Great Plains*, pp. 196–208, for efforts toward readjustment in the west-river region of South Dakota.

[6] N. E. Hansen, "Originating and Importing Hardy Plants for South Dakota" in *South Dakota—Fifty Years of Progress, 1889–1939* (Sioux Falls: South Dakota Golden Anniversary Book Co., 1939), pp. 45–47. See also Mrs. H. J. Taylor, "The Life and Work of Niels Ebbesen Hansen," *South Dakota Historical Collections,* XXI (1942), 185–290, for a detailed account of Hansen's activities.

Alfalfa soon became a highly valued crop for both stock-raiser and farmer throughout the entire state. In subsequent years, the production of alfalfa seed was an important source of income west of the 100th meridian.

The work in plant exploration and plant improvement was carried on along a wide front. Other drought- and cold-resistant forage crops introduced by Hansen included several varieties of millets as well as kaoliang, a grain sorghum valuable as a supplementary feed crop during dry seasons. At the same time improvements were made in sweet clover and native alfalfa strains.

Plant scientists also studied new varieties of spring wheat for the Northern Plains area. There was a strong shift to the durum or macaroni variety after it had proved its resistance to drought and rust. By 1914 over 20 per cent of all the wheat grown in South Dakota was of durum varieties. The durum wheats accounted for 42 per cent of the total wheat production in 1921 and 58 per cent in 1923. The Marquis variety, a strain of the Red Fife which had been popular during the 1870's and 1880's, was widely planted because it resisted drought and rust. In subsequent years, new varieties bred from Marquis also were widely grown in South Dakota.

The homesteaders' invasion of the west-river area after 1900 forced the stockmen to accept a modified system of ranching with an emphasis on forage and feed crops. With miles of fence in all directions, the ranchers were faced with the alternatives of going out of business or reconciling themselves to limited operations. Aside from occasional fence-cutting incidents and altercations over crop damages caused by stockmen's herds, the transition from the open range to the new order was made without the violence experienced in neighboring states.

The droughts of 1910 and 1911, which left abandoned or vacated claims available for stockmen's herds, meliorated the impact of the homesteaders. As fences fell into disuse, miles of barbed wire were rolled up by the stockmen to enclose their enlarged pastures. Many ranchers built up private ranges by buying several adjoining tracts and leasing others. Additional pasturage became available through the leasing of Indian allotments. The size of the herds generally ran from fifty to a few hundred head. One of the best known of the large ranches to survive the homesteading era was the Diamond A. Its range, acquired mostly through leases in Armstrong, Dewey, and

Ziebach counties, covered up to 300,000 acres. The Diamond A was dissolved in 1939.

Many ranchers, discouraged with the low prices prevailing in the cattle market after the Panic of 1907, sold their herds and turned to sheep-raising. Some ran both sheep and cattle, using separate ranges. Sheep-raising did not require so large an outlay of capital as cattle-ranching, and it provided quicker returns. It possessed an additional virtue in the double source of income derived from wool and lambs. The sheep industry became especially important in Butte, Harding, and Perkins counties where an abundance of grazing space was available for range flocks.

The requirements of larger units for farming operations on the Northern Plains led to modifications of the public land laws. In 1915 Congress applied the Enlarged Homestead Act of 1909 to South Dakota, thus enabling settlers to acquire 320-acre tracts. Its application was delayed because South Dakotans were reluctant to have areas with an annual rainfall of fifteen inches designated as semiarid. The State Legislature, which had expressed opposition to the extended homestead principle in 1909, supported it by 1913 in the hopes of attracting settlers to public lands left unoccupied following the droughts of 1910 and 1911. In 1912 Congress gave further recognition to environmental problems in the Great Plains region by lowering homestead residence requirements from five to three years, and by permitting a continuous leave of absence for a period of five months each year. It also reduced the requirements for cultivation. To aid the cattle industry, Congress passed the Stock-Raising Homestead Act in 1916, providing for 640-acre homesteads on lands officially designated as nonirrigable grazing lands.

The boom in the west-river section also extended into the region east of the Missouri. It especially affected the central counties lying between the 99th and 100th meridians where the collapse of the Great Dakota Boom had slowed down settlement. What was left of the public domain in this region passed into private hands soon after 1900, and large areas of grassland went under the plow. In Brule, Buffalo, Hughes, Hyde, and Sully counties the combined total of improved lands increased from 475,744 to 908,725 acres between 1910 and 1920.

The outbreak of World War I in 1914 and the United States' entry into the war in April, 1917, stimulated both farmer and rancher to greater activity. War demands pushed farm prices to higher levels and led to a greater volume of production. The following statistics show the price trend:

Year	Wheat (per bushel)	Corn (per bushel)	Hay (per ton)	Beef Cattle (per head)
	South Dakota Farm Prices, 1910–1919[7]			
1910	$ .89	$ .40	$ 7.10	$21.50
1911	.91	.53	8.50	21.80
1912	.69	.37	6.10	22.20
1913	.71	.56	6.50	32.30
1914	.94	.50	5.70	39.50
1915	.86	.49	5.30	39.50
1916	1.50	.77	5.40	38.40
1917	1.96	1.20	10.60	43.70
1918	1.99	1.10	10.00	49.80
1919	2.40	1.10	13.50	53.90

The war stimulus was especially reflected in the utilization of a larger acreage and a corresponding increase in the production of livestock and field crops. The total amount of improved lands increased from 9,805,000 acres in 1914 to 11,190,000 acres in 1919. Although the figures available are not entirely reliable, it has been estimated that the wartime expansion accounted for an increase of 929,000 acres in the semiarid west-river region and 515,000 acres in the eastern half of the state.[8]

Wheat acreage rose from 3,469,000 in 1914 to 3,725,000 in 1919, while corn acreage climbed from 3,000,000 to 3,200,000 during the same period. Local sources indicate expanded plantings in wheat even among cattlemen on western ranches during the period, warranting the conclusion that considerable grassland west of the 100th meridian was converted into wheat fields. The increased production of hay and livestock is of even greater significance. The land devoted to hay production increased from 9,805,000 to 11,190,000 acres between 1914 and 1919. The number of cattle (other than milch cows) increased from 967,000 in 1915 to 1,496,000 in 1919, while sheep increased from 635,000 to 801,000 for the corresponding years.

The heavy demand for farm products during World War I placed

[7] From annual volumes of *Yearbook of Agriculture,* published by the United States Department of Agriculture.

[8] See Lloyd P. Jorgenson, "Agricultural Expansion into the Semiarid Lands of the West North Central States during the First World War," *Agricultural History,* 23 (January, 1949), 30–40.

South Dakota farmers and ranchers in a most favorable position. Except in 1917 when drought plagued the western part of the state, weather conditions were favorable, assuring excellent returns from the land. Farmers again showed a tendency to extend a cash-grain pattern westward into semiarid areas. Where the stock-raising economy prevailed, the ranchers began to extend their operations with resulting overstocking and overgrazing. Sheep production on the western range doubled between 1915 and 1920, when the price of wool went from 68 to 91.5 cents a pound. Stockmen invariably went into debt as they expanded their herds and bought additional land at inflated values. Rentals on leased school lands had skyrocketed from eight to twenty cents an acre by 1920.

The continued rise in farm prices at the war's end led to a speculative land boom that affected the entire state. Land values rose rapidly during 1919 and 1920, prompting city-dwellers to invest in farm lands for speculative purposes in competition with farm owners who sought to increase their holdings. Farm lands rose in value from $9.90 in 1900 to $64.43 per acre in 1920. In Beadle County, with a low of $4.60 in 1900, the appreciation in value was even greater, increasing from $42.45 to $93.75 per acre in the decade ending in 1920.[9]

The boom in agriculture came to an abrupt end by the latter part of 1920 when farm prices dropped sharply in the face of a declining world market. In the two-year period from 1919 to 1921, wheat dropped from $2.40 to 87 cents and corn from $1.10 to 26 cents a bushel, while the average price of cattle declined from $53.90 to $29.20 per head. The cattle and sheep industry was especially hard hit. The deflationary movement shown in the collapse of farm prices during 1920 and 1921 left agriculture in a depressed and precarious condition. The farming patterns in South Dakota, however, remained relatively unchanged except for minor adjustments due to natural price fluctuations peculiar to such commodities as cattle and sheep. Weather conditions were generally favorable during the period.

The farmers found themselves in an anomalous position during the 1920's. Although prices rose again after 1921, the farmers' crop receipts remained low in relation to the cost of farm machinery and other commodities needed on the farm. Faced with a fixed over-

[9] Beryl Rogers McClaskey, *A Social and Economic Survey of Beadle County, South Dakota* (Chicago: privately printed, 1940), p. 106.

head in high taxes and heavy interest charges and with increased production costs as a result of a declining purchasing power, they had to farm more intensively and increase their volume of production in order to make ends meet.

A greater use of power machinery, in particular the tractor, was largely responsible for the increase in production which helped to swell still further the price-depressing farm surplus. It has been estimated that the number of acres that could be harvested by a single worker in South Dakota as a result of the transition from animal to mechanical power increased from 33.2 in 1920 to over 100 by 1929.[10] Land in crops increased from 16,441,000 acres in 1924 to 19,003,000 acres in 1929. The acreage in corn increased from 3,520,000 to 4,982,000 acres between 1920 and 1932. Wheat acreage rose to nearly four million acres in 1932.

This acceleration in farming activities during the 1920's again promoted a tendency to extend cultivation beyond the margin of good land into areas unsuited for crops. Submarginal lands were farmed along with the better grades where several types of land intermingled. Moreover, the unit of production in many areas was too small for economical and efficient operation.

The reverses sustained during the early thirties during the depression and drought focused attention once again upon the problem of proper land use. The dust storms of 1933 and 1934, which removed soil in some places to the depth of the plowline, underscored the need for conservation practices, while the serious economic plight of the central counties, reflected in a heavy relief load and high incidence of farm foreclosures and tax delinquency, strongly suggested a close relationship with improper patterns of farm management.

Numerous agencies of the federal government participated in long-range conservation and rehabilitation programs. Their activities included efforts to shift cropped lands to grazing and to reclaim drought-damaged and overpastured range lands; grappling with the problem of wind and water erosion; restoring and maintaining soil fertility; and determining proper land-use patterns throughout the entire state. A total of $55,280,000 was disbursed in South Dakota as benefit payments between 1936 and 1947 under the Agricultural Adjustment Acts of 1936 and 1938 in a soil- and range-building

[10] Harold V. Faulkner, *The Decline of Laissez Faire, 1897–1917* (New York: Rinehart and Co., 1951), p. 333.

program. The payments were made for planting soil-building crops, reseeding abandoned lands with permanent grasses, and for constructing stock dams in grazing areas. To restore to fertility areas badly damaged from wind erosion and to promote a program of erosion control, the federal government in 1935 established at Huron a demonstration and control project covering 190,000 acres in central South Dakota, mostly in Beadle County. A little later in the same year a second project, comprising an area of 49,280 acres in Gregory and Tripp counties, was started with headquarters at Winner.

Under another conservation program the Department of Agriculture between 1935 and 1942 planted 3,206 miles of shelterbelt in the central part of the state with a total of 41,599,000 trees, including 13,817,000 for replacement. Five Civilian Conservation Corps camps carried on demonstration work in erosion control directed by the Soil Conservation Service. These were located at Alcester, Chamberlain, Fort Meade, Huron, and Presho. Sixteen other camps, operating in the Black Hills, also conducted some phase of conservation, including the collection of seed for shelterbelt nurseries. About 87 per cent of the cultivated cropland in the state was covered by soil conservation programs in 1936.[11] In subsequent years over a thousand artificial lakes were to be constructed, most of them under a water-conservation program fostered by local, state, and federal agencies. By 1960 about 100,000 small stock-water dams had been built under the various conservation programs.

In 1937 a state organization was created to coordinate the activities in conservation conducted under the auspices of the federal government. The State Legislature enacted a Soil Conservation Districts Law, providing for conservation districts set up under the supervision of a state soil conservation committee. The committee included the director of extension and the director of the experiment station at South Dakota State College.

A two-thirds majority in a public referendum was required for the creation of a conservation district. By the end of 1942 a total of 76 districts were in existence, representing a land area of nearly eight million acres. More than five thousand individuals had developed conservation plans for their farms. Although soil conserva-

[11] The problem of conservation is covered in Roger J. Thomas, "A History of Soil Conservation in South Dakota through 1942" (unpublished Master's thesis, University of South Dakota, Vermillion, August, 1949).

tion districts were empowered to enact land-use regulations, they refrained from exercising the authority.

Another phase of the conservation movement was a land-utilization program instituted in a small way by the federal government in 1935 and extended under the Bankhead-Jones Farm Tenant Act of 1937. Its authorized purpose was the retirement of lands considered submarginal or not suitable for cultivation in order to correct inappropriate land use. Supervision was at first exercised by the Soil Conservation Service, but was transferred to the Forestry Service in 1954. Under this program the federal government acquired title to 986,000 acres of land, mostly in western South Dakota, between 1936 and 1940. The owners made the sale voluntarily, generally receiving from three to eight dollars per acre, and were furnished aid in resettlement whenever required. Most of the land was reseeded with crested wheat grass and other grasses, and restored for grazing and feed production.

Three land-utilization projects were set up: the Perkins-Corson, the Badlands-Fall River, and the South Central South Dakota projects. The acquired lands were formed into community pastures and placed under the administration of cooperative grazing associations governed by locally elected groups of stockmen in accordance with state legislation enacted in 1935. Some of the land was leased directly to individual operators. The use of the pasture areas was restricted through a system of permits. In 1955 about 620,000 acres of the purchased lands were under the land-utilization program, involving 660 ranchers. The rest of the lands purchased by the federal government were administered mostly as recreation areas and game refuges.[12]

The acreage acquired by the federal government under the emergency measures of the 1930's was intended to become a permanent addition to the public domain. A subsequent improvement in the national economy and the return of favorable weather conditions, as well as the administrative difficulties inherent in land-utilization programs, led to sentiment in many quarters in favor of public sale. By 1968, however, no provision had been made for the

---

[12] See Loyd Glover, *Experience with Federal Land Purchases as a Means of Land Use Adjustment* (Brookings: Agricultural Experiment Station, Agricultural Economics Pamphlet No. 65, August, 1955), for a discussion of the land-utilization program.

return of any portion of the lands to private ownership except by trade.

Because of the improvement in economic conditions during World War II and after, there was a tendency to forget many of the protective conservation practices of the thirties, but nevertheless the conservation and rehabilitation agencies had played an important part in helping to establish a rational and stable economy more in conformity with the soil structure and rainfall supply. Moreover, the Soil Conservation Service continued its activities. In 1968 there were 70 soil and water conservation districts actively engaged in carrying out conservation practices. At that time 97 per cent of the farmland was included in conservation districts. During the ten-year period from 1948 to 1958 conservation districts had planted 57,000 acreas of trees, mostly in the form of field and farmstead windbreaks.[13]

The agricultural situation improved rapidly after 1939 and continued its upward trend throughout the forties and fifties. Production reached a record level for the state in 1948. The output of farm products in South Dakota from 1940 through 1953 increased 81 per cent, in contrast with an increase of 31 per cent for the country as a whole during the same period. The state achieved this production with a slightly smaller acreage in major crops, with fewer farms, and with a smaller farm population.

The increased production was due in part to the adoption of improved crop- and livestock-production practices. Increased mechanization was also a significant factor. By 1951 from 30 to 50 per cent of the wheat farmers had combines. At the same time 95 per cent of the corn crop was being harvested with mechanical pickers. The predominantly level terrain over large areas had made possible a high degree of mechanization and a maximum production in terms of manpower. A greater utilization of the activities of the Extension Service and other educational agencies in converting the findings of agricultural research into farming practices was likewise an important factor in the improvement shown by South Dakota agriculture. While cash-grain crops remained important, livestock production greatly exceeds them as the major source of farm income in the state. In 1966 the cash income from livestock and livestock products was 79 percent of the total farm income, or nearly four times as large as that derived from crops.

The livestock industry developed a high degree of specialization

[13] Sioux Falls *Argus Leader,* January 31, 1959.

over the years. While stock-raising continued to dominate the economy in the west-river section, by the middle of the century the final feeding operations had become a specialty of the east-river region. Approximately two-thirds of the cattle reported by the South Dakota Crop and Livestock Reporting Service for 1966 were located east of the Missouri River. Dairy cattle were of minor importance. The short-grass region west of the Missouri was raising beef cattle primarily for sale to stock-feeders for intensive feeding on the surplus corn and other feed crops raised in the eastern and southeastern sections.

At the end of its first hundred years, South Dakota was still essentially an agricultural state. Nine out of every ten acres of land were in farms. The federal census of 1970 listed 368,879 persons, or approximately 55 per cent of the total population of 665,507, as rural; of this number, 315,723 lived on farms or in small communities closely identified with the farming economy.

Significant changes have occurred in the state as a whole. The number of farms dropped from a high of 83,157 in 1935 to 43,500 in 1974, while the average size of farms rose from 439 to 1,046 acres during the same period. Especially noteworthy was the increase in the average size of farms from 672 to 997 acres between 1950 and 1969. By the early 1970's farms were declining in number at the rate of about 2 per cent each year.

The state derived about 30 per cent of its total income in 1974 from the sale of crops and livestock. High prices and record yields, attributable to favorable weather conditions, explain the advantageous position enjoyed by South Dakota agriculture at the time. It ranked first in production of rye and second in production of flaxseed. It held third place in durum wheat and oats production and fourth in the production of other spring wheat. It also ranked high in the production of corn, alfalfa seed, sweet clover seed, and crested wheatgrass seed. In the production of Kentucky bluegrass seed, a relatively new cash crop for the state, South Dakota ranked first in 1960, producing more than half of the nation's supply at that time. The main operations, which began extensively in 1950, centered in the area between Brookings and Pierre.

The major systems of farm management that have developed reveal marked variations from east to west and from north to south, especially in the eastern part of the state. The gradations and variations from area to area may be seen in the type-of-farming classification used by the South Dakota Agricultural Experiment Station in its investigations of farm management problems.[14]

Any discussion of South Dakota agriculture must include a consideration of irrigation farming. Three main factors have generally militated against the establishment of large-scale irrigation projects: the rugged terrain of the semiarid portion of the state; the costliness of construction and maintenance of irrigation projects; and the unwillingness of agriculturists in areas of favorable rainfall to adopt irrigation practices during periods of drought except on a supplementary basis.

Irrigation began in the Black Hills region in 1877 when settlers from Montana acquired water rights along Spearfish and Spring creeks in the Spearfish Valley.[15] By the end of the second year some fifteen irrigation ditches had been completed. Projects were also installed on other tributaries of the Belle Fourche and Cheyenne rivers. By 1899 a total of 38,318 acres was under irrigation in the extreme western part of the state, utilizing the gravity flow from running streams. This acreage represented 179 separate projects. There were also sporadic efforts at irrigation along the Missouri in the central part of the state during early drought periods, but the excessive cost of pumping plants made stream irrigation impractical in the region. The unsuccessful efforts to utilize an underground supply of water by means of artesian wells in the James River Valley has been discussed above.

Most of the early efforts in the Black Hills area were directed toward the irrigation of pasture lands. By 1912 Rapid Creek Valley had supplanted other areas in importance with some twenty irrigation systems extending along a thirty-mile stretch and capable of irrigating some seventeen thousand acres of cropland. The practice of cattlemen in impounding water for irrigation at points upstream to the detriment of downstream water-users led to legislation in 1905 and 1907 designed to standardize and systematize the use of water for irrigation as well as other purposes. The law of 1905 pro-

[14] Ray F. Pengra and Gabriel Lundy, *Fifty Years of South Dakota Agriculture* (Brookings: Agricultural Experiment Station, Agricultural Economics Pamphlet 56, November, 1954), p. 4. This classification was established by the Bureau of the Census. See also Lyle M. Bender, *The Rural Economy of South Dakota* (Brookings: South Dakota Extension Service, South Dakota State University, Special Report No. 1, September, 1956).

[15] For an extended discussion of irrigation activities, see Lowell E. Whiteside, "A History of Irrigation in South Dakota" (unpublished Master's thesis, University of South Dakota, Vermillion, June, 1955).

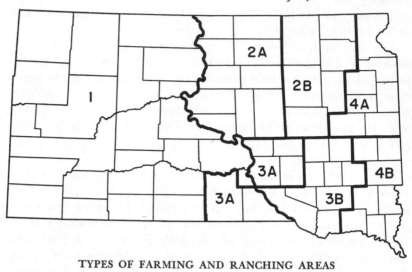

TYPES OF FARMING AND RANCHING AREAS

(Exclusive of Black Hills. Statistics from 1950 census. Chart adapted from Lyle M. Bender, *The Rural Economy of South Dakota*, Special Report No. 1, September, 1956, South Dakota Extension Service, Brookings, South Dakota, pp. 81–84.)

Area   1—Grazing region with islands of wheat production. Average rainfall (outside Black Hills) : less than 16 inches. Average farm size: 1,962 acres.

Area 2A—Transition area; wheat the dominant crop. About 60 per cent of land in pasture and hay. Rainfall average: 18 to 20 inches. Average farm size: 829 acres.

Area 2B—Cash grain area; wheat an important crop; annual rainfall average: 20 to 22 inches. Average farm size: 470 acres.

Area 3A—Southern transition area between feed grain farming and extensive ranching areas. Beef production leading enterprise. Rainfall average: 18 to 20 inches. Average farm size: 666 acres.

Area 3B—Western corn belt fringe; moderately intensive crop and livestock farming area; corn main crop. Rainfall average: 20 to 24 inches. Average farm size: 324 acres.

Area 4A—General farming area; wheat, flax, and barley important cash crops; corn, oats, main feed crops. Rainfall average: 22 to 24 inches. Average farm size: 309 acres.

Area 4B—Intensive livestock feeding, hogs, dairy, poultry production. Corn, oats, soybeans main crops. Rainfall average: 24 to 26 inches. Average farm size: 214 acres.

vided for a state engineer with full supervisory powers over the waters of the state.

The Reclamation or Newlands Act, passed by Congress in 1902, included South Dakota' among sixteen western states in which the federal government was authorized to construct irrigation facilities for the reclamation of arid and semiarid lands. After an examination of several prospective locations, including the Angostura site on the Cheyenne River, the Bureau of Reclamation chose the valley east of the city of Belle Fourche as the most promising site. The construction of Orman dam between 1905 and 1911 created a reservoir from which water was to be carried through 500 miles of canal to irrigate a total of 90,000 acres in an area thirty miles long and averaging about twelve miles in width. The first water for the project was made available in 1908. In order to provide irrigators with information regarding crops raised under dry-land and irrigation systems, the Bureau of Reclamation established an experimental farm near Newell in 1907. Irrigation research was started in 1912.

Although the Belle Fourche project was of great economic significance for the area, mistakes made during the planning and early development stages handicapped it for years. Inexperience in irrigation methods on the part of settlers who had no farming background, the play of speculative forces in the acquisition of irrigation tracts, a failure by the Bureau of Reclamation to make a proper land classification with the result that unmanageable heavy gumbo soil made up 47 per cent of the project area, costly errors in construction and maintenance, and an unrealistic plan for repayment of construction charges were major causes of failure during the first two decades of operation. The project was further plagued by a deflationary movement during the 1920's and by periodic water shortages during seasons of severe drought a decade later. The cumulative results of these shortcomings were financial insolvency for the project, the abandonment of numerous irrigated farms, and a large turnover in the farm population.

More lenient contracts in 1914 and 1926 relieved the farmers from paying construction charges during certain years and extended the time for repayment, at first from ten to twenty years, later from twenty to forty and even in some instances to eighty years.

The economic status of the project began to improve after 1937 as a result of more favorable conditions and an improvement in irrigation practices. In accordance with the original agreement made with the irrigation district in 1904, the Bureau of Reclamation negotiated a new contract in 1949 which gave the district a greater degree of self-government. A reclassification of the land and the abandonment of one extension also reduced the project area to slightly over 57,000 acres. Whereas the original cost of the project was based on a project area of 90,000 acres, the land actually irrigated never exceeded 60,000 acres.[16] In other words, less than two-thirds of the project had been carrying the entire repayment load. The new contract remedied this situation. As a result of several charge-offs, together with some subsequent additional funding by Congress, the contractual repayment obligation stood at a total of $4,230,000. Of this amount, the irrigators had repaid $2,197,000, or 52 per cent, by 1974.

An important factor in the economic rehabilitation of the Belle Fourche project was the sugar-beet industry, introduced to the district in a small way in 1910. Until 1927 the beets were shipped to Scottsbluff, Nebraska, for processing; then the Utah-Idaho Sugar Company constructed a $1,500,000 sugar factory at Belle Fourche. In that year 13 per cent of the irrigable cropland went into the production of sugar beets, which had become the major cash crop. After World War II, alfalfa began to replace sugar beets as the major crop. Sugar beet culture continued to decline and, in 1965, the sugar factory ceased operations. This ended sugar beet production in South Dakota. Barley, corn, oats, and wheat also became important crops for the Belle Fourche Valley. Livestock was another major source of income on the irrigation project during the 1960's.

In 1950 the completion of Angostura dam on the Cheyenne River seven miles southeast of Hot Springs made an area of 12,154 acres, divided into some eighty farms, available for irrigation in Fall River and Custer counties. Water from the Angostura reservoir was

---

[16] Marvin P. Riley, W. F. Kumlien, and Duane Tucker, *50 Years Experience on the Belle Fourche Irrigation Project* (Brookings: Agricultural Experiment Station, South Dakota State University, Bulletin 450, May, 1955), is an attempt to analyze the experiences gained from the project. An excellent critique is F. C. Youngblutt, "Let's Profit from Past Mistakes," *Dakota Farmer*, LVI (April, 1946), 6–7, 22–23. At the time the article was published, Youngblutt had served as superintendent of the Belle Fourche project for twenty-two years.

first released to the project in 1952 in accordance with a water-users contract negotiated between the Bureau of Reclamation and the Angostura Irrigation District. Future plans called for an increase in the total acreage for irrigation to 25,000 acres by means of pumping units along the Cheyenne.

The Angostura project was part of the multipurpose Pick-Sloan Plan for the development of the Upper Missouri Basin, authorized by Congress in December, 1944. The plan originally called for the irrigation of nearly a million acres of land in South Dakota, including 750,000 acres in the James River Valley, with water supplied from a reservoir created by Oahe dam above Pierre. In addition to the Angostura project, dams and reservoirs were to be constructed in the trans-Missouri region along the Bad, Cheyenne, Grand, Moreau, and White rivers. Dams at Deerfield and Pactola in the Black Hills were designed to make supplemental water available for irrigation units already in operation. Whereas irrigation projects were formerly confined to semiarid areas, the Pick-Sloan Plan contemplated the extension of irrigation to the glacial soils of sub-humid areas in the eastern part of South Dakota.

The ambitious irrigation program led to extensive exploratory work by the Bureau of Reclamation in the form of land classification and surveys in the James River Valley and other areas of eastern South Dakota, as well as in areas along the Grand, Cheyenne, and White rivers in the western part of the state. Plans for irrigation along the Moreau River were found impractical.

Development work on the Oahe project has assured the suitability for eventual irrigation of 445,000 acres in the James River Valley and 50,000 acres in the Missouri Slope area, mostly in Sully County. The initial stage, authorized by Congress in 1968, provides for the irrigation of 190,000 acres in Brown and Spink counties as well as a water supply for seventeen municipalities. The completion of this initial stage, begun in 1974, will require about seventeen years. It will take about fifteen additional years for the consummation of the entire project, which calls for irrigation in Brown and Spink counties, besides small acreages in Marshall, Day, and Sully counties.

The Oahe project provides for a main pumping plant whereby water is to be lifted an average of 122 feet from the Oahe Reservoir to the nearby bluffs on the east. From this point, the water will flow by gravity to the irrigable lands within the James River Valley.

While plans were being laid for the impounding of large bodies of waters to stabilize agriculture in the James River Valley, aquifers were giving new impetus to irrigation on a supplementary basis in other parts of eastern South Dakota. In some instances, the underground waters were utilized by means of wells and ditches. More prevalent, however, was the use of sprinkler systems, employing portable equipment. The irrigated acreage for the entire state increased steadily after 1960. A total of 129,000 acres, over two-thirds of which were located west of the Missouri, were under irrigation in 1973. Alfalfa has continued to be the leading crop under irrigation, mostly in the western counties. Corn has ranked second, with most of the irrigated acreage in Spink County and the south central section, including Charles Mix, Clay, Turner, and Union counties.

In common with other states preponderantly agricultural in their economy, South Dakota began to suffer population losses following the decade of the 1920's. The state reached its peak in population in 1930 with 692,849 inhabitants. By 1945, according to the state census of that year, the population had dropped to 589,920, indicating a loss of nearly 103,000 people during a fifteen-year period.

The initial decline began during the drought and depression of the 1930's. Only Sioux Falls and the Black Hills region gained population during this period; nearly every county showed a loss. Further losses came during World War II. Although federal census figures show a slight increase during the 1940–1950 decade, this increase is due to a rising birth rate: the state had actually sustained a net loss of approximately 79,000 persons in interstate migration.[17]

The census return for 1960 indicated a continuation of this trend of migration out of the state. The total gain in population for the state as a whole was only 27,774, or considerably less than the excess of births over deaths during the decade. More significant than the net migration out of the state was the continued movement from the farm to the city. The three counties which showed the greatest increase for the 1950–1960 decade contained fast-growing urban communities: Pennington, with a gain of 23,000; Minnehaha, with a gain of 14,000; and Hughes, which gained 4,600. Brookings, Brown, and Codington counties also showed substantial increases. This trend generally continued during the next decade, with Brookings, Brown, and Minnehaha counties again showing marked increases. For the state as a whole, however, the census of 1970 revealed a declining trend.

The following table shows the population growth of South Dakota since statehood:

Census Year	Total Population	Percentage of Increase or Decrease
1890	328,808	234.6[18]
1900	401,570	15.2
1910	583,888	45.5
1920	636,547	9.0
1930	692,849	8.8
1940	642,961	-7.2
1950	652,740	1.5
1960	680,514	4.0
1970	665,507	-2.2

Emigration from South Dakota's rural areas resulted from the trend toward larger and fewer farms, and from a lack of employment opportunities. With the loss of population from their trade areas, hamlets and small villages also declined. Of 377 hamlets in existence in 1911, only 148 remained forty years later. Rural trade centers shrank faster following World War II.

This movement out of rural communities increased the social and economic importance of the larger cities. Sioux Falls with a population of 72,488 was the largest city in 1970. It is the largest trade center in South Dakota, and employs 60 per cent of the state's workers in manufacturing industries. Rapid City, the second-ranking city, has had a phenomenal growth in recent years. Between 1940 and 1970 its population rose from 13,844 to 43,836. It is the eastern gateway to the Black Hills and the metropolis of western South Dakota. Near Rapid City is Ellsworth Air Force Base. Aberdeen, with a population of 26,476 in 1970, is the third largest city. Located on the transcontinental line of the Chicago, Milwaukee, St. Paul and Pacific Railroad Company, it commands the retail and wholesale trade of the north central part of the state. Other cities with populations above 10,000 in 1970 were Huron, Brookings, Mitchell, Watertown, and Yankton, ranking in that order.

The greater use of trucks and automobiles in marketing and merchandising has been an important factor in the decline of rural trade centers and the corresponding growth of urban communities.

[17] John P. Johansen, *The Influence of Migration upon South Dakota's Population, 1930–1950* (Brookings: Rural Sociology Department, South Dakota Agricultural Experiment Station, Bulletin 431), pp. 13–14.
[18] Based on population figures for the area of present-day South Dakota.

Trucks first began to be widely used at the end of World War I when favorable farm prices gave farmers the means and the incentive to buy them to expedite the marketing of their products. The number of trucks increased from 8,277 in 1921 to 14,445 in 1926. In 1966 there were 110,026 motor trucks in operation. Automobiles were in general use by 1921 when 110,997 cars were registered. By 1966 the number had risen to 280,147.

Driving regulations soon followed the appearance of the automobile around 1900. A Sioux Falls ordinance in 1903 placed a speed limit of seven miles per hour for city driving, with a reduction to four miles at street corners. Two years later a state law prescribed a twenty-mile speed limit in the country and ten miles in towns. Subsequent early legislation declared twenty-five miles per hour a prudent rate of speed.

The introduction of motorized transportation led to a movement for better highways. At first roads were the responsibility of local government units. Instead of paying road taxes in cash, citizens were given an opportunity to work out their levy. This wasteful and inefficient system of road maintenance was abolished in 1911. Beginning in that year all road taxes were collected in cash and road work was placed on a contract basis. Rural residents lessened their opposition to changes in the law as they began to appreciate that mail delivery was facilitated by good roads. However, real progress in road-building had to await the adoption in 1916 of a constitutional amendment which permitted the state to construct public roads. The following year a good roads law provided a system of trunk highways connecting county seats and towns of over 750 people, and created a state highway commission. Two years later, legislation was enacted to comply with the requirements for federal aid on a dollar-matching basis in accordance with the 1916 Federal Aid to Highways Act. There were no graveled roads before 1921. With the aid of federal funds, the first concrete road was built between Sioux Falls and Dell Rapids in 1923, and hard-surfaced roads were constructed at an accelerated rate in subsequent years.

In 1966 the road system of South Dakota included 8,490 miles of state trunk highways, 20,040 miles of county roads, and 50,690 miles of secondary rural roads. This constituted approximately a mile of road for every eight inhabitants. This network of roads includes the interstate highway system, authorized by Congress in 1956, which crosses the state from east to west and from north to south with 675 miles of four-lane, limited-access, divided freeways. Plans for the interstate highways call for their completion by 1982, with 90 per cent of the construction costs to be borne by the federal government. About 540 miles were constructed by 1974.

Early plans for a modern highway system included proposals for bridging the Missouri. Although the river was spanned with railroad bridges in 1907 at Pierre and Mobridge and a pontoon bridge at Chamberlain, all vehicular traffic between the two sections of the state was carried by ferries until the middle of the 1920's. A privately owned toll bridge was completed at Yankton in October, 1924. A month later, the first of five highway bridges was opened to traffic at Mobridge. During the next two years bridges were completed at Wheeler, Chamberlain, Pierre, and Forest City. The total cost for the five public bridges approximated two million dollars. Funds were raised through a special tax levy authorized by the Legislature in 1921. The original plans which had called for three bridges were changed to avoid a deadlock over the selection of prospective sites. In order to hasten construction, counties and municipalities were permitted to advance funds which were to be reimbursed later out of the bridge fund. The Yankton bridge became the property of the city of Yankton in 1953 and was made toll-free.

The construction of the four multiple-purpose dams across the Missouri forced the relocation of the original bridges at Chamberlain, Forest City, Mobridge, and Pierre. The bridge at Wheeler was moved up the river to form one of the two spans for a new bridge at Chamberlain. As a replacement for the Wheeler bridge, a mile-long structure known as the Platte-Winner bridge and said to be the longest bridge in the United States west of the Mississippi, was opened in 1966. The crests of the four dams also serve as highways spanning the river. Including the Yankton bridge which was not affected by the Missouri Basin development projects, motor traffic in the state could now cross the Missouri at ten different points.

The improvements in road construction, the developments in motorized transportation, and the decline in trade centers forced the railroads to adjust themselves to a loss of business, abandoning depots in small towns and curtailing train service in general. Nearly three hundred fifty miles of railroad were abandoned between 1928 and 1968. All passenger service had been discontinued by 1968 except for a single train on the transcontinental line of the Milwaukee road serving Aberdeen and Lemmon. The extensive use of trucks had also cut heavily into the freight business. The proportion of livestock carried to Sioux Falls by truck increased from 12 per cent in 1930 to 98 per cent in 1950. By 1960 all shipments of hogs to the Sioux Falls market were made by motor truck.

The reduction of railroad service was a stimulant to air transportation. Eighty-three approved airports were developed with federal and locally sponsored funds between 1940 and 1974. Four commercial airlines were operating in 1974 from nine certified passenger air terminals. In addition to regular airline service, charter service was available from many South Dakota airports. South Dakota residents owned 1,081 planes.

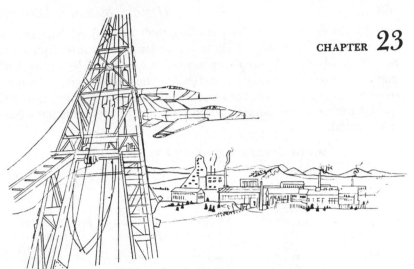

CHAPTER 23

Reappraisal: Developments in Manufacturing and Mining

FROM THE EARLIEST BEGINNINGS, the settlers of South Dakota sought a diversified economy. They had visions of building up manufacturing establishments as well as exploiting the timber and mineral resources of the Black Hills. The industrial development, however, remained slow in getting under way and small in extent. In 1899 only 2,224 or about eight-tenths of one per cent of the total population were industrial wage-earners. By 1958 the number of wage-earners had risen to about ten thousand. The ratio in proportion to total population had, however, increased but slightly; less than one and a half per cent of the total population were classified as wage-earners.

The table on the following page indicates the rate of industrial growth since statehood.

In tracing the state's industrial development, the first half century must be viewed as a period of experimentation when the region was still in a frontier stage of development. Many manufacturing ventures were victims of a "boom and bust" economy during the early 1890's. In attempts to attract industry during the first fifty years of the state's history, various towns vied with each other in making civic improvements, seeking additions to their rail-

367

way facilities, and generally parading their alleged advantages before the world. Commercial clubs and other groups of businessmen, as well as private individuals, sponsored promotional literature and made overtures to interested parties. In their eagerness to become industrial centers, communities offered generous bonuses, granted special tax exemptions, and raised local funds to supplement outside capital.

SOUTH DAKOTA MANUFACTURES, 1899–1958[1]

Year	Total Establishments	Wage-Earners	Wages Earned	Value Added by Manufacturing
1899	624	2,224	$ 1,130,000	$ 3,046,000
1909	1,020	3,602	2,298,000	6,394,000
1919	1,054	5,588	6,751,000	17,070,000
1929	615	6,535	8,132,000	22,681,000
1939	450	5,421	5,905,000	19,619,000
1947	494	8,062	19,193,000	51,398,000
1954	546	8,414	27,977,000	77,692,000
1958	577	10,000	38,000,000	108,000,000

Most early manufacturing activities were concerned with processing raw materials produced in the area and fabricating materials in local demand. The potentialities were well stated by the territorial commissioner of immigration in 1889:

There is no better field for investments in manufactures than in Dakota. We have wool and flax, we have cattle, sheep and hogs, and we have wheat and corn. We have nearly all the minerals known to geologists. We need more flouring mills, we need . . . woolen factories, we need wood working shops, implement factories, iron foundries, and machine shops. There is room for legions of capitalists and workers.[2]

Flour-milling was the major industry for many years. One-half of the entire valuation of the state's industrial products in 1890 was represented by flour and gristmill products. Although by 1910 the ratio had dropped to one-third, flour-milling was still the leading industry. At least 180 flour mills were in existence at some time or other, nearly all of them established prior to 1910.

The first mill appeared in the fall of 1867 in Union County on the

[1] *United States Census of Manufactures, 1954*, Volume II, Industry Statistics (Washington: Government Printing Office, 1957), p. 48; U. S. Department of Commerce, *1958 Census of Manufactures: Preliminary General Statistics* (Washington: Bureau of Census, 1959), pp. 2, 3. Statistics for 1958 represent preliminary estimates.

[2] Frank H. Hagerty, *A Dictionary of Dakota* (Aberdeen: *Daily News Print*, 1889), p. 11.

Big Sioux southeast of Elk Point. At the outset it operated two run of burrs and served portions of four states. It was said to have drawn patronage from Minnesota, a hundred miles away. In September, 1868, the Bloomingdale mill began operations on the Vermillion River about ten miles north of Vermillion. Additional mills in the southeastern counties appeared in quick order during the 1870's following the steady influx of settlers into the region. By the time the Great Dakota Boom had run its course, over a hundred mills were supplying the needs of the state.

Although usually regarded as a mining country, the Black Hills area also had its share of flour mills. These were powered mostly by water. In the eastern part of the state the majority of the mills were steam operated. Several mills, mostly in the James River Valley, utilized for a time the energy released by deep wells in the artesian belt of Central South Dakota. The largest flour mill to operate with artesian power was located at Woonsocket.

The flour mills played a vital part in the local economy. The wheat they bought was locally grown; much of their product was locally marketed. South Dakota millers, as a rule, paid the farmers a slightly higher price than the shippers. The wheat grown in South Dakota enjoyed the reputation of possessing superior milling qualities, and was therefore also in heavy demand with the large flour mills at Minneapolis and St. Paul. Even though the volume of production was constantly increasing up to 1900, the South Dakota mills were able to process only a small portion of the entire wheat crop. Of a total production of nearly 42,000,000 bushels grown in the state in 1899, slightly less than 4,500,000 bushels was used by local flour and gristmills. The rest of the crop had to be shipped outside.

The South Dakota mills, generally speaking, supplied the home markets, meeting very little competition from the outside, even from the large commercial mills of the Twin Cities in Minnesota. In view of the state's relatively small population, a considerable portion of the output had to be marketed elsewhere. By 1900 the merchant mills in the eastern part of the state had to find an outside market for about five-sixths of their total production.

Most of the South Dakota flour was marketed in the Upper Mississippi Valley. Some millers were able to build up a special trade in suburban areas of Chicago. South Dakota mills also enjoyed a share of the export trade to the United Kingdom, where high patent

American flour, the product of new milling processes that included the use of differential rollers, commanded a favorable market. The trade names under which Dakota patent flour found a market were, as a rule, quite distinctive. The "Swans-down" brand, first brought into usage in 1889 by the Rapid City Milling Company, was the most famous of all South Dakota flour brands. After 1929, the Tri-State Milling Company, which had acquired ownership of the Rapid City mill, registered the brand in nine different states under the name "Swan's Down." In December, 1941, the firm sold all rights to the trade name to General Foods, Incorporated. Representative flour brands of other mills were "Snow White" and "Ermine" (Aberdeen); "Artesian Queen" (Springfield); "Dakota Silver" (Eureka); "Dakota Straight" (Madison); "Prairie Lily" (Mt. Vernon); and "Queen Bee" (Sioux Falls).

The most ambitious undertaking in flour-milling during territorial times was the Queen Bee Mill at Sioux Falls. A seven-story building of Sioux Falls granite constructed at a cost of nearly three hundred thousand dollars, it was reputedly the second largest mill in the United States when it began to grind wheat in October, 1881. It had a potential daily capacity of 1,200 barrels. The mill, however, operated only at intervals and never at full capacity. After initial operations from October, 1881, to January, 1883, it shut down until 1911 when, after some modernization, it resumed grinding on a small scale for several years. Operations ceased permanently at the close of World War I. The large structure remained standing by the falls of the Big Sioux until its destruction by fire in 1956.

Only a few of the mills in operation at the turn of the century exceeded a daily capacity of 200 barrels. The mill operated at Watertown by the W. H. Stokes Milling Company was the largest in the state until the Tri-State Milling Company constructed one of the country's most modern and efficient mills at Rapid City in 1937.

Electricity was not a source of motive power for milling before 1900, but it was employed for lighting mills as early as 1887. In that year the Cascade Milling Company of Sioux Falls began to operate an electric light plant in addition to its mill. By the early 1890's a number of mills were generating electricity as a by-product. Besides the Sioux Falls company, milling firms in such towns as Beresford, Bowdle, Springfield, Tyndall, and Vermillion became the local light companies. In some instances, flour-milling gave way entirely to the production of electricity.

By 1910 the milling industry was in a state of decline.[3] Only about eighty mills were in actual operation at the time. The trend toward large-scale manufacturing was already under way, forcing the smaller mills to confine themselves to the grinding of feed or to tailor their operations to local needs. Moreover, by relying primarily on a local supply, the South Dakota miller had placed himself at a disadvantage in competing with the large commercial mills whose product came from carefully blended wheat. In 1961 the plant operated by the Tri-State Milling Company was the only commercial flour mill left in operation.

The creamery industry also played a prominent part in the economic life of the state. The factory system of making butter and cheese, which had its beginnings in the middle of the nineteenth century, was slow in getting established in the early Dakota settlements because of the emphasis on grain farming. Dairying did not become important until adverse weather conditions induced a trend toward diversified farming. Cheese making, presumably on a community basis, was reported in Turner County as early as 1872.

According to federal census reports, there were four establishments making butter and cheese in 1880, including a Vermillion creamery which was operating on a twelve-month basis. A creamery boom occurred during the following decade, but the establishments generally lacked sufficient patronage. The usual explanation offered for the short life of early creameries was that there was not enough milk to make it pay. A creamery required the milk of at least a thousand cows for economical operations, but most early establishments began with considerably less patronage. The large production of butter and cheese on farms in 1880 indicates that farmers still preferred to take their own butter to local stores in trade. Moreover, milk was produced primarily during the summer months when the cows grazed on the native grasses. The creameries usually ran from May 1 to November 1. Whatever milk there was during the winter was usually processed into cheese. The census of 1890 indicated only sixteen creameries for the whole state.

The creamery business continued in a state of flux until about 1895. The low price level, reflected in forty-cent wheat, and the ad-

[3] For a more comprehensive survey of the early flour-milling industry, see Herbert S. Schell, *South Dakota Manufacturing to 1900* (Vermillion: Bulletin No. 40, Business Research Bureau, University of South Dakota, May, 1955), pp. 4–31.

verse effects of protracted droughts led to a greater degree of diversification, especially in the spring wheat area, where creameries became more numerous between 1890 and 1910. A number of creameries also made their appearance in the homesteaded areas west of the Missouri River after 1910.

Most of the creameries were established on the cooperative or stock company plan. During the 1890's the widespread use of the centrifugal separator led to a change in creamery techniques with the "skimming station" replacing the cream gathering that was in vogue earlier. At convenient points throughout the countryside, the creameries set up one or more power separators to accommodate the farmers of the locality. From the skimming station the cream was carried to the central factory for curing and churning. Some of the larger creameries had as many as eight skimming stations. With such changes in creamery management, butter production lost its seasonal character.

Although South Dakota did not hold so high a rank in butter production as the neighboring states of Iowa and Minnesota, its creamery industry commanded sufficient prestige to prompt the selection of Sioux Falls in 1899 and 1903 for national buttermakers conventions. The Legislature gave support to the creamery movement in 1901 by providing for a food and dairy commissioner who, among other duties, was to furnish encouragement and assistance in the organization of creameries. All creameries had to be licensed. The Legislature also placed restrictions upon the sale of colored oleomargarine. In 1919 there were eighty-six creameries in operation, with 223 wage-earners and a production value of $10,805,000. Although the creamery industry had undergone revolutionary changes in production techniques by 1954, it still comanded an important position in South Dakota with forty-one establishments and a production value of $20,643,000.

The processing of cereal products other than flour received only sporadic attention during early times. A small oatmeal mill was in operation at Parker from 1884 to 1886, and a larger establishment appeared at Sioux Falls during the early nineties. For the brief space of a month during the year 1892 a cornstarch factory was also in operation at Sioux Falls.

Canning factories operated for a short time at Springfield and Sioux Falls before the Panic of 1893. Canneries were also undertaken for short periods in several communities subsequent to 1900.

The only canning plant in continuous operation on South Dakota soil was established in 1904 on the state boundary line at Big Stone City by the Big Stone Canning Company which was originally incorporated under the laws of South Dakota. Although Ortonville, Minnesota, subsequently became the mailing address for the plant, the establishment began as a South Dakota enterprise. Among the several improvements pioneered by the canning plant at Big Stone City was the perfection of machinery that made it possible to pack whole-kernel corn.

Despite several early efforts to establish meat-packing plants, none was in operation at the turn of the century. The first establishments were butcher shops which shipped their surplus east after supplying the local neighborhood market. Their operations were seasonal and mostly limited to the processing of hogs. Such pork-packing plants were in operation for brief periods during the eighties in Huron, Mitchell, Pierre, Rapid City, Scotland, Sioux Falls, Watertown, Woonsocket, and Yankton. The Sioux Falls plant also processed beef for a short time.

A more modern packing plant was established in 1888 at Oelrichs by the Anglo-American Cattle Company as a part of the firm's extensive grazing operations in Fall River County. The project included a modern slaughter house and extensive feeding pens whereby the company could condition its range cattle and process its own animals for eastern markets. The plant operated at full capacity for several months and then shut down. High freight rates to distant markets, the price-cutting tactics of eastern packers, and a large overhead due to the high cost of imported feed were major factors in the failure.

At the same time that the project at Oelrichs was failing, plans were under way for a large packing center at Sioux Falls. Enlisting the support of Maine capitalists, R. F. Pettigrew organized the Sioux Falls Stockyard Company, purchased over a thousand acres of land in the southern part of the city, and began the construction of a six-story building. The financial stringencies of the period, however, caused numerous delays. When finally finished, the plant was one of the most completely equipped packing houses in the entire Northwest. Although pork was processed for a short time in 1899, continued financial difficulties compelled the abandonment of the project, and Pettigrew's dream of a million-dollar packing house in South Sioux Falls was never realized. Forty years later, the massive building of Sioux Falls granite was razed by the W.P.A.

The efforts made by Pettigrew and his associates to develop an industrial center in South Sioux Falls included the oatmeal mill and cornstarch factory mentioned above, a soap factory, an axle-grease factory, and a woolen mill. None of the projects succeeded. The woolen mill ran intermittently after August, 1889, until the Panic of 1893 forced it to shut down permanently. Following unsuccessful efforts to revive the project in 1898, the machinery was finally dismantled and shipped to a New England mill. During its period of operation, the Sioux Falls mill manufactured fifty different styles of cloth, including blankets, flannels, skirting, and cassimeres.

The attempts to establish woolen manufacturies represented an effort to utilize the raw wool that was produced in increasing volume by Dakota farmers. A woolen mill was also in operation at Yankton, then an important wool-purchasing center, which ran seasonally for ten-month periods from 1883 to 1891. The growth of the range sheep industry in Fall River County led also to the establishment of a short-lived woolen mill at Edgemont in 1890.

The extensive production of flax in the southern portion of Dakota Territory during the decades of the eighties and nineties led to the establishment of tow mills in order to utilize the flax straw. Serious efforts to build up a fiber industry in the United States provided a ready market for tow. Eastern firms interested in fiber manufacturing generally promoted the tow mills. The first mill was built at Scotland during the summer of 1883. Within the next six years thirteen additional plants appeared. The higher market price enjoyed by flax during most of these years gave it a distinct advantage over wheat and was undoubtedly a major factor in the promotion of the tow industry on the Dakota frontier. More tow mills were erected during 1892 and 1893 when flaxseed again went up to about a dollar a bushel.

Most of the nineteen tow mills founded in South Dakota from 1883 to 1893 remained in operation only a short time. None was in business after 1895. One of the larger mills, built at Wentworth by a Milwaukee firm, ran for about a decade. During good seasons, the Wentworth plant processed about six thousand tons of straw, frequently shipping out two carloads of tow a day. The tow mills ran during the fall and winter season, beginning whenever sufficient straw was on hand, usually in November or December. Over a thousand tons were required for economical operations. The mills paid from $2.50 to $4.00 per ton for the straw and received from

$10.00 upward for the tow, depending upon the grade. The product went to eastern points, particularly New York, where it was extensively used in making upholstery. Some of the coarse tow was utilized for making binder twine.

Despite all the promotional activities in various South Dakota communities for the establishment of linseed oil mills, only two projects materialized—one at Yankton in 1887, the other at Groton in 1888. Each remained in operation for only a short period. A large part of the flaxseed raised on South Dakota farms prior to 1900 was shipped to Sioux City where the third largest oil mill in the nation was producing from 250 to 300 barrels of linseed oil per day.

The interest in building up an American fiber industry led to the promotion of a linen mill in Sioux Falls in 1892. The owner of a small linen mill in Minnesota was given inducements to move his weaving machinery to the South Dakota city where a three-story structure was built near the future site of the Morrell packing house. The mill, equipped with fifty looms, was designed for both weaving and spinning. The spinning looms were imported directly from Belfast, Ireland. During its existence of about fifteen months, the linen mill employed sixty-five persons. Its products included various kinds of pure linen crash. It was advertised widely as the only mill in the country to manufacture huck toweling on a large scale. The Sioux Falls Linen Company commanded considerable attention at the Chicago World's Fair in 1893 with its display of products made exclusively from flax grown and processed in South Dakota. One of four or five linen mills in operation at the time, the Sioux Falls plant was a victim of the Panic of 1893.

Brickmaking was also an important pioneer industry. The clays found in glacial drifts in the eastern part of the state as well as in alluvial deposits in the Black Hills furnished the materials. Despite a serious drawback, the occurrence of small pebbles and limy matter which interfered with the molding and burning process, the "brick clays" became a valuable asset in communities where building materials were scarce or not readily available. Brick was especially needed for the construction of chimneys and foundations and was extensively used for residences and other construction in the towns when the product became more plentiful. Later the use of brick for sidewalks increased the demand for the clay product.

Bricks were made on a large scale by the late 1860's and early 1870's. Brick residences began to appear in Yankton by 1870 and in Sioux Falls by 1874. No less than eighteen communities in the eastern part of the state and at least six in the Black Hills had brick-yards at some time or other prior to 1900. With the exception of Rapid City where fire brick was also made, the product was of the common red clay variety. Occasionally, as at Yankton, a white sand-lime brick was also manufactured. Because of the impurities in the clays, brickmaking remained highly experimental in character. Constant search was made in the early settlements for superior clays, but these were not always found in places convenient for a manu-factory. Although eleven brickworks were listed in the census of 1900, only eight plants, three of them in the Black Hills, were in business in 1902.

By 1910 the early brickmaking industry had come to an end. It was not revived until 1927, when a clay products plant was put in operation at Belle Fourche, manufacturing brick, building tile, and drain tile.

A cement plant operating at Yankton from 1890 to 1909 repre-sented an effort to exploit the extensive outcroppings of chalk or limestone material, known as the Niobrara formation, that is espe-cially accessible between Fort Thompson and Yankton. The cement factory was located four miles west of Yankton. Most of the financial support came from English capitalists. Yankton citizens paid a subsidy of about $13,000 and procured the right of way for a spur track to the plant. Although the Western Portland Cement Com-pany controlled about 3,000 acres of chalkstone property, the in-dustrial plant itself covered only about ten acres, including the main building, mud basins, dry kilns, and storage and shipping warehouses. A broad-gauge railway was built along the river bottom to Yankton, which served as the shipping point as well as the place of residence for the employees. At the time of its construction, the establishment was said to have been the largest portland cement factory in the United States.

The Yankton cement plant began with a daily capacity of 250 barrels. It was usually closed down for two months during the winter season. When running at full capacity, it furnished employ-ment for seventy men. There was a constant demand for the prod-uct, much of which was used on government buildings throughout the Middle West. The plant gained further prestige when its prod-uct received first premium at the World's Fair in 1893.

Following a reorganization of the company in 1896 because of financial difficulties, the plant was sold to New York and Chicago capitalists. Production costs were so high that the original company had been operating at a loss from the very beginning. In 1904 improvements and changes in equipment increased the plant capacity fourfold. The efforts at modernization, however, served to increase the operational costs further. In 1909 a Sandusky, Ohio, cement company secured title to the property. After a survey of the situation, the new owners decided to shut down the plant and dismantle the machinery. During its period of operations the Yankton plant produced nearly two million barrels of cement, valued at $3,000,000. Of this output, 325,000 barrels, valued at $750,000, had been sold before 1901.

A number of other manufactories commanded the interest of the early settlers. Among the several establishments possessed by Watertown during its boom period was a paint factory. Besides mixed paints, it made carriage paints, varnishes, and putty, mostly for a South Dakota market, during its period of operation between 1887 and 1893. A paint factory operating at Custer from 1897 to 1905 processed dry paint from oxidized iron ores and graphite obtained from nearby mines. The powdered pigment was shipped to a mixing plant at Aurora, Illinois. Several soap factories were also in operation for short periods prior to 1900, as were plow and wagon factories. Woodworking establishments, foundries, and machine shops proved to be of a more permanent character.

Cigar-making was undertaken at an early date. There were few towns in South Dakota that did not at some time or other have at least one cigar factory. The industry was usually carried on in rented rooms, requiring little capital for land and buildings. The work was done by hand; the main equipment was a set of molds and a hand press. The materials consisted chiefly of leaf tobacco bought from importers and wholesalers in such limited quantities as to be quickly worked up and disposed of locally and in neighboring communities. Most of the plants were small, employing only a few persons. For a number of years Sioux Falls was the state's cigar manufacturing center. By 1900 Huron was in the front rank of the industry, with an annual output of over a million cigars.

Cigar-making was one of the few expanding industries at the turn of the century. Between 1900 and 1909 the number of cigar factories increased from twenty-seven to fifty-nine. During the next decade came the inevitable decline as the smaller establishments were forced to yield ground to large tobacco companies operating under the economies of quantity production and highly systemized methods of distribution.

The brewing industry likewise began to flourish at an early date. Yankton had a brewery as early as 1866. According to semiofficial statistics released in 1887, the southern part of Dakota Territory possessed at least eight brewing establishments, two of them located at Yankton. When prohibition went into effect in 1890 under the state Constitution, all the breweries shut down with the exception of an establishment at Sioux Falls which continued to operate at full blast despite strenuous efforts by local enforcement committees to compel compliance with the law. Only two breweries were in operation in 1919 when national prohibition went into effect.

In surveying the early industrial activities of the state, one must note the failure to build up large industrial plants. The businesses represented by the various establishments in 1900 were small in scope and generally restricted to neighborhood or regional trade. Of the several ambitious projects that had been undertaken, only the cement plant at Yankton was in operation at the turn of the century. Although speculative ventures continued during the next fifty-year period, the period of experimentation was over by 1900.

The outstanding industrial development during the second half century of the state's history was the establishment of the meatpacking industry. As a result of the technological changes in flour-milling and the growing importance of beef cattle in the farm economy, the processing of meat gradually replaced flour-milling as the state's major industry. It represented about 38 per cent of the value added by all manufacturing activities in South Dakota by 1960.

The modern meat-packing industry in South Dakota began in 1909 when John Morrell and Company opened a branch plant in Sioux Falls. Originally an English corporation, the Morrell firm established its main plant at Ottumwa, Iowa, in 1877. Thirty years later it decided to expand its facilities into a region better able to supply a northern bacon-type hog that was especially suitable for its English customers. After looking over several prospective sites in Minnesota and South Dakota, the company in 1909 selected Sioux Falls for the new location. Leasing the property of a small local establishment that was idle at the time, the Morrell Company during its first year of operations processed 89,000 hogs and nearly

2,000 cattle. In 1911 it moved into its own plant, which had a larger capacity. Further expansion followed in 1920 and subsequent years until by 1960 the Sioux Falls packing house had attained a daily slaughtering capacity for 6,500 hogs, 1,000 cattle, and 2,000 sheep. Its operations provided employment for 3,500 men and women.

Besides the Morrell plant, nine other meat-packing establishments were in operation in 1968, three of them having several hundred employees. In addition to these larger establishments, at least thirty-three smaller plants, mostly lockers, were in existence, engaged in meat-packing and employing less than twenty-five people.

The depression of the thirties interrupted the steady growth in manufacturing that had followed World War I. Although the number of establishments declined from 1,054 to 615, the labor force had increased from 5,588 to 6,535 and the value added rose from $17,000,000 to $22,680,000 between 1919 and 1929. Meat-packing was responsible for two-thirds of the growth in value during this period. The onset of the depression, accompanied by the adverse effects of drought, caused a drop in value added to $19,619,000 by 1939. The number of establishments declined to a low of 450 during the depression period.

The demands of the war years 1941–1945 enabled South Dakota manufacturers to recoup the losses sustained during the depression days. Noteworthy gains were made in almost every type of activity. The number of industrial wage-earners increased from 5,421 to 8,062 between 1939 and 1947, while the value added by manufacturing jumped from $19,619,000 to $51,398,000. Even before the United States entered the war in December, 1941, machine shops and foundries in Aberdeen were profiting from defense needs for tools and cutter grinders and other items of shop equipment, some of the orders coming directly from England and France.

In the absence of large defense plants, South Dakota made a notable contribution to the war effort by converting garages, machine and woodworking shops, and electrical appliance shops into small war plants. Some seventy-eight machine shops and other establishments produced materials valued at approximately $50,-000,000 during the years from 1941 through 1945. In addition to machine tools of various kinds, the small war plants turned out hand grenades, rifle slings, engine parts, ammunition cases, punches and dies, and many other small items. The Smaller War Plants Corporation assisted the firms in securing government contracts as well as subcontracts from larger defense plants. Besides their direct services in the war effort, the small defense plants also slowed down the migration of workers from the state to defense centers in more highly industrialized areas.

The war experiences gave impetus to a program for industrial expansion in the postwar period. A natural resources commission, authorized by the Legislature in 1945, undertook a survey of the state's potentialities for small industry. This was followed a decade later by the creation of an Industrial Development and Expansion Agency. Local industrial foundations and chambers of commerce supplemented the activities directed by the state government. As a result of these efforts to attract and promote industry, manufacturing was becoming of increased importance by 1968. Small plants rather than large establishments were sought in the effort to develop a more balanced economy for the state. As a further means of attracting new industries, the Legislature in 1964 passed a law authorizing cities to issue revenue bonds for industrial development. Although industry's share of the state's total income was still only about 4 per cent during the 1960's, the value added by manufacturing had increased from $51,398,000 in 1947 to $226,000,000 in 1971, with a labor force of approximately 16,000 in the latter year.

The lumbering industry had its beginnings at an early date. Since the timber resources are mostly limited to the Black Hills, the industry has been generally confined to that region. Extensive groves of cottonwood, ash, elm, and box elders found on the bottoms along the lower portions of the Missouri and Big Sioux rivers as well as in steep gulches and ravines and along lakes in the eastern part of the state also supplied the needs of the early settlers for fuel and lumber. The local sawmill became the first manufactory wherever a community possessed a supply of timber and was without railroad connections.

When the Black Hills were opened up, lumber was indispensable not only for the construction of buildings, but also for sluicing boxes and for the timbering of mines. The first sawmill in the region was established at Custer in February, 1876. According to an early Deadwood resident, men sat on logs at the sawmills, with money in hand, waiting to pay seventy dollars per thousand feet for lumber needed for the erection of buildings.[4] In 1883 there were forty-three sawmills in the region in addition to some twenty-five

[4] George W. Stokes, *Deadwood Gold: A Story of the Black Hills* (Yonkers, N. Y.: World Book Co., 1926) , p. 58.

shingle mills. During the early 1890's Custer was the largest lumber shipping station in the Black Hills.

The greater portion of the lumber was shipped to the Northern Hills, where it was used in the mining industry. The Homestake Company alone required 2,000,000 running feet of timber annually. Large quantities of Black Hills lumber were also shipped to Nebraska and Wyoming towns. After the establishment of a forest reserve by the federal government in 1897, the United States Forest Service supplied the bulk of the timber supply under a system of regulated cutting. By 1960 the annual production of lumber was about 45,000,000 board feet. The industry then consisted of about sixty small mills, half of which had an annual production capacity of 200,000 board feet or over. Three of them produced over five million board feet each.

Production of both metals and nonmetallic materials continued to increase after 1900, the value of minerals produced in the state rising from $5,200,000 in 1910 to $26,870,000 in 1950. By 1963 mineral production had increased in value to $55,100,000, over half of which was represented by metals. Gold production with a value of $20,185,000 accounted for 97 per cent of the total metal value.

The depression of the thirties and the action of the federal government in raising the price of gold in 1934 provided the impetus for a short-lived gold-mining boom and the appearance of several new companies, none of which was able to survive. By the fifties only two mines remained, the Homestake and the Trojan Mine, owned by the Bald Mountain Mining Company. After thirty years of continuous mining activities, the latter company closed down its operations in 1959, leaving the Homestake Mining Company as the only gold-producer in the state.

The Homestake Company was a large producer at an early date. From its small beginning in 1878 it was able to expand its operations until by 1960 it possessed over 6,000 acres of patented and 300 acres of unpatented mining claims. Also included in the company's holdings at that time were a semilignite coal deposit in Wyoming, extensive timber lands, and water rights along several northern Black Hills streams. Its greatest period of expansion occurred during the years 1893 to 1900, when it absorbed and consolidated the properties of four corporations with which it had been engaged in an intense rivalry earlier. The Homestake became the largest gold mine in the western hemisphere. Over a seventy-three year period up to the end of 1949 it had yielded approximately 19,190,000 ounces of gold.

Gold mining virtually ceased in June, 1943, in compliance with orders from the War Production Board, and was not resumed until July, 1945. In the meantime, the Homestake Company confined its activities to other minerals more vital to the war effort, such as coal and tungsten. It also produced lumber and made hand grenades, monkey wrenches, and forgings for use in defense plants. Its large maintenance shops and foundry were frequently in operation on a twenty-four-hour basis during World War II.

By 1968 the Homestake Mining Company was the only major straight gold producer left in business in the fifty states of the Union. Its volume of production had made South Dakota the leading gold-producing state in the Union. Through its selective mining methods and constant improvements in milling practices, the Homestake Mining Company was enabled to recover 97 per cent of the gold from each ton of the low-grade ore produced from its mine. The continuation of a fixed-selling-price policy by the federal government during a highly inflationary period became, however, a serious handicap to the company's operations during the postwar years. In the hope of arresting the course of declining profits, the 1967 Legislature suspended for a two-year period the major portion of the ore tax imposed on the gold-mining industry under a measure enacted in 1935. In 1970 the law was repealed.

The war demands gave impetus to the production of critical or strategic materials throughout the entire Black Hills region. Of the sixteen minerals and mineral products generally regarded as of commercial importance, bentonite, feldspar, and mica especially benefited from the war boom. The war needs for glass greatly stimulated the production of feldspar, which was first mined during the twenties. Ground feldspar, most of it processed at Custer, continued in demand throughout the fifties for use in glass, pottery, and enamel industries, giving South Dakota second rank in production.

Bentonite, a peculiar claylike substance which readily absorbs water, finds wide use in the manufacture of cosmetics, paints, paper, plastics, and soaps, and as a filtering agent in petroleum refining. Half the state's production of bentonite found its way into war plants for foundry use as a drilling mud and for bonding purposes. The major deposits occurred in Butte County near Belle Fourche. By 1968 bentonite production was in a decline.

Following intermittent production subsequent to its discovery near Custer in 1879, mica assumed sudden importance when it was classified as a strategic material during World War II. It was used in condensers for electric generators and in radar. Sheet mica also goes into the production of electrical heater elements. In its ground form, mica is used in the manufacture of roofing, paint, plastics, and wallpaper. In 1958 about ten per cent of the national output came from sixty-two mines in Custer and Pennington counties, giving the state second rank in production. The mica industry suffered a setback when the federal government in June, 1962, terminated its domestic purchasing program. The following year only two mines were in operation. In 1967 the state produced no mica.

Gypsum was one of the first nonmetallic minerals to be used in the Black Hills. The period from 1895 to 1915 has been termed the golden age of the gypsum industry. The largest plant at the time was located at Hot Springs. Wall plaster and stucco were the chief products provided by the raw gypsum. For a short time a high grade of dental plaster was also produced. By the end of the 1930's the industry was virtually nonexistent. The only gypsum in production in recent years has been used by the state-owned cement plant.

The cement plant at Rapid City also utilizes the extensive hard limestone deposits of the Black Hills. The state-owned enterprise started operations in January, 1925, representing an investment of $2,000,000. Although the plant made a profit from the beginning, its greatest period of prosperity occurred subsequent to World War II. The Legislature in 1949 authorized a program of expansion, enabling the plant to double its capacity. In 1958 it produced nearly three and a half million barrels of portland cement, netting a profit of nearly $5,000,000. By that time the South Dakota Cement Plant had an estimated replacement value of $20,-000,000. In 1966, because of an extended slump in the cement industry, production was down to two million barrels yielding a net profit of slightly over $3,000,000.

The red quartzite, a variety of sandstone commonly known as Sioux quartzite or Sioux Falls granite and found extensively in the southeastern part of the state, gave rise to a stone-quarrying industry of considerable commercial importance prior to 1900. The durability of the stone, together with the ease with which it could be excavated and dressed, made it especially suitable for paving. It also became a favorite stone for building because of its strength and its attractive, unchangeable color.

Although the Sioux quartzite was put to use locally from the beginning of settlement in the Big Sioux Valley, it was not until 1886 or 1887 that the quarrying industry began to flourish. The most extensive quarries were opened up east of Sioux Falls, at Dell Rapids, and near Spencer in Hanson County. The paving blocks found a ready market throughout the entire Middle West. Many of the skilled stonecutters came from England and Scotland. During the early nineties, the quartzite industry was hard hit by the panic and tightness of money. Shortly after 1900 it came to a virtual standstill as the market for paving and building blocks had all but disappeared. Although quartzite continued to be used extensively in a crushed form for making concrete and for surfacing roads, the industry never regained the prominence it commanded prior to 1891. An extensive quarrying industry also flourished for several years at the turn of the century in Fall River County, utilizing the rich deposits of Dakota sandstone in the region.

The quartzite deposits in the Big Sioux Valley also led to the establishment of a stone-polishing works at Sioux Falls in 1883. In addition to the preparation of quartzite blocks for monuments, the firm added the polishing of chalcedony in the form of petrified wood to its operations during the late eighties, obtaining the product from a large field of petrified wood in Arizona. Sioux Falls chalcedony products were widely used for table tops, counter and fireplace adornments, and for shelving. The polishing works ceased operations shortly after 1900.

The outcrops of a granite formation in the northeastern part of the state gave rise to a granite industry in Grant County. The first large commercial quarry was opened near Milbank by the Robert Hunter Granite Company in 1908. Because of its rich, dark color, the stone bears the trade name "Mahogany Granite." Over half of the production from the Grant County quarries is used for monuments. The product is also used for building stone, curbing, and paving blocks. In 1967 six different firms were engaged in quarrying granite in the Milbank area; three of them, however, processed the product at Minnesota plants. At that time, the South Dakota quarries produced about 30 per cent of the total dressed monumental granite in the United States.

Among the mineral resources that remained undeveloped in 1968 were tin and manganese. Following the short-lived Harney Peak tin-mining boom which occurred between 1883 and 1893, small amounts of the low-grade ore were produced intermittently in both the northern and southern parts of the Black Hills until about 1940. Large deposits of low-grade manganese occur along the Missouri River in the vicinity of Chamberlain. Like the tin found in the Black Hills, manganese cannot be mined economically in competition with the richer ores supplied by foreign countries. The exploitation of South Dakota manganese must await the development of cheaper metallurgical methods of treating the ore. Research undertaken by the federal government during the forties to find out whether manganese mining could be made practical proved unsuccessful.

The coal or lignite deposits of South Dakota are confined to the northwestern counties and a small area near Edgemont in Fall River County. The United States Geological Survey has estimated that the deposits in Harding and Perkins counties alone contain a billion tons of lignite. The first recorded production of coal occurred in 1895 near Edgemont. The lignite provided a cheap local supply of fuel during the homesteading period after 1900 as well as during the depression days of the thirties. In 1934 over 42,000 tons valued at $76,000 were produced from twenty-one mines. Lignite production reached a peak of 70,800 tons in 1941. Most of the coal was obtained through surface mining or stripping from open pits. The discovery during the 1950's that much of the lignite contains traces of uranium gave new importance to the state's coal resources. Their exploitation, however, must await metallurgical improvements.

Extensive uranium-bearing ores other than lignite lie scattered across the western part of South Dakota. Uranium ore was first discovered near Edgemont during the summer of 1951. A uranium rush followed the disclosure of the news. During the next three years more than two thousand claims were filed in Fall River County alone, and intensive prospecting occurred in other areas. The federal government opened an ore-buying station in Edgemont in 1952, and shortly thereafter constructed a mill for processing the uranium-bearing ores. About 72,000 tons were produced in 1963, mostly from mines in Fall River County. By the middle of the 1970's, however, the production of uranium was being phased out.

The discovery of petroleum in the Williston Basin in North Dakota in 1951 reawakened an interest in prospecting for oil that had started with the discovery of natural gas in the state in 1880. After many years of costly exploration in various parts of the state, oil finally began to flow from two wells in Harding County in 1954. By 1958 there were four producing wells, including one in Custer County, with a total annual production of 62,000 barrels. The following year ten additional wells in Harding County began to produce oil in commercial quantity. By 1967 the cumulative production ran close to 2,000,000 barrels with 93 per cent produced from the Buffalo Field in Harding County. During 1966 some 25 producing wells in the Buffalo Field yielded 220,000 barrels; 5 wells in the Barker Dome Field of Custer and Fall River counties produced 20,000 barrels. In 1973 there was a total production of 285,200 barrels. The total cumulative production from the early 1950's to 1974 was nearly 3,418,000 barrels.

The critical energy shortage facing the entire country during the early 1970's focused special attention on the vast lignite deposits of the Dakotas as a potential source of gas. Sufficient progress had been made by 1974 at an experimental coal gasification plant at Rapid City to place a pilot plant in operation for converting the low-quality coal gas into pipeline quality.

Interest has also been directed to the possible use of thermal waters from the artesian basin west of the Missouri River for heating purposes. The town of Midland, famed for years for its hot mineral baths, has utilized since 1962 artesian waters with a constant temperature of 156° in heating its public school building.

South Dakota, moreover, in common with the rest of the nation, could look forward to benefits from the use of earth-orbiting satellites for the collection and distribution of physical data concerning the earth. An advanced phase of such technological developments was the launching of an experimental Earth Resources Technology Satellite (ERTS) by the Department of the Interior under its Earth Resources Observation System (EROS) in July, 1972. The data gathered through highly sensitive cameras and remote-sensing instruments were converted at receiving centers into photographic images and then deposited at the EROS data center established at Sioux Falls, where they were stored as well as processed for distribution.

CHAPTER 24

Reappraisal: Social and Cultural Aspects of South Dakota Life

IN LOOKING BACK over the social and cultural developments of the hundred-year period from 1861 to 1961, it seems appropriate to begin with mention of the state's rich Old World heritage. Thousands of European immigrants of a dozen major nationalities and from every walk of life came to the Dakota frontier, bringing with them their native tongues and social customs. In the words of one writer:

Cultivated, restless young men from Europe made incongruous figures among the hard-handed breakers of the soil. . . . Knut Hamsun, the Norwegian writer who was awarded the Nobel Prize for 1920, was a "hired hand" on a Dakota farm . . . . Colonies of European people, Slavonic, German, Scandinavian, Latin, spread across our bronze prairies like the daubs of color on a painter's palette. They brought with them something that this neutral new world needed even more than the immigrants needed land.[1]

In 1890 one-third of the white population was foreign-born; and although by 1940 only one out of every ten had been born in a foreign country, nearly half the population was only two or three generations removed from the Old World.

The immigrants, for the most part, were a homogeneous group, a majority of them being of Teutonic and Alpine stock. About one-

[1] Willa Cather, "Nebraska: The End of the First Cycle," *The Nation*, Sept. 5, 1923.

half of the foreign-born came from western Europe and slightly more than one-fourth from central Europe. Because the state's economy was lacking in diversification, South Dakota did not share in the heavy immigration from eastern and southeastern Europe that contributed so heavily to the growth of population in other parts of the United States after 1890. Although immigration to South Dakota had almost ended after World War I, Old World customs and speech persisted in many communities, a reminder of national heritages.

Among the foreign groups, the Germans are the most widely dispersed and are found in all parts of the state. They are numerous enough in many localities to give the entire community a predominantly Germanic character, and have given German names to many townships and towns. In 1940 about one-sixth of the state's population was either German-born or of German parentage. Although this figure includes migrants from southern Russia, the so-called German-Russians, the majority came directly from Germany. Among the German-Russians were the Mennonites and Hutterites. The Hutterites have attracted considerable attention because of their communal social organization: they hold all goods and property in common, and each Hutterische or Hutterite colony maintains a large farm. In 1918 seventeen colonies were in existence, but because of the manifestations of anti-German prejudice and the treatment accorded them during World War I, most of the Hutterites moved to Canada. They returned to South Dakota to re-establish their religious communities two decades later. Sixteen colonies were in existence in 1955 when a legislative enactment prohibited the formation of additional colonies or the expansion of existing corporations.

The Scandinavian element, comprised of Norwegians, Swedes, and Danes, makes up about one-third of the foreign stock. The Norwegians have been especially important in South Dakota's history, and have furnished many outstanding leaders. Up until 1880, one-tenth of the state's population was of Norwegian nationality. Because of their social solidarity as well as their numbers, the Norwegians exerted a strong influence upon the development of community life. Except in early settlements in the southeastern part of the state, the Swedish settlers formed less compact communities than the Norwegians. The Danish settlements, like those of the Swedes, were scattered throughout the state. The heaviest concentration of Danes is found in Turner and Yankton counties.

The Bohemians or Czechs formed another important early immigrant group. In 1930 nearly two per cent of the state's population was of Bohemian or Czech extraction. At first the Czechs settled mostly in Bon Homme and western Yankton counties, but as the line of settlement swept westward, they moved into Charles Mix, Douglas, Brule, and Buffalo counties, and ultimately into Gregory and Tripp counties west of the Missouri. The Czechs likewise brought with them many Old World customs, which their local lodges helped to preserve.

Many Dutch settled in the western part of Douglas County, where a colony of Hollanders from Orange City, Iowa, located in the early eighties. Four whole townships were taken over by the Dutch colonists, a number of whom came directly from Holland. From Douglas County the Hollanders spread into the neighboring counties of Aurora, Bon Homme, and Charles Mix. They also established settlements in Lincoln and Minnehaha counties and in the Upper Big Sioux Valley.

Other smaller groups which made distinct contributions to the culture of their areas include the Finns in Hamlin and Lawrence counties and the Welsh in Edmunds County. Immigrants from English-speaking lands tended more than other foreign groups to locate in urban communities.

South Dakota's religious life has been strongly influenced by its immigrants. It has been estimated that about half of the state's churches were established by foreign groups. Their religious organizations not only promoted social solidarity, but also played an important part in the acculturation process. Irrespective of their national origins, most early settlers were deeply concerned with their spiritual welfare. Each new settlement had its nucleus of devout individuals who banded together for religious service. In the absence of pastors the settlers sang hymns and read the Scriptures in their homes. Although itinerant preachers appeared in the settlements along the Missouri in 1860 and a log church was erected by the Presbyterians at Vermillion, there were no formal church organizations for several years. By 1869 the Baptist, Congregational, Episcopalian, Lutheran, and Methodist denominations were serving Protestants in the older settlements. In 1867 a Catholic church was erected at Jefferson and a resident priest appointed to serve the southern part of Dakota Territory.

The Great Dakota Boom provided an excellent opportunity for

missionary endeavor. As soon as new communities came into existence, the missionaries appeared. In central Dakota a band of nine
missionaries from Yale was particularly active, carrying the gospel
to new settlements and organizing Congregational churches. Catholic
clergymen and representatives of other organizations were equally
active in the numerous communities that sprang up along the new
railway lines.

By 1890 there were twelve religious groups in the state. Most numerous were the Catholics, while the Lutherans were a close second.
The Congregationalists, with their New England heritage, were
third, and the Methodists ranked fourth. The 1936 census of religious
bodies in the United States showed that 278,567, or 42 per cent of
South Dakota's population, were church members. By 1960, according to the National Council of Churches, the proportion of church
members had risen to 63.4 per cent of the total population. The
leading church groups with their respective memberships in 1936
were:

Lutheran	96,604	Baptist	8,521
Roman Catholic	89,001	Reformed (Dutch)	5,627
Methodist	23,928	Evangelical and Reformed	5,003
Congregational	14,595	Mennonite	2,071
Presbyterian	11,430	Evangelical	2,001
Protestant Episcopal	8,269	Disciples of Christ	1,179

Among the several Lutheran bodies, the Norwegian Lutheran
Church ranked first with a membership of 45,084. The Missouri
Synod was second with 19,771 members, while the American Lu-
theran Church held third rank with 13,043 members.

Closely related to their religious activities were the efforts of pioneer church bodies to establish academies and colleges, which were
warmly welcomed by townsite boomers and local boards of trade.
The movement for private colleges during the 1880's paralleled
the excitement over locating public institutions. Lack of support
doomed some institutions to a brief existence, and forced others to
merge or consolidate. In 1961 there were nine church-related institutions, including three junior colleges, all but two established prior
to 1900. The four-year institutions were Augustana College at Sioux
Falls, Dakota Wesleyan University at Mitchell, Huron College at Huron, Yankton College and Mount Marty College at Yankton, and
Sioux Falls College at Sioux Falls. The two-year institutions were
Freeman Junior College at Freeman, Presentation Junior College at
Aberdeen, and Wessington Springs College at Wessington Springs.

State-supported institutions of higher learning include the University of South Dakota at Vermillion, South Dakota State University at Brookings, South Dakota School of Mines and Technology at Rapid City, Black Hills State College at Spearfish, and Northern State College at Aberdeen. Southern State College at Springfield was placed under the administration of the University of South Dakota in 1971, as was Dakota State College at Madison in 1974.

Although they were too busy making a living to devote much attention to the creative arts, the early South Dakota settlers were by no means isolated from the main stream of American life. Local newspapers kept them informed about current happenings on both the national and international scenes, and provided an outlet for literary expression on the part of gifted editors. Musical and dramatic performances by traveling artists were staged in local halls and opera houses, while nationally known lecturers, booked by lyceum bureaus, presented popular topics on the public platform. Inspirational lectures were especially in vogue.

Among the several summer Chautauqua assemblies that were established in South Dakota, the one organized in 1891 by the Lake Madison Chautauqua Association was the best known, and continued to function until 1933.[2] Sessions usually lasted three weeks, until the middle of the 1920's when eight-day schedules became common. Programs included drama, readings, musical entertainment, and public lectures in which the speakers discussed political and social problems of the day. Often sessions were given over to church organizations and temperance societies. Chautauqua assemblies also served large crowds for a few years at Big Stone City, Canton, Hot Springs, and Ruskin Park, near Forestburg. The Chautauqua circuit, whose sessions were held in tents instead of stationary pavilions, also found South Dakota fertile territory. Tent Chautauqua moved into the state in 1905, within a year after its beginnings at Marshalltown, Iowa. From that time until the early thirties the Vawter-Redpath circuit carried its balanced programs of entertainment and education into numerous communities throughout the entire state.[3]

[2] W. Cory Christenson, "The Early History of the Lake Madison Chautauqua" (unpublished Master's thesis, University of South Dakota, 1956), covers the topic in a comprehensive manner.

[3] See Harry P. Harrison, *Culture under Canvas: The Story of Tent Chautauqua* (New York: Hastings House, 1958), for Chautauqua activities in South Dakota. Harrison was a booking agent for lyceum courses in South Dakota for a few years before he became manager for the Vawter–Redpath Chautauqua circuit.

Early settlers were interested in libraries, and formed reading circles and library associations. Their books were kept in small reading rooms that also served as social centers. From such modest beginnings developed the leading public libraries of South Dakota. In 1887 a law was passed which permitted towns to establish public libraries and to collect taxes for their support. Aberdeen and Sioux Falls were among the first to take advantage of the legislation. In 1958 there were eighty-six public libraries in the state, most of them tax-supported. There were also seventeen libraries maintained by state and private institutions, in addition to the library of the State Historical Society at Pierre. A traveling library system was set up in 1913 under the direction of the Free Library Commission.

The literature of South Dakota may be said to have begun with the publication of the *History and Resources of Dakota, Montana, and Idaho* by Moses K. Armstrong in 1866. The publication bore the imprint of the Yankton *Union and Dakotaian* and at the time was acknowledged to be the first book printed in the Missouri Valley above Omaha.[4] More than half its contents pertained to history. Armstrong, a surveyor, had settled in Yankton in 1859 and played a prominent part in the early legislative sessions. He was a prolific and colorful writer who turned out many newspaper articles during his sixteen-year residence in the Territory. *Early Empire Builders of the Great West,* which he published in 1901, is mostly a compilation of his earlier writings. Armstrong's *History* was the forerunner of a number of publications, mostly of a promotional nature. Of special importance was James S. Foster's *Outlines of History of the Territory of Dakota and Emigrant's Guide to the Free Lands of the Northwest,* published at Yankton in 1870, when the author was commissioner of immigration.[5] More than a third of the text consisted of historical material. In 1884 A. T. Andreas published a *Historical Atlas of Dakota* containing a general sketch of the Territory with a special section on the Black Hills, and a historical sketch of each county. The most ambitious historical project was George W. Kings-

[4] Armstrong's *History* was reprinted in *South Dakota Historical Collections,* XIV (1928), 9–69. Armstrong drew heavily on a series of historical articles published by him during July and August, 1864, in *The Dakota Union,* a short-lived newspaper started by him and George W. Kingsbury as a rival to *The Dakotian.* The two papers were merged to become the *Union and Dakotaian* in November, 1864.

[5] The Foster publication likewise appears in *South Dakota Historical Collections,* XIV (1928).

bury's *History of Dakota Territory,* published in 1915. Most of its two volumes were compiled by the author from his own file of the Yankton *Press and Dakotaian* with which he had been associated since 1862. The volumes by Kingsbury were accompanied by a third volume, *South Dakota, Its History and Its People,* edited by George M. Smith, and two biographical volumes.

The first systematic research in the history of South Dakota began in 1901 when the State Historical Society was established and Doane Robinson appointed its secretary. During his twenty-five year tenure, Robinson made a major contribution in collecting and compiling historical records, and also wrote a number of volumes dealing with the state's history. Notable among these were a two-volume *History of South Dakota,* published in 1904; a *History of the Sioux Indian* (1904) ; and an *Encyclopedia of South Dakota* (1925) ; and another two-volume *History of South Dakota* (1930).

The first fiction writer of distinction to deal with the South Dakota scene was Hamlin Garland, who launched his literary career in Brown County. Out of his experiences on a homestead claim and as a clerk in his father's store at Ordway came a series of short stories which he began to write in 1887 for *Harper's Weekly.* In 1891 they were collected under the title *Main-Travelled Roads.* "Boomtown," which is the setting for his earliest fiction, can easily be identified as Ordway. Although the public was slow to accept Garland, some critics immediately recognized his work as an advance in American realism. An exponent of the single-tax philosophy, he used the ugliness and frustrations of pioneer life to dramatize the need for political and economic reform; his emphasis upon the "intellectually stifling nature of western life" may be regarded as an exemplification of single-tax principles.[6] He identified himself with the Populist movement and made several unimpressive appearances on the hustings in South Dakota during the Populist campaign of 1892. His short stories depicting hard times in Dakota were utilized as campaign literature. Although he turned to other themes after 1894, he occasionally reverted to the Brown County setting for local color as he did in a novel, *The Moccasin Ranch,* published in 1909. In *A Son of the Middle Border* and *A Daughter of the Middle Border,* he recalled his experiences as a young man on the Dakota frontier.

---

[6] Donald Pizer, "Hamlin Garland in the *Standard,*" *American Literature,* XXVI (November, 1954) , 415.

Writing a generation later than Garland, Ole Edvart Rölvaag emphasized the psychological rather than the sociological in his portrayal of pioneer life. His *Giants in the Earth,* which was first published in Norwegian, became an immediate and phenomenal success when it appeared in English in 1928. With *Peder Victorious* (1929) and *Their Fathers' God* (1931), it comprises a trilogy dealing with emotional aspects of Norwegian immigrant life. The setting of this classic work is Minnehaha County, near the present-day town of Colton. The twenty-year-old Rölvaag arrived in South Dakota from Norway in 1896, and worked for three years as his uncle's farm hand before entering a Lutheran academy at Canton. He attended St. Olaf College, Northfield, Minnesota, and from 1906 until his death in 1931 was Professor of Norwegian on its faculty.

During the early 1900's a number of novels set in South Dakota were well received. Will O. Lillibridge, a young Sioux Falls dentist who practiced his profession by day and wrote by lamplight, produced seven novels in the course of a few years. His premature death cut short a promising career. In the opinion of some critics, his first and most popular work, *Ben Blair* (1906), took rank over Owen Wister's great success, *The Virginian.* Several of his novels dealt with life in Sioux Falls at the turn of the century when the bustling young city was the divorce mecca of the United States.

Equally well known for their writings at this period were Kate and Virgil Boyles, a sister and brother who lived at Yankton. Like Lillibridge's *Ben Blair,* their first and best novel, *Langford of the Three Bars* (1907), concerned the South Dakota cattle domain along the White River and the adjacent valley of the Missouri. In this widely acclaimed work Virgil Boyles drew upon his own experiences as a Lyman County court stenographer during the cattle-rustling era. In *Homesteaders* (1909), the authors depicted the land rush into the Rosebud country.

Although a resident of the Black Hills for only a few years, Stewart Edward White made the rowdy, boisterous mining community of Keystone the background for *The Westerners* and *The Claim Jumpers,* both of which appeared in 1901. Kennett L. Harris, publisher of an early-day Hot Springs newspaper and one-time resident of Oelrichs, gained national fame as a writer of magazine fiction. Most of his stories were based on incidents in the early history of western South Dakota. In his *Meet Mr. Stegg,* a collection published in 1920, an old bullwhacker spins yarns about the Old West in a manner reminiscent of that of O. Henry.

A number of other writers made literary capital out of short-term residence in the state. Most of them wrote about the forces of nature that beset South Dakotans, with blizzards, droughts, dust storms, and grasshopper plagues moving monotonously across their pages. Rose Wilder Lane made the vicinity of DeSmet, where she spent her childhood, the locale of her best novel, *Let the Hurricane Roar* (1933), and of a later volume, *Free Land*. Ethel Hueston, a prolific novelist, lived long enough in the Black Hills to pick up a fund of local color sufficient for three books, one of which was *Calamity Jane of Deadwood Gulch* (1937). Frances Gilchrist Wood made use of her experiences as a pioneer in Potter County in *Turkey Red* (1932), while Edith Eudora Kohl drew so heavily on her homesteading days in the west-river country after 1900 that her novel, *Land of the Burnt Thigh* (1938), is close to being autobiographical. J. Hyatt Downing recalled his boyhood experiences in *A Prayer for Tomorrow* (1938), placing the characters in the small town of Rudge, a fictionized Blunt. In a second novel, *Hope of Living* (1939), Downing made the low hills west of Blunt the locale.

The South Dakota scene is also represented in many works of nonfiction. Joseph Mills Hanson, native of Yankton and writer of verse and fiction, became best known for his biographical account of Grant Marsh, famed Missouri River steamboat pilot, in *The Conquest of the Missouri* (1909). Archer B. Gilfillan rose to literary fame when *Sheep*, his account of life on the South Dakota range, was published in 1929. Writing with humor, philosophy, and charm, Gilfillan tells of his eighteen years as sheepherder in Harding County. Selections from his account have appeared in a number of anthologies of American literature. Other autobiographical works of merit dealing with the west-river range include Ike Blasingame's *Dakota Cowboy: My Life in the Old Days* (1958) and *A Man from South Dakota* (1950) by George S. Reeves.

Professor Herbert Krause of Augustana College in Sioux Falls has made valued contributions to regional literature. His first novel, *Wind without Rain* (1939), written in a prose style that approaches poetry, won an award as the year's best book by a Midwestern author. His second novel, *The Thresher* (1946), also received critical kudos, several authorities terming it a literary milestone. The author's native Pockerbrush country in western Minnesota is the scene of both works. *The Oxcart Trail,* a historical novel of merit, appeared in 1954.

Frederick Manfred, who grew up in a Frisian community in northwestern Iowa and whose writings appeared under the pen name of Feike Feikema prior to 1951, has drawn heavily upon the "Siouxland" region for his characters and locales. His first novel, *Golden Bowl,* appeared in 1947, dealing with South Dakota's depression years. His Buckskin Man Tales, comprising *Lord Grizzly* (1954), *Riders of Judgment* (1957), *Conquering Horse* (1959), *Scarlet Plume* (1964), and *King of Spades* (1966), have been widely acclaimed.

Vine Deloria, Jr., member of a distinguished South Dakota Indian family, has treated the various problems arising from cultural conflicts between Indian and non-Indian. His first book, *Custer Died for Your Sins: An Indian Manifesto,* was published in 1969, followed by *We Talk—You Listen* (1970), and *God Is Red* (1973).

Native South Dakotans have also shown great interest in writing poetry. In 1937, Badger Clark, whose cowboy ballads are well known, was named poet laureate of South Dakota. Some of his many poems appear in *Sun and Saddle Leather* (1915), a collection which celebrates life in the open spaces and the Black Hills region of which he was long a resident.

Dramatic productions made their appearance in Dakota Territory at an early date, staged by both professional troupes and home-talent dramatic associations. Many a town featured its local Opera House which booked variety shows and legitimate drama played by traveling companies. The mining population of the Black Hills at the peak of the gold rush found diversion in the legitimate theater as well as in the turbulent dance hall. The dramatic arts have continued their appeal through the media of community and summer theaters. Most notable among the summer theaters has been the Black Hills Playhouse, organized in 1946 by Warren M. Lee as an adjunct of the Department of Dramatic Art at the University of South Dakota. Since its first performance in Custer State Park the Black Hills Playhouse has served a dual purpose in bringing legitimate drama to a wider audience and, at the same time, affording professional training to personnel participating in the project.

Quite apart from ordinary drama, yet spectacular and with universal emotional appeal, is the Black Hills Passion Play. The play was introduced to Spearfish in 1939 by a German troupe which left

Germany in search of more favorable conditions for its annual portrayal of the dramatic events during the last seven days in the life of Christ. This widely acclaimed production has been held annually during the summer months except for a brief interval during the 1940's. The Passion Play with Josef Meier in the role of Christus is staged in a specially constructed amphitheater on the outskirts of Spearfish. The entire ensemble consists of 250 persons including 40 professional players.

The graphic arts have, likewise, not been neglected. Such artists as George Catlin and Karl Bodmer visited the region during the early 1830's, recording Indian life and the scenery along the Missouri through numerous sketches and paintings. They were followed by other artists of the fur-trading frontier including John James Audubon in 1843 and Rudolph F. Kurz in 1851. Gradually, as permanent settlements made their appearance, local artists tried their hands at expressing themselves on canvas. A number of them reached professional status, exhibiting their works in local and national shows.[7]

Two native-born artists, Harvey Dunn and Oscar Howe, devoted their talents to interpreting South Dakota life. Harvey Dunn, who was reared on a Kingsbury County homestead, was one of the nation's leading illustrators at the time of his death in 1952. He had gained wide recognition both as an artist and as a teacher of art, and was especially well known for his paintings of pioneer life. Thirty-eight canvases in the Harvey Dunn Collection are on permanent display at South Dakota State University.

Oscar Howe, a full-blood Sioux whose forbears were Yanktonnais chiefs, was born on the Crow Creek Reservation. His artistic talent was discovered while he was studying in an Indian high school in New Mexico and his paintings were on exhibit in many American cities, in London, and in Paris even before he graduated. After several years of hardship and frustration on the reservation during the depression years, he found a satisfying outlet in painting murals. After serving in the armed forces during World War II, he was graduated from Dakota Wesleyan University and took a Master's degree in art at the University of Oklahoma. After serving as art director at

[7] Frances Cranmer Greenman, *Higher Than the Sky* (New York: Harper & Bros., 1954) is an autobiographical account by a native of Aberdeen who moved on to fame as a portrait painter. In a sprightly style Mrs. Greenman recounts her early life during pioneer times in Aberdeen as well as her varied experiences as a successful artist.

a Pierre high school, in 1957 he was named Assistant Professor of Fine Arts and Artist-in-residence at the University of South Dakota. Employing modern media and techniques, Howe makes use of the motifs and symbolism of his Indian heritage in paintings of native rituals and dances and sketches of tribal figures. He has been the recipient of various awards and trophies from the Philbrook Art Center, Tulsa, Oklahoma, as well as awards from several art museums. His paintings are on permanent exhibit in several noted art centers. In 1960 he was named artist laureate of South Dakota.

One of the best-known American sculptors, Gutzon Borglum, created the world-renowned stone carvings on Mount Rushmore in the Black Hills. In 1927 Borglum set out "to carve a great national shrine dedicated to the principles and ideals of America"[8] on the granite mountainside 6,000 feet above sea level. After fourteen years of labor, the colossal carvings—the faces of Washington, Jefferson, Lincoln, and Theodore Roosevelt—were completed and have since become one of the leading tourist attractions in the United States. Conceived by the artist as a shrine of democracy, the mountain sculpturing, high up among the clouds, may be regarded as a symbol of greatness and durability which embodies the dreams, ambitions, and accomplishments of the American people.

[8] See Gilbert C. Fite, *Mount Rushmore* (Norman: University of Oklahoma Press, 1952), for the story of the Mount Rushmore National Memorial.

References

Appendix I

SOUTH DAKOTA COUNTIES

County	Land Area in Sq. Miles	When Orga-nized	County Seat	Population 1960	Population 1970
Aurora	709	1882	Plankinton	4,749	4,183
Beadle	1,259	1880	Huron	21,682	20,877
Bennett	1,181	1912	Martin	3,053	3,088
Bon Homme	560	1862	Tyndall	9,229	8,577
Brookings	800	1871	Brookings	20,046	22,158
Brown	1,674	1881	Aberdeen	34,106	36,920
Brule	818	1875	Chamberlain	6,319	5,870
Buffalo	482	1885	Gann Valley	1,547	1,739
Butte	2,250	1883	Belle Fourche	8,592	7,825
Campbell	732	1883	Mound City	3,531	2,866
Charles Mix	1,097	1879	Lake Andes	11,785	9,994
Clark	964	1881	Clark	7,134	5,515
Clay	405	1862	Vermillion	10,810	12,923
Codington	687	1878	Watertown	20,220	19,140
Corson	2,470	1909	McIntosh	5,798	4,994
Custer	1,557	1877	Custer	4,906	4,698
Davison	432	1874	Mitchell	16,681	17,319
Day	1,030	1881	Webster	10,516	8,713
Deuel	639	1878	Clear Lake	6,782	5,686
Dewey[1]	2,351	1910	Timber Lake	5,257	5,170
Douglas	435	1882	Armour	5,113	4,569
Edmunds	1,154	1883	Ipswich	6,079	5,548
Fall River	1,743	1883	Hot Springs	10,688	7,505
Faulk	996	1883	Faulkton	4,397	3,893
Grant	681	1878	Milbank	9,913	9,005
Gregory	997	1894	Burke	7,399	6,710

401

Appendix I

County	Land Area in Sq. Miles	When Organized	County Seat	Population 1960	1970
Haakon	1,816	1914	Philip	3,303	2,802
Hamlin	511	1878	Hayti	6,303	5,172
Hand	1,432	1882	Miller	6,712	5,883
Hanson	430	1871	Alexandria	4,584	3,781
Harding	2,682	1909	Buffalo	2,371	1,855
Hughes	748	1880	Pierre	12,725	11,632
Hutchinson	815	1871	Olivet	11,085	10,379
Hyde	863	1883	Highmore	2,602	2,515
Jackson	808	1915	Kadoka	1,985	1,531
Jerauld	527	1883	Wessington Springs	4,048	3,310
Jones	973	1917	Murdo	2,066	1,882
Kingsbury	818	1879	DeSmet	9,227	7,657
Lake	567	1873	Madison	11,764	11,456
Lawrence	800	1877	Deadwood	17,075	17,453
Lincoln	576	1867	Canton	12,371	11,761
Lyman	1,683	1893	Kennebec	4,428	4,060
McCook	575	1878	Salem	8,268	7,246
McPherson	1,147	1883	Leola	5,821	5,022
Marshall	848	1885	Britton	6,663	5,965
Meade	3,465	1889	Sturgis	12,044	16,618
Mellette	1,306	1911	White River	2,664	2,420
Miner	570	1880	Howard	5,398	4,454
Minnehaha	813	1868	Sioux Falls	86,575	95,209
Moody	523	1873	Flandreau	8,810	7,622
Pennington	2,779	1877	Rapid City	58,195	59,349
Perkins	2,860	1909	Bison	5,977	4,769
Potter	869	1883	Gettysburg	4,926	4,449
Roberts	1,108	1883	Sisseton	13,190	11,678
Sanborn	570	1883	Woonsocket	4,641	3,697
Shannon	2,100	Unorganized		6,000	8,198
Spink	1,505	1879	Redfield	11,706	10,595
Stanley	1,414	1890	Fort Pierre	4,085	2,457
Sully	1,004	1883	Onida	2,607	2,362
Todd	1,388	Unorganized		4,661	6,606
Tripp	1,620	1909	Winner	8,761	8,171
Turner	612	1871	Parker	11,159	9,872
Union	452	1862	Elk Point	10,197	9,643
Walworth	718	1883	Selby	8,097	7,842
Washabaugh	1,061	Unorganized		1,042	1,389
Yankton	519	1862	Yankton	17,551	19,039
Ziebach	1,981	1911	Dupree	2,495	2,221

[1] Dewey County was enlarged in 1951 when Armstrong County (population 42) was consolidated with it.

Appendix II

ORIGIN OF COUNTY NAMES

COUNTY	NAMED IN HONOR OF
Aurora	Aurora, Roman goddess of the dawn
Beadle	William H. H. Beadle
Bennett	Granville G. Bennett, territorial judge
Bon Homme	French word meaning "good man"
Brookings	Wilmot W. Brookings, pioneer legislator and judge
Brown	Alfred Brown, territorial legislator
Brule	Brule tribe of Teton Sioux
Buffalo	The wild buffalo
Butte	Numerous buttes in the region
Campbell	Norman B. Campbell, territorial legislator
Charles Mix	Charles E. Mix, Commissioner of Indian Affairs in 1858
Clark	Newton Clark, territorial legislator
Clay	Henry Clay, famous stateman
Codington	The Rev. G. S. Codington, territorial legislator
Corson	Dighton Corson, Justice of State Supreme Court, 1889–1913
Custer	General George A. Custer
Davison	Henry C. Davison, early resident of county
Day	Merrit H. Day, territorial legislator
Deuel	Jacob S. Deuel, pioneer legislator
Dewey	William P. Dewey, territorial surveyor-general
Douglas	Stephen A. Douglas, famous statesman

403

County	Named in Honor of
Edmunds	Newton Edmunds, second territorial governor
Fall River	River of same name
Faulk	Andrew J. Faulk, third territorial governor
Grant	General Ulysses S. Grant
Gregory	John Shaw Gregory, Indian agent and early territorial legislator
Haakon	King Haakon VII of Norway
Hamlin	Hannibal Hamlin, Vice-President and United States Senator
Hand	George H. Hand, early settler and territorial official
Hanson	Joseph R. Hanson, Yankton pioneer and territorial legislator
Harding	J. A. Harding, territorial legislator
Hughes	Alexander Hughes, territorial legislator
Hutchinson	John S. Hutchinson, secretary of territory, 1861–1865
Hyde	James Hyde, territorial legislator
Jackson	J. R. Jackson, territorial legislator
Jerauld	H. A. Jerauld, territorial legislator
Jones	Jones County, Iowa
Kingsbury	George W. and T. A. Kingsbury, early Yankton pioneers and territorial legislators
Lake	Many lakes in the vicinity
Lawrence	Colonel John Lawrence, territorial legislator
Lincoln	Abraham Lincoln
Lyman	Major W. P. Lyman, territorial legislator
McCook	Edwin S. McCook, secretary of territory, 1872–1873
McPherson	James B. McPherson, Civil War general
Marshall	Marshall Vincent, early settler of county
Meade	General George G. Meade
Mellette	Arthur C. Mellette, territorial and state governor
Miner	Nelson and Ephraim Miner, early territorial legislators
Minnehaha	Indian word meaning "laughing water"
Moody	Gideon C. Moody, territorial legislator
Pennington	John L. Pennington, territorial governor
Perkins	Henry E. Perkins, state legislator
Potter	Dr. Joel A. Potter, territorial legislator
Roberts	S. G. Roberts, territorial legislator
Sanborn	George W. Sanborn, railway official
Shannon	Peter C. Shannon, Chief Justice of territorial Supreme Court, 1873–1882
Spink	S. L. Spink, territorial official

Stanley	Brigadier General David S. Stanley, for many years commander at Fort Sully
Sully	General Alfred Sully, who established Fort Sully
Todd	J. B. S. Todd, early pioneer
Tripp	Bartlett Tripp, outstanding lawyer and territorial judge
Turner	John W. Turner, early pioneer and territorial legislator
Union	Sentiment for the Union cause during the Civil War
Walworth	Walworth County, Wisconsin
Washabaugh	Frank J. Washabaugh, territorial legislator
Washington	George Washington
Yankton	Yankton tribe of Sioux Indians
Ziebach	Frank M. Ziebach, Yankton pioneer and territorial legislator

Based on *South Dakota Place Names* (Vermillion: South Dakota Writers' Project, 1941), pp. 15–33. This publication was reissued in revised form in 1972 by Brevet Press, Sioux Falls, S.Dak., under the title *South Dakota Geographic Names*.

Appendix III

A. GOVERNORS OF DAKOTA TERRITORY

William Jayne	(R)	1861–1863
Newton Edmunds	(R)	1863–1866
Andrew J. Faulk	(R)	1866–1869
John A. Burbank	(R)	1869–1874
John L. Pennington	(R)	1874–1878
William A. Howard	(R)	1878–1880
Nehemiah G. Ordway	(R)	1880–1884
Gilbert A. Pierce	(R)	1884–1887
Louis K. Church	(D)	1887–1889
Arthur C. Mellette	(R)	1889

B. GOVERNORS OF SOUTH DAKOTA

Arthur C. Mellette	(R)	1889–1893
Charles H. Sheldon	(R)	1893–1897
Andrew E. Lee	(Fusion)	1897–1901
Charles N. Herreid	(R)	1901–1905
Samuel H. Elrod	(R)	1905–1907
Coe I. Crawford	(R)	1907–1909
Robert S. Vessey	(R)	1909–1913
Frank M. Byrne	(R)	1913–1917
Peter Norbeck	(R)	1917–1921
William H. McMaster	(R)	1921–1925
Carl Gunderson	(R)	1925–1927

407

William J. Bulow	(D)	1927–1931
Warren E. Green	(R)	1931–1933
Tom Berry	(D)	1933–1937
Leslie Jensen	(R)	1937–1939
Harlan Bushfield	(R)	1939–1943
M. Q. Sharpe	(R)	1943–1947
George T. Mickelson	(R)	1947–1951
Sigurd Anderson	(R)	1951–1955
Joe Foss	(R)	1955–1959
Ralph Herseth	(D)	1959–1961
Archie M. Gubbrud	(R)	1961–1965
Nils A. Boe	(R)	1965–1969
Frank L. Farrar	(R)	1969–1971
Richard M. Kneip	(D)	1971–1979

Supplementary Reading

CHAPTER 1

THE NATURAL SETTING

The standard reference covering institutional developments within the Great Plains region is Walter Prescott Webb, *The Great Plains* (New York: Houghton Mifflin Co., 1936). The sociological implications of the Great Plains environment upon modern society is the special theme of Carl F. Kraenzel, *The Great Plains in Transition* (Norman: University of Oklahoma Press, 1955). Publications of the South Dakota Geological Survey, located at the State University of South Dakota, dealing with the natural setting, are Stephen S. Visher, *The Geography of South Dakota* (Bulletin No. 8, 1918) and E. P. Rothrock, *A Geology of South Dakota* (Bulletin No. 13, Part I, The Surface, 1943). Valuable for understanding the relationship between the Great Plains environment and land-use problems is Mary Wilma M. Hargreaves, *Dry Farming in the Northern Great Plains, 1900–1925* (Cambridge: Harvard University Press, 1957), pp. 3–36. Also useful is S. W. Jones, *A Graphic Summary of Land Use, Physical and Economic Features of South Dakota* (Extension Circular 182, South Dakota State College Extension Service, July, 1938). A characterization of the soils of South Dakota appears in *Soils and Men*, United States Department of Agriculture *Yearbook of Agriculture* (Washington: Government Printing Office, 1938), 1019–1180, and Fred C. Westin, Leo F. Puhr, and George J. Buntley, *Soils of South Dakota* (Brookings, S. Dak.: South Dakota Agricultural Experiment Station, Soil Survey Series No. 3, March, 1959).

CHAPTER 2

THE FIRST PEOPLE ON THE LAND

A good general account of the culture and social organization of the Plains Indians is Robert H. Lowie, *Indians of the Plains* (New York: McGraw-Hill Book Co., 1954). Clark Wissler, *Indians of the United States* (Garden City: Doubleday and Co., 1953) and Frederick Webb Hodge (ed.), *Handbook of American Indians North of Mexico*, Bulletin 30 Bureau of Ethnology (Washington: Government Printing Office, 1907–1910), 2 vols., are standard references. *Archaeological Studies*, Circulars 1 to 8, published by the South Dakota Archaeological Commission under the direction of Dr. Wesley R. Hurt, relate to excavations con-

409

ducted in the Upper Missouri Basin by the joint efforts of the William H. Over Museum at Vermillion, the South Dakota Archaeological Commission, and the National Park Service. Especially useful is the monograph by Dr. Hurt, *Report of the Investigation of the Swan Creek Site, 1954–1956* (Circular No. 7, 1958). Donald J. Lehmer, *Archaeological Investigations in the Oahe Dam Area, South Dakota, 1950–51,* Bulletin 158, River Basin Survey Papers No. 7, Bureau of American Ethnology (Washington: Government Printing Office, 1954) likewise concerns the work of excavating village sites prior to the inundation of the region by the Missouri River Development Project under the Pick-Sloan Plan. A good account of the Arikaras, written in 1855–1856, appears in Edwin Thompson Denig, *Five Indian Tribes of the Upper Missouri,* edited by John C. Ewers (Norman: University of Oklahoma Press, 1961). This publication consists of a manuscript written by a fur trader at Fort Union after twenty-one years of residence in the Indian country. A definitive study of the Poncas is James H. Howard, *The Ponca Tribe* (Washington: Bureau of American Ethnology, 1965). George E. Hyde, *Red Cloud's Folk: A History of the Oglala Sioux Indians* (Norman: University of Oklahoma Press, 1937) and Scudder Mekeel, "A Short History of the Teton-Dakota," *North Dakota Historical Quarterly,* X (1943), 137–205, are the best printed accounts of the Teton Sioux. Still useful is Doane Robinson, "A History of the Dakota or Sioux Indians," *South Dakota Historical Collections,* II (Pierre: South Dakota State Historical Society, 1904), 15–58. Of special interest are two works by Frank Gilbert Roe: *The North American Buffalo: A Critical Study of the Species in Its Wild State* (Toronto: University of Toronto Press, 1951) and *The Indian and the Horse* (Norman: University of Oklahoma Press, 1955).

CHAPTER 3

FRENCH AND SPANISH SOVEREIGNTY ON THE UPPER MISSOURI

The period of French exploration is covered in John B. Brebner, *The Explorers of North America, 1492–1806* (New York: The Macmillan Co., 1933) and Clarence Vandiveer, *The Fur Trade and Early Western Exploration* (Cleveland: Arthur H. Clark Co., 1929). The best and most recent biography of the elder Verendrye is Nellis M. Crouse, *La Verendrye: Fur Trader and Explorer* (Ithaca: Cornell University Press, 1956). The Spanish activities are well covered by A. P. Nasatir (ed.), *Before Lewis and Clark—Documents Illustrating the History of the Missouri, 1785–1804* (St. Louis: St. Louis Historical Documents Foundation, 1952), 2 vols. Articles by Nasatir on Spanish explorations on the Upper Missouri appear in the *Mississippi Valley Historical Review,* XIV (1927–1928), 47–71, and XVI (1929–1930), 359–382, 507–530. Truteau's journal may be found in *South Dakota Historical Collections,* VII (1914), 412–474. Annie Heloise Abel, *Tabeau's Narrative of Loisel's Expedition to the Upper Missouri* (Norman: University of Oklahoma Press, 1939), covers the Spanish activities at the turn of the century. An extensive account by Charles E. DeLand, "The Verendrye Explorations and Discoveries," appears in *South Dakota Historical Collections,* VII (1914), 99–402. The whole subject of French and Spanish activities in South Dakota is also treated by Donald Dean Parker, "Early Explorations and Fur Trading in South Dakota," *South Dakota Historical Collections,* XXV (1951), 1–47.

CHAPTER 4

OPENING THE WAY TO THE WESTERN SEA

The major events for the period from the accession of the Louisiana Purchase to the end of the War of 1812 can be conveniently followed in Doane Robinson,

Supplementary Reading 411

History of South Dakota (Chicago: B. F. Bowen and Co., 1904), I, pp. 52–92.
John Bakeless, *Lewis and Clark, Partners and Discoverers* (New York: William
Morrow and Co., 1947), and Bernard De Voto, *The Course of Empire* (Boston:
Houghton Mifflin Co., 1952), pp. 383–553, are good recent accounts of the Lewis
and Clark Expedition. These can be supplemented by James K. Hosmer (ed.),
History of the Expedition of Captains Lewis and Clark, 1804–5–6 (Chicago: A. C.
McClurg and Co., 1924), 2 vols., and Bernard De Voto, *The Journals of Lewis
and Clark* (Boston: Houghton Mifflin Co., 1953). Ethel Hueston, *Star of the
West: The Romance of the Lewis and Clark Expedition* (Indianapolis: Bobbs-
Merrill, 1935), is a work of fiction written with scrupulous care with respect to
both historical setting and details. Washington Irving, *Astoria* (New York:
John B. Alden, 1887), is a literary classic covering the expedition headed by
Wilson Price Hunt on its way to the Columbia in 1811. It is available in various
editions. The impact of the War of 1812 upon the region can be traced in Louis
Arthur Tohill, "Robert Dickson, British Fur Trader on the Upper Mississippi,"
North Dakota Historical Quarterly, III (October, 1928, January and April, 1929),
5–49; 83–128; 182–203.

CHAPTER 5

THE SAGA OF THE FUR TRADE

The best account of the western fur trade is Hiram Martin Chittenden, *The
American Fur Trade of the Far West* (New York: Francis P. Harper, 1902), 3
vols.; it is also available in a reprint edition, with a new introduction by Grace
Lee Nute, published in 1954 by Academic Reprints, Stanford, California. This
can be supplemented with Vandiveer, *The Fur Trade and Early Western Ex-
ploration*, and Everett Dick, *Vanguards of the Frontier* (New York: Appleton-
Century Co., 1941); Richard Oglesby, *Manuel Lisa and the Opening of the
Missouri Fur Trade* (Norman: University of Oklahoma Press, 1963), and John E.
Sunder, *The Fur Trade on the Upper Missouri* (Norman: University of Oklahoma Press, 1965). The part played by the Teton Sioux in the fur trade is
treated by Merrill G. Burlingame, "The Buffalo in Trade and Commerce,"
North Dakota Historical Quarterly, III (July, 1929), 262–291. Scudder Mekeel,
"A Short History of the Teton-Dakota," *ibid.*, X (July, 1943), 137–199, is also of
value. Concise biographical sketches of such outstanding fur traders as William H. Ashley, Pierre Chouteau, Jr., Manuel Lisa, and Jedediah Smith may be
conveniently found in the *Dictionary of American Biography* (New York:
Charles Scribner's Sons, 1928–1958), 22 vols. The events in connection with the
so-called Yellowstone Expedition of 1819 are covered by Edgar Bruce Wesley,
Guarding the Frontier: A Study of Frontier Defense from 1815 to 1825 (Minneapolis: University of Minnesota Press, 1935), and "Some Official Aspects of the
Fur Trade in the Northwest, 1815–1825," *North Dakota Historical Quarterly*, VI
(April, 1932), 201–209. For documentary materials on the Leavenworth Expedi-
tion against the Arikara villages in 1823, see *South Dakota Historical Collections*,
I (1902), 179–256. Allan Nevins, *Fremont, Pathmarker of the West* (New York:
Appleton-Century Co., 1939), pp. 29–45, covers the visits of Nicollet and Frémont
to the region. Reprints of the writings by Brackenridge, Bradbury, and Maxi-
milian concerning their travels in the Upper Missouri Valley appear in R. G.
Thwaites (ed.), *Early Western Travels* (Cleveland: Arthur H. Clark Co., 1905),
V, VI, XXII–XXIV.

CHAPTER 6

THE WHITE MAN COMES TO STAY

George W. Kingsbury, *History of Dakota Territory* (Chicago: S. J. Clarke Publishing Co., 1915) 2 vols., is the standard detailed work for the territorial period. The developments leading to the opening of the Territory are covered in Volume I, Chapters 9 and 13. Doane Robinson, *History of South Dakota*, I, pp. 149–184, covers the same ground in briefer fashion, as does Herbert S. Schell, *Dakota Territory during the Eighteen Sixties* (Vermillion: Governmental Research Bureau, Report No. 30, University of South Dakota, 1954), pp. 1–16. Hyde, *Red Cloud's Folk: A History of the Oglala Sioux Indians*, pp. 56–98, is an excellent presentation of the conflict between red man and white along the overland trails. The events forming the background for the establishment of military posts at Fort Pierre and Fort Randall can be followed in *South Dakota Historical Collections*, I, 263–315; 381–440. William H. Goetzmann, *Army Exploration in the American West, 1803–1863* (New Haven: Yale University Press, 1959), pp. 406–426, is useful for the explorations conducted by Lieutenant G. K. Warren and Captain William F. Raynolds in the Sioux country. For documentary materials concerning the activities of the Dakota Land Company in the Big Sioux Valley, see *ibid.*, VI, 133–180. Howard Roberts Lamar, *Dakota Territory, 1861–1889: A Study of Frontier Politics* (New Haven: Yale University Press, 1956), pp. 28–66, gives special attention to the speculative motives that led to white settlement in the region.

CHAPTER 7

THE SIXTIES—DECADE OF UNCERTAINTY

The nonpolitical events of the sixties can be conveniently followed in Schell, *Dakota Territory during the Eighteen Sixties*, pp. 17–60. The study includes an extensive bibliography. Hyde, *Red Cloud's Folk: A History of the Oglala Sioux Indians*, pp. 101–184, and Robinson, "History of the Sioux Indians," *South Dakota Historical Collections*, II (1904), 269–399, cover the relations with the Sioux tribes. Kingsbury, *History of Dakota Territory*, I, pp. 233–432; 744–769, gives extended coverage to the period, but is too detailed for the general reader. W. Turrentine Jackson, *Wagon Roads West: A Study of Federal Road Surveys and Construction in the Trans-Mississippi West, 1846–1869* (Berkeley: University of California Press, 1952), pp. 279–311, has a full account of the wagon roads projected through the southern part of the Territory. Lucile M. Kane (trans. and ed.), *Military Life in Dakota: The Journal of Philippe Regis de Trobriand, 1867–1869* (St. Paul: Alvord Memorial Commission, 1951), has special value for its faithful portrayal of military life on the Indian frontier.

CHAPTER 8

ORGANIZING THE TERRITORIAL GOVERNMENT

Lamar, *Dakota Territory, 1861–1889: A Study of Frontier Politics*, pp. 67–126, previously mentioned, is especially concerned with an interpretation of political behavior. It is an excellent study of the period, based on an examination of the Territorial Papers of Dakota, housed in the National Archives at Washington, as well as other documentary collections. Schell, *Dakota Territory during the Eighteen Sixties*, pp. 61–88, likewise covers the period. Moses K. Armstrong, *The Early Empire Builders of the Great West* (St. Paul: E. W. Porter, 1901), is a contemporary account of the early sixties, based in part on newspaper articles appearing originally in the *Sioux City Register*.

CHAPTER 9

THE EARLY SEVENTIES—PROGRESS AND PROBLEMS

The extended accounts of the period by Kingsbury, *History of Dakota Terri-tory*, I, and Robinson, *History of South Dakota*, I, can be supplemented by such county histories as Dana R. Bailey, *History of Minnehaha County, South Dakota* (Sioux Falls: Brown and Saenger, 1899) and William H. Stoddard, *Turner County Pioneer History* (Sioux Falls: Brown and Saenger, 1931). Harold E. Briggs, *Frontiers of the Northwest* (New York: D. Appleton-Century Co., 1940), pp. 485–594, includes much material dealing with pioneer agricultural life in Dakota Territory. Studies by Herbert S. Schell include: "Official Immigration Ac-tivities of Dakota Territory," *North Dakota Historical Quarterly*, VII (October, 1932), 5–24; "The Dakota Southern: A Frontier Railway Venture of Dakota Ter-ritory," *South Dakota Historical Review*, II (April, 1937), 99–125; and "The Grange and the Credit Problem in Dakota Territory," *Agricultural History*, 10 (April, 1936), 59–83.

CHAPTER 10

OPENING THE BLACK HILLS

Of the many books dealing with the Battle of the Little Big Horn, the follow-ing are especially useful: Colonel William A. Graham, *The Story of the Little Big Horn* (Harrisburg: Military Service Publishing Co., 1941); Charles Kuhl-man, *Legend into History: The Custer Mystery* (Harrisburg: The Stackpole Co., 1952); Edgar I. Stewart, *Custer's Luck* (Norman: University of Oklahoma Press, 1955); and Frederick F. Van de Water, *Glory Hunter: A Life of General Custer* (Indianapolis: Bobbs-Merrill, 1934). Martin F. Schmitt (ed.), *General George Crook, His Autobiography* (Norman: University of Oklahoma Press, 1960), is of value for the general military campaign. George E. Hyde, *Red Cloud's Folk: A History of the Oglala Sioux Indians*, pp. 205–293, and Stanley Vestal, *Sitting Bull, Champion of the Sioux* (Boston: Houghton Mifflin Co., 1932), pp. 132–205, give special consideration to Sioux activities during the military campaigns. Joseph Mills Hanson, *The Conquest of the Missouri, Being the Story of the Life and Exploits of Captain Grant Marsh* (Chicago: A. C. McClurg, 1909), pp. 171–375, covers the military activities in the Yellowstone and Powder River valleys. This is a biographical account of a famed steamboatman who captained the *Far West* employed in various capacities during the Sioux campaign. The book was reissued by Rinehart and Co. in 1946. Annie D. Tallent, *The Black Hills, the Last Hunting Ground of the Dakotahs* (St. Louis: Nixon, 1899), is an account by a member of the Gordon Party which entered the Black Hills in December, 1874. Custer's explorations in the Black Hills are the subject of a special study by W. M. Wemett, "Custer's Expedition to the Black Hills in 1874," *North Dakota Historical Quarterly*, VI (1932), 292–302. A more definitive account is Donald Jackson, *Custer's Gold—The United States Cavalry Expedition of 1874* (New Haven: Yale University Press, 1966).

CHAPTER 11

THE BLACK HILLS GOLD RUSH

Much of the literature concerning the Black Hills gold rush is ephemeral in character. Harold E. Briggs, *Frontiers of the Northwest: A History of the Upper Missouri Valley* (New York: D. Appleton-Century Co., 1940), pp. 25–124, is an excellent account covering the gold rush in its various aspects. Annie D. Tallent, *The Black Hills, the Last Hunting Ground of the Dakotahs*, previously mentioned, is a detailed contemporary account by the first white woman to enter the region. Estelline Bennett, *Old Deadwood Days* (New York: J. H. Sears and Co., 1928), is autobiographical in nature and represents an attempt to portray early Deadwood life. A well-researched study of great merit is Watson Parker, *Gold in the Black Hills* (Norman: University of Oklahoma Press, 1966). The subject is also covered in Rodman W. Paul, *Mining Frontiers of the Far West, 1848–1880* (New York: Holt, Rinehart & Winston, 1966). The colorful story of transportation can be followed in Agnes Wright Spring, *The Cheyenne and Black Hills Stage and Express Routes* (Glendale: The Arthur H. Clark Co., 1949); Harold E. Briggs, "Early Freight and Stage Lines in Dakota," *North Dakota Historical Quarterly*, III (July, 1929), 229–261; and Arthur J. Larsen, "The Northwestern Express and Transportation Company," *ibid.*, VI (October, 1931), 42–62. The part played by steamboat transportation is admirably treated in William E. Lass, *A History of Steamboating on the Upper Missouri* (Lincoln: University of Nebraska Press, 1962). Richard B. Hughes, *Pioneer Years in the Black Hills*, Agnes Wright Spring (ed.) (Glendale: The Arthur H. Clark Co., 1957), is the best autobiographical reference available to date. A well-written colorful account of the mining region, designed for the tourist, is Robert J. Casey, *The Black Hills and Their Incredible Characters* (Indianapolis: Bobbs-Merrill Co., 1949). The general economic developments can be followed in R. E. Driscoll, *Seventy Years of Banking in the Black Hills* (Rapid City: The Gate City Guide, 1948). For works dealing with the cattle industry see the Supplementary Reading Notes for Chapter 17. J. Leonard Jennewein, *Black Hills Booktrails* (Mitchell, S. Dak.: Dakota Territory Centennial Commission and Dakota Wesleyan University, 1962), is an exhaustive bibliographical work dealing with the Black Hills region.

CHAPTER 12

THE GREAT DAKOTA BOOM, 1878–1887

The period of the Great Dakota Boom can be followed in Kingsbury, *History of Dakota Territory*, I, pp. 1060–1079; 1125–1147; 1293–1335. Briefer treatment appears in Harold E. Briggs, *Frontiers of the Northwest* (New York: D. Appleton-Century Co., 1940), pp. 410–429; 454–484; and Charles Lowell Green, "The Administration of the Public Domain in South Dakota," *South Dakota Historical Collections*, XX (1940), 136–153; 199–228. Briggs also covers the story of settlement in an article, "The Great Dakota Boom," *North Dakota Historical Quarterly*, IV (January, 1930), 78–108. Robert J. Casey and W. A. S. Douglas, *Pioneer Railroad* (New York: McGraw-Hill Co., 1948), gives an excellent picture of the part played by the Chicago and North Western Railroad Company in the settlement of South Dakota. A good county history is Dana Harlow, *Prairie Echoes: Spink County in the Making* (Aberdeen, S. Dak.: privately printed, 1961). Noteworthy county histories published in the *South Dakota Historical Collections* include Marc M. Cleworth, "Twenty Years of Brown County Agricultural History," XVII (1934), 17–176; John H. Bingham and Nora V. Peters, "A Short History of Brule County," XXIII (1947), 1–184; S. S. Judy and Will G. Robinson, "Early History of Sanborn County," XXVI (1952), 1–180; and Wright Tarbell, "The Early and Territorial History of Codington County," XXIV (1949), 276–469.

CHAPTER 13

PIONEER LIFE

An excellent account of social pioneering on the Northern Plains, including South Dakota, is Everett Dick, *The Sod-House Frontier, 1854–1890* (New York:

D. Appleton-Century Co., 1937, reissued by Johnsen Publishing Co., Lincoln, Nebr., 1954). Seth K. Humphrey, *Following the Prairie Frontier* (Minneapolis: University of Minnesota Press, 1931), pp. 77–154, is a lively narrative by an individual who resided at Aberdeen during the early eighties and later served as field representative in the Dakotas and neighboring states for an eastern mortgage company. Edwin C. Torrey, *Early Days in Dakota* (Minneapolis: Farnham Printing and Stationery Co., 1925), presents a series of sketches and incidents concerning pioneer life in eastern South Dakota. The author was an early Aberdeen newspaperman. William J. Hyde, *Dig or Die, Brother Hyde* (New York: Harper and Bros., 1954), is a personal account by a Methodist clergyman who served charges at Groton and Faulkton during the early days of the boom period. Laura Bower Van Nuys, *The Family Band: From the Missouri to the Black Hills, 1881–1900* (Lincoln: University of Nebraska Press, 1961), covers the Vermillion flood of 1881 and also portrays early life in Pennington County. Contemporary glimpses of pioneer life in Spink County appear in J. Leonard Bates (ed.), *Tom Walsh in Dakota Territory: Personal Correspondence of Senator Thomas J. Walsh and Elinor C. Clements* (Urbana: University of Illinois Press, 1966). Reminiscences of the boom period can also be found in scattered volumes of the *South Dakota Historical Collections*.

CHAPTER 14

POLITICS IN THE SEVENTIES

Lamar, *Dakota Territory, 1861–1889*, previously mentioned, pp. 100–176, has a brilliant analysis of the intricacies of Dakota politics for the period. Kingsbury, *History of Dakota Territory*, I, pp. 521–564; 597–647; 718–743; II, pp. 985–1051; 1080–1124, includes much material of a documentary nature reprinted from the files of the Yankton *Press and Dakotaian* of which he was editor and part owner. Schell, *Dakota Territory during the Eighteen Sixties*, pp. 73–88, covers the political campaigns of 1870 and 1872. A study of high merit is W. Turrentine Jackson, "Dakota Politics during the Burbank Administration, 1869–1873," *North Dakota History*, XII (July, 1945), 111–134.

CHAPTER 15

PRELUDE TO STATEHOOD

Kingsbury, *History of Dakota Territory*, II, pp. 1293–1313; 1598–1939, covers the political developments for the period in great detail, but with an obvious bias. Doane Robinson, *History of South Dakota* (Chicago: B. F. Bowen and Co., 1904), I, pp. 313–337, and *History of South Dakota* (Chicago: American Historical Society, Inc., 1930), I, pp. 305–320, cover in brief fashion the movement for division and separate statehood. The part played by W. H. H. Beadle in linking the school lands issue with the statehood movement can be traced in Beadle's autobiographical account, "Personal Memoirs of General William Henry Harrison Beadle," *South Dakota Historical Collections*, III (1906), 85–246, and Barrett Lowe, *Twenty Million Acres: The Story of America's First Conservationist, William Henry Harrison Beadle* (Mitchell, S. Dak.: Educator Supply Co., 1937). A useful, although inadequate, account of the period is Carrol G. Green, "The Struggle of South Dakota to Become a State," *South Dakota Historical Collections*, XII (1924), 503–540.

The removal of the capital from Yankton to Bismarck is covered in dramatic but superficial fashion by Bruce Nelson, *Land of the Dacotahs* (Minneapolis: University of Minnesota Press, 1946), pp. 127–133, and Merle Potter, "The North Dakota Capital Fight," *North Dakota Historical Quarterly*, VII (October,

1932), 25–36. John Elmer Dalton, *A History of the Location of the State Capital in South Dakota* (Vermillion: Governmental Research Bureau, State University of South Dakota, Report No. 14, January, 1945), has an excellent discussion of the capital removal of 1883 as well as the capital fights of 1889 and 1890. The copyrighted study was made available in mimeographed form and is, unfortunately, no longer available.

Earl S. Pomeroy, *Territories and the United States, 1861–1890* (Philadelphia: University of Pennsylvania Press, 1947), is an excellent study of the territorial system as it functioned during the period of federal tutelage for Dakota Territory. Lamar, *Dakota Territory, 1861–1889*, pp. 177–284, attempts to give larger meaning to the movement for division and statehood. It is especially concerned with techniques and patterns of political behavior developed on the agricultural frontier of the Northern Plains. John D. Hicks, *The Constitutions of the Northwest States* (Lincoln, Nebr.: University of Nebraska Studies, Vol. XXIII, Nos. 1–2, 1923), is a study of the constitution-making of the two Dakotas as well as the other states admitted during 1889 and 1890, making meaningful the provisions placed in the frames of government.

CHAPTER 16

THE FARMERS' ALLIANCE AND THE POPULIST PARTY

Fred A. Shannon, *The Farmer's Last Frontier: Agriculture, 1860–1897* (New York: Farrar and Rinehart, Inc., 1945), pp. 125–267; 291–338, has excellent background material. The standard reference on the Populist movement is John D. Hicks, *The Populist Revolt: A History of the Farmers' Alliance and the People's Party* (Minneapolis: University of Minnesota Press, 1931, reissued 1961 by the University of Nebraska Press, Lincoln). Hallie Farmer, "The Economic Background of Frontier Populism," *Mississippi Valley Historical Review*, X (March, 1924), 406–427, and "The Railroads and Frontier Populism," *ibid.*, XIII (December, 1926), 387–397, are scholarly articles of special value for the economic background of Populism in South Dakota. A full-scale history of the Populist movement in South Dakota remains to be written. Its influence on South Dakota politics is treated in Kenneth E. Hendrickson, Jr., "Some Political Aspects of the Populist Movement in South Dakota," *North Dakota History*, XXIV (Winter, 1967), 77–92. This article is based on the author's doctoral dissertation in the Department of History, University of Oklahoma, 1962, "The Public Career of Richard F. Pettigrew." Pettigrew was United States Senator from 1889 to 1901 and the acknowledged leader of the Silver Republicans in South Dakota. Charles J. Dalthorp (ed.), *South Dakota's Governors* (Sioux Falls, S. Dak.: The Midwest-Beach Co., 1953), pp. 1–11, covers briefly the administrations of the first three governors under statehood.

CHAPTER 17

THE END OF THE OPEN RANGE

Standard works dealing with the cattle industry are Edward Everett Dale, *The Range Cattle Industry* (1930) and *Cow Country* (1945), published by the University of Oklahoma Press; Ernest S. Osgood, *The Day of the Cattlemen* (Minneapolis: University of Minnesota Press, 1929); and Louis Pelzer, *The Cattlemen's Frontier* (Glendale, Calif.: The Arthur H. Clark Co., 1936). John O. Bye, *Back Trailing in the Heart of the Short Grass Country* (Everett, Wash.: Alexander Printing Co., 1956), and Bert L. Hall, *Roundup Years: Old Muddy to Black Hills* (Pierre: privately printed, 1954), and Bob Lee and Dick Williams, *Last Grass Frontier: The South Dakota Stock Grower Heritage* (Sturgis, S. Dak.: Black

Hills Publishers, Inc., 1964), cover the South Dakota scene. A. H. Schatz, *Opening a Cow Country* (Ann Arbor: Edward Brothers, 1939) and *Longhorns Bring Culture* (Boston: The Christopher Publishing House, 1961) describe the early cattle industry in Fall River County. Ike Blasingame, *Dakota Cowboy: My Life in the Old Days* (New York: G. P. Putnam's Sons, 1958) is an excellent autobiographical account by one who came to South Dakota with the Matador Land and Cattle Company in 1904. Walker D. Wyman, *Nothing but Prairie and Sky* (Norman: University of Oklahoma Press, 1954), based on original notes of Bruce Siberts, South Dakota rancher until 1906, is also a good personal account of early ranching days. The events concerning the movement of homesteaders into the trans-Missouri region can be followed in detail in Charles Lowell Green, "The Administration of the Public Domain in South Dakota," *South Dakota Historical Collections* (1940), XX, 155–184. William Williamson, *An Autobiography* (Chicago: The Lakeside Press, 1964), gives a good picture of the problems of law enforcement in pioneer times. Williamson as state's attorney played a prominent part in the crusade against cattle rustlers in Lyman County in the first decade of the present century. From 1921 to 1933 he represented the west-river district in Congress. Mary Wilma M. Hargreaves, *Dry Farming in the Northern Great Plains, 1900–1925*, pp. 439–484, and Carl Frederick Kraenzel, *The Great Plains in Transition*, pp. 103–148, previously mentioned, note the impact of homesteading upon the cattle industry.

CHAPTER 18

THE PROGRESSIVE ERA, 1903–1924

The major political events from 1900 to 1915 can be followed in George Martin Smith, *South Dakota, Its History and Its People* (Chicago: The S. J. Clarke Publishing Co., 1915), Chapters 6 and 18. This reference is usually cited as the third volume of Kingsbury, *History of Dakota Territory*. Calvin Perry Armin, "Coe I. Crawford and the Progressive Movement in South Dakota" in *South Dakota Historical Collections*, XXXII (1964), 22–231, is a scholarly study of the first phase of the Progressive movement, based on the manuscript papers of Coe I. Crawford. An excellent account covering the entire period is Gilbert C. Fite, *Peter Norbeck: Prairie Statesman* (Columbia: University of Missouri Studies, XXII, No. 2, 1948). Russell B. Nye, *Midwestern Progressive Politics: A Historical Study of Its Origins and Development, 1870–1950* (East Lansing: Michigan State College Press, 1951), pp. 181–309, is an interpretive study viewing Progressivism as a regional movement.

Robert L. Morlan, *Political Prairie Fire: The Nonpartisan League, 1915–1922* (Minneapolis: University of Minnesota Press, 1955), and Theodore Saloutos and John D. Hicks, *Agricultural Discontent in the Middle West, 1900–1939* (Madison: University of Wisconsin Press, 1951), pp. 149–218, cover the story of the Nonpartisan League. Special studies by Gilbert C. Fite include "Peter Norbeck and the Defeat of the Non-Partisan League in South Dakota," *Mississippi Valley Historical Review*, XXXIII (September, 1946), 217–236; "South Dakota's Rural Credit System: A Venture in State Socialism, 1917–1946," *Agricultural History*, 21 (October, 1947), 239–249; and "The History of South Dakota's Rural Credit System," *South Dakota Historical Collections*, XXIV (1949), 220–275. Joseph Mills Hanson, *South Dakota in the World War, 1917–1919* (Pierre: South Dakota State Historical Society, 1940), has some value for the general reader despite its major emphasis on the military activities. The movement for a state-owned hydroelectric project is covered in Donald L. Miller, "The History of the Movement for Hydro-Electric Development on the Missouri River in South Dakota" (unpublished Master's thesis, Department of History, University of South Dakota, 1930). Dorinda Riessen Reed, *The Woman Suffrage Movement in South Dakota* (Vermillion: Governmental Research Bureau, Report No. 14, University of South Dakota, 1958), originally prepared as a Master's thesis in the Department of History, covers the topic admirably.

CHAPTER 19

THE TWENTIES AND THIRTIES—HARD TIMES AND
THE NEW DEAL

For general references dealing with the depression period, Dixon Wector, *The Age of the Great Depression, 1929–1941* (New York: The Macmillan Co., 1948) and Broadus Mitchell, *Depression Decade: From New Era through New Deal, 1929–1941* (New York: Rinehart and Co., 1947), will be found useful. Gilbert C. Fite and Jim E. Reese, *An Economic History of the United States* (Boston: Houghton Mifflin Co., 1959), pp. 547–629, is especially helpful in analyzing economic problems and policies as they affected Midwestern farmers. The "farm strike" of the 1930's can be followed in Saloutos and Hicks, *Agricultural Discontent in the Middle West, 1900–1939* (Madison: University of Wisconsin Press, 1951), pp. 404–451, and John L. Shover, *Cornbelt Rebellion: The Farmer's Holiday Association* (Urbana: University of Illinois Press, 1965).

The South Dakota Planning Board, in operation during the Berry Administration, published a number of informative studies dealing with economic and social problems facing South Dakota during the depression days. Especially pertinent to a consideration of land-use problems are *Agricultural Resources* (January 1, 1936) and *Tax Delinquency Status of Farm Land in South Dakota* (July 1, 1937). Publications of the Agricultural Experiment Station at South Dakota State University, showing the financial plight of South Dakota farmers, include Harry A. Steele, *Farm Mortgage Foreclosures in South Dakota, 1921–1932* (Circular 17, May, 1934), Supplements to Circular 17, published in 1934 and 1939, and Gabriel Lundy, *Farm Mortgage Experience in South Dakota, 1910–1940* (Bulletin 370, June, 1943). Other highly informative bulletins are W. F. Kumlien, *A Graphic Summary of the Relief Situation in South Dakota, 1930–1935* (Bulletin 310) and Agricultural Economics Pamphlet 91, *Farm Price Programs* (October, 1957).

Unpublished Master's theses at the University of South Dakota of special interest for the period are Leonard C. Andersen, "An Analysis of State Bank Failures in South Dakota" (1937); W. A. Person, "Federal Relief through the Works Progress Administration with Special Reference to South Dakota" (1939); Robert S. Thompson, "The History of the South Dakota Farmers Union, 1914–1952" (1953); and J. E. Wickstrom, "A History of the Depositors Guaranty Law in the State of South Dakota" (1951). In addition to Fite, *Peter Norbeck: Prairie Statesman,* previously mentioned, Charles J. Dalthorp (ed.), *South Dakota's Governors* (Sioux Falls, S. Dak.: Midwest-Beach Co., 1953), is of some use in following the political trends. For an understanding of the philosophy underlying rural rehabilitation and resettlement activities, Paul K. Conkin, *Tomorrow a New World: The New Deal Community Program* (Ithaca: Cornell University Press, 1959), is especially helpful. Also of value is Rexford G. Tugwell, "The Resettlement Idea," *Agricultural History,* 33 (October, 1959), 159–164.

CHAPTER 20

WORLD WAR II AND AFTER

South Dakota's war activities can be followed in *South Dakota in World War II* (Pierre: World War II History Commission, 1947). Recent political developments are well covered in Alan L. Clem, *Prairie State Politics: Popular Democracy in South Dakota* (Washington: Public Affairs Press, 1967). Useful sketches of Bushfield, Sharpe, Mickelson, and Anderson appear in Dalthorp (ed.), *South Dakota's Governors*, pp 69–83. Annual articles on South Dakota in *Britannica Book of the Year, Collier's Encyclopedia Year Book*, and *The Americana Annual* cover the major events for each year. Henry C. Hart, *The Dark Missouri* (Madison: University of Wisconsin Press, 1957), is an excellent analysis of the various problems presented by the Missouri Basin development project. Also useful for the historical background and an understanding of conflicting viewpoints are M. Q. Sharpe, "History of the Missouri River States Committee," *South Dakota Historical Collections*, XXII (1946), 400–409; Will G. Robinson, "The Development of the Missouri Valley," *ibid.*, 445–544. and Thomas H. Langevink, "Development of Multiple-Purpose Water Planning by the Federal Government in the Missouri Basin," *Nebraska History*, XXXIV (March, 1953), 1–21.

CHAPTER 21

REAPPRAISAL: THE TRANSFORMATION OF THE SIOUX

J. P. Kinney, *A Continent Lost—A Civilization Won* (Baltimore: Johns Hopkins Press, 1937), and Loring Benson Priest, *Uncle Sam's Stepchildren: 1 ne Reformation of United States Indian Policy, 1865–1887* (New Brunswick: Rutgers University Press, 1942), trace the formulation of Indian policy following the Civil War. Hyde, *A Sioux Chronicle*, previously mentioned, and *Spotted Tail's Folk: A History of the Brule Sioux* (Norman: University of Oklahoma Press, 1961), are well-written accounts of reservation life from 1878 to 1890. James C. Olson, *Red Cloud and the Sioux Problem* (Lincoln: University of Nebraska Press, 1965) is a well researched and scholarly treatise based on archival materials hitherto not utilized. The best study of the Messiah Craze and its impact on the Teton Sioux is Robert M. Utley, *The Last Days of the Sioux Nation* (New Haven: Yale University Press, 1963). Of special interest for South Dakota are Francis E. Leupp, *The Indian and His Problem* (New York: Charles Scribner's Sons, 1910), James McLaughlin, *My Friend the Indian* (Boston: Houghton Mifflin Co., 1910), Julia B. McGillycuddy, *McGillycuddy, Agent: A Biography of Dr. Valentine T. McGillycuddy* (Palo Alto: Stanford University Press, 1941), and Flora Warren Seymour, *Indian Agents of the Old Frontier* (New York: D. Appleton-Century Co., 1941). For an understanding of the allotment policy under the Dawes Act, Sister Mary Antonio Johnston, *Federal Relations with the Great Sioux Indians of South Dakota, 1887–1933* (Washington: Catholic University of America Press, 1948), has special value. For an excellent study of adjustment problems under reservation life, see Gordon Macgregor, *Warriors Without Weapons: A Study of the Society and Personality Development of the Pine Ridge Sioux* (Chicago: University of Chicago Press, 1946). The transformation of the Cheyenne River bands into a reservation people is admirably covered in Harry H. Anderson, "A History of the Cheyenne River Indian Agency and Its Military Post, Fort Bennett, 1868–1891," *South Dakota Historical Collections*, XXVIII (1956), 390–551. Winifred Barton, *John P. Williamson* (New York: Revell Co., 1919), and Sister Mary Claudia Duratschek, *Crusading Along Sioux Trails: A History of the Catholic Missions of South Dakota* (Yankton, S. Dak.: Benedictine Convent of the Sacred Heart, 1947), deal with missionary activities among the Sioux. Wesley R. Hurt and William E. Lass, *Frontier Photographer: Stanley J. Morrow's Dakota Years* (Lincoln: University of Nebraska Press, 1956), contains much photographic material dealing with the Teton Sioux, based on the Morrow Collection in the W. H. Over Museum at the University of South Dakota. Other references of special interest are Luther Standing Bear, *My People, the Sioux* (Boston: Houghton Mifflin Co., 1928); Elaine Goodale Eastman, *Pratt, the Red Man's Moses* (Norman: University of Oklahoma Press, 1935); and Stanley Vestal, *New Sources of Indian History, 1850–1891* (Norman: University of Oklahoma Press, 1934).

CHAPTER 22

REAPPRAISAL: THE GROWTH OF FARM AND RANCH ECONOMY

No adequate agricultural history of South Dakota has been written. Lyle M. Bender, *The Rural Economy of South Dakota* (Brookings: South Dakota Extension Service, South Dakota State College, Special Report No. 1, September, 1956), a publication of great merit, gives some attention to the historical background. Mary Wilma M. Hargreaves, *Dry Farming in the Northern Great Plains, 1900–1925*, previously mentioned, is indispensable for the serious student of agricultural history. The various studies published by the South Dakota Agricultural Experiment Station and the reports and bulletins of the State-Federal Crop Livestock Reporting Service provide much valuable information. Several useful studies have been mentioned in footnotes in this chapter. Gilbert C. Fite, *The Farmers' Frontier, 1865–1900* (New York: Holt, Rinehart & Winston, 1966), a work of great merit, has several chapters dealing with the Dakota frontier.

Ladd Haystead and Gilbert C. Fite, *The Agricultural Regions of the United States* (Norman: University of Oklahoma Press, 1955), pp. 179–203, includes an excellent discussion of the Northern Plains region in relation to its farming and ranching economy.

CHAPTER 23

REAPPRAISAL: DEVELOPMENTS IN MANUFACTURING AND MINING

No general work treating the nonagricultural features of the South Dakota economy is available. Early activities in manufacturing can be followed in Herbert S. Schell, "Early Manufacturing Activities in South Dakota, 1857–1875," *South Dakota Historical Review*, II (January, 1937), 73–95, and *South Dakota Manufacturing to 1900* (Vermillion: Bulletin No. 40, Business Research Bureau, University of South Dakota, May, 1955), p. 1–87, by the same author. The periodic publications of the Business Research Bureau at the State University cover various phases of the economic developments. Especially helpful numbers include V. E. Montgomery, *The South Dakota Economy at Mid-Century, 1900–1950* (Bulletin No. 26, June, 1952), and *The Granite Industry in South Dakota* (Bulletin No. 28, April, 1953); Montgomery and Beatty, *The Precious Metals Mining Industry in South Dakota* (Bulletin No. 33, December, 1953); Montgomery, *The Economy of Southeastern South Dakota* (Bulletin No. 48, August, 1956); Montgomery and Volk, *The Economy of the Black Hills of South Dakota* (Bulletin No. 52, October, 1957); Paul C. Mathis, *The Meat Packing Industry in South Dakota* (Bulletin No. 54, November, 1957); and Montgomery, *The South Dakota Cement Plant* (Bulletin No. 62, May, 1959). Also useful is Francis Church Lincoln *et al.*, *The Mining Industry of South Dakota* (Rapid City: Bulletin No. 17, Department of Mining, South Dakota School of Mines, February, 1937). Lawrence O. Cheever, *The House of Morrell* (Cedar Rapids, Iowa: The Torch Press, 1948), gives a good insight into the history of the meat-packing industry.

CHAPTER 24

REAPPRAISAL: SOCIAL AND CULTURAL ASPECTS OF
SOUTH DAKOTA LIFE

There are few references covering the cultural and social development of South Dakota. Various aspects are well covered for the territorial period in J. Leonard Jennewein and Jane Boorman (eds.), *Dakota Panorama* (Sioux Falls: Midwest-Beach Printing Co., 1961). This is a publication of the Dakota Territory Centennial Commission. It includes an extensive reading list of about 1,100 titles dealing with South Dakota. Pertinent materials may be found in the Federal Writers' Project, *South Dakota: A Guide to the State*, first published in 1938 and reissued by Hastings House with revisions in 1952. Sections dealing with education, literature, and religion as well as communications appear in York Sampson (ed.), *South Dakota: Fifty Years of Progress* (Sioux Falls, S. Dak.: Golden Anniversary Book Co., 1939). R. W. Kraushaar *et al.*, "Studies in South Dakota Education," *South Dakota Historical Collections*, XVIII (1936), is a useful compilation of materials dealing with various phases of educational history. Published county histories also contain valuable information on significant social and cultural developments. Of value also are Doane Robinson, *History of South Dakota* (Chicago: American Historical Society, 1930), 2 vols.; *Encyclopedia of South Dakota* (Pierre: privately printed, 1925); Geroge Harrison Durand, *Joseph Ward of Dakota* (Boston: Pilgrim Press, 1913); and M. A. DeWolfe Howe, *Life and Labors of Bishop Hare, Apostle to the Sioux* (New York: Sturgis & Walton, 1911). Unpublished Master's theses at the University of South Dakota with relevant materials on early social and cultural growth include Joseph H. Cash, "A History of Lead, South Dakota, 1876–1900"; Robert J. Hagan, "LeBeau: Old and New"; Donald K. Harkcom, "Social and Economic History of Yankton, 1859–1879"; and Ross P. Korsgaard, "A History of Rapid City, South Dakota, during Territorial Days."

NEW REFERENCES

A unique picture history of the Oglala is Amos Bad Heart Bull, *A Pictographic History of the Oglala Sioux*, text by Helen H. Blish (Lincoln: University of Nebraska Press, 1967). This pictographic record consists of a series of more than 400 drawings and script notations originally made in an old ledger book on the Pine Ridge Reservation between 1890 and 1913.

Robert G. Athearn, *Forts of the Upper Missouri* (1967; reprinted Lincoln: University of Nebraska Press, 1972) describes the part played by both military and trading posts.

Roy W. Meyer, *History of the Santee Sioux* (Lincoln: University of Nebraska Press, 1967) is a definitive study of the Santee tribes.

Joseph H. Cash, *Working the Homestake* (Ames: Iowa State University Press, 1973) tells the story of the Homestake Mining Company and its working force.

Joseph H. Cash and Herbert T. Hoover (eds.). *To Be an Indian: An Oral History* (New York: Holt, Rinehart and Winston, 1971) is a collection of interviews based on oral history techniques and presenting the Indian point of view.

Acknowledgements

THIS BOOK is the culmination of many years of research. In some measure it has grown out of the preparation and experience incidental to classroom instruction in South Dakota history. The keen interest in the subject shown by students, both graduate and undergraduate, has been a constant source of inspiration. The writing of a state history, however, rests largely upon the combined efforts of a whole corps of workers. The final product must be a composite of all the research conducted in the field. One can be especially grateful in this connection for the graduate students who have been willing to elect local and regional topics and make available their findings in the form of theses. Microphotography has been a godsend in making accessible dissertations written on South Dakota topics on distant campuses.

The author is indebted to many individuals in the preparation of this volume. Staff members identified with the libraries of several state historical societies were most helpful in making manuscript and newspaper collections available. He is especially grateful to Will G. Robinson, Secretary of the South Dakota State Historical Society, for his assistance and counsel. During his search for manuscript and newspaper materials, the author encroached upon the time of many other people, and to all these he expresses his deep gratitude.

For immediate help in the preparation of the book the author owes thanks to a number of colleagues at the University of South

Dakota for their willingness to read with critical eyes portions of the manuscript in its raw form. He also profited greatly from suggestions by a former student, Dr. Gilbert C. Fite, Research Professor of History at the University of Oklahoma and an outstanding authority on various phases of South Dakota history. The manuscript also benefited materially from the incisive comments of another former student, Harry H. Anderson, assistant secretary of the South Dakota State Historical Society, with regard to the military events of 1876 and 1877. Congressman Benjamin Reifel, former area director of the Bureau of Indian Affairs at Aberdeen, South Dakota, supplied constructive advice and criticism with reference to Indian policy. At the University of South Dakota, Professor Joseph H. Cash, Duke Research Professor of History, and General Lloyd R. Moses, former Director of the Institute of Indian Studies, have been helpful in making recent Indian history meaningful. Preston L. Funkhouser, Jr., and Everett M. Jennewein of the Bureau of Reclamation office at Huron have generously supplied up-to-date information about the Belle Fourche and Oahe irrigation projects.

Numerous individuals lent assistance in the gathering and reproduction of photographic materials. Among them should be mentioned Will G. Robinson and Harry H. Anderson of the South Dakota State Historical Society, Lloyd I. Sudlow of the *Bison Courier,* Paul G. Kretschmar, Sr., of Eureka, William W. Slattery, formerly of the News Bureau of the University of South Dakota, Mike Sougstad of the publicity division of the South Dakota Department of Highways, and the personnel in charge of the photographic sections of the National Archives and the Bureau of Ethnology at Washington, D. C. The author is also indebted to Mrs. Patricia L. Rist for her expert drawing of the map on the endsheet.

The author also wishes to acknowledge his debt to the University of South Dakota for a seven-month leave of absence from administrative and instructional duties in 1957 and to the University Research Committee for a grant to enable him to examine materials in the National Archives at Washington as well as in other localities and to assist him in the preparation of the manuscript. And, finally, he wishes to thank his wife, Mildred Senour Schell, for her deep interest in the book and her generous acceptance of long working hours. Her constant encouragement helped to keep spirits buoyant while the manuscript was taking form.

Index

425

Index

Home Owners Loan Corporation, 291
Homestake Mine, 146, 147, 153
Homestake Mining Company, 148, 381, 382
Homestead Act, 79, 170–174, 176
"Honest Caucus Law," 260
Hoover, Herbert, 281, 283
Horses: importance of, to Sioux Indians, 22, 23; raising of, 246
Hosmer, 169
Hot Springs, 218, 383, 391, 394
Hotch City, 247. See also Kennebec
Hotels, 185
Howard, William A., 198–201, 212
Howe, Oscar, 397, 398
Howes, William W., 274
Hueston, Ethel, 395
Hughes, Alexander, 210
Hughes, Richard B., quoted, 151
Hughes County, 345, 362
Hughitt, Marvin, 161, 162
Hump, Indian chief, 325
Humphrey, Hubert H., 317
Hunkpapa Sioux, 91. See also Teton Sioux
Hunt, Wilson Price, 47, 61
Huron, 162, 163, 165, 166, 170, 174, 209, 213, 216, 217, 224, 225, 293, 363, 373
Huron College, 390
Hutchinson County, 109, 116, 117
Hutterites, 117, 271, 388
Hyde County, 182, 214, 345
Hydroelectric plant: proposals for, 268, 275; rejection of, 275

I

Idaho Territory, 82
Igloo Ordnance Depot, 299, 300
Illinois Central Railroad, 165
Immaculate Conception School, 331
Immigration, foreign: nationalities concerned in, 115–117; promotion of, 118, 160
Immigration bureau, 117, 118
Indebtedness, farm. See Farm indebtedness
Independent party, 227–235. See also Populist party
Indian agents: corruption among, 329; administrative problems of, 330

Indian commissions: (1882), 322, 323; (1888), 323; (1889), 323
Indian Defense Association, 338
Indian police, 324
Indian policy: during fur trade, 45, 48, 57, 59, 60; under Governor Edmunds, 106; formulation of reservation system, 320–322; distribution of rations, 333; formulation of allotment system, 333–337; under New Deal, 338, 339; present-day goals, 340, 341
Indian Reorganization Act of 1934, 338, 339, 340
Indian reservations: Cheyenne River, 91, 251, 252, 253, 255; Crow Creek, 90, 91; Great Sioux, 88, 89, 139, 322–324; Lake Traverse (Sisseton), 92, 320, 333, 334; Lower Brûlé, 91, 253, 254; Pine Ridge, 253, 255, 320; Rosebud, 253–255, 320; Standing Rock, 251, 252, 253, 255; Yankton, 71, 72, 320, 333, 334
Indians, prehistoric, 20
Industrial Development and Expansion Agency, 380
Industrial Workers of the World (I.W.W.), 271, 272
Initiative and referendum, adoption of, 238, 241, 260
Insane, care of, 200
Institutions, public. See Public institutions
Insurance: bank-deposit, 265, 277, 278, 284; hail, 266, 268, 286; on crops, 290; unemployment, 296
Inter-Agency Committee. See Missouri Basin Inter-Agency Committee
Interior, 247
Intermediate Credits Act (1923), 277
Interstate highway system, 364, 365
Ipswich, 164, 166, 167
Iroquois, 162
Irrigation: artesian, 344, 345; in early Black Hills, 357; in Belle Fourche Valley, 359, 360; under Pick-Sloan Plan, 360, 361; by use of aquifers, 362
Isabel, 252

Index 441

Scandals in Indian service, 107, 108
Scandinavians. *See* Norwegians; Swedes; Danes
School lands, movement to restrict sale of, 212, 213, 221, 222
School of Mines and Technology, 391
School reorganization, 310
Schools, early, 102, 183. *See also* Education
Schools, public, state aid for, 309, 310
Schurz, Carl, 201, 329
Scotland, 373, 374
Sedition Law of 1917, enforcement of, 272, 273
Selective Service Act, 299
Selkirk colony, 57
Senn, E. L., 256
Seventh Cavalry, 136
Severalty Act (1887). *See* Allotment Act
Sewall, Arthur M., 235
Shannon, Peter C., 101, 192, 193, 322
Sharpe, M. Q., 282, 283, 313
Sheep Breeders and Wool Growers Association, 246
Sheep-raising, 245, 246, 351, 374
Sheidley Cattle Company, 251
Sheldon, Charles H., 231, 232, 233
Sheldon, Stewart, quoted, 165, 166
Shelterbelt, 353
Sheridan, 195
Sheridan, Philip H., 126, 129
Sheridan Lake, 293
Sherman, W. T., 13
Short Bull, Indian leader, 326
Shoshone Indians, 42
Sioux Agreement of 1889, 247
Sioux City, 70, 80, 83, 87, 153, 375
Sioux City and Pacific Railroad, 83, 84, 109, 110
Sioux City Times, 125
Sioux Falls, 73–76, 79, 85, 110, 165, 200, 236, 240, 363, 364, 370, 372, 375, 377, 378, 383, 392
Sioux Falls *Argus Leader*. See *Argus-Leader*
Sioux Falls College, 390
Sioux Falls Linen Company, 375
Sioux Falls Training Base, 299, 302

Sioux Indians: migration of, from Minnesota, 19–22; general characteristics of, 22, 23; early contacts of, with French, 24–26; importance of, to fur trade, 23; brought under military control, 68, 69, 91, 138; at war with whites, 84–87, 133–138, 327, 328; acculturation of, 320–322, 324, 329–341. *See also* Santee Sioux; Teton Sioux; Yanktonnais Sioux; Yankton Sioux
Sioux quartzite. *See* Quartzite industry
Sisseton Agency, 320, 333, 334
Sisseton Reservation: creation of, 92, 320; surplus lands of, made available, 333, 334
Sitting Bull, 86, 138, 139, 143, 325, 326
Slim Buttes, battle of, 137
Smaller War Plants Corporation, 379, 380
Smith, Alfred E., 281
Smith, Henry W., 230
Smith, Jedediah, 53
Smithsonian Institution, scientific expedition in Big Badlands, 7; meteorological observations, 14
Smithwick, 250
Smutty Bear, 70, 72
Soap factories, 374, 377
Social Security Act, 286, 292, 296
Social Welfare, financial support of, 296, 311, 312
Socialist party, formation of, 241; activities against during World War I, 272
Soil Conservation and Domestic Allotment Act (1936), 289, 290
Soil Conservation Service, 354, 355
Soils, description of, 8–10; first maps, 14
Soldiers bonus. *See* Veterans bonus
South Dakota State University, 205, 209, 391
Southern Alliance. *See* Farmers' Alliance
Southern State College, 391
Spanish: acquire Louisiana, 30; fear foreign aggression, 30–32; explorations in Upper Missouri Valley, 31–36; transfer possessions to

A Note about the Author

HERBERT S. SCHELL was born in Bernville, Pennsylvania, and educated at Muhlenberg College (A.B., 1920), Columbia University (A.M., 1923), and the University of Wisconsin (Ph.D., 1929). In 1925 he joined the faculty at the University of South Dakota where for a number of years he was Dean of the Graduate School and Professor of American History. During thirty years of research in the history of the state he has examined a mountain of primary source material, has covered numerous newspaper files, and spent weeks in Washington looking over documents in the Library of Congress and the National Archives. His publications have included *South Dakota, Its Beginnings and Growth* (1942), *Dakota Territory During the Eighteen Sixties* (1954), and *South Dakota Manufacturing to 1900* (1955).

In 1949 Dr. Schell participated in educational workshops conducted by the American Military Government at Heidelberg and Stuttgart; and in 1950 he served again with AMGOT in the Ryukyu Islands as educational consultant in the establishment of the University of the Ryukyus at Shuri, Okinawa.

His hobbies are gardening and philately. He is a member of Phi Beta Kappa.